Responses to Drama

AN INTRODUCTION TO
PLAYS AND MOVIES

Responses

to Drama

AN INTRODUCTION TO

PLAYS AND MOVIES ❀

by *Thelma Altshuler and*
Richard Paul Janaro

MIAMI-DADE JUNIOR COLLEGE

HOUGHTON MIFFLIN COMPANY · BOSTON
NEW YORK   ATLANTA   GENEVA, ILL.   DALLAS   PALO ALTO

48824

ILLUSTRATIONS BY NATE GOLDSTEIN

Contents

PART ONE · *Audience and Reader*

The comic spirit and its scope. Laughter, the essense of life. Comedy, satire and malaria. The principle of comic unity. Two comic climaxes — Single and double comedy and tragedy in America. Out of context. The variations on character. The romantic comedy. Wit, farce and satire.

The idealism of the exhibit stage on the audience. Three revolutions: sentimentality and melodrama. Work Ibsen: the Moldavsky Drakons. Ibsen, Chili and social problems. Theater and the theater of ideas. Professionalism in acting.

The causes of new forms of theatrical expression. Eliot's comic disguise. "Heightened realism." Chekhov's naturalistic theater. Dostoevskian tragedy. The realist social psychology theater. Expressionism. Epic theater. Theater as revolution. The philosophy of experimental theater.

Realistic actors reacting to the audience's interest, etc. Three fans, tension and movement. The social qualities of classical: Elizabethan, French, Classical, sentimental, problematic, natural, naturalistic, little theater, comedia house, idealized comical forms of acting.

The role of directing and related arts.

The musical, professional director, the style director needs for play-acting debating. The director's vision. Transference in production. The comic character role, mime and costume. Setting the social limits.

❧ SUPPORTING CAST

❧ LIST OF ILLUSTRATIONS

❁ Prologue

In some theater at this moment a small audience is watching a few, nearly motionless actors on a bare stage. In a movie house a larger audience watches a favorite star in a filmed remake of a story with the proven appeal of sex, tears, and horses. In a civic auditorium the road show company of a hit musical is playing before an audience which whistles and shouts its approval. In a small art theater is a foreign film with a "daring theme" and sub-titles. In a small community theater created from an old barn a packed house laughs generously at friends and neighbors pretending to be sophisticated aristocrats in a drawing-room comedy. Somewhere a small boy is sitting close to a television screen, his eyes opened wide in delighted horror as an undersea monster, huge and radioactive, crushes bridges between its paws. On a college campus there is a revival of a neo-classical tragedy, attended by students who hope to get extra credit for the reports they will write and by faculty members who are enjoying a seldom-performed work but making allowances for the inexperience of the players. At the same time, in a large Broadway theater, a famous actor is playing Hamlet before a varied audience: hypercritics, familiar with every line of the play and with other interpretations; well-dressed illiterates who have come to be seen at the season's most fashionable production; and at least one viewer who is a little nervous about whether she is expected to applaud after "To be or not to be."

In the theater lobbies at intermission the familiar remarks are murmured:

"I don't get it."

"Did you ever hear such language?"

"The door is a symbol of — "

"Her clothes are gorgeous."

"Life is bad enough without — "

"Where's the orangeade?"

"Nobody would do that in real life."

"I wonder how they learned all those lines."

Away from the crowd, a critical viewer leans against the wall, watching the others but saying nothing. The play is not yet over. He is using the intermission time to sort out his varied reactions, quietly reflecting on what he has seen so far and preparing to make a more definite evaluation — later.

It is the purpose of this book to assist playgoers (or readers) and film viewers in the making of such evaluations. While the uncritical are likely to offer the old argument that they just want to be entertained and that there is little point in becoming perceptive, the book hopes to encourage all who read it to explore the pleasures of greater sensitivity to dramatic experiences. The truly critical viewer is *not* a wallflower, forever standing apart, an outcast from the convivial society of others in the lobby. When the play is over, he and his friends will get together for coffee and discuss what they have seen. Theirs is a fellowship even stronger than that of the talkers in the lobby, for it is predicated on the assumption that he is most alive who is most aware.

Insensitivity to dramatic experience is symptomatic of a much larger deficiency. To be uncritical of stage and screen is the exclusive right of those who would be uncritical of life in general. The book therefore has something to say about the state of contemporary American culture as it is reflected in popular drama and popular taste.

The book is intended to increase critical perception in a gradual way. It assumes no previous systematic thought on the subject of theater, but rather a lively interest, accompanied perhaps by some embarrassment in the attempt to formulate opinions about what has been seen or read. It assumes that most people would really prefer to say something intelligent about drama and to become increasingly articulate critics; thus it moves from a consideration of the most fundamental aspects of the theater to the more complex matters of theatrical history and technique.

Above all, this book strives to cut through the mystique normally associated with the aesthetics of drama as encountered in an exclusively literary approach. It offers, instead, a critical terminology that is based upon what the drama honestly is and that can be understood and applied by everyone.

THELMA ALTSHULER

RICHARD PAUL JANARO

Miami, Florida

PART ONE ❀ ❀ ❀

Audience
and Reader

PROGRAM NOTES

This book is intended for all viewers of plays and movies who would like to become critical viewers. Those who already have settled tastes and prefer definite kinds of entertainment may find in the following chapters insight into their preferences. Those who are less sure of their preferences will find some important considerations in the development of critical standards.

Part One, Audience and Reader, indicates what can be said about plays that are seen or read and motion pictures and television shows that are viewed, without any special knowledge of the historical development of the drama or of the technical aspects of stage and screen production.

Interwoven throughout the seven chapters which comprise Part One are observations on some of the values current in our society which tend to make certain dramatic forms, certain themes, and certain types of characters more popular than others. Since the drama has traditionally been a social art, its contemporary condition necessarily interacts with its audience. The one, in short, illuminates the other.

Since the screen media — movies in particular — are as significant as today's theater and, on occasion, make important contributions to the art of drama as a whole, the term "drama" has been expanded in this book to include any work which tells a story through action, not narration, while the term "theater" is assumed to cover all of the dramatic media. When the context obviously deals with live stage performances, "theater" may be referred to in its traditional sense.

1 ❀ ❀ ❀

The World, A Stage

Man is endowed with an instinct for the dramatic. This gift helps turn the demands of day-to-day existence into little dramas which he constantly re-writes and recasts, usually with himself as the star. From the mother who is convinced that "nobody will ever know how much I have suffered and sacrificed for my children" to the gangly adolescent making the difficult transition from Little League to big girls, each, in Shakespeare's words, "in his time plays many parts."

Nor is age the only cause for a changing role. A man can be more than one person during the same day as he reacts to different people and situations. He can feel like a tycoon as he tips his shoeshine boy, a confused incompetent as he tries to balance his checkbook, a coward as he contemplates a repairman's estimate, and winner of the Grand Prix as he drives on the expressway.

In turn, he causes people to treat him according to the role he plays in their lives. The same man is lover, little boy, genius, tyrant, etc. Even the same situation calls for different responses as people react and inter-act. A man arriving late for an appointment may expound at length on the reason for his tardiness; apologize briefly; dismiss it loftily; or explain that his habit of being late is really a part of his charm. And his friends, according to their own natures, will be disappointed, amused, outraged, or forgiving. The variations are almost infinite.

In a sense, each one of us is a dramatist, continually writing scripts for ourselves and the people around us, and drama is one of the basic conditions of life. It is a game; it is serious business; it is make-believe; it is reality. However one wishes to view the process, it is theater, and it is all around us every day of our lives.

Limitations of the Dramatic in Real Life

When a child is given a coloring book, he turns the mailman green, the grocery boy purple, and the dog orange. As he matures, he becomes less imaginative in his use of color. He learns that mailmen and grocery boys should look a certain way, and there are just so many colors one can use for dogs. The world of earliest childhood is a stage filled with dazzling scenery and oddball characters.

3

Growing up means using fewer crayons; it means making decisions which are often based upon evaluations of other people and upon some definite conception of the self. Though in reality everyone could have an infinite variety of colorings, the choices inevitably have to be narrowed down. A parent, for example, must decide what he is going to be to his children. Firm yet reasonable? Permissive yet disciplining? Liberal to a point? Tyrannical for their own good? Indeed, if he does *not* so decide, his children are likely to decide *for* him.

Decisions are more often wrong than we realize. Most of the time we just fail to find out. Since events have happened in a certain way, there seems to be no point in looking backward. "If I had not said that, he would not have done that and believed that I was . . ." Nothing alters what is or what was, but the pity is that the past and the present do not usually help to alter the future. We go on making mistakes because we cannot see ourselves and others in all possible shades.

The recognition of character in the theater, on the other hand, is a more stable experience. Though a vast difference exists in stage life, as in real life, between simplified and complex characterizations, no play can possibly survive with characters who can be all things to all people at all times. Nor can the opposite — a play in which each character is all-good or all-bad — sustain continued interest and respect. Shakespeare's Iago is the most interesting, many-sided of all stage villains; for centuries critics have disagreed over the precise motivation for his evil practices; but just as he would be less interesting if he were too simple, with only one reason for his evil, it is folly to suggest that he is not a villain at all. Othello, deceived by Iago into murdering his wife, draws forth our compassion, but not our forgiveness. In snuffing out a completely innocent life, he has done a monstrous and terrifying deed. Nor does he ask for quarter. In a magnificent final gesture, he executes himself, making sure that we remember him in all of his grandeur. We leave the theater emotionally spent, but not confused. There couldn't be an Othello trial. Not even Perry Mason would take the case because his client would insist on admitting his guilt.

Maturity in real life means possessing more "understanding" of others — that is to say, seeing the possibilities for variant rather than specific coloring. In the theater we "understand" characters in the sense of coming to know why they do what they do, and we are expected to react to them in one way or another, not to suspend all judgment. The point is that role-playing and role-casting in real life are hazardous affairs, fraught with many chances for error. In theaters and movie houses role recognition is easier. The theater world, in other words, even in the subtle hues painted by such dramatists as Anton Chekhov or in the massive brush strokes of Shakespeare, is not the bewildering place that our world so regularly becomes.

In real life, too, there are people we "know" — people we see, nod to, smile at, exchange inane remarks with — but who somehow never assume any roles at all for us. They inspire in us nothing but emptiness. In a play or movie, however, it is the business of the writers, actors and directors to give to each character who figures prominently in the plot a set of noticeable attributes. Some directors insist that each member of the cast must see himself as the central character of the play so as to be as dynamic as possible on the stage or on the screen.

The genius of great dramatists like Shakespeare and Chekhov is that they almost never allow a character to appear, even briefly, without giving him a certain coloration. Even Sophocles, centuries ago, had the astonishing instinct to turn the sentry in *Antigone* (440 B.C.) into the theater's first comic figure.

What playwrights do perhaps is to file away in their semi-conscious minds any unusual, exciting, provocative people they encounter in their day-to-day existence. Later, much later, they find occasion to remember this one's face, that one's way of walking, somebody's gravelly voice, an old woman lighting up a cigarette, a rotund man with a ruddy face looking as if it had just been rubbed down with baby oil, who sprawled across two seats of a subway train and read the Bible. Indeed one of the great pleasures that plays and movies have to offer is the instinctive response we all have to the role-playing of others. Since role-casting seems to be a deeply rooted mechanism, we are entertained in theaters by the mere awareness that a figure up there on the stage or on the screen has a certain definite identity. The more "striking" the identity, the more we should be entertained; and "striking" in this instance does not mean the run-of-the-mill roles with which we cast the drama of everyday living.

The theater — and here it is the great, enduring dramas which are meant — has an important function in thus alerting us to the existence of types and categories of people. Other forms of art do this too (literature, painting, sculpture) but not precisely as the theater can do it, for the theater offers a facsimile of the real world, the illusion that what is happening on the stage or the screen is really happening. By becoming regular theater-goers, we learn to respond to every important character of the plot, and we ought to carry the habit out of the theater with us. By degrees we learn to see humanity in everyone, even the people we had failed to notice before.

The theater is an improvement on reality in yet another respect. Real life does not usually fall into definite scenes. To be sure, there are memorable moments, such as the announcement at graduation that one has been chosen most likely to succeed, but for the most part the things we say happened to us never did happen in quite the way we describe. Not only do we cast ourselves and others into certain roles, but we habitually alter the shape of events so as to make them more dramatic. At some time or other each one of us has fabricated a story about, say, receiving a rather tepid insult and then parrying with a well-timed, beautifully worded passage of our finest prose which utterly squelched our antagonist. And we have heard our audience say, "Did you really say that? Did you dare?" And we smiled, triumphantly, having already persuaded ourselves that we did. As a matter of fact, witty stage dialogue is sometimes called by a marvelous French phrase, *l'esprit d'escalier*, the spirit of the stairs — the remark we think of after the party is over, as we are going down the stairs, the remark we later tell people we did make at a most miraculous moment, the remark which, however, is made only in the world of the theater where everything is more compressed and intense than our lives ever can be.

Scenes in real life have too many loose ends. Everything fizzles out, from the toastmaster's emotion-choked stammering of a few inadequate words which attempt to sum up what somebody feels about somebody to the tearful goodbye we bid to an old, old friend whom we meet again, seconds later, around the corner in the drug store. Scenes in real life never seem to end just when they should. The curtain somehow will not fall; the lights refuse to fade. The young girl cannot enter the living room to inform her unsuspecting parents that she is secretly married to the young man next door and expect their horrified faces to dissolve like images on the movie screen.

Scenes in real life, just like the people we know before we cast them into their roles, tend to possess variant colorings. Unable to cope with the variance, we make them more specific than they were. But when they are happening, we seldom experience them as we think we did. Thus, if we find out there was a prowler in the neighborhood the night before, we might think back and suppose that we were "in danger." We become characters in a suspense thriller. In the movies the audience is aware of both prowler and innocent victims inside the house. The scene takes on the dark and ominous coloring of suspense.

Similarly, in real life, we cannot experience things in broad perspective. When Tennessee Williams was actually living through events which might resemble those of his frankly autobiographical play *The Glass Menagerie* (1945), it is doubtful that the woman he was later to immortalize as Amanda Wingfield, one of the indestructible stage mothers, was *always* seen as Amanda is now seen by the audience. Interestingly enough, the conclusion of the play offers us brilliant insight into the process by which the dramatist, through the filtering process of time and distance, comes to see his past in a new light. The stage directions are a duplication of the process:

The interior scene is played as though viewed through soundproof glass. AMANDA appears to be making a comforting speech to LAURA who is huddled upon the sofa. Now that we cannot hear the mother's speech, her silliness is gone and she has dignity and tragic beauty.

In other words, the conversion of real life into drama cannot take place exactly as things are happening. Real life thus lacks both the filtered qualities and the perspective which plays and movies can give.

A young man in real life who finds himself continually being harped on by his mother, as Tom Wingfield is by Amanda, could not be expected to find the rich vein of humor which underlies much of *The Glass Menagerie*. Williams' play is short as plays go; each scene is like a finely cut gem which sparkles in the dim light of the theater and then is removed before we are quite through looking at it. In real life friction between mothers and sons is less like a shining jewel than it is like sandpaper. One usually has quite enough of it quite soon.

The Act of Theater-Going

Since the origins of the theater in Greece in the sixth century B.C., it has remained one of the enduring popular social institutions. Even during the early Middle Ages, when there was no drama for people to go to, the church Mass served for many the dual purpose of providing spiritual uplift and being a source of entertainment. When one considers the theatrics of Masses and services even now, one becomes aware of the aesthetic pleasure provided by dim lighting, candles, organ music, choir singing, the various kinds of special garments often worn, and the generally solemn atmosphere — all of it above and beyond the metaphysical and theological reasons for being there. It is not at all surprising that, after the centuries-long absence of formal theater during the medieval period, dramatic art was reborn directly *from* the Mass.

The Greeks made an all-day affair out of theater-going, arriving at sunrise and sitting in tiers of hard stone benches hewn out of the side of a mountain and leaving at sunset, having viewed four complete plays, three tragic and one comic. The Romans, somewhat more sophisticated if not more sensitive to tragic grandeur and poetry, made theater-going one of the true arts of civilization. The London and Paris high society of the seventeenth century, borrowing many of their standards of living from the Romans, had the further advantage of the first indoor theaters, artificially lighted by chandeliers. Theater became at last the essentially nighttime thing it has remained — a place of make-believe on both sides of the footlight.

From the time we enter the theater lobby to the time we slam the car door and turn the ignition key for the trip home, we experience a number of sensations that are all essential to the total act of theater-going, that are, in fact, all part of the total function and significance in society of the theater. Analyses of plays themselves are likely to ignore many of the peripheral delights of the theater — moments which sometimes compensate for a play (or movie) which fails to satisfy.

Though we tend to turn real life into a play, we are not entirely conscious of so doing — or, at all events, not at the appropriate moment.

Dialogue is "edited" in memory; scenes are re-staged in memory; roles are cast unconsciously. Therefore, most of the joy of the theater is really absent from the play of life. As soon as we are inside a real theater, however, there occurs within us a remarkable change. Unless our personal problems are so pressing that they prevent our thinking of anything else, we enter almost immediately into the spirit of the occasion. We have already left one plane of existence and are on the threshold of another. The air all around us is charged with a kind of electricity. We have the gratifying sense of being looked at. We experience the comfortable feeling of "belonging" and the immediate pleasure of conviviality as we blend into random, excited conversation and the dynamic colors of people dressed in their finest, moving back and forth from friend to friend; the sweep down the aisle, preceded by a smiling usher who hands us a program with the traditional "I hope you enjoy the show," which tells us that we are important and that our favorable opinion is something the entire production cannot afford to scorn; the mounting tension as curtain time draws closer and closer; the realization that house-lights are dimming; the hush that spreads from one end of the theater to the other; and finally that silence which is felt just before the curtain rises — the silence of many questions, such as "Will it be a hit?" "Can he outdo himself?" "What will the set look like?" "What will happen first?"

Movie-Going, a National Pastime

Unfortunately the most glamorous kinds of theater-going are confined to the large metropolitan centers of the United States: New York, primarily, followed by San Francisco, Chicago, Los Angeles, Boston, Philadelphia, and other cities such as Atlanta and Minneapolis which are slowly coming to the forefront in the move to decentralize the American theater. In a nation so vast as ours it is absurd to suppose that the dramatic experience should be confined to a relatively small number of regular spectators. Thus the majority of Americans go to the movies, or else stay home and watch television. The latter has, of course, displayed its potential on more than one notable occasion and may become the dominant mode of theater-going of the future. But, while television drama can accomplish a great deal, people will always want to attend stage and screen performances that will get them out of the house. Since the home is often the locale of our real life role-playing and role-casting, the loss of oneself in the darkness of an auditorium may always be the necessary factor for the greatest personal response to drama.

The movie theater is dark, but it cannot offer the other elements of play-going. People dress more casually to go to the movies. Since the audience is comprised of a larger cross-section of the population than is the audience for live drama, we miss that "in-group" feeling and the sparkling conversation of intermission time. Die-hard supporters of the legitimate stage insist that movies can never match the theater for immediacy, that the complete engaging of all our senses which theater offers at its very best can never be achieved from even the greatest movies.

Nonetheless, a glance through the amusement pages of the local newspaper reveals movies as by far the most popular form of theater-going available. Nor is it unrealistic to expect an exciting, rewarding experience at the movies. With a careful selection of films, based on the reputation of the movie-maker, the opinion of a discriminating critic, or our own previous experience, we may be attending a screen drama that will someday be read and analyzed as the great live plays of the past are now preserved and studied.

So exuberant and creative is the current Renaissance of the Cinema that more and more personalities from the world of the theater are becoming converts. The distinguished reviewer Judith Crist has said that the live theater is a static art form, neither making notable advances nor experimenting with new dramatic forms in anything like the profusion one finds in film-making centers around the world. Movie clubs specializing in classic films of the past and present can be found on almost every college campus, while academic courses in cinema appreciation are springing up everywhere.

Enthusiastic supporters of films point proudly to the fact that *their* medium can do almost anything it wishes; it can lead us into a make-believe existence that the three-dimensional flesh and blood reality of the stage cannot equal. It is true that technical innovations in film provide few limits to the imagination. Films can use close-ups, metaphor, repetition of a scene, juxtaposition, flashbacks, change in color or combination of color and black and white, and deliberate distortion of the picture to do almost anything the director wants. They force scrutiny of details that would have been missed on stage: for example Cocteau's *Beauty and the Beast* (1947) and *Orpheus* (1950) with their candelabra held by human arms thrust out of strangely undulating walls and mirrors one can walk through to enter a world that does not exist in any time and space one has ever known. Movies must count as important dramatic experiences and, from this hour forth, they must be included in discussions of theater.

What matters most is the *level of theater* to which one responds as well as the type of response. The playgoer who visits New York and sees every big-time musical from Forty-fourth to Fiftieth streets is surely not more highbrow than his jean-clad sister, who prefers a rerun of Fellini's 8½ (1963) at a small movie house on the lower East side. On the other hand, a mature response to a musical, one that recognizes in it dishonest optimism as well as casual entertainment, is no doubt preferable to an uncritical acceptance of 8½.

Judith Crist *on the N.B.C. Today Show, September 20, 1966**

CRIST: I have a feeling that there has been a change in the last three years — that today movies are where the action is. Movies have had a great renaissance, as far as people's interest goes. I wish the renaissance were carried on into production but I think it has only partially. The theater in the meantime to me has become quite static. This does not mean that I have lost any of my love or even passion for the theater but I *think* there is far more to think about and be interested by in movies — consider just sheer numbers. You see 300 movies a year, let's say. (You don't; I do.) But out of that, there are a hundred movies that are possible. There are fifty movies that have not been a waste of time.

WALTERS: But the theater critic is, used to be, well, still is, *the* prestige critic — more so, in general . . .

CRIST: I think that is snobbery and also I think it is a leftover from the days when theater was the dominant force. But what are you getting — 60 plays on Broadway — and really, if there are *five* that you could sort of survive, you've had a great season. Also I think that so many of our young writers, the exciting writers, are writing for movies today. In my generation creative young writers wanted to write a play or a novel. Today they want to do movies.

WALTERS: What about . . . I know you teach a writing, a journalism class at Columbia. Do they want to come out and be theater critics or movie critics?

CRIST: Well, what's interesting is, when I began the critical writing workshop about eight years ago everyone wanted to be a theater critic. Maybe there were odd balls who wanted to be dance or music critics but now out of the dozen graduate students I take, I would say a minimum of ten want to do movies. There may be one or two odd balls who still want to do theater or music or something else. Now it's all movies. This is *the* art of the moment, I think.

HUGH DOWNS: Do you think that movies will be getting better from the writing standpoint eventually?

CRIST: Yes. Now there are close to 600 colleges and universities that are giving very *specific* movie courses.

DOWNS: That could mean something.

CRIST: And an important thing. It means that we are getting a more critical audience . . . and its demands are getting higher.

* Reprinted by permission of Judith Crist.

Like the rest of the arts or "humanities," theater is more than a decoration on the façade of civilization. Like a stately column that is perhaps beautiful in itself, theater must *do* something, even as the column supports a roof. As a matter of fact, theater is one of the most versatile of all arts, capable of doing a great many things — from whiling away a dreary, rainy afternoon to creating more critical responses to the drama of real life; from helping in the escape from awareness of unpleasant realities to heightening that awareness and so enabling us to cope better with those realities. Theater can remain nothing more than the extension of a childhood love of making believe, or it can be one of the dynamic pleasures of maturity — indeed one of the basic conditions of maturity. Theater can fill the mind with all those ancient stereotypes — like the nagging mother-in-law or the thoroughly rotten cattle baron — and all those ancient lies that tell how the good always triumphs over the bad or that good and bad can be so easily separated in the first place. But it can also alert us to the more delicate shadings in real life characterizations and and scenes and so assist us in being less apt to make decisions based upon scant reflection. When one considers that the art of theater includes names like Sophocles, Shakespeare, and Molière, one recognizes that some of the keenest, most profound, and most enduring insights into human existence have come from plays. A hundred years from now it may be seen that these insights have come from films as well.

Sometimes the world and the stage are mirrors of each other. Sometimes they do not resemble each other at all, either because the dramatist has lied or because his imagination has created a world of its own. But they always interact, and therefore it is impossible to leave theater alone. An important part of the process of maturation is coming to understand what theater can do and how it can best be used toward making each of us more sensible, more humane, and more appreciative of life in the short time we have to live it.

For I like to be entertained, and I think that
a movie that is not entertaining cannot be considered as art . . . The question is what is entertaining ('To hold the attention agreeably')? For
me, *Marienbad* is, Jerry Lewis isn't.*

Dwight MacDonald

2 ❀ ❀ ❀

Popcorn and Caviar

The very pleasures of theater-going encourage the same kind of uncritical acceptance common to most spectator sports. There is almost as
much appeal in the surroundings as in the advertised attraction. Even a
neighborhood movie theater, less plush than the first-run houses, offers
an evening out, away from home responsibilities, and the mood of most
audiences is to think no more than they would if they were attending
the stock-car races rather than a drama. The lobby, the refreshments, the
welcoming darkness, and meeting with friends — everything combines to
put the emphasis on comfort rather than criticism. Even a not-very-good
movie is dismissed with a few words and a shrug as the uncritical viewer
heads for his car. Going out was as important as being there; besides,
many people consider close viewing, "talking back," observation of
technique, and comparisons with similar dramas as an infringement on
their right to "enjoy."

For the "average viewer" there has been little to encourage critical
thinking about the movies, anyway. He is unlikely to have encountered
serious consideration of a film in newspaper reviews. His only other
experience with criticism may be a grim memory of an academic course
which required his learning much that was peripheral and hard to
pronounce before he was considered worthy of having an opinion.

It might be supposed that an evening at a play would encourage
critical viewing, if only to check on whether the long-range planning and
additional expense for tickets had been worth it. But the public makes

* Reprinted by permission of *Esquire Magazine*. © 1965 by Esquire, Inc.

few demands on a play either. Perhaps ready acceptance comes from having waited until a handful of critics pronounced the verdict. Or perhaps it comes from the glitter of the lobby, the well-dressed audience, the theater program itself, with selected gossip and advertisements for luxury items. In the case of a musical, the noise and colorful costumes, as mindless as a display of fireworks, seem to enforce the notion that it is impossible to think and have fun at the same time.

The uncritical acceptance of American theater audiences is shared by neither their European counterparts nor by professional critics. European audiences have been known to register disapproval by jumping on chairs, making jeering noises, and even driving a performer from the stage. But the enthusiastic response of an American audience at an opening is so unreliable that producers have learned not to trust even a standing ovation. The colder, more cerebral response of the professional critic is more likely to determine the success of a new play. Even the occasional exception, when "Nobody liked it except the public" does not prove the superiority of uncritical viewing, though it is surely of great commercial interest. The professional critic should represent all those who expect a worthwhile return on their investment of time and money for an evening out at the theater. He has an obligation to prevent himself from being swept along by the excitement of crowd and color. Though he may have applauded along with the audience, as he writes an opinion he can reflect and re-evaluate. He may decide that what was momentarily interesting in spots did not provide a satisfactory whole; or that the play had greater value than was immediately apparent.

Like any expert, including the knowledgeable football fan, the critical viewer carries with him the memory of previous performances and a vision of the ideal. Even while watching, he refuses to be led astray by his surroundings. The novice at a football game sees cheerleaders, hotdog vendors, marching bands, and an occasional spectacular run for the goal line. The experienced football fan can enjoy all these things and get additional pleasure from knowing more about what he sees, for he does see more. His eyes pick out a deceptive play unobserved by the novice, for whom all is a mere blur of bodies. He is conscious, he is aware, and he would deny his ability to enjoy a game simply because he can tell the difference between the good players and the bad.

The Popcorn Syndrome

The first step towards becoming a more critical viewer, therefore, is to learn to resist the immediate pleasure of being just another member of an audience and hold out for what the play or movies itself may have to offer. One can return to the enjoyment of pre-curtain festivities after he has learned not to confuse one experience with another. One man even derives pleasure from viewing bad drama by first being part of the audience and then withdrawing from membership, considering why what is being viewed is not working. In order to reach this level, one must stop being a popcorn eater.

There is something about the purchase of a tall, warm, brimful box of popcorn in a movie lobby that seems to get the evening off to a good start. Or perhaps when one enters the auditorium, his mouth wide open to receive the first stinging taste of the salty wonder drug, he has already lost his defenses. For what happens is that the impact of the theater itself (where the popcorn is figurative) or of the action on the screen is so immediate and so great that the popcorn eater forgets to close his mouth at all. Such obvious unconsciousness of the self, surrendered into without the least struggle, is the leading characteristic of the popcorn syndrome, the disease which is often incurable and fatal to critical sensitivity.

The syndrome can first be detected in children confined to playpens. They are easily bored but just as easily diverted by the silly, unrehearsed dramaturgy of the parents: funny faces, hopping around, baby talk, loud noises of any kind. Some people grow up only apparently; inside they retain the uncritical outlook of the child and are always willing to be interested in the events taking place outside them — at a moment's notice and to the exclusion of inward reflection about the things that happen.

The syndrome, finding fertile ground for expansion in the uncritical adult, is particularly fond of dark places — like theaters. Danger signals for the theater-goer to heed are:

accepting any story that is shown, even one which makes no sense

falling for the basic tricks which actors are prepared to thrust at the unsuspecting

The unbelievable plots and characters which are most often available are far too numerous to list and need not be anyway, since the amusement page of the daily newspaper provides a good start for anyone wishing to make the investigation. Extreme care should be taken, however; entering the darkened theater means running the risk of catching the disease. One begins to believe in poverty-stricken heroines with lavish wardrobes; heroes who meet all adversity with a song; hardened villains who have a change of heart under the tutelage of a lovable child; and all the other mindless make-believe of popular theater. Only a strong inoculation of critical taste can counteract the virus.

Recognition of actors' tricks is worthwhile. It is a kind of reward for alertness, because noting the things actors are doing wrong can turn an extremely dull evening into an amusing game. It is particularly pleasurable to be a member of an audience which seems to be taken in, to know that one is not being fooled, and to understand why. There are times when the labeling of a performance as bad is relative; two viewers of equally high degrees of perception may sharply disagree about the effectiveness of a particular approach to a role. Sometimes knowledge of the historical background of a style of acting is necessary before an intelligent decision can be made about it. But the performers in popular farce comedies, musicals, or television variety shows (especially the stand-up comics) do resort to easily detectable tricks about which there is little disagreement.

Loudness is an old stand-by. "I'm not good but I'm loud" is one of the common mottoes in American show biz. Everyone who has seen a Broadway musical is familiar with the slam-bang kind of production which seems more often to be attacking the audience than attempting to divert it. The entrepreneurs of the old brassy tradition are probably counting heavily on the well-known tendency of American audiences to revert to the playpen outlook, which is peculiarly susceptible to amusement through noise. Loud sound also makes thinking difficult and discourages critical analysis during the act of viewing.

Excessive movement is another trick and operates on the theory that bad acting is less noticeable when the actor moves around constantly. Everyone knows that children in playpens cannot be kept interested unless something or someone is kept in motion before their eyes. The television comic is famous for skipping onstage — accompanied by deafening music — and thereafter never keeping either his hands or his legs still. Amateur actors usually wander all over a stage, trying to conceal their awkwardness, but succeeding only in advertising their lack of physical and mental co-ordination. If a recently observed bad performance is compared with one that seemed convincing, it is more than likely that the believable actor either moved less or was less noticeable in his movements. Performers who know what they are doing on a stage move only when they must, when the logic of the speech or the action warrants motion.

Mugging is hitting lines too hard that are supposed to "get a laugh"; it is being over-expressive with the face; and it is making the voice sound odd. Actors usually resort to mugging in an attempt to warm up a cold audience. When the coughs, the fanning of programs and shifting in the seats, indicate restlessness, fear may set in, with a corresponding loss of integrity. On stage as off, trying too hard is pathetic.

Closely allied to mugging is the rapid-fire speech to cover poor material. Stand-up comics are notoriously guilty of this deceptive speed. Gags about the wife, the mother-in-law, the stingy employer, the tiny hotel room — all follow in dizzy profusion. Hopefully the audience will not realize how deadly each joke would be by itself. Rapid speech is also charactertisic of the farce comedy and the musical and is virtually a signature of slick directors. Talking fast yet enunciating clearly is something only seasoned performers can do and it can be delightful in patter songs of complex terminology. But it almost always is a cover-up for a lack of genuine acting, lack of subject matter, lack of originality, and, above all, innocence of any appeal whatsoever to the intellect.

In non-comic theater such blatant trickery is less prevalent. Since an audience witnessing a serious play is quiet, its presence is less oppressive to the actor. This of course leads to yet another kind of bad acting: excessive emotionalism, which the uncritical viewer may applaud as good because it is so "hard" to do. In reality, over-emoting comes quite easily to the actor, and he must be constantly on his guard against falling in love with himself in a role, against seeing himself as he would like the audience to see him. The popcorn eater — with his defenses down — may be as impressed as the actor himself by unbridled emotionalism. He may believe that, because someone actually weeps on the stage or cries out in a high pitch of frenzy, the proceedings are praiseworthy. It stands to reason, however, that it is not difficult for a performer to become a parrot and reproduce certain facile methods for projecting joy or grief or passion.

It is not possible here to list comprehensively the characteristics of a good performance, but surely some attributes of a bad one are worth noting. These can be found in screen as well as stage acting:

1) the representation of a type that is so familiar the audience usually expects and gets familiar vocal patterns and gestures
2) failure to communicate with other actors
3) excessive consciousness of the presence of the audience
4) mobile face, immobile body; expressive voice, deadness in face and body; grace of speech, awkwardness of movement — in short, any trait that does not appear to be in harmony with the role
5) the showing, instead of feeling, of emotion. (For a rule of thumb, this warning will carry anyone safely through: *the tear must be in the character, not the eye or the voice.*)

One of the dangerous side-effects of the popcorn syndrome is the tendency to confuse the actor with the roles he characteristically plays. Perhaps it does not seem possible for otherwise intelligent people to make such a mistake, but nonetheless there are those who will say, "She's too nice a girl to play a role like that," or "No matter what part he plays, I always love him."

The person who confuses actors with their roles or who finds himself uncritically accepting obvious tricks has been afflicted by the popcorn syndrome. And the susceptibility to such affliction is by no means limited to people who might be termed unsophisticated. Everyone who goes to the theater or the movies or turns on the television set can be "had," and it's a good feeling while it lasts. One of the most depressing experiences in the world is the popcorn hangover, the recognition the next morning

that one has been tricked the night before by a piece of maudlin sentimentality. The only thing worse is never to be aware or never to experience a sobering morning after.

  Erich Fromm *on Cultural Escapism**

> Suppose that in our Western culture movies, radios,
> television, sports events and newspapers ceased to func-
> tion for only four weeks. With these main avenues of
> escape closed, what would be the consequences for
> people thrown back upon their own resources? I have no
> doubt that even in this short time thousands of nervous
> breakdowns would occur, and many more thousands of
> people would be thrown into a state of acute anxiety, not
> different from the picture which is diagnosed clinically
> as "neurosis."

> * From *The Sane Society* by Erich Fromm. Copyright © 1955 by
> Erich Fromm. Reprinted by permission of Holt, Rinehart and
> Winston, Inc.

What Is "Entertainment"?

Does thinking spoil entertainment? The statement "I don't go to the
theater to think, I'd rather be entertained" makes a wide separation between analyzing and having a good time. Even people who are engaged
regularly in pursuits that are termed "mental" — professors, scientists,
students — may remember times when they have sought the relaxation of
a movie or a television show after a particularly strenuous day. They
may also remember that they began with no desire to be critical, to peek
behind the façade of showmanship and find out the reason something
was not working. Yet a viewer with developed tastes not only will decline
to sit for very long without making critical judgment but will ultimately
derive his maximum pleasure from knowing the reasons for his having
enjoyed or failed to enjoy what was seen.

Perhaps the word "thinking" is itself responsible for much of the confusion. People who say they want to have fun, not think, are referring
to the act of reflecting upon what is being said rather than what is being
seen. There is an enormous difference; and the fun-seekers are actually
right. It *is* the business of the theater and of motion pictures to offer
the audience an absorbing experience, one that must hold the interest
and attention each passing moment. Dramas which require intense
speculation about meanings beyond the immediate experience force the
viewer to choose between being absorbed and being enlightened. Both
cannot take place at the same time.

The kind of thought which the critical theater-goer revels in is that which pertains to the experience itself. Why, for example, does this scene appear to be dragging? Is the fault that of the script? the actors? the director? the subject matter rather than the dialogue? Why does that scene appear to be throbbing with vitality? Is it a particular personality in one of the roles? the staging? the photography? And the recognition that the events being witnessed possess wider significance offers pleasurable anticipation for later reflection. After the show, either in solitude or in the company of friends who have also viewed critically, one can look back. Many, many times the post-mortem is more fun than going to the theater itself.

In reality, to be diverted is not to be entertained. It is like taking a shot of one of those drugs that affect the memory, whereby one feels pain but does not recall that he did. The popcorn eater, willing to yield up all awareness of self as soon as his foot is inside the theater door, may never remember that he was bored sometimes, that he dozed here and there, or that he found one scene funnier than another. Such "relaxation" can be more than rivaled by alcoholism or sleep.

Reprinted from the Miami News by permission of Bell-McClure Syndicate. Artist, Fred Neher.

Entertainment in the sense that best applies to drama means playing the game along with the author and the actors; it means agreeing to believe that everything is true, while at the same time remaining aware that everything is not true. Drama works best when it affects the total self: as relaxation or "play" it surely is beneficial to the body; as intensified experience it excites the emotions; and as art it stimulates the critical sense and thus affords the pleasure which only the act of thought can give.

Entertainment in the sense of forgetting one's troubles is not the primary function of the drama. If plays and movies are able to lull us into euphoric escape from worrying about paying the rent or finding a job or patching up a quarrel, they are doing only what alcohol and drugs do; they may be more legal but not less harmful. The well-known unhappy housewife down the street, with the husband whose affection has waned, with the six children in school, with creditors continually pounding on the door, with her own youth and good looks vanishing, rushes in the afternoon to the dark, cool sanctuary of the local movie emporium. For two hours she inhabits a technicolor, cotton-candy world of Las Vegas swimming pools and Rock Hudson kisses — only to return home to squalor which somehow seems more squalid. The reason is that the escapee never really escapes from her problems: she only covers them up for a time, as one might place a lid over boiling water. The steam will disappear briefly, but sooner or later an explosion is bound to take place.

Surely nobody *wants* to worry himself sick. If escape were possible or if an afternoon's diversion could help straighten out one's tangled affairs, then the drama would have to be hailed as the greatest achievement of man. It is not. No human institution can lay claim to being the one which makes civilization possible, but like any of the humanities — that is, like music or art or the dance, the drama contributes to our total well-being. The enthrallment of our attention is the theater's first duty, but this must be counterbalanced by an unwavering critical consciousness. When both of these factors are present equally, we may say that we are being entertained. When only the first occurs, we run the risk of taking the uncritical attitude back into real life, whereas what we should strive for is to be increasingly more conscious in day-to-day existence.

The double-self — enthralled viewer and perceptive critic — has been experienced in some degree by everyone who has ever been to a theater. Everyone has felt the mounting suspense of watching an actor dangling from a ledge seventy stories above the ground without *really* believing the actor would fall. Indeed it is possible to shudder even as one is enjoying the technique and possibly comparing it with many other similar scenes. It is even possible to shudder while realizing that the cliff-hanging is another corny trick.

It is also possible to experience a delightful trip backward to scenes one had almost forgotten and to forgive a contrived plot because it is accompanied by the familiar sights and sounds of an earlier time — an old-fashioned stove, dance craze, or the emotionalism of the end of tension in world events. In a period of affluence one remembers the small economies practiced by the characters in a play about another time. It is quaint, picturesque, and appealing in the same way a piece of antique furniture may be forgiven ugliness because of its age. The critic is pleasantly wrung out, but at the same time knows how much he owes to the joys of nostalgia.

The reason this is possible is that the critical viewer goes to the theater to be deceived in precisely the same way that someone watches the magician perform his tricks in the hopes of *not* being immediately aware of the fakery involved. The card specialist who removes the queen of hearts from the observer's inside pocket is the one who merits the applause, not the fumbling amateur who is unaware that the missing card has fallen from his own sleeve.

Empathy and Alienation

If one should arrive late for a circus performance, making his entrance during the tightrope-walker's act, what he would see is not only the death-defying stunter on high but hundreds of seated patrons swaying back and forth. Each one of them would be projecting himself into the precarious journey across a thin wire; each of them, no matter how clumsy, would feel that he possessed the performer's skill and grace as he inclines now one way, now the other to maintain his careful balance.

In similar fashion does the movie-goer — especially in this era of super screens and Cinerama — share the ride with the frenzied heroine, tied up in the back seat of a driverless car careening wildly down the mountain. And because of this remarkable phenomenon whereby the viewer can be in two places at once, an entire audience of sophisticated people in the trade rose to their feet cheering lustily during the chariot race sequence at the premier of *Ben-Hur* (1959).

This projection is called *empathy*, and, while it is often shamefully exploited by movie directors, it has a more subtle counterpart in the live theater. It enables the play-goer to have gooseflesh and a tingling of the spine during the suspenseful moments or to feel that inward surge of joy when wonderful things occur — as, for example, when the blind and deaf young Helen Keller says her first word at the conclusion of William Gibson's *The Miracle Worker* (1957). During periods of lesser emotional intensity empathy means sustained audience involvement in the action.

The opposite of empathy is *alienation*, sometimes referred to by the word *verfremdung* because the condition is the one described by the German playwright Bertolt Brecht. According to Brecht's theory of drama, the intellectual, not the emotional, component of drama constituted its entertainment value; theater was for thinking people, not those who wished either total escape from themselves or merely to derive all of the complex benefits experienced by witnessing drama's heightened and ordered reality. As a Marxist, Brecht believed that man could effect changes in society, could help to bring about a better way of living, and so could not afford to waste his time enjoying make-believe. Since the world of the theater was evidently not real, its existence could be justified only if the play made the audience more aware of the social evils still to be eradicated. In this respect the Communist theory of the function of drama is similar to the literary theories of the seventeenth-century Puritans who insisted that literature have moral value for the reader. A poem was never to be enjoyed for the beauty of its language or the subtle effects of its rhythms.

There are many, however, who believe that Brecht maintained one thing only to practice another. They insist that one cannot read or see a play such as *The Caucasian Chalk Circle* (1944) and not feel intense sympathy for the peasant girl who raises another woman's child only to face the possibility of a heartbreaking loss when the real mother insists upon taking her offspring back. The statement Brecht is making through the play is unmistakable: property belongs to those who take care of it, not to those who claim it as a birthright. The parable of Grusha and her adopted baby is not intended to have a very human level, but it is questionable whether a dramatist can deal with such fundamental emotions as a mother's need for her child without inviting audience involvement. Brecht's methods are deliberately anti-realism in an effort to discourage empathy, yet the enduring popularity of *The Caucasian Chalk Circle* in particular suggests that the author's work has an appeal even where Communism does not.

In developing the theory of alienation Brecht was making a conscious break with that set forth by Aristotle regarding the purpose of tragedy. According to the theater's first critic, the value of tragedy for the audience was that it permitted an expenditure of emotions toward a make-believe situation. The benefit was the same as in real life when, after an intense emotional experience, a person reaches a state of tranquillity. The idea was that everyone had a point beyond which no more grieving or being afraid or being excited was possible. Aristotle called this restoration of inner equilibrium after emotional release the *catharsis* and considered it to be the major aim of tragic drama. Since his time most critics and scholars of the theater have tended to accept the theory as being broadly applicable to all forms of drama; to regard the catharsis as the primary benefit of theater-going; and to maintain that tragedy — because it deals with the extremes of human suffering — still best serves the purpose of drama.

Critical viewing means being two people at once; it means swaying back and forth with the tightrope artist and deciding that he is better than his counterpart in the circus across the street. It means enjoying the pleasure of becoming excited and fearing for the man's life even as one is nodding with approval of the improvements in "the act." In a sense, then, critical viewing is combining the two theories of drama: the theory of empathy and that of alienation.

Over-involvement with the events in a play or movie can be just as unsatisfying as that total withdrawal of sympathy for the characters in which Brecht professed a belief. Arthur Miller's *Death of a Salesman* (1949) is the subject of much critical controversy because many believe that its subject matter — the thwarted efforts of the little man in society to make a respectable living for his family — comes too close to home for comfort of most American viewers.

Miller intended, by writing the play, to show that tragedy could still be written even though few kings and princes exist anymore. But many critics argue that the kind of empathy Aristotle was talking about is not possible when there is a direct identification between viewer and character. In other words, a distinction is often made between empathy and identification on the grounds that sympathetic involvement presupposes for the audience that the characters keep their distance. If the tightrope walker, for example, were one's own father, not only would critical detachment be difficult to achieve but it is probable that no pure pleasure would be inspired. Similarly, people who attend funerals can actually enjoy the release of emotion through sympathy for the bereaved — as long as they are not too directly affected by the death. The ancient Greeks who attended the first theaters in Western civilization were mainly free citizens, not aristocrats; yet the tragedies they witnessed all dealt with persons in high places, most of whom were descended from the gods. The common people who stood in the pit and watched the tragedies of Shakespeare could not have put themselves in the places of Hamlet and King Lear any more than we can today. Over-participation in the action blurs critical perspective and should not be the aim of theater-going. The famous chariot race in *Ben-Hur* worked effectively because the rest of the action took place in the remote past and happened to types who are familiar to anyone who has ever seen a Hollywood Biblical epic. Rooting for the hero was a game that could be played without serious consequences, but thousands of viewers have left performances of *Death of a Salesman* talking about unfair interest rates, not about Miller's beautiful writing.

Ben-Hur notwithstanding, it is not always easy to play the game that has to be played, to be willing to enter into the joy or the terror of what we are viewing. It is especially difficult in the case of Hollywood movies, for the star system allows major performers to be paid astronomical salaries merely to be themselves. The public more often than not goes to see personalities like Richard Burton and Elizabeth Taylor. When the latter appeared as Martha in the movie version of *Who's Afraid of Virginia Woolf* (1966), fans all over the country hailed her performance for a number of reasons, not the least of which was that the famous beauty had allowed herself to look fat and homely for the first time. Such veteran performers as James Stewart and Spencer Tracy have personality traits which can never be disguised. Thus real involvement with a Hollywood movie featuring one's favorite star cannot occur when it is all too evident that the film character is an old friend who can be visited some other time. He can never die or, what is perhaps more important, can never be poor. Until recently foreign films seemed more honest, at least in part, because they offered unfamiliar faces on the screen. Now the foreign films, too, have stars, and Marcello Mastroianni, Jean-Paul Belmondo, Claudia Cardinale, Max von Sydow, and Simone Signoret are seen as personalities rather than as characters playing a role.

 Colin Young *from a review of "On the Beach"** (1959)

> The casting fails not because the actors are ill-chosen but because known actors were used at all. We cannot believe in the end of the world when it is represented by such flagrantly successful heroes and heroines of our escapist fiction. We know we shall see *them* again, and if we have been primarily aware of them as themselves rather than as the characters they represent (as is usual), the film is bound to flounder as it reaches its conclusion. As the movie's end is telegraphed, we are reaching for our coats, not searching our consciences. We wonder what Peck's next movie will be, and whether he will get the girl, and keep her, this time.

> * Reprinted from *Film: Book 2, Films of Peace and War*, edited by Robert Hughes, by permission of Grove Press, Inc. Copyright © 1962.

Alienation in Contemporary Drama

Brecht may have been trying to produce alienation, but he sometimes achieved empathy instead. This inconsistency between theory and practice does not mean that alienation is never desirable or possible in the theater. It does not mean that pleasure can never be derived from a work which is viewed as from a distance, without involvement in the fate of the characters.

During the last two decades a movement which has been broadly labeled "Theater of the Absurd" has risen mainly in Europe. If its member dramatists have any common ground at all, it is certainly their terror of creating plots that could be called "sentimental." The stage world of writers like Ionesco and Beckett is full of irrationality. Dramatic dialogue, which in traditional works is compressed, stays directly on course. In theater of the absurd it may begin sensibly enough but rapidly deteriorates into apparent nonsense. Characters are often hard to pin down; their sense of identity is amorphous and shifting. In Edward Albee's *The American Dream* (1960), for example, a woman named Mrs. Barker is referred to as "they" and calls herself "we." She does not seem to know who she is or what she is there for. This presentation of dialogue and character is consistent with contemporary philosophical attitudes concerning the self and society.

Faced with proceedings on the stage that are radically different from those of other plays, the viewer naturally feels detached. He can be interested in them because what is happening at each moment may be funny or just bizarre, but he cannot be concerned with the people on the stage as people or with the outcome of a plot that has been deliberately constructed so as not to move in a straight line like the plots of the past. The initial reaction to such unavoidable alienation may be an uneasy feeling of bewilderment. Knowing that he is supposed to become involved when he goes to a theater, the viewer who is accustomed to the conventional, straightforward stories of Broadway and Hollywood with their familiar characters wandering from plot to plot like freeloaders at New Year's Eve open houses may deny himself the chance to be entertained. Inability to become attached to the characters may erroneously be called "not understanding the show," when the whole point may be that "understanding" in the traditional sense is not necessary. The far-out dramas, in this respect, are like non-objective paintings, which sometimes give novices at art exhibits a hard time of it as they stubbornly search for the story which a painting is not telling.

One of the works of the new drama is Samuel Beckett's *Waiting for Godot* (1952), which was given its American premiere in 1956 at the Coconut Grove Playhouse in Miami. It was a gala evening, with socialites and theater celebrities gathered from all over the country to welcome two events: the raising of the curtain on a million-dollar theater and the arrival of a play from Paris written by a close friend of James Joyce and a writer apparently destined to be one of the literary giants of the twentieth century. But the play itself proved to be a great anti-climax to a highly publicized and highly social event. If the actual performance had been omitted altogether, there might have been less disappointment. The reviewers could have discussed the theater itself, the carpeting, the lighting, and the important personalities seated in the comfortable chairs. As it was, *Waiting for Godot* — one could tell from the tone of the reviews — proved to be a strange choice for such a gala premiere. It was clear that most members of the audience had not found the good time they had expected, and this was duly reported in the newspapers. The chemistry between stage stars and the audience which is so much a part of American show business had not taken place, even though the star of *Godot* was Bert Lahr, the cowardly lion of the enduring *Wizard of Oz* (1939) and certainly a beloved figure to the American public. The first critical reaction, then, was that the play, not the audience, was to blame. The audience expected empathy, got alienation, and did not know what to do with it.

Godot has since won the admiration of both theater and literary critics all over the world, but it could well be that reading the published text of the play and listening to the remarkable recording made by Mr. Lahr with E. G. Marshall and Kurt Kasznar have helped to bring out the play's many subtleties. William Saroyan's comments relative to this recording are greatly useful for a better comprehension of audience and reader responsibility toward avant-garde drama in general.

> You will observe that your friends who most bitterly protest that a work of art is crazy are themselves quite daft and disorganized, if in a very boring manner, whereas the maker of the work is quite clear-eyed, clear-minded, and a master at his work. The maker could make in another manner. Then why does he make in a crazy manner? That question is the beginning of impatient scorn, or of decent study — the beginning of rejection, or of an essay at acceptance, if the thing made is not instantly irresistible.

"Irresistible" is the contagious delight and the wide-eyed innocence of musical-comedy stars Mary Martin and Carol Channing. They project instant charm in vehicles which demand little. But Bert Lahr will not play to the audience in *Godot*. He cannot have the audience's whole-hearted sympathies because then the audience will not have been able to stand back far enough to see *Godot* as a whole.

Thus it is that plays and even movies of recent vintage which leave one cold at first viewing may have to be re-read or re-seen and under-stood from the standpoint of alienation, the opposite of involvement. The trick is to be able to decide whether a feeling of alienation was intended or not. If it was, the play is worth reconsidering, for the theater of aliena-tion must be reckoned with. But finding that one cares little about the events on the stage may be the sign of a chaotic, unintentionally purpose-less play. The difference is important and will be discussed further in the chapter on modern drama.

Theater Is a Game of Conventions

Aristotle made certain assumptions about tragedy and its effect upon the audience, and for the most part these have been endorsed by theater critics ever since. Yet, if alienation is not an impossible response to drama, then it follows that the Aristotelian approach is not necessarily the one set down by heavenly decree. Feeling empathy or alienation are theatrical *conventions,* which vary from age to age and drama to drama.

When two strangers find themselves partners in a bridge game, it is customary for one to ask the other whether he plays the conventions of Goren, Gerber, Stayman, or Blackwood. In the game there are many different bidding and playing procedures that can be followed; but one can never win unless he uses the same conventions as his partner.

A convention of any game is the set of rules which determine the moves and objectives. People can have fun playing games with all sorts of rules, logical and illogical, as long as they know what the rules are.

Critical viewers in the theater are also distinguished for displaying a broad toleration for different conventions in the drama. A stage convention — such as characters singing instead of talking to each other in a musical — is a rule, one we should not mind obeying since it is not a legal decree. It makes the game possible, and the only alternative to abiding by the rules is not playing the game at all. It is as silly to demand that the world of the theater follow only certain rules as it is to insist that the winner in a poker game return all the money to the losers.

Anything that we are willing to believe constitutes a convention of the drama. The list is almost infinite, and each play, each movie, each television show or musical may impose new rules to be accepted. The difficulty is that popular entertainment usually fails to make enough demands on the viewer. Only a limited number of rules are set down. The viewer becomes spoiled, attached to the prevailing conventions and may naturally resist different rules, such as those which govern the strange world of *Waiting for Godot.*

Verisimilitude

Popular stage plays, films, and television shows generally are dominated by the most common single convention of twentieth-century drama: *verisimilitude* or the depiction of surface realism. In a play this convention means that the scenery must look authentic. Every possible effort must be made to disguise the fact that an apparently solid brick wall is made of painted canvas. When a period piece is to be performed, the scene designer must present to the audience an acceptable facsimile of appropriate furniture styles, colors, and room decor; the costumer must study the historical background of the play so thoroughly that even small articles of jewelry will not be found unbelievable to even the most discerning and knowledgeable member of the audience.

Cinema and television have an easier time appearing authentic, for it is now possible for cameramen to be transported to any part of the globe in order to photograph stories in their actual locale. Movie-goers would never accept an African film with *papier-maché* lions. Even underwater episodes, which used to be "shot" through the sides of glass tanks, are usually filmed at the real bottom of the real sea by specialists in underwater photography. Hollywood studios spend millions of dollars making movies look as real as possible. For *Gone with the Wind* (1939), which is still one of the most spectacular of all movie epics, the whole city of Atlanta was reconstructed as it must have looked in 1864 — and then it was actually burned to the ground to comply with the facts of history. (Fortunately the director did not need to shout "Cut!" in the midst of the conflagration.)

A Broadway musical comedy, on the other hand, is not required to have verisimilitude. The audience expects fifteen or twenty different scenes, presented imaginatively and usually with two-dimensional backgrounds, sometimes whisked on and off stage by means of rollers. Such unreality makes it easier to accept a hokum plot and characters who are unlike any that ever existed. The fun begins when a musical hit is transferred to the movie screen and a different set of rules has to be imposed. Against a real background, the nonsense of story and characters is suddenly seen for what it is. It is hard to play the game with the producer and director of the movie, as it is always hard to play a game when one knows one is being deceived.

The opening scene of the film version of Rodgers and Hammerstein's *The Sound of Music* (1965) is a case in point. The enormous screen suddenly was turned into an airplane in which the audience slowly floated over a breathtaking expanse of Austrian mountains. The effect had been used in the first Cinerama production in the early fifties, in which three projectors flashed onto a huge curved screen three images which became one shot giving a remarkably three-dimensional illusion. This process, clearly created to invoke maximum audience empathy, was then imitated successfully by the director of *The Sound of Music* — too successfully, as a matter of fact, for no sooner had the audience accepted the cineramatic convention than it was suddenly asked to accept the fact that the film's heroine was standing atop the highest hill, singing her heart out with a full orchestra accompaniment!

Several scenes later, the Prioress of a convent rebuked the heroine for her habit of singing within what were established as sacred confines. Yet the Prioress herself was to come forth with a booming mezzo-soprano in the middle of the film and in the middle of the convent. In the stage version of the same musical, both she and the heroine sang a duet almost immediately after the censure for singing was issued. But this was more acceptable against an obviously phony backdrop depicting the Prioress' study.

The argument is sometimes advanced that the complete verisimilitude of the movies is more enjoyable than the necessarily limited illusionism of the live theater. Hollywood producers evidently believe the public in general holds such an opinion. Yet accepting conventions can be a source of pleasure for its own sake, just as children have always had fun

BAITING THE TRAPPS DEPT.

In times past, Hollywood has turned out some big, corny movie musicals. But the biggest, corniest movie musical of all is now playing. Sure, the songs are lovely, but take them away and what have you got? Nothing but a collection of the same old dull clichés and boring tear-jerker gimmicks that you've been seeing in movie musicals for years. (We're even falling asleep writing this introduction about it!) It's obvious that this motion picture was made with only one goal in mind: Mainly to hear

THE $OUND OF MONEY

*How come I'm alone, and there's so much music?
High up on a hill, with no one in view?
So how do they get all this sound and music?
A musical quiz I now pose to you.

Just see how I race up this steep mountainside
Without ever losing a beat!
You'd think that my lungs would give out up here
Over ten thousand feet!

To do all these things
  with a wide-mouthed **grin**
Really should not amaze;
I've had lots of rest,
'Cause they filmed it on five different days!

I'm not singing now; I am pre-recorded!
I'm just mouthing words I have sung before!
And how does it feel to be singing nothing?
It's an aw-ful bore!

ARTIST: MORT DRUCKER
WRITER: STAN HART

Sung to the tune of "The Sound of Music"

Reprinted from *MAD*. Copyright © 1966 by E. C. Publications, Inc.

putting on shows in the cellar by ignoring the steam pipe or else turning it into the Brooklyn Bridge.

Conventions are *not* a necessary evil, even though the movies — and now, television — seem to consider verisimilitude as the crowning glory of the drama, that toward which all forms of theater have really been working. But the viewer who accepts this premise is betting all his money on one horse. Much of the original popularity of Thornton Wilder's *Our Town* (1940) stemmed from the delight audiences took in the simplicity of the production — the charm of the bare stage which became the town of Grover's Corners by the merest snap of the imagination, the stepladders which represented neighboring houses, or the boy perched atop one ladder naïvely wooing the girl next door, perched a foot away from him

One of the lightest musicals ever created, *The Fantasticks* (1960), became an enduring New York institution because of its method of presentation. Much of its charm derives from the fact that its tiny cast of nine performers sings and dances on a miniature stage without any scenery, using an obviously marked "Prop Box" from which objects like the moon are drawn as needed for the story. This fanciful tale about two young lovers separated from each other by a wall even employs an actor holding his arm out to represent the wall. The reason? Nothing but the recognition that audiences love the chance to make believe.

When Hollywood filmed *Our Town,* it photographed a very real Grover's Corners and stole from the play its most admirable feature. Yet film viewers who simply accepted what they were given may not have realized that even verisimilitude is a convention. It is a simple little fact that nonetheless bears constant reiteration: VERISIMILITUDE IS ONLY ONE OF MANY POSSIBLE CONVENTIONS.

There is, of course, nothing really wrong with enjoying scenic grandeur in a movie. The vast, frozen emptiness of Siberia, as shown in the film *Doctor Zhivago* (1965), had an undeniable impact that certainly could not have been equalled by any other medium. There is nothing wrong with enjoying *any* convention as long as it is recognized as a convention. The difficulty arises when verisimilitude is mistaken for reality.

Before the advent of television, housewives listened devotedly to radio "soap operas" in which both voices and conversation were made to sound very lifelike. Thousands of listeners wrote letters of advice to characters who were in trouble and even sent gifts to expectant mothers. At the end of each year all the networks donated these presents to charitable institutions, no doubt a worthy and laudable practice, yet rendered possible by a frightening price — the inability of people to distinguish between fantasy and reality.

All drama is fantasy, no matter how much it may resemble real life and no matter how significant it may be. The critical viewer may agree with Keats that art is a heightened reality, is realer than real, but he would scarcely knit bootees for a paid actress' non-existent baby. To those who maintain that it is better not to be aware of the fantasy element, that total escape from reality is, after all, what is most desired, it can be said that the total surrender to illusion is just not possible for a thinking person in full command of his wits. Since this is the case, it makes sense to play a game of make-believe and know that it *is* a game.

Other Conventions: Scene, Tone, Character, Action, Language

The critical viewer is able to suspend his disbelief as long as the conventions used are consistent with each other. Since verisimilitude was the first convention discussed, it can be said that *scene* is no doubt the first element of make-believe that we are asked to accept as real. Every story told in dramatic form, whether on stage or on the screen, has to be taking place somewhere. A bare stage and a few simple props or none at all can suffice if the play is powerful, the acting believable, and the audience sophisticated enough. But when props, for example, are missing in the first scene, they may not be used in the second. This would be an example of inconsistency in the handling of conventions.

Time, also, can pass as slowly or as rapidly as the writer requires, but a mixing up of time sequences calls attention to the whole unreality of drama-going. Half of the work should not be assumed to take place in one day, while the other half covers a sixty-year time span. In plays and movies with action that is supposedly continuous in time, one character may say to another after a three-minute dialogue, "We've been arguing now for twenty minutes." But later in the play a twenty-minute dialogue should not be spoken of as a three-minute interval. Time can go backwards or forwards, or there may be no time at all — as in *Waiting for Godot*. But the rules cannot change once they are set down.

Closely allied to scene is the convention of *tone*, but no convention can be more difficult to describe. Tone has its pure forms: the tragic, the somber, the serious, the lighthearted, the absurd. And normally a drama committed to one or another should not stray too far, except that the giants of the theater are sometimes able to commit grievous sins against tonal purity and not only be forgiven but actually achieve an extraordinary sense of reality.

Traditionally, however, the light moments in tragedies are used for contrast, to make the sense of ominous doom more effective. Serious moments in comedies provide needed relief from laughter; otherwise the things that are supposed to be funny would become increasingly unfunny. Tone is a commitment made to the audience by the writer and the director, in exchange for the audience's agreement to accept the conventions of the drama. It is a promise that what started out ridiculous will remain ridiculous; it is the assurance made to the audience that it may laugh at everything that happens. Nothing is more disappointing to the critical viewer than to recognize that this commitment has not been met, that a character who was introduced as a bungling idiot has become elegant and witty because it was convenient for the script.

Charlie Chaplin's famous "little fellow" with his ducklike walk, spinning cane, and proud derby offered a unique combination of absurdity and pathos that were not inconsistent with each other. The character he created was a complete misfit in the elegant world he wanted to inhabit and was therefore funny. But there was more than comedy: the larger implications of the great Chaplin films involved society as a whole, even existence itself, forces that overwhelmed the little tramp and robbed him of his dignity. The loss of human dignity is not hilarious; thus Chaplin's character could be two things at once, an achievement not unusual in great comedy. Tonal inconsistency, however, occurs when a character or plot is one thing now, another later on.

Judy Garland became famous for the way she concluded her television and night club act. After wearing dazzling gowns for most of the evening she came out costumed as the Chaplinesque little tramp, sat on the floor and sang "Over the Rainbow" and so expressed the pathetic fantasies which unhappy people everywhere must have in order to live. It was a tonal change that worked because it did not involve an illogical switch in perspective. Miss Garland's expressive face, her extraordinary eyes that retain their child-like look of innocence no matter how many years go by, give continual promise that the dream inside will cry out, even though the voice will quiver from a thousand past disappointments.

Character is a third convention of the drama — or, more specifically, the approach to character is. In a work controlled by the convention of verisimilitude the people on the stage or the screen should make us forget that they are players, sometimes famous stars. It is their obligation to work towards creating this illusion. In a musical comedy, on the other hand, the stars can be themselves. It is their personalities we have come to enjoy. Bob Hope, one of the major comic artists of our time, has always professed a burning desire to play Hamlet. "Inside" sources insist he is really being serious. This is a land in which the mailman can become president but a comedian cannot do a Shakespearean tragedy. Bob Hope has had to pay the high price of fame: to be cast forever in a certain role by all of his admirers. Jack Benny is expected to be stingy and to turn green every time the subject of money comes up. But Richard Burton is supposed to be a serious actor and need not resemble himself in every role he plays. Unfortunately, his distinctive mannerisms, his vocal precision, his way of tossing barbs from the side of his mouth without seeming to alter the rhythm of his breathing, have become so well known that directors appear to exploit them at every possible opportunity. As a result, Richard Burton has become a personality actor whom the audience is willing to accept as Richard Burton, no matter what the conditions of the plot may be.

The critical viewer, the person who can handle empathy and detachment at the same time, can enjoy Richard Burton's performances, can play any game Richard Burton wants him to play. It is, conversely, the uncritical viewer, who is more likely to wonder why Mr. Burton should be playing an American character with a British accent.

The convention of character in drama has changed as attitudes toward human identity have changed. The confusion which can be engendered by not recognizing conventions for what they are is illustrated by the vast amount of words which scholars have poured forth regarding Shakespeare's people. "Did Hamlet have an unnatural fixation on his mother?" "Why did Hamlet so mistreat Ophelia?" "Was Hamlet really in love with Ophelia?" are questions that probably can never be or should be answered since they involve assumptions about the human ego and human motives which belong to a psychological age like our own, not Shakespeare's.

There is also a profound difference between the drama of the past and that of the present in the matter of character continuity. Ever since Chekhov expanded the province of the play to include what was happening off-stage as well as on-stage, it has become customary for dramatists, directors, and actors to think in terms of what happened before the plot begins and what will happen in the future. Thus the question of the "pre-play" Hamlet is familiar in academic circles. When he was attending school at Wittenberg, was Hamlet idealistic? Was he pure? Did he place women on pedestals? Those who believe he did may argue that Hamlet's disillusionment with his mother, expressed in his first soliloquy, clearly suggests what kind of young man he has been and is now. But the astonishingly simple truth is that there is no pre-play Hamlet. Nothing, of course, prevents a modern actor's interpreting the role in the context of contemporary character creation — in which the past has to be carefully reconstructed; but it is still legitimate for the Shakespearean actor to play each scene at face value, to believe that each speech says what it says instead of being an oblique indication of sadism, masochism, or homosexuality, dating back to an unhappy childhood.

That all characters in a drama should even be taken for human beings is a matter of convention, not necessity. Dinosaurs seem quite at home in the living-room of Mr. and Mrs. Antrobus in Thornton Wilder's *The Skin of Our Teeth* (1942), which deliberately aims to bewilder audiences stubbornly clinging to the expectation of seeing verisimilitude. In Oriental drama it is traditional for players to imitate animals or forces of nature, such as rainstorms, just as in medieval drama characters could have names like Good Deeds, Fellowship, or Vice and so were not to be regarded as actual people.

In Greek tragedy actors wore masks that did not pretend to be replicas of real faces, and they did not offer themselves as facsimiles of persons that might have existed in real life. Moreover, Greek plays had a Chorus that sang and danced and watched all of the action but had more than human powers of understanding. The Chorus was there in the sense that other characters spoke to it, interacted with it; but the players who comprised the Chorus were supposed to be a collective voice of reason, not individual persons who ate breakfast, had toothaches, and worried separately about the fate of the kingdom.

Thus the comment "Nobody would do that" or "Why didn't he do this?" may or may not be apt. It depends upon the prevailing conventions of character. It is hopeless to suppose that all the dramas of the past could be completely changed every time conventions change. The viewer who thinks a masked performer or a dinosaur huddling before a fire for warmth is silly is missing the benefits which theater can offer him. Furthermore, inability to accept differing character conventions has a striking parallel in the real life unwillingness to accept unconventional people because they too are different and seem strange.

Another convention is that of *action*. It is only verisimilitude which requires that a movie fist-fight be authentic, right down to the broken nose and the spurting blood. That we are willing to believe a fight is really taking place at all on a piece of white material called a movie screen represents a temporary adjustment in what we can believe. Yet, once again, the expectation of verisimilitude can interfere with the enjoyment of dramatic action presented in other ways. Audience members who would titter during the stabbings and poisonings that occur in wholesale amounts in Elizabethan tragedies might accept unquestioningly the code whereby the villain in a western calls out before he shoots, so that his victim will not have been shot in the back.

Shakespeare's characters sometimes talk directly to the audience, but this is supposed to represent their inmost thoughts. Characters in Shakespeare, as well as in seventeenth-century plays, talk to each other in the presence of others who presumably hear nothing. In a modern musical the girl might tell the boy in song that she is stepping out of his life so as not to stand in the way of his singing career, yet he never notices what a fine voice she herself has. Characters kiss each other and shoot each other; armies — in Shakespeare — cross the stage making token, simulated combat; the Chorus — in Greek tragedy — speak or sing in unison, and their constant presence never seems odd to the other characters; in opera nearly every single line is sung, even, as in modern opera in English, innocuous comments like "Do you take sugar or cream in your coffee?" In short, anything that happens in play or film and the way in which it happens are matters of convention and must be judged on the basis of a full understanding of what the rules are that each work imposes.

It is even possible for a character to express everything through movement. Pantomime, the art of expressing something entirely through facial expressions and bodily movements, is an ancient, venerable, and enduring form of drama, which along with dance was an integral part of early theater.

On the stage or on the screen movement, face, and gesture are under the intense scrutiny of the audience and so must all mean something that can be interpreted at every moment.

However, it is dialogue that the audience most expects and *language* is perhaps the most universal convention of the theater. Nothing resembling a play would have been possible without the words. Since language-making and language interpretation are universal human instincts, a respectful attention to words is characteristic of the audience participation in even the most primitive kind of ceremony. From the witch doctor with his magical incantations to the most soaring poetry in Shakespeare, words have always had a greater impact upon people gathered *en masse* than any other single element of communication.

In the beginning, when the Greek drama was intimately connected with a festival, when its origins were obviously religious, there was no question at all that the words spoken should be dignified, elevated far above the language of real life — in short, poetic. Poetry was for centuries the only acceptable kind of stage talk. Nor was dramatic poetry written with only the intellectuals in mind. The entire population of Athens attended the theater, and in Shakespeare's time no play could be a hit without the enthusiastic support of the common people who paid their penny to stand and watch it. Perhaps Greek and Shakespearean audiences did not understand or were not excited by every line they heard, but they had the *habit of listening,* something which modern audiences do not have.

Today's theater-goers have been spoiled by verisimilitude in dramatic language. The criteria for accepting stage talk as real-life conversations have changed with society, so that a line like "I have adored only you, Millicent, throughout this whole wretched existence" could have been taken for realistic — even daringly so — in 1895, while we are not surprised to hear once forbidden words coming from even the movie screens of today. As the language spoken by characters has become homelier, franker, and closer to the monosyllabic vocabulary that all of us use in our casual daily conversations, the convention of dialogue has tended to have less and less impact as something to be enjoyed for its own sake. Even in the most distinguished of modern plays, language is likely to be merely functional, because the playwrights usually limit themselves to the kind of talk that is probable. In the days of poetic drama — that is, in almost all theater prior to the late eighteenth century — dramatists used language that was possible.

This distinction between the probable and the possible is a very great one and involves all the other conventions as well as that of language, for once an audience is willing to believe in things that are only possible, its sphere of enjoying the imagination of playwrights is widened almost infinitely.

The insistence upon dramatic dialogue's fidelity to the way people talk in real life creates for the theater a task that is both impossible to accomplish completely and undesirable to attempt at all. Somewhere along the line the concept developed that drama is more believable when people sound prosaic, not poetic. The prose of the late-nineteenth-century realists like Ibsen was no doubt an improvement over the pseudo-poetics of earlier nineteenth-century plays in which Plainjane Trueheart from Peoria was given a ridiculously elevated lingo to deliver. The apologists for prose over poetry in the theater maintained, rightly, that elevation of language was proper when stage characters were aristocrats. The change-over to prose was in many respects a part of the common-man movement as a whole, with cultivated diction sounding snobbish and more conventional dialogue suggesting that the playwright was very much in sympathy with the cause of democracy.

But no matter how plainly a thing is said on stage or screen, dramatic dialogue can never be a true equivalent of real-life conversation. All one has to do to test the validity of this statement is to listen closely to what people say. It is rare that a complete sentence of any complexity is spoken. The sound of ordinary speech would not hold an audience long. An accurate transcription of dialogue would include many silences, grunts, yawns, irrelevant remarks, and references to people unidentified except by nickname or some other special code known only to those present. Even the sound of a crisis in real life contains the kind of aimless "undramatic" sounds which would be extremely difficult to communicate.

Real conversationalists either do not fully express what they might or do not finish what they try to express. Since the responses of the people being spoken to are not controlled by a playwright, the subjects of conversations tend to change from one minute to the next. People are required to talk entirely too much for the brief amount of time that can be spent in carefully considering what is to be said. If one does take the time, the opportunity to speak often goes by and the chance to tell a favorite story is lost as the subject changes. The speakers who are able to dominate conversations are usually the intrepid ones who open their mouths first and then worry about what to say.

In contrast, stage dialogue, whether prose or poetry, has compression of thought, intensity of feeling, and a more logical sense of direction and purpose. In the last scene of Ibsen's *A Doll's House* (1879) the wife tells the husband to sit down because she has some things to tell him. There follows a famous conversation about women's rights, the double-standard in a society, and the fact that an individual's freedom is more important even than family obligations. In real life no conversation can make such definite points without any extraneous commentary. The reason is obvious. Nobody pays admission to hear real-life conversations. When a group of people gather in a body to hear someone else talk, the conditions immediately become theatrical. Thus the minister toils in advance over his Sunday sermon and the politician pays someone else to plan what he is to say. For both, economy and precision of language are necessary in order to hold the attention of their listeners. For the most part, talk in real life is motivated by the need to express onself or the need to socialize; in drama, talk is controlled communication. Everything said must advance the plot, reveal character, or raise the pertinent issue.

When the conventional quality of theatrical language is understood, there is less and less reason to limit oneself to hearing the imitation monosyllabic chit-chat that abounds in drama today. As one becomes not only a more critical viewer but a viewer more knowledgeable in the drama of past ages, one discovers yet another, greater dimension that is possible to achieve in theatrical language: sound. One learns that a major reason for Shakespeare's immortality is not only what his characters say, which is part of the inherited wisdom of Western man, but the rhapsody of sound through which they say it.

The Critical Viewer

Where Critical Standards Come From

The twilight zone between critical viewing and popcorn eating is an uncomfortable place to exist, but everyone goes through it during the stage when he knows that he intensely likes or dislikes what he is seeing but wishes he knew why. He has risen above the search for a security that waits for him in the darkness of the auditorium; he is trying to feel empathy but at the same time to maintain the needed critical detachment. He is uncomfortably aware of all his reactions. At times he laughs at one undeniably funny sequence and comments to himself, "This means I like what I see." Five minutes later he may catch himself nodding, unable to keep his eyes open: "This means the plot is deplorably dull." The next scene is filled with unbearable tension. The girl was told not to open the locked door because something terrible would happen, and there she is, slowly doing it now. "This means the plot is filled with suspense. Is that good?" If, as the contents of the room seem about to be revealed, the movie cuts to another scene, is the director being original? needlessly prolonging the agony? cheating the audience? And so on through a night of self-conscious, decidedly unenjoyable, almost-critical theater-going. It hardly seems a worthwhile substitute for the bliss of ignorance.

There are times when anyone will emerge from a theater without a definite opinion at all — just some vague sensations that are hard to put into words and yet an appeal to authority is unsatisfactory. One can look around at the face of a friend, secretly hoping for a clue. Jerry, the respected one, is frowning; perhaps the film was not good after all. But to parrot the opinion of someone else — whether friend, journalist or academician — is dishonest. Once a definitely new level of awareness is reached, there is never any going back.

Hence the familiar complaint of those who have begun a study of the theater and the movies: "Now that I've started really trying to look at what's going on and how it is affecting me, I can't enjoy myself anymore." No comforting answer is possible. It is easier to accept the fact that, at the outset, there will be misunderstanding of principles as they are applied to work seen. Thus: "I saw *Oedipus* produced at the university theater last night, and I can see now what is meant by classical tragedy. It means that you are not supposed to have any emotions toward it because everything dramatic happens off-stage." Such a response confuses displayed violence and feeling; the apprentice critical viewer may fear any emotion at all in an attempt to curb excess. No one expects him to leave the theater having felt no empathy whatever.

Where then does it all begin? It would be horrible if there were one supreme critical authority, a critical encyclopedia, to which we would all refer whenever we had doubts; a compendious tome that would offer an annual supplement to bring it up to date. It would be as inhibiting as fear of hanging a picture without a decorator's advice or (worse) planning devastating remarks before a date through the aid of an authority on love. Half the pleasure of taste in theater as in any other activity stems from making up one's own mind. Though reading a favorite professional critic is a pleasure, we do not read criticism in order to discover how to react to the play seen the night before. The professionals do not help that much, because they themselves make certain assumptions about their readers. When Judith Crist, for example, comments that a certain play concludes with the characters' being sadder but wiser, while the audience "is merely sadder," she is assuming that her followers understand for themselves all of the ways in which a good play might leave them wiser and all of the reasons that seeing a bad play leaves one feeling sad. She is therefore reporting that mature viewers will not find anything satisfying about the play, no matter what particular elements each may tend to notice.

A critical viewer is someone who has mastered the basic vocabulary of theater-going, including the elements of play structure. He can note the elements as he views the work without destroying his sense of the whole. These elements are not the invention of any one critic of the theater but are intrinsic to the very nature of drama.

All of them derive from the logic of the art form itself; what it has to have in order to do what it must do. In the twenty-five centuries since drama began as live theater, the stage has naturally been the main source of interest, and critical terms are stage terms. In our own era, as movies became important, some stage terms remained the same for the new medium.

The Protagonist

From the first, every drama tended to center on one character more than the others. It is easy to take this for granted and not consider it a phenomenon; that is, not recognize that herein lies a very essential difference between the drama and real life. In reality there are central figures only occasionally. At a shower the bride-to-be is the Cinderella girl of the day; at a ceremony honoring a war hero, no one else seriously exists; at a funeral the deceased is the unwavering object of attention. The emotions of the others — the "supporting cast" — are intensified and normally very sympathetic ones. Who will talk about the faults of the bride-to-be, the war hero, or the deceased?

The unpleasant details save themselves for a rainy day and may soon crop up once more. A year after her marriage, the bride is no longer the special girl, no longer even a newlywed, receiving the warm applause of the audience when the night club master of ceremonies points to the honeymooning couple. War heroes would soon become bores if they walked around jangling their medals, and after the burial, the memory of even the most beloved dims.

That a drama should have one figure, the protagonist, around whom most of the action revolves, probably has much to do with the hero-worship of less democratic ages than ours. The Athenians, who were the world's first theater-goers, did have a democracy, in many respects the purest one that has ever existed; but they admired and respected greatness in a manner that cannot be matched today.

A study of the development of Greek religion suggests a movement away from supernaturalism towards humanism — that is, the gods increasingly resembled human beings. Conversely, this tended to raise the image of man. The subject matter of many of the early tragedies, such as Aeschylus' *Prometheus Bound* (c. 465 B.C.), is the warfare between man and gods. Based on the myth of the punishment of Prometheus for his audacity in stealing fire from the gods and presenting the gift to mankind, the play ends with a prophecy that one day someone (Hercules) will come and release Prometheus from his bondage. Of course, there are many other factors which played their part in so complex a development as the roots of protagonism in drama, but the idea of singling out one man as the hero could be compared to the common practice whereby two warring groups settled their differences by having their two most skillful fighters battle to the death.

Greek literature in general possesses the champion-as-hero; qualities that might be termed "likable" are certainly not insisted upon. In Homer's *Iliad* (c. 850 B.C.), for example, of the three central figures, Agamemnon, Achilles, and Hector, only Hector has characteristics that would be sympathetic by today's standards. That is, he is shown against a domestic background and seems to love his wife. But when she begs him not to desert her and go to fight Achilles, he rejects her plea, thereby elevating personal honor to a position above that of the home or even love. The other heroes are hard-headed, vain, and murderous. In one memorable scene, one that virtually captures the whole essence of the classical world, Agamemnon comes upon his brother Menelaus, who has his foot planted on top of a fallen Trojan warrior and his lance poised, ready for the inevitable and expected thrust. But Menelaus hesitates. For a fleeting moment he sees no sense in reckless killing, and it appears almost as if Homer were about to make history. But Agamemnon then administers a severe scolding to his brother, who promptly apologizes for his unheroic lapse and disposes of the captive with cool efficiency. Today the question of morality would inevitably arise, but for Homer's listeners the moment simply generated some suspense. The matter was not one of right or wrong but one of being or not being a hero.

The connotations which the word "hero" has acquired in popular entertainment have their roots, not in the classical, but in the Christian world. In the medieval romances the dashing knight risking all for his God, his country, and his lady fair was a hero quite as much in the moral sense as in the physical. One implied the other as a matter of fact. In the western it is the self-sacrificing town marshal who is fastest on the draw, who "cleaned up this here town and made it fittin' fer decent women to walk the streets again."

But there is enormous confusion about protagonism now. Quick-draw Slade is a combination of Achilles and Sir Galahad (though about as close to the original as a TV dinner is to a banquet on the French Line), and he is meant to inspire empathy by his murderous skills and moral approbation by being on the right side, which means the side of right. In this respect he is a descendant of the perfect popular hero — Robin Hood.

The ideal feminine protagonist for popular entertainment is a descendant of Cinderella, demure, pretty, and thoroughly brainless — as man's ideal companion has always been pictured. But she goes a step beyond her male counterpart, Robin Hood, by having nice things happen to her just because she herself is so nice. Her inexorable rise to the height of economic and sexual success in the palace of Prince Charming offers proof that all of us live in a moral universe, in which goodness is rewarded.

But the modern theater has inherited one other kind of hero from the past, and in many respects he is becoming the dominant protagonist of today: the charming rogue. No doubt a close first cousin to the knight-hero who was as pugnacious as he was virtuous, the rogue simply sheds the virtue but retains the skills of maneuvering his adventurous way through life. He became the darling of the jaded audiences of the seventeenth-century theaters, who cared little about Christian morals and a lot about having fun. Their hero became the one most proficient at finding pleasure, and his habits became models to strive for or at least to dream about in secret.

The middle-class, who filled the theaters in the late eighteenth and early nineteenth centuries, began, as might be expected, by going along with the Sir Galahad and Cinderella figures. The male protagonist was manly-because-virtuous and virtuous-because-manly, a perfect champion of middle-class values in every respect. He retained the heroic qualities of his ancestor by triumphing over those with more wealth and social status, but he did so in the name of truth, honesty, purity — graces which upper class people could not be expected to match. The female protagonist was forever in danger of being ruined by upper class immorality. But she was always saved in time and raised considerably in the social scale. Thus began the practice of equating goodness with economic advancement, something earlier knight-heroes and ladies fair at least did not have to worry about.

Contemporary rogue heroes, such as James Bond, are sometimes referred to as "spoof heroes" or "mock heroes" — an indication of changing tastes, but not necessarily developing sophistication on the part of audiences. As the champion of the populace because he is above the petty morality which governs their lives, the rogue hero offers no truer portrait of a man than did Robin Hood. Actually, Achilles makes a far more acceptable rogue hero because he mirrors the true custom of admiring the champion. More realistic heroes in the classic sense would be the holder of the heavyweight title or a crafty murderer who has, with the aid of a clever lawyer, evaded punishment for his crimes.

Just as annoying as the unworthy protagonist is the "accidental" protagonist, the one who simply happens to be around all the time and who claims audience sympathy because he is familiar to them. To say that every person is important because he is human may be good philosophy but it is bad drama.

It is not a simple matter to decide that a given protagonist is the right one. Since he is the only one at hand, the problem becomes that of determining, first, that he is possible and, second, that what he is, says, or does is interesting. In dramas that deliberately inspire alienation, the protagonist may be a symbol of an idea, and it is the idea that must have appeal.

When a protagonist is possible, he is believable within whatever kind of framework the author has created. If the work is a musical, for example, he must have charm, personal magnetism, warmth. The audience for a musical likes to be caught up in high spirits, the feelings engendered whenever people are in a good mood and bear each other no malice. If the protagonist is callous and exploits his fellowman with a "dog-eat-dog" philosophy of life, the drama must belong to a world in which goodness does not prevail.

But there has to be something special about a protagonist: wit, ingenuity, perception, or else involvement in a conflict that seems typical of many men, important in its own right because of its originality, or worthy of concern because the stakes are high. There is almost no limit to the list of qualifications held by protagonists that "work" for us.

Fidelity to real life is sometimes important, but it is not the sole criterion. Or, to put it in proper historical perspective, the heroes of the past were rather more celebrated for their uncommonness; and one cannot help believing that the workability of T. E. Lawrence as the protagonist of the admirable motion picture *Lawrence of Arabia* (1963) can be attributed in no small measure to the fascinating uniqueness of the man. On the other hand, Arthur Miller obviously intended that his salesman, Willy Loman, should be a mirror in whom the average citizen might see reflected his own unhappy existence. The decision regarding the protagonist must be made on the basis of each drama's intentions and possibilities. The matter is a pragmatic one. If we are willing to accept the hero, the author has succeeded. The trick is to resist the cliché heroes who come with ready-made heroic credentials culled from a million previous plots.

Finally, there doesn't have to be one protagonist at all. The significance of a playwright like Chekhov becomes doubly impressive when it is recognized that, instead of doing away with a hero (as has sometimes been said), he creates a drama of many heroes — plays that fall into tiny units, each of which has its own protagonist. Thus our sympathetic concern eventually gets around to almost every character on the stage. Perhaps Chekhov's work represents the logical handling of protagonism in this age without champions.

The Villain

If nearly every play has a single protagonist, the main character who attracts audience concern, it does not follow that nearly every play must contain his unsympathetic counterpart. The formula plots of movies and television make all dramas become battles between good guys and bad guys, but such villainy, in the sense of personal, human, throughly malicious evil, is rare in quality theater.

Most dramas have antagonistic elements which are responsible for the conflict in which the hero is involved, but the conflict in great dramas is seldom between man and man. While it is not impossible for one man to be dedicated to the ruin of another, the major dramatists, over the centuries, all appear to have found the truly destructive aspects of life to be larger and more inescapable forces than individual characters.

Even the propagandistic plays and films which abound during time of war need to treat their callous and sadistic torturers as "the enemy" — in other words, as a force greater than any one man. It is through individual characters that "the enemy" is given dramatic life, but without representing something vast and omnipotent, the torturers become minimal as true threats. Of course, many war dramas do indeed become displaced westerns. Instead of inspiring the deep-rooted alarm which an ideological enemy might give, the other side becomes "them" — silly-looking snipers hiding in trees, getting shot one by one just like Indians or the cattle rustler and his gang.

The trouble with such confined antagonism is that it is so predictably and easily surmounted. The great dramatists know that evil is a basic condition, not an occasion, of life; and therefore the great plots offer conflicts that cannot be resolved by a carefully aimed rifle or by a hair-breadth escape over the barbed-wire fence.

In that specialty of Hollywood, the light romantic comedy, antagonism often comes from such improbable barriers to immediate marriage as the rich but unfeeling father of the girl, who wants her to marry a solid and dull businessman or from the "other woman," who wears leopard skin pajamas and drinks straight gin; (in post-censorship "adult" versions of this genre she may even be a vindictive wife, representing an early mistake of the hero).

In mystery thrillers there is invariably a stalking fiend, who waits in London fogs to strangle Cockney show girls, or a hood, who is finally out on parole and vows to get even with the cop who sent him up the river.

Even musical comedies and the wildest farces have their antagonists. Usually, the more weary, stale, flat, and unprofitable the plot, the more specific and personal the antagonism. It is more reassuring to the audience to find that the bad things of life are really just people and can be taken care of.

An example of the difference in the handling of evil between an honest stage drama and a popular television show is provided by two adaptations of Henry James' classic ghost story *The Turn of the Screw* (1898). In William Archibald's stage version, *The Innocents* (1950), the two ghosts who are supposedly trying to seduce the souls of two young children are never actually seen by the audience. The viewer feels continually that he is about to witness a hideous materialization, but the terror evoked by the play is self-induced. An empty stage becomes frightening to look at, as is a flight of steps half shrouded in darkness. But nothing definitely supernatural ever occurs. The play is a masterpiece of horror primarily because its evil is nameless, everywhere and nowhere, and therefore unconquerable.

A television version, however, used an actor and an actress as the ghosts. Their faces were properly horrid in the white clown makeup, exaggerated eyebrows, and the cruelly drawn mouths, but after they were once seen, their menace diminished noticeably. One man and one woman, however dead, do not have the impact, because they do not offer the conflict of larger forces.

Antagonism is not really equated with evil in pre-Christian drama. The humanistic Greeks saw dramatic conflict in terms of man, in his desire to assert his greatness, and the fatal weakness of pride which led to his downfall. Or else they saw it in terms of man against the dark, inscrutable, and universal fate which refused to allow him to achieve perfection. Even in *The Iliad,* which preceded the origins of the theater by several centuries, there was dramatic conflict between men — Achilles and Hector, for example — but it is not villainous antagonism. Homer was Greek, and thus technically Hector was "the enemy." Nonetheless he is handled with as much sympathy as Achilles, possibly even more. It is the gods who are responsible for the Trojan war. Though Achilles, the Greek champion, slays Hector, the weeping of Hector's widow as she sees her husband's body dragged ignominiously around the walls of Troy by Achilles' chariot tells the reader that no great victory has been won. The war has solved nothing.

In Sophocles' *Oedipus the King* (c. 430 B.C.) antagonism comes from two sources: the past itself, in which Oedipus did in fact murder his father and marry his mother according to the prophecy; and his own pride, which leads him to insist that he, the world-renowned king, could not have done such deeds. Both forces are inescapable and lead the hero inevitably to destruction.

In Sophocles' *Antigone* (440 B.C.) the plot concerns a clash between two characters: Antigone, the daughter of Oedipus, and Creon, her uncle and king of Thebes. The reason for the conflict is Antigone's belief in the sacredness of the individual and Creon's arrogant assertion that the king's authority must be total. Though Antigone says all the right things about human dignity, her stubborn refusal to bow before Creon's power becomes an antagonistic force. By bringing out the worst in the king, by defying him and making it impossible for him not to condemn her to death, she becomes the lure which leads him on to his own tragic end.

At times sympathy rests with Antigone, but by the time we reach the conclusion, we cannot help but feel pity for the king, who has lost his son and his wife as well as his high estate. The play thus illustrates the Greek preoccupation with the fact of human suffering rather than an easy division between the perfectly good and the perfectly bad. It also points up the characteristic Greek concept of destruction through pride, which is at once the reason for man's tragedy and the source of his greatness.

Christianity was responsible for the eventual development of stories and plays about goodness against wickedness. Virtue, in the Christian sense of purity and holiness, became the outstanding trait of the hero, while the antagonist was a treacherous character, who represented the power of Satan on earth. In other words, it now became possible to say that evil *could* reside in particular persons, Satan's disciples, and as such could be successfully fought and overcome.

The villain, as a stock element in a dramatic plot, owes his birth partly to the evil agents in medieval Christian plays and partly to the interpretation of the character and writings of Niccolo Machiavelli (1468–1527).

In *The Prince* (1532), Machiavelli stated his conviction that a ruler ought to have absolute control, gained and retained through any means. He based this belief on his view of men as being basically evil, requiring a firm hand to protect them from each other. But when Machiavelli rose to great literary fame, particularly in England, he himself became confused with what he had observed about mankind and his name became a synonym for evil. Sixteenth-century English literature abounds with mention of him as the devil's advocate.

The evil antagonist of English drama came to be the "Machiavellian" figure and was given his most memorable forms by Shakespeare himself. Usually of Latin background, the Machiavellian had the black hair and flashing eyes and teeth that became the trademark of the villain on stage and screen.

What distinguishes the Shakespearean villains, such as Richard III and Iago, from those of lesser Elizabethan playwrights is that they are far from two-dimensional in their evil. They are human beings with an extraordinary ability to justify their actions to themselves. They see themselves as heroes, triumphing over the less skillful and the less imaginative. They do not slither about, laughing horrendously, admitting they are villains. Richard III and Iago are both geniuses at their craft. The evil of the former is a political philosophy, leading him to murder after murder with cold and methodical dispatch. Iago is so successful in his efforts to become Othello's master that all the damage is done before Othello learns the truth. We are left with no sense whatever that the villain has destroyed himself or been defeated by a superior adversary. Iago's end seems much more the inevitable burning out of a magnificent fire. He has run out of terrible things to do. He does not repent; he is not converted. He does not offer a last-minute sermon against wickedness as a way of life.

Shakespeare does about as much as a writer can do with personal evil. His greatest villains represent total depravity. In contrast, the villains of popular movies and television shows are bad in simple and specific ways. We are meant to believe that they are incorrigibly wicked, but we never see them in solitude, expressing a complete philosophy of evil. Thus they are far more likely to be defeated, since their kind of villainy demands certain bold steps. The cattle rustler must rustle. Because the challenge is obvious it can be met. Head him off at the pass.

What makes the Shakespearean villain so terrifying is that he is a monster that is believably human. He seriously raises the possibility that there can be personal, dedicated iniquity. The ultimate effect of a Shakespearean villain on the audience is to make them aware that real-life evil is never superficial or easily overcome. The Hollywood formula is to suggest, on the other hand, that existence is always morally efficient. One can walk the West with confidence: he will never be shot in the back. In time of war the enemy will prove thoroughly incompetent when the chips are down.

The trend in serious drama — that is, drama not specifically aimed at the commercial market — has been toward erasing hard and fast distinctions between good characters and bad ones. The heyday of the monster of iniquity is by now well past, and he has been succeeded by an increasingly psychological antagonist. Shakespeare himself had paved the way for the newer concept in his creation of Macbeth, the ambitious politician who, like Richard III, commits murder for a throne but experiences the pangs of conscience for it. Macbeth is both hero and villain at the same time. Near the end of the play, when it is obvious that he has lost everything, that his dedication to evil has proved futile, he has a frightening vision of existence as empty and meaningless. The play is the tragedy of a man who could come to such nihilism, not the story of a villain's defeat.

The major dramatists of the late nineteenth and twentieth centuries tend to think of good and bad in relative terms, sometimes doing away with the difference altogether. The Theater of the Absurd, for example, sometimes finds that the whole idea of human identity is founded on a misconception of reality, so that it is "truer" for the playwright to provide no focal point either for sympathy or unsympathy.

Chekhov, who stayed with no single hero throughout the course of a play, had no villains either. He once said that evil "flows through people not from them." If there is a constant force of antagonism behind his plots, it is nature herself, which does whatever she has to do without taking man into consideration. Life is not full of iniquity; it is neutral, but man is not. Man has hopes and dreams that are continually being thwarted. No human agent is responsible, and this is what makes man's plight so pitiful. There is no one — not even a monster of iniquity — to seek out in order to restore life's moral balance. This fundamentally cynical view of the real antagonism in human existence is shared by most of today's dramatists.

Enjoyment of theater, however, does not depend upon an acceptance of the contemporary attitude. If the thoroughly wicked Machiavellian of Shakespeare's time is a convention of drama, so too is the Chekhovian capacity for making every character an object of sympathy. Enjoyment of theater becomes a matter of the extent to which the dramatist is able to make us share his vision of life and the extent of his honesty about his vision. The superficial division between good guys and bad guys is deplorable because it *is* superficial. It is hard to believe there ever was a time when anyone seriously thought evil would roll over and die for Sir Galahad or Cinderella. The great writers share one common belief: the source of evil in life is not the work of a black-caped villain in league with Satan.

Conflict and the Must-Mustn't Factor

It would seem that the easiest element to achieve in drama would be the most essential one: conflict. The word suggests clash, struggle, search, argument — all actions which can be inserted into almost any story. But conflict is not necessarily where the action is. One can spend two hours watching a wartime spectacular with a cast of thousands and a budget of millions, and still come away dissatisfied. The cause of dissatisfaction is likely to be the fact that, despite the noise and violence depicted, the basic conflict was weak. Indeed, as has been proved many times, it is possible to be temporarily diverted by great displays of violence — as in the chariot-race sequence in *Ben-Hur* — only to be less pleased with the underlying tension than in a gentle story which contains little or no violence at all. In *The Bicycle Thief* (1948), the search of the father and son through the streets of Rome for the bicycle so important to the family's welfare is more exciting and impressive throughout than most dramas marked by bone-crushing fights. The same is true for the scene marking the end of *David and Lisa* (1963), in which the girl manages to break through her isolation and clasp the hand of the boy who helped her.

In its most essential definition, conflict need not involve people at all. It can be felt when a dot in an animated cartoon tries to reach a corner on the side of the screeen but is held back by unseen forces. What is needed is some kind of believable tension to maintain audience interest. But while the audience will remain temporarily interested in any kind of conflict, a series of unconnected individual scenes, no matter how great their separate conflicts, leaves a sense of disappointment at the end.

Conflict in drama may exist between two characters — usually the protagonist and the antagonist — between the protagonist and a larger force, such as fate, war, an economic system, or between warring aspects of the protagonist's own character. It is always dangerous to make wholesale generalizations about which is more effective, for the theater is pragmatic. If something works for a knowledgeable audience, there is little use in pointing out that it should not have worked or that something else would have had greater impact.

Nonetheless, there are some criteria by which the stage potential of the conflict in a new play may be judged. A professional director knows, for example, that a brittle distinction between hero and villain is dated by now and that few dramas of the past have survived without more complex kinds of conflict. He knows that, even though Iago is a Machiavellian, a man of confirmed, unrelenting evil, the conflict in *Othello* (1604) is not simply between Othello and Iago as hero and villain. Othello considers Iago his friend until after he has been driven by the villain's subtle devices to murder his wife. Thus the conflict which builds the play towards its climax is between Othello and the dark, inscrutable, and irrational forces which lie buried deep inside him — indeed inside every man — and which, once awakened, overcome his civilized self. Conflict generated by the protagonist himself can be more effective than any other kind, because it *limits the alternatives* to the outcome of the action.

Too many alternatives are as bad as none at all. If a plot is so loose that almost anything might happen, the audience is hard put to remain interested in it. Ideally there should be one outcome that seems to be clearly promised from the beginning but that is not completely inevitable. Iago makes his plans very plain in several speeches to the audience early in the play. As soon as Othello shows himself to be an easy victim of Iago's hypnotic influence, the death of Desdemona appears certain. But there is always an alternative to a murder — not committing it. Besides, the great advantage to having murder as the anticipated outcome of the dramatic action is that the conflict within the potential murderer is transferred to the audience itself, which is torn between the natural, civilized wish not to see the crime committed and the secret thrill that violence and brutality can provide.

Audiences also enjoy watching a character going down to his own destruction. The tremendous popularity of prison movies is a case in point, for these almost never fail to provide a "last mile" sequence in which a condemned man is led down the long corridor by grim-faced guards and the solemn warden with his "Go like a man, Eddie." Then there are the inevitable closing of the door, the camera panning from face to face of the frightened prisoners behind the bars, the close-up of the overhead light, the torturing pause, and finally the dimming of the lights.

When it is over, the audience is not going to be glad that Eddie was pierced from all sides by those throbbing and excruciating electric volts. The audience, for the most part, would be quite willing to testify that it never wanted Eddie's death, that it hoped for a last-minute reprieve from the governor. But everyone in his heart of hearts will admit that eleventh-hour pardons are dramatically disappointing.

The great success of the film *I Want to Live!* (1957) can be directly attributed to the skillful plotting and direction which capitalized on the two-alternative outcome. On the one hand, the heroine, a woman wrongfully convicted of murder, is handled so sympathetically that only the most sadistic member of the audience could have wished her harm. The movie seemed even to crusade for the abolishment of the death penalty and so to belong in the category of highly responsible, socially-minded drama. But on the other hand, the method of convincing everyone that execution was a barbaric, outmoded ritual was to take the viewers inside the cell in Death Row and allow them to spend every last minute of waning life with the condemned woman. As the hour of doom grew nearer, the shrill ringing of the telephone offered the hope that pardon might come and the promise that it would not. The woman was taken step by step to the door of the dreaded chamber. Again the telephone rang; again the inevitable was delayed so that the audience might hope for a happy ending all the better to enjoy the disaster. Finally, with all prospects for the reprieve gone, the audience was taken inside the chamber and given the chance to see every ghastly detail: the strapping of the heroine in the chair, the faces of the onlookers pressed tight against the side windows, the closing and bolting of the huge door, the torturing pause again, the warden, soberly hesitant at first, plunging down the lever which released the cyanide pellets, the pellets dropping into a small vat of acid under the woman's chair, the rising cloud of vapors, and finally the heroine's face contorted as she struggled desperately for breath.

The film was both hailed as a triumph of realism and condemned as another piece of tasteless Hollywood sensationalism. Its advocates argued that the long and agonizing execution scene was necessary in order for the point to be made most forcefully. Furthermore, the movie was based on an actual case, and the telephone had rung twice!

The truth is that the film was neither realistic nor tasteless. That it actually happened in real life is superfluous to critical judgment. What matters is that the long and agonizing execution scene had tremendous impact because it made the audience both want and not want the woman to die. The principle by which either the dramatist or the director creates within the audience this fierce concentration on two alternatives is called the *must-mustn't factor*. The heroine must die: the plot has promised this from the outset. But she must not die: it is cruel to put a woman in the gas chamber; such barbarism must not take place in a civilized society. For centuries the must-mustn't factor has been one of the major causes of theatrical excitement, and important modern playwrights have learned how to turn it to their advantage.

There are two versions of this factor, conflict from an outer and an inner force. *I Want to Live!* is one example of conflict from the outer forces of the legal system, circumstantial evidence, the death penalty. It is believable that they should combine to cause the execution of the heroine. A death sentence carried out in a carefully guarded prison is so real that its alternative — that is, the heroine's escaping death — can reasonably be hoped for.

But in most conflicts caused by an outside force there are too many choices available. The two men who face each other in a gun duel on a western street did not have to meet. Another place, the interference of other people, other codes of values, and variations in character would prevent the showdown in a way that the prison execution could not have been prevented. There is a greater sense of the dramatist's hand deliberately manipulating the characters to force them to face each other when too many alternatives are available. There is always the recognition that, since the dramatist has arranged the plight, he can easily arrange its solutions. Thus an infinitude of alternatives becomes at the same time no alternatives. We know that the hero will make it all right, because the author will never let him down. The author is a god, and in such a well-run world no one is ever really up against anything. Inner conflict, emerging from a struggle between the protagonist and some weakness within himself, is usually better.

In *Othello* the antagonism of Iago creates the must-mustn't factor but is not one of the forces involved in it. The audience is not saying to itself, "Iago must deceive Othello, but he must not." The moment of Desdemona's death is the moment the plot works toward; it is this we do and do not want to occur. And it is Othello's own character which makes the murder seem inescapable, just as it is Othello's own character which offers the possibility that it will be escaped.

As the climactic moment approaches, Othello, dressed in a white robe to symbolize what he believes is the purity of the sacrifice he is going to make, walks slowly and deliberately to the bed on which Desdemona sleeps. He delivers a speech, indicating his convictions, not a wavering back and forth. His intentions are to strangle or smother her as methodically as possible — without passion. But Shakespeare has Desdemona wake up. The thought strikes us that she will explain everything to him; he will understand and beg her forgiveness. All will be well, for Othello has been shown to be a reasonable and lucid being and deeply in love with his wife. How *can* he kill her now?

Yet Othello's deliberation at the beginning of the scene, we soon realize, was not a return of his earlier dignity, control, and clarity of thinking. It was the final stage of his susceptibility to Iago's influence, the very opposite pole from rationality. Thus Desdemona's pleas go unheeded. They must. Othello is going to kill her. He must. The more she pleads, the more irrational he becomes. It is totally believable; it was predictable long ago. But it still must not happen. Shakespeare appeals to a universal moral principle.

The tension between the must and the must not is what provides the utter absorption in the action which great dramas inspire as they near their climactic points. It is not all a great drama must have, but it is hard for any play or movie to succeed without it. It is completely missing from the works of Chekhov, but its ghost still haunts the critical evaluation of Chekhov. "Find what these plays have since they don't have me," says the ghost of conflict.

That the phenomenon exists is hard to deny. Why it exists is hard to explain, except that it roots lie buried deep in the subconscious of people who go to the theater, people who can be eminently human and civilized and at the same time be fascinated by the inexorable coming of disaster. Because the must-mustn't factor is strongest in dramas with tragic endings, tragedy — far from being "morbid" and "depressing" — is to the critical viewer the most deeply satisfying form of theater.

Pyramidal Structure: The Classic Dramatic Plot

Though the terms are often used interchangeably, the story of a play is not the same as the plot, in precisely the way that a house is not the same as the architect's blueprint. When someone says, "Tell me what your house is like," a description is given of some of the rooms or perhaps of the general style of the house or perhaps of a distinguishing feature such as an indoor garden. When someone says, "What was the plot of the movie?" the reply usually deals with a few of the memorable events. Yet just as a house may have one or two magnificent rooms and still fail for many reasons to be completely satisfactory, a drama can have interesting and exciting moments and still not add up to a successful piece of theatrical art. A trained eye — whether that of architect or viewer — sees the structure, the design, the underlying logic, in addition to eye-catching features.

In the theater or on the screen it is the plot which must be examined first whenever the critical viewer suspects that the drama is not working. The story is less important than the plotting — the arrangement of the events in a sequence. The same story could be told in two different ways with totally different success.

A famous German film *The Cabinet of Dr. Caligari* (1919) illustrates what superior plotting can do for a story. The movie is narrated in flashback by the inhabitant of a town which has been in the throes of a supposedly mad scientist and a monster which he controls. On the face of it, the story idea is not unlike that of *Frankenstein* (1818) and innumerable imitations. The potential for generating high excitement is obviously there but so is the danger of losing the attention of the critical viewer on the grounds that the undoing of the fiends is all too predictable. Or, it might be thought, this kind of movie may have been all right in 1919, when movies were still a novelty, but it will not do for a generation fed up with stories of emotionless Martians and their programmed mechanical killers. What distinguishes *Dr. Caligari* from every other work of its kind is the fact that the narrator turns out to be a mental patient and Dr. Caligari, not a fiend at all but the head of the institution. The events have been the wild fantasies of a disturbed mind, not a chronological record of what actually happened. If the sequence had been reversed by the writer — that is, if the audience had to understand from the beginning that an inmate is about to tell a story, the impact of the film would have been substantially lessened.

Sophocles' *Oedipus the King,* written twenty-five hundred years ago, has the most effective plot ever devised by a playwright. Based on an ancient story of a man who murders his father and marries his mother, the play begins many years after these deeds have taken place. Oedipus, the king of Thebes, still does not know, however, that his queen is really his mother, for whose hand in marriage a strange prophecy long ago destined him. In the first scene of the action we learn that a plague is raging in Thebes; the oracle sends word that the plague will not abate until the murderer of the former king has been apprehended and punished. Not knowing that he is himself the murderer and that the former king was his father, Oedipus vows to his subjects that he will bring the culprit to justice. The audience, of course, knows in advance that the big scene in the play will have to be Oedipus' discovery of his own identity and his terrible crimes. Scene by scene brings the protagonist inexorably closer to a doom from which no escape is possible, a doom already sealed in the past.

The flawless structure of the plotting, the elimination of all alternatives except the must and the must not which the audience experiences, has caused critical historians of the drama to speak of such a thing as a classic plot and to use this as a point of departure in evaluating all subsequent plots. The Greeks, who were meticulous about the symmetry of their art, perfected in an astonishingly short time the art of telling a story in the theater. They invented the *pyramidal structure,* one that still works, that has saved many an unlikely story and turned it into respectable drama.

Since the Greeks were opposed to excessive ornamentation, it is only natural that their idea of a dramatic plot was that it should be as simple as possible. The pyramidal structure begins with a scene in which the alternatives of the action are (or at least seem to be) as many as they will ever be and step by step eliminates them until an inevitable climactic point is reached. Thus in the first scene of Oedipus there are these possibilities: Oedipus need never find out who he is and what he has done; the reason for the plague need not be the presence in the kingdom of the murderer of the former ruler; and Oedipus need not commit himself to the unrelenting pursuit of the killer. Like the base of a pyramid, this opening scene is the broadest part of the structure. The discovery scene becomes the apex of the pyramid, reached after a progressive narrowing of the sides (alternatives).

What makes *Oedipus* the purest example of the classic pyramidal plot is that the three possibilities at the outset are more apparent than real. Oedipus' own pride will make it impossible for him not to find out who he is. He has heard the prophecy but resolutely denies that it could have been fulfilled. He propels himself toward the discovery. What causes many unsuccessful imitations of this structure is the evident hand of the author in contriving the sequence of events so as to eliminate alternatives that need not logically disappear. The movie heroine who is being relentlessly stalked by the psychopath invariably backs into a corner of the room. On a somewhat more sophisticated level — but nonetheless contrived — there was the competent journeyman dramaturgy of Sidney Kingsley's *Detective Story* (1949), which presented in the beginning a hardnosed bastion of the law, a crook-hating police officer, who never seems to want to know the extenuating circumstances behind a crime. It is not hard for the audience to predict that the play will work towards a scene in which a compromise in ideals becomes necessary. The author provides such a scene by having the man discover that his own wife, whom he considered exemplary, has herself committed a felony. The crispness and clarity of the plotting are conducive to a modest amount of pleasure, but the audience is required to forgive the heavy-handed use of coincidence.

The beautiful logic which the Greek plots have at their best seems to belong to another, more distant age, when the universe itself was thought to be put together with rational coherence. The Greeks, for example, are fond of "sins of the father" stories. These not only provided good bases for pyramidal plots but were entirely possible in a world not governed, as so many of the modern dramatists believe, by chance; a world in which a deed committed generations before can set in motion an inescapable chain of consequences.

The classic structure is divided into four parts: *prologue, intensification, obligatory moment,* and *resolution.* Most plays contain at least some of these elements.

The Prologue and The Problem of Exposition

The prologue is that part of the drama which comes before the action really begins; the opening scene (or scenes) in which the background of the story is given to the audience. This is called *exposition,* and the playwright usually has a problem in how to interest the audience by starting things happening almost as soon as the curtain goes up and yet introduce them and their relation to each other at the same time.

The great advantage which the Greek dramatists had is their use of myth; this helped them to get over the expository scene as rapidly as possible and move almost at once into the action proper. Since the Greek theaters lacked both marquees and programs, the dramatist had the obligation of letting the audience know what they were seeing before many moments had elapsed. Thus *Oedipus* begins with the figure of the king emerging from the entrance to the palace and asking a group of assembled citizens what they want of him, "world renowned Oedipus." Immediately the Greek audiences, familiar with the old legend, would have known that this man has killed his father and murdered his mother.

The modern playwright is in a quandary. He sometimes alienates our interest before he has a chance to show us what he has in store. Long stage exposition may include obviously planted references as a means of letting the audience know who the characters are. At its clumsiest, exposition has two people telling each other what they already know ("I understand your brother Al will be here tonight for the reading of Aunt Maud's will ...") in order to let the audience know too. A convenient device, popular with Ibsen and other playwrights, is to make the opening scene a meeting between people who have been separated for some time and can therefore naturally fill each other in on recent developments in their lives. Movies have an opportunity for quick exposition because the camera can fade in on a close-up of a sign, reading "J. Frippington Wentworth, Psychologist," and then offer an immediate cut to the anxious face of the obviously disturbed girl who is about to open the door to the office.

One of the most notable prologues in contemporary drama is that of Arthur Miller's *Death of a Salesman,* with its curtain rising on an empty stage on which Willy Loman presently appears, walking slowly and wearily, dragging his two torn suitcases, while above him tower the skyscrapers of the city. From far away comes the sound of a mournful flute which he does not quite hear. Since the title of the work has already announced what this man is and what his ultimate fate is to be, Miller has prepared us for what is in store as well as a modern dramatist, lacking myth, can do.

But even with the advantage of the audience's pre-knowledge of the story, the Greek dramatist had to break into it at some point. In the opening scene of *Antigone* the heroine and her sister are shown together, discussing Creon's edict against the burial of the women's dead brother Polyneices. In just six single lines of poetry, the first six of the play, Sophocles tells the audience that the woman being spoken to is named Ismene, that the speaker is Antigone, that they are living under the same curse which destroyed their father Oedipus, that their brothers killed each other, and that the present king, Creon, has come forth with a new law which will greatly multiply their grief.

What Sophocles was free from was the necessity of introducing a lot of small talk to foster the illusion of real life. In a typical Broadway or Hollywood romantic comedy we have to be shown the rental of an apartment by two pretty young girls and listen to the superintendent and look at the view of the city; perhaps before we reached that point, we were forced to ride up in the elevator, observing the other riders and listening to random snatches of conversation, all of which relates not at all to the plot, which is still non-existent.

Sometimes what is finally presented does not ever fit together; it fails to give the audience a sense of direction. This is one thing the Greeks were never without. The very mention of the name Oedipus would have been enough to charge the air with electricity. Little happens to an audience of today when a man enters a room and says, "My name is Steve." As a result, modern dramatists may go all out for fast-moving action at the outset. The man might announce his name and be immediately stabbed. Everyone is familiar with the current device in movies and television whereby a scene of pulsating action is hurled at the audience before even the title is given. This is known as a "teaser," and its primary weakness is overuse, so that extravagantly exciting openings often have as little impact as straight, undramatic exposition.

In evaluating the handling of exposition, the critical viewer is concerned with two things: The first is whether a simple, Greek prologue to the action has been employed with success — that is, with at least a semblance of dramatic tension, to provide a modern counterpart of the Greek "instant interest." The second is whether or not the desire of the dramatist to hold our interest from the outset has resulted in a hazy, directionless plot. One failure is hardly less serious than the other. A plot that is too imitatively Greek, in an age without mythology, runs the risk of being tiresomely obvious as it unfolds neatly from one scene to another. But just as bad is the plot that is not predictable and that suddenly arrives somewhere via a series of unrelated contrivances, to the dismay of the critical viewer, who usually likes to have the pleasure of anticipating his destination in the theater.

Intensification and Episodic Plots

The main part of the play — between the exposition and the climactic high point — is the intensification, which takes up the major portion of the drama. From scene to scene, as it develops, the alternatives to the outcome progressively narrow. It is the element of the drama that must be the most successful if we are to sustain our interest. A play or movie may have a smashing start and a shattering climax but somehow weave around uncertainly in between. It is the structuring of the intensification that tells whether the drama is going in any direction.

Aristotle, the first drama critic, defined a tragedy as an imitation of an action that is "serious, complete, and of a certain magnitude." By "complete" he meant "having a beginning, a middle, and an end." The beginning of the play — the prologue — needs nothing before it. It explains itself; it is instantly acceptable and puts the cards right on the table. By "middle" Aristotle means the intensification of the drama, the part that must be preceded by something and is followed by something — namely, the climax or high point of the plot.

Just as many dramas fail to begin in the classic sense of the word — despite the shock openings that attempt to lure us into an easy acceptance of the action — so too may they fail to intensify. For there is a profound difference between true intensification and mere continuation of the story.

Antigone intensifies at the moment in which the Sentry enters to tell Creon that someone has disobeyed his decree forbidding burial to Polyneices. During the prologue we learn from the conversation of the two sisters that such a decree exists and that Antigone intends to proceed with the burial anyway. If she never does as she promises or if Creon never discovers her deed, the plot cannot move forward. But once the arrogant king learns that his authority has been challenged, it is inevitable that he must take appropriate steps. The first is to apprehend the rebellious subject, who turns out to be his own niece.

The confrontation scene between Antigone and Creon reintensifies the plot — that is, it adds much greater excitement to what has already begun to involve us. The scene offers Creon the alternatives of backing down from his position or having to condemn his niece to death. Since specifically dooming a certain person — and a relative at that — is more interesting than the promise in the earlier scene that someone will be given the ultimate punishment, Sophocles has not only carried the plot forward but moved it higher on the pyramid. In other words, when a drama possesses so perfect a structure as *Antigone,* it should be impossible for the viewer who arrives late to experience the same excitement as the viewer who has watched the action from the outset, for the intensifying is something that happens inside the spectator. It is a gradual quickening of the pulse, instead of the steady but more casual interest offered by the play or movie that moves but is not moving, that has activity rather than action.

In the classic sense at least, action can be judged only relatively — that is, in terms of plot intensification. It is possible for a drama to be full of action though it is confined to a single room in which three characters sit on three sofas and do very little moving around. Such a work is Jean-Paul Sartre's *No Exit* (1945).

Three people are ushered into what appears to be a tasteful and comfortable hotel room, a man and then two women. During the prologue it is made clear that each has died and has been condemned to spend eternity in hell. But the seemingly pleasant nature of hell puzzles both the characters and the audience. The moment at which the first realization occurs that their hell is to torment each other is a moment of intensification in the classic tradition, because it raises the immediate question of how the torment will take place, what its exact nature will be. After all, the situation seems to be anything but desperate: a young man, two young and attractive women, all three of them pleasant strangers bearing no malice to each other. Recognizing that they are supposed to inflict mutual pain, they agree to remain seated on their respective sofas, never interacting, never even speaking. Out of so apparently static a situation Sartre has fashioned one of the most absorbing and intensifying of modern plays. He virtually defies the viewer not to care what happens next. As in *Oedipus,* the outcome is certain from the beginning. In a sense it has already happened, for the people are already in hell and have only to discover what hell really means. There is no way for the plot to advance except in the direction of this discovery. Moment by moment the drama weaves a subtle web of involvement among the characters as we see how utterly incompatible they really are, how the personality of each is absolutely wrong for the happiness of the other two. It is an extraordinary play, filled with action — that is, for the viewer who is willing to accept the idea that action is not the same as motion.

In strikingly sorry contrast is the kind of plot structure that dominates the screen and television markets: the episodic or the "and-then" plot. As a principle of bad story-telling, it is also known as the "one fine day a stranger rode up to the ranch" structure, whereby the author keeps running out of momentum and must re-begin rather than re-intensify the story. The usual way is to have a series of disasters: the robbery *and then* the landslide *and then* the explosion *and then*. . . for as long as necessary. There are two serious objections to such plots. One is that it is hard for the viewer to anticipate a certain outcome, a high point of the action. It becomes a matter of saying "I wonder how it will turn out," rather than — as in the case of *No Exit* — "I wonder how the action will reach its certain destination." The second objection is that, with each new beginning, new characters and character relationships have to be introduced, and this requires additional, time-wasting expository material. "Excuse me. My name is Kincaid. Sixteen years ago your father and I played poker, and I won this here ranch . . ."

Once a Greek play begins, it moves. To reverse the pyramid metaphor, one might compare classical intensification to the act of rolling a rock downhill. Once it has been pushed over the precipice nothing can stop it. In *Oedipus*, for example, within a few minutes of the play's beginning, the king swears that he will rid his land of the plague by apprehending the murderer of the former ruler. Since he is the murderer, the action has intensified almost at once and committed itself irrevocably to one course of development. Unfortunately many plots require the audience to kick rocks uphill all the way. It becomes difficult to be entertained when one's toes are hurting.

The Obligatory Moment and the Classical Principle of Suspense

The climax of a classically constructed drama is called the obligatory moment because it has been promised to the audience from the prologue, or at least from the beginning of the intensification. The plot of *Oedipus* offers the most perfect climax in all of drama. Since the theme of the play has been recognition and non-recognition, Oedipus resolutely refuses to see the truth as it comes closer and closer with increasing clarity and inescapability. Total understanding is the only point which the plot may reach.

The surprise ending, familiar to all viewers of Alfred Hitchcock motion pictures and television plays, is sometimes an acceptable substitute for an obligatory moment. It may indeed compensate for a weak plot. The surprise factor tends to outweigh the lack of strong interest generated by earlier portions of the drama. But a sudden twist can never be as good as an obligatory moment, since by its very nature it robs us of the chance to anticipate. Besides, once seen, the plot with a sudden twist tends to lose its charm. The secret is out, while foreknowledge of the ending does not prevent enjoyment of more than one viewing of a great play.

The classical principle of *suspense* in drama is not achieved by making the audience wonder how everything will turn out. By all rights suspense should be called "suspension." It is the deliberate holding back of the big moment in order to make the audience appreciate it all the more when it arrives. It is an element which must accompany the obligatory moment in order to sustain and intensify audience involvement.

In the concluding aria of the heroine in Wagner's *Tristan und Isolde* (1865) the singer reaches a magnificent high note, which is actually the climax of the entire musical score. Isolde, grieving over the body of her dead lover, sings of her passion for him; as she does so, the power of her love turns grief into ecstasy. She transcends time and space and the physical barrier of death that has separated them, reaching always closer for one final moment of total spiritual union. In the earlier portions of his score, Wagner introduces bits of the love theme, always hinting at the fulfillment of the melody but never completing it. Soon it becomes apparent that the fulfillment will be one soaring note. As the final aria progresses, the singer keeps coming near, but then backs away from, the note. The final achievement of it justifies the extreme length of the opera and makes it one of the glories of the musical theater. Certainly without that note, the audience would feel a distinct let-down.

Making a promise to the audience and then finally keeping it (after some deliberately injected doubt) is perhaps the most fundamental aspect of telling a story on stage or screen. In the case of *Oedipus,* the doubt takes the form of the arrival of a messenger from the land of Corinth with news that the king has died. Since Oedipus has been raised by this man and always supposed him to be his real father, the fact that Oedipus had nothing to do with his death seems to prove the prophecy false. But the hope the scene raises is immediately shattered when the messenger informs Oedipus that the king of Corinth was not his real father.

In *Antigone* Sophocles has a scene between Creon and the blind prophet Teiresias, who warns him of the fatal consequences of refusing to compromise his ideals. Suddenly changing his mind, Creon acts quickly to avert Antigone's death, in the same manner that Shakespeare has Desdemona awaken and create the false hope that she will be able to reason with Othello. In both cases these are delaying tactics. The promised disasters eventually come about.

Only the popcorn eater hopes that everything will always turn out for the best. He is the person who allows his insecurity to guide his response to the drama. The critical viewer is most resentful of an unkept promise no matter where it leads. He can forgive some lapses early in the evening, even an unbelievable performance here and there, so long as the time spent at the theater proves ultimately to have been justified by the integrity of plotting.

If a play begins with a wife happily vacuuming her rugs and then being stabbed to death by a burglar who stuffs her into the closet, if it continues with the husband's coming home and finding her gone, the playwright has incurred the obligation of making the husband open the door and discover the disaster. There will be the inevitable tension between the must and the must-not, as any humane viewer naturally is against both murder and bereaved husbands, but any tampering with the logical direction of the plot toward the promised moment will invite audience scorn, not rejoicing.

One might also imagine a hypothetical play about a defense attorney who automatically sympathizes with the underdog. He takes a case involving an immigrant accused of murder, and at the beginning of the intensification, it becomes evident that his true reason for taking the case is his prejudice in favor of his client, who belongs to a minority group. Despite the evidence the lawyer believes the arrest and trial are a form of persecution. With such a premise, the play incurs the obligation of concluding with a scene in which the ideals of the attorney undo him. The author, in other words, must have the immigrant really be guilty.

The critical viewer knows he must solve his own real-life problems whenever and however he can. He does not expect the theater to solve them for him by offering the pretense that they do not really exist, or at all events that they will miraculously solve themselves. Actually, it is the almost paradoxical truth that, even though the obligation of a great tragedy is to culminate in catastrophe, the pleasure of experiencing the fulfillment of the promise has a very stabilizing effect upon one's emotions. The involvement in a slowly intensifying line of action which works toward an undesirable but unavoidable high pitch of excitement wrings the emotions out and renders the spectator tranquil and better able to cope with his problems.

On the other hand, a delicate and graceful comedy, such as Oscar Wilde's *The Importance of Being Earnest* (1895), incurs, just as strongly, the obligation of concluding with the embracing of the lovers and the falling of the curtain on happiness and exuberance. While tragic endings are perhaps the most deeply satisfying, it is better to be able to enjoy many forms of theater so long as the dramatists can interest us in where they are going and reward our interest by taking us there.

Perhaps the most deplorable sin of all is the use of the *deus ex machina,* a serious violation of the agreement made between drama and audience at the outset. The phrase means "god out of a machine" and referred originally to a pulley device which enabled Greek dramatists to end their plays by having a supernatural deity lowered to the stage, as though from heaven, and resolve a plot which had become too tangled up for the playwright to resolve logically. Euripides was especially famous for such careless endings. In the contemporary theater the phrase refers to the author's crawling out of his obligation with an implausible but convenient event. Nineteenth-century audiences were accustomed to last-minute conversion of the villain. An eleventh-hour reprieve from the governor, an unexpected inheritance, a "judicial" lightning bolt, even the arrival of an interesting new romance in the life of a spinster — all are examples of the *deus ex machina,* if they are the means of saving or killing off characters the author seemed unable to handle in a more believable way. Coincidences do, of course, occur in real life, but in the theater, where there is such intense focus on what is possible, coincidences seem unforgivable.

The Resolution

The resolution in the classical plot structure corresponds to what Aristotle called "the end." While it may sound unnecessary to comment on such an element in a plot, it is nonetheless true that many dramas fail to end though the curtain may fall amid thunderous applause or the words THE END may glow upon the screen in red letters. Aristotle considered a proper ending that which cannot logically be followed by anything else. In other words, it is a scene that completely satisfies the audience, causing no further concern about the fate of the characters.

Once again, it is *Oedipus* that furnishes the perfect example. If the promised obligatory moment is self-recognition, the hero's realization of his terrible deeds, the play cannot end here. One final scene is absolutely required — the revelation of what Oedipus plans to do. In the prologue he has vowed to his subjects that he will appease the gods and so end the plague by bringing the unpunished murderer to justice. Now that he has found the murderer to be himself, he must either make good his promise or try to escape punishment. Sophocles thus re-intensifies the plot one more time beyond the climactic high point. The king rushes from the stage. There is a terrifying cry, and then a messenger relates that the queen has hanged herself and Oedipus has gouged out his eyes. Oedipus re-appears — in modern productions a horrendous figure with empty eye sockets and dried blood on his face — to plead for banishment; so wretched a creature does not deserve the comforts of death. The wish is granted by Creon, the new king, who admits the rightfulness of the harsh sentence Oedipus has given to himself. Oedipus is allowed to say goodbye to his ill-fated children in what remains one of the most moving scenes in all of drama.

None of this final scene is extraneous. It is not merely a matter of tying together the loose ends. It is a legitimate part of the drama. In symphonic music there is a "coda" or "tag" appended to the fourth and final movement, which sometimes was used by classical composers to wake up the dozing members of the audience. Usually it was loud and vigorous and singularly empty of musical content. But as music developed, many composers made the coda an integral part of the score itself. In great plays like *Oedipus* the last moments are sometimes referred to as the "falling action," and this has the same effect as the quiet codas in music which restore the listener's emotional equilibrium after the climax has passed. As Oedipus slowly gropes his way from their midst, the Theban citizens dolefully comment that no man ever really finds happiness until he dies.

Another need was thus served by the classical resolution: that of making a final moral assertion. Sophocles is not certain how benevolent the gods are, but he knows that the arrogance of man is fatal. Rightly or wrongly, the universe has order, and when man attempts to shatter this order, he reaches disaster.

Shakespeare did not adhere to the symmetry of the pyramidal structure; nevertheless his greatest tragedies have definite resolutions which neither leave the audience wondering about the fate of the characters nor question the justice of what has happened. His major protagonists — Hamlet, Othello, Lear, Macbeth, Cleopatra — have inflicted doom upon themselves, but no quarter is asked. There is no indication that they have deserved less. On the other hand, there is no repentance. They and the universe have been "mighty opposites," and they have lost. Everything is over.

The contemporary dramatist has difficulty ending his works. The whole view of the universe and of nature has changed so radically from that of the Greeks and Shakespeare that it is now almost impossible to concoct a symmetrical plot or at least one that resolves itself completely without its seeming to be a contrivance. Happy endings are, of course, common in popular movies and television, but they are seldom logical. Total disaster can seem equally unmotivated, for the modern dramatist lacks both the Greek assurance that the universe is rational and the Renaissance admiration for towering individuals, who were irreplaceable when gone. In modern drama the audience is often left with the feeling that even the bitterest tragedy is not of great consequence, that if Arthur Miller's salesman, for example, could not make the grade, another salesman might.

It is perhaps for this reason that, of all the Greeks, Euripides has been the most popular with contemporary writers. Traditionally accused of careless plot construction, particularly in his use of the *deus ex machina*, Euripides with his unresolved action seems to have the most to say to the modern world. An apparent atheist who saw human life as governed by chance and man himself as driven on by uncontrollable passions and secret drives, Euripides was able to devise marvelous stories without quite knowing how to end them. He appears to have found real life to be without purpose and could not be serious in giving to his plays a moral resolution. His most famous tragedy, *Medea* (431 B.C.), the story of a woman driven to murder her two sons through hatred of her husband, has one of the theater's most terrifying climaxes but a casual ending in which the heroine goes off to become another man's mistress, leaving her husband to mourn the death of his heirs. In a modern adaptation by Robinson Jeffers, Medea leaves her grieving husband with the scornful reminder that he is alone in his sorrow — without even a remote god to watch or care.

Like Euripides, the contemporary dramatist is sensitive to conflict and to the anguish of existence; like Euripides, he can create exciting plots but can seldom reach a satisfying conclusion. The unresolved or "open" ending is one of the trademarks of modern plays and movies. It has been praised by critics — Eric Bentley, for example — who prefer an ending which leaves the resolution up to the audience. According to this view, once a social problem has been presented, a happy ending encourages false optimism and an unhappy ending leads to pessimistic despair. Those playwrights and critics of the "committed" school believe that a deliberately unresolved "ending" may arouse an audience to work for satisfactory change. Charlie Chaplin's tragi-comic little tramp is perhaps the most memorable example of the modern unresolved ending as he duckwaddles down a long street, swinging his cane and disappearing from view, ever hopeful yet ever certain to be victimized once again by a world he never made.

Irony: Sophoclean and Euripidean

In choosing the myth of Oedipus as the subject for a play, Sophocles could have handled the story in a variety of ways. He might have told, for example, a tale of a king who knew he was guilty of the dreaded sin of incest and who was torn between his desire to place the responsibility on the gods and the human pride that drove him to blame none but himself. Instead, Sophocles capitalized upon the audience's familiarity with the legend and gave to the theater henceforth and forevermore one of its most potent devices, so characteristic of his work that it has become called by his name — Sophoclean irony. It is the principle of plot construction whereby the audience knows the hero's fate from the outset but the hero does not.

A playwright's use of Sophoclean irony does not always guarantee that the evening will be well spent. When the outcome of the plot is very evident, there must be a strong must-mustn't factor to counteract the possibility of the drama's becoming monotonous. What Oedipus is to discover is so appalling that we are grateful for any delay, such as the coming of the messenger from Corinth. This, in turn, re-intensifies the action.

There is another form of irony that is more widely employed, especially in modern drama. Sometimes the single term "irony" itself refers to this device. It is closer to what is often called the "ironic" in real life.

A ship flounders helplessly in a fog, after having been buffeted by a storm. All communication has been cut off. Since the situation is apparently hopeless, the captain allows the crew to abandon the vessel; but he himself insists upon staying behind. The morning light, however, reveals that there is land only a few hundred yards away. The "ironic" is thus a twist of fate that is grim but sometimes sardonically funny.

From the first, dramatists have been sensitive to life's consistent ability to prevent the success of man's schemes with almost flawless timing. The Greeks were particularly aware of this perverseness at the heart of existence, for their earliest mythology shows man as a victim of fate. The legend of the three sisters — spinning, drawing out, and then arbitrarily cutting the thread of life — haunted them even when they were most productive and sophisticated. For the purpose of theatrical excitement, it would have been hard for a playwright to resist the certain impact of moments when a line of action takes a cruel reversal.

Sophocles uses this more specific and bitter kind of irony as part of the delaying tactics whereby the plot is reintensified so as not to reach its destination too swiftly and too directly. In *Oedipus* the false hope generated by the messenger from Corinth is immediately dashed to the ground. In *Antigone* the king's decision to save the heroine happens just minutes after her death.

But it was Euripides, the most cynical of the early dramatists, who loved the bitter twist, and for this reason it is sometimes called Euripidean irony. One of its most famous manifestations occurs in *Medea,* when the anxious Jason, having discovered the full extent of his wife's treachery, rushes home to prevent her from doing harm to his sons only to find that they are already slain.

Shakespeare also makes use of Euripidean irony. The device was responsible for Samuel Johnson's later condemning *King Lear* (1605) as a barbarous play. The old king and his beautiful young daughter have been sentenced to death; the daughter's husband, the king of France, arrives upon the scene to save the day. The villain, Edmund, admits what he has done, and a stay of execution is hastily dispatched — but too late. King Lear enters, bearing the corpse of his daughter, and the audience is lashed by two ironies, one more horrible than the other. It is ironic that the pardon should not have arrived in time and that the old man's life has been spared instead of the young girl's. Logically the order of executions could have been reversed. Logically they need not have taken place at all. Euripidean irony in a conclusion is thus the opposite of the contrived happy ending: it is a contrived unhappy ending. The universe in which the characters of both Euripides and Shakespeare meet their dooms is a harsh place. Frustration is the condition of life, not an occasional inconvenience.

In his youthful tragedy *Romeo and Juliet* (1595), however, Shakespeare uses Euripidean irony more awkwardly and less believably than in *King Lear*. The only reason Romeo does not know that Juliet is not really dead is that the message is never delivered to him: there is a quarantine in effect in the city where he is hiding. The musical *West Side*

Story (1957), a modern version of *Romeo and Juliet,* motivates the death of Tony by having Anita, the lovers' go-between, deliberately lie after she has been roughly handled by Tony's gang. Actually the authors have improved upon Shakespeare in this one instance, since Anita's desire to inflict suffering upon Tony by making him believe Maria is dead stems from deep-rooted race hatreds. When assaulted by the native Americans, Anita realizes that she is, after all, Puerto Rican and so reacts believably.

Euripidean irony is frequently shocking because it is not readily anticipated. There is nothing wrong with shock in the theater so long as it does not outrage the audience's intelligence and stretch its credulity beyond all reasonable limits.

Plausibility and Focus

It should be quite evident by now that the informed viewer does not go to a play or movie with the express intention of sneering at every opportunity. Those who are so motivated do not deserve to be called critical in the best sense of the term, for criticism is not derogation; it is enlightened appreciation. Primarily the critical viewer wants to enjoy himself. He is willing to suspend his disbelief, to play the game with the dramatist and the actors so long as they allow him to. When the rules change without a logical reason, however, he finds himself all too painfully aware that he is sitting in a theater watching nonsense.

The action in a play or film must be *plausible,* that which could possibly happen under the prevailing rules of the game. In Alice's Wonderland a cat is able to swallow itself as long as Alice is allowed to grow larger and smaller by taking pills. In *Oedipus* the instigation of the conflict comes from a prophecy, which we are willing to accept as true even in our scientific age. In Edward Albee's *The American Dream* the grandmother carries on stage a number of small boxes. When asked what they contain, she replies that she has wrapped up a television set, a blind Pekingese, a set of false teeth, and some memories. But the world of the play is one in which rooms disappear for no apparent reason, in which memories are as real as a television set, and both can be placed in boxes.

The audience wants to believe, but two factors can spoil the illusion: one, a theater-goer's naïve literal-mindedness, his inability to stretch the meaning of plausibility to include anything he does not believe could happen in real life; and two, inconsistency in the handling of the conventions by either the dramatist or the production itself. For the critical viewer, who is neither naïve nor literal-minded, the problem is restricted to a breach of contract between him and the makers of the drama.

The sudden intrusion of a new convention not on the same level of make-believe is the most obvious sin of implausibility. In the movie *Tom Jones* (1963) the director established very early the habit of having the characters directly address the audience. Not only was this convention carried through consistently throughout the film but it was entirely compatible with the other conventions such as the speeding up of the action at times to look like the old Mack Sennett chase scenes and the sudden freezing of the action so as to suspend a moment beyond its natural span. It would have been implausible for the characters to stop looking straight into the camera, just as it would be implausible for an actor in a serious play, one in which the presence of the audience has been steadily ignored, to turn front without warning and deliver a few lines which the other actors are not supposed to hear.

Another crime against plausibility is the changing of a character's nature without reason. People normally change through experience, and in drama the rules of the game require that uncharacteristic behavior be accounted for. It is unacceptable to the critical viewer to have a man steeped in villainy suddenly repent at the final curtain or at the fade-out. Where experience does not motivate character changes, as in Theater of the Absurd, the very amorphousness of human identity makes the uncharacteristic become the characteristic. The two tramps in *Waiting for Godot* are called Estragon and Vladimir in the program but call each other Gogo and Didi and seem unaware that they are supposed to have other names.

The laws of nature, of the real world, of "life as it is," are invoked if the dramatist so wishes, and once he makes the commitment of fidelity to actuality, he cannot switch universes. In general, the contemporary dramas which are dominated by the convention of verisimilitude tend to invite comparison with the probabilities of human experience more than dramas of the past or of the present which utilize different conventions. Once reality — the scientifically investigated material reality of today — becomes the rulemaker, the probability of the characters and what they do becomes essential to the critical viewer. Thus the sin of improbability can be committed by the theater but only under certain circumstances, and it is important to know whether to look for such a sin or not.

More prevalent throughout the different periods of theater history is the sin of obscurity, of a character's being made to act through motives which are not plausible or implausible but puzzling. When this happens, the critical viewer generally discovers that a certain event was needed by the dramatist for the convenience of his plot. He allowed it to happen without first consulting the characters. Few examples come to mind from the great dramas of the past, for those which contained serious obscurity have long since reaped the wages of sin. But movie-goers can readily provide their own recent instances.

Both the film and stage versions of the musical *My Fair Lady* (1956) did considerable violence to Shaw's *Pygmalion* (1914), on which they were based, in the matter of the ending. Henry Higgins, a woman-hater as a result of many factors including an overriding mother, is made by

Shaw to seem well rid of Eliza Doolittle, the Cockney flower girl whom he has turned into an aristocrat. In the world of Shaw the women are usually very capable of taking care of themselves, and men have to put up a stout defense.

The musical also makes use of Shaw's own unforgettable Henry, so set in his ways and so philosophical a bachelor. But for the obvious benefit of audiences who seem to be unable to accept a musical without any "romantic" elements whatsoever, the authors allow Henry to sing "I've Grown Accustomed to Her Face" after Eliza has left him, a song which, though fine in itself, suggests a capacity for sentimentality in the hero which is inconsistent with what we know of him or human nature. His determination to "throw the baggage out" should she try to return is consistent with his character, but the musical allows the curtain to fall upon a scene of domesticity ("Eliza, get my slippers!") which would have appalled Shaw, evidencing as it does an extremely masculine and dominant Henry and a properly mousy Eliza, who would give up a fortune and an easily bullied dolt of a husband like Freddie to endure Henry's verbal lashings forevermore.

Closely allied to implausibility is a blurring of focus. Since the reality on stage or screen, no matter how faithful it may try to be to real life, is a channeled one, controlled by the author and the director, we the audience are permitted to know only so much of what is going on as they want us to. In the real world we look anywhere and everywhere; we see this, not that, and not always for explainable reasons. As a result, life itself is not focused as a drama is. But in the theater there would be nothing entertaining about random happenings.

The writer of fiction has a much easier time of directing our attentions, however, because there is nothing but his words on the page to attract the eye. In play and movie there are scenic elements and minor characters who can become noticed without having an important function. An exceptionally beautiful "extra" in a movie could easily divert attention from the stars if she should happen to come into camera range. (Indeed many personalities who later became stars were discovered in this way.) In fiction, if Sinclair Lewis is describing George F. Babbitt shaving himself in the morning, we have no business wondering what his next-door neighbor is doing. He has no next-door neighbor. Literature may relate to life and truth, but it is not life and truth; its horizons are determined by authors. Whatever exists within these horizons does not exist continually or independently of the use the author wishes to make of it.

The vantage point from which the reader is meant to read a novel or short story is called "viewpoint," and this exists in the theater too, though the controls on the audience have more variable factors than those on the reader. The stage offers less of a problem than movies because it must work within broader limits that remain fixed throughout the evening. We come to know how to experience the play through the plot itself. In a film the drama is likely to be made up of individual moments, each with its own purpose, each with its own focus. The camera becomes a phantom awareness — that of the director in most cases — but within that awareness it may enter into the mind and mood of different characters. Detecting sins against screen focus is a task for a highly experienced critical viewer of movies.

On the other hand, too-easy acceptance of the screen convention of the cut — the camera's moving from one scene to another without visible transition — can cause blurred focus to go uncensured. A movie may start off with an unseen narrator talking while the camera pans over technicolor vistas of rolling hills and quaint meadows. "My name is Jim Randall. This is the valley where I was born and grew up." This is fine, and so far there is no confusion. Yet the next shot may be that of a lanky young man walking up a mountain path. We surmise that this is Jim Randall. Who is seeing him? Why is he being seen objectively now, when a moment before the camera was his subjective vision? There may or may not be a rationale behind the shots. The viewer must learn to ask the right questions and be properly puzzled if no apparent answer seems at hand.

In a play the viewpoint has to be the playwright's vision. Whatever we see on the stage was once in his mind, now given three-dimensional life by the director and the actors. The director has studied the play thoroughly and has decided what kind of reality it is offering. He has either accepted the conventions dictated by the author or imposed some of his own which he believes will better serve the purpose. But there are times when the audience is still confused over what it sees; it knows what it sees but does not always know why something is being shown.

Tennessee Williams' *The Glass Menagerie* employs the device of a narrator, speaking directly to the audience. The scenes that follow are to be the memories of his youth. The first scene played is such a recollection, but the second scene, which takes place only between the mother and the daughter, could not have been remembered by the narrator. However, only the most rigid viewer would object to believing in the convention. The play as a whole operates within a specified framework; the Wingfield home, impressionistically presented on the stage, contains the constant, brooding presence of the poetic Tom, dreamily wandering through his past.

Plays go out of focus generally when they have episodic plots. That is, they begin by seeming to be about one character — a possessive mother who keeps nagging her son about his lack of ambition, for example — and force us to view the action from a certain viewpoint. Then the subject matter changes to the son's need for a young ballet dancer he happens to meet. Then we are asked to become involved with the dancer's family problems. She has an alcoholic father and is ashamed to ask the boy to her home. Then the play seems to take the side of the rejected parent and ask for broader toleration of human weakness. It is not merely a matter of changing themes, but of changing protagonists. Only a genius like Chekhov is able to make us care about each of his characters in turn, to make us experience a hundred tiny dramas, each complete in itself and therefore not constituting a breach of the focus contract.

Careful listening to the dialogue in a play can aid the critical viewer to decide whether the train is staying on the track. Dramatists have continually to fight against the natural human tendency to wander from the point. A conversation in real life among several people is likely to end up nowhere, because each thought has suggested another with which it may have only a tenuous connection. Dramatists sometimes forget that their characters are not real people but exist within a certain framework. Once their characters are given the breath of life they may be allowed to structure their own conversations. Reality becomes the model at the wrong time. One of the great advantages that theater has over reality should be precisely the intensity and compression that reality lacks.

Live theater also has the disadvantage of using real actors performing as make-believe characters. Naturally they will bring their own actuality to the stage with them. Nothing is to stop an actor from giving a line of dialogue a certain inflection, suggesting a certain connotation that the author or director might not have intended. The need for separating the player from the play is one of the many reasons that critical detachment must accompany emotional involvement in the action.

The nature of movie-making — that is, the possibility of a scene's being shot many times until it accomplishes exactly what the director wishes — greatly increases the chances that blurred focus — where it exists on the screen — is at least deliberate. But it also increases the opportunity for artistic directors to have their final product exactly what they hoped for. Television shows, working under the sword of demanding deadlines, are likely to be far more careless and inscrutable in their viewpoints. The *reductio ad absurdum* is surely the daytime serial, or "soap opera," with its endlessly drifting dialogue, its lack of a constant protagonist, and its continual shifting from plot to plot, character to character for no apparent reason other than the actors' union requirement that each player be given his share of work.

4 ❀ ❀ ❀

Page, Stage, and Film

The Importance of the Medium

Although critical viewing can begin with any of the dramatic media — stage, film, or television — live drama has more to recommend it because of age, prestige and an established vocabulary of analysis. Many of the terms of live drama can be used for judging the other forms as well. A screen plot that makes a definite promise only to break it is just as disappointing as a stage plot that does the same thing. The *deus ex machina,* which backs away from its obligation by finding improbable solutions for interesting problems, is as bad in one form as another. And thought, characters, dialogue and the other elements of live theater are all involved to some degree in film.

The separation of the media according to what each is able to do best becomes valuable at a more advanced stage of critical viewing. It is helpful, for example, to realize that there are very rewarding films which do not attempt to tell a story in the same way that plays do. Knowing that plot can be disregarded if there are compensatory moments of quiet insight helps to increase one's tolerance for innovations of the screen. Realizing that the screen requires the elements of drama in different degrees helps to broaden one's ability to enjoy a greater variety of drama — particularly the avant-garde films which so often puzzle the un-prepared.

Because live theater has such a long history as an art form and as a discipline in the humanities, the film has been scorned by scholars and theater people alike. It is considered a novelty, a business, a destroyer of talent, and Hollywood has been the target of countless attacks from people lured by the money but repelled by the medium. The live-theater contingent would usually prefer a second-rate stage play to a first-rate film.

More recently films have found defenders in those who believe that the live theater has been doing less exciting and significant things from year to year. They point out that there is little to praise on Broadway, that each new crop of musicals and superficial romances, though presented by actors on a legitimate stage, can hardly be said to be maintaining a tradition begun by Sophocles, Shakespeare, and Molière, and that only snobbism prevents defenders of the stage from acknowledging the superiority of film, which will be the important drama of the future.

It is true that the glories of live drama lie mainly in the past. If it were not for the university theaters and the small experimental groups, the critical viewer might well prefer the movies. But assuming that there will always be enough live theater around, one can make an intelligent choice from the best of both media, and make a case for either side.

The Live Presence and the Screen Image

Partisans of live theater point out that a shadow on a white screen or a relatively tiny picture inside a piece of furniture at one corner of the living room cannot match the effect of a real human being on a stage. They insist that there is no substitute for action on the stage, happening now as we experience it. Only theater can sustain illusion over long periods of time.

It is true that the theater-going experience is far less casual than either movie-going or television-watching. In the theater, the whole tradition of curtain time, intermission time, lobby chatter, and after-theater get-togethers creates a unifying atmosphere, not only encouraging but positively demanding more intense concentration than the screen media are in a position to require. The activity of people getting up to go outside or arriving in the middle of a film does not promote attention, whereas once the audience at a live play has settled down there are few distractions. Besides, the live presence calls for the courtesy of attentive watching and listening. Even the most bored spectator seldom will leave in the middle of an act. The live theater operates under physical conditions highly favorable for entertainment.

The fact that actors on a stage retain their size and have a continuing presence does help build the illusion of reality. Once the house lights are dimmed and the curtain has risen, we have made the adjustment to this artificial form of experience and need not keep making further adjustments. Theoretically, however, every time the screen image changes we could be required to suspend our disbelief once more. Now a face is enormous, taking up almost all of the screen — a close-up; now the camera moves back to a half-shot, so that the torsos of several actors are seen; finally there is a long-shot, taken from a camera positioned high above a crowd at a beach. What is the point of view? Through whose eyes do we see these things?

If the critical viewer accepts, without reservation, the *Gulliver's Travels* world of film which jumps from Lilliput to Brobdingnag, he has not experienced any illusion to begin with. Perhaps it is harder for him to lose himself in a movie and harder still in front of a television set, while the uncritical viewer, unaccustomed to thinking in terms of shifting conventions, has no trouble whatever. The kinds of illusion possible in the two media are vastly different and are not comparable from any viewpoint.

Words and Pictures

One definition of a stage play is the telling of a story by means of live actors who move and use language. The same definition cannot apply to the screen media, for the screen does not need spoken language. (There never was an era of silent theater as there was of silent films.) The advent of sound in 1927 added another means of creating effects, but the visual language of the screen came first and remains primary.

Probably everyone has had the experience of lying on a sofa, closing his eyes, and "listening" to television. Those who can remember what it used to be like to listen to stories on the radio and imagine the people and places that could not be seen, can testify to the profound change that television has brought. Listening to television is very unsatisfying and definitely unstimulating to the imagination. There are long, long stretches of silence, usually with background music punctuating whatever is happening on the screen, so that at length the listener is forced to sit up, open his eyes, and watch the pictures that were selected for him.

Since the motion picture became a serious art form, it has produced a number of important works, but few, if any, memorable lines of dialogue. There was, of course, Lauren Bacall's comment to Humphrey Bogart in the screen version of Hemingway's *To Have and Have Not* (1945): "If you want anything, all you've gotta do is whistle." But the line was celebrated less for its sound than for the extremely provocative look on Miss Bacall's face. In *Gone with the Wind* (1939), in reply to Vivien Leigh's desperate question, "If you leave me, where'll I go, what'll I do?", Clark Gable said, "Frankly, my dear, I don't give a damn." But the fame of the line was not caused by its eloquence. Even before the movie opened, there had been much controversy over whether the Hays office would permit such profanity to be heard by a mass audience.

During its two decades of existence, television has had even fewer memorable lines than movies. Old-timers still watch *I Love Lucy* re-runs with loving nostalgia because they like the situations or the irresistible look on Lucille Ball's face whenever Desi Arnaz catches her in some innocent form of intrigue. The gag lines assume the mellow charm of old friends from the past who drop in occasionally — good to visit with, but easily forgotten.

In striking contrast, the stage has for centuries been the home of great language. What is the printed version of Shakespeare but sheer language? There are hardly any stage directions, and those we have do not describe actions in much detail. The Elizabethan actor simply stepped onto a bare platform, opened his mouth, and spoke. For the Greek audiences the situation was even more dependent on words. Their actors were hidden behind grotesque masks which could not be seen in detail from six hundred rows up anyway. His face of no consequence, the Greek actor was chosen for the carrying power and clarity of his voice.

Die-hard theater advocates insist that movies and television discourage any great interest or pride in language, that, tasteless as the Broadway stage usually is, it is still more "literate" than the screen media. In other words, the convention of communicating through language remains honorific, while that of "resorting" to purely visual communication is sometimes construed as a shameless pandering to mass illiteracy.

But the deverbalization which is an inevitable consequence of a visual medium *can* be looked upon as another, not necessarily lower, form of communication. Pictures can get at things which neither books nor lectures can reach. The screen medium fails when it attempts to be verbal as well as visual — that is to say, when words and pictures are directly parallel. Thus the film opens, and we hear a narrator: "This is my town. I was born at the end of this drab and dingy street, littered with refuse." If the camera does nothing but show what the words are talking about, either the pictures or the words are not necessary. A picture is not really worth a thousand words. If the visual media function as they should, if they utilize their own means of communicating, if they stop attempting to offer "word-pictures," pictures and words become non-equivalents; a picture should need no verbal equivalent because none should be available.

  John Bigby *on the Art of the Film**

> Film is strongest when it makes greatest use of what is peculiarly its own — the ability to record time and space, slice them up into fragments, and glue them together in a new relationship.

> * Reprinted from "Language in the Age of Zworykin," *Studies in the Mass Media*, Vol. IV, no. 4 (January, 1964), published by the National Council of Teachers of English.

The memorable moments from the films and from television are not lines, but images. Silent films like Eisenstein's *Potemkin* (1925) or Charlie Chaplin's comedies of the 1920's continue to have appeal for new audiences. Much has been said and written about the Chaplin figure, but it is almost impossible to capture in words the extraordinary fusion of farce and pathos, of idiocy and dignity which made him famous.

Television at its height of creativity lacked the technical facilities to do much to advance the art of imagery, but it offered character insights through intense close-range photography. An actor's reaction to someone else's speech was usually more significant than the speech itself.

The issue is not whether the visual media have failed in their linguistic obligations, but whether what they have done and are still doing with pictures is itself worth doing. The extraordinary visual effects in memor-

Scene from stage production of A Streetcar Named Desire. *The people in the audience are free to look anywhere they wish and to see whatever they care to.*

able films — the close-ups, lyrical images, variations in speed, the blurring and sharpening of focus — are testimony to the special quality of pictures.

Just as playwrights are less insistent on visual effects than they are on dialogue, so the film director, who is the major creative force behind the movie, is less intent on camera imagery, which is *his* contribution, than he is on the actual dialogue.

"Stage pictures" — that is, the configurations of characters which the director arranges — are added pleasures of play viewing, but many scenes achieve impact with little movement to none at all. In the fourth act of O'Neill's *Long Day's Journey into Night* (1956), the father and the younger son sit at a table, play cards, drink and talk. There is no way for a director to inject movement into the scene; none of the lines suggests a change of location. The scene runs nearly thirty minutes. Yet it does not bore. The more the father drinks, the more he tells his son of his past, and the son comes to understand his father for the first time. The rapport which the two reach is touching indeed. This scene is pure theater; it could not have been done through camera imagery. In the film version of the same play, the camera merely reported the scene as the theatrical sequence it is.

Perhaps someday a dramatist will emerge who can combine the power of both words and pictures. Shakespeare, working with no scenic element to speak of, having to accomplish everything through words, nonetheless recognized the force of visual impact. To compensate for the bare platform on which the actors performed, he created his own visual medium through the imagery in his language.

Close-up from movie version of A Streetcar Named Desire. *The audience is required to watch the expression on Blanche's face as well as the unsympathetic immobility of the man.*

If even the most imaginative innovator in films were to attempt *Antony and Cleopatra,* it is doubtful that his prolific camera-eye imagination could improve much upon this description of the heroine given by Enobarbus:

> The barge she sat in like a burnish'd throne,
> Burn'd on the water. The poop was beaten gold;
> Purple the sails, and so perfumed that
> The winds were love-sick with them. The oars were silver,
> Which to the tune of flutes kept stroke, and made
> The water which they beat to follow faster,
> As amorous of their strokes. For her own person
> It beggar'd all description: she did lie
> In her pavilion — cloth-of-gold of tissue —
> O'er-picturing that Venus where we see
> The fancy outwork nature. On each side her
> Stood pretty dimpled boys, like smiling Cupids,
> With divers-color'd fans, whose wind did seem
> To glow the delicate cheeks which they did cool,
> And what they undid did.

When Shakespeare has Enobarbus say that Cleopatra "beggar'd all description," he is really sidestepping the issue. He has to; he has reached an impasse. Language has gone as far as it can go. The "cloth-of-gold" image offers a suggestion of how the listener might complete the scene in his own mind. Shakespeare makes *us* see the queen, but his words do not really create her with pictorial completeness. "O'er-picturing that Venus" is a mythological allusion that works for literature, but it does not do what a camera can do. Shakespeare's most complex female figure is all but unplayable. Perhaps she lives best in the imaginations of those who read about her.

When the playwright's words open doors in the mind for which there exist no pictorial equivalent, he is working at the summit of his medium. Conversely, when the film director finds an image for which there exists no verbal equivalent, he is doing the same in his medium. The critical viewer dislikes the trespassing of one medium into the domain of another. If a play is a movie in disguise, it clutters up the stage with much fast-moving action and little memorable dialogue; when a movie is a play in disguise, it is endlessly talky and the camera has been used simply to photograph actors with their lips moving.

The Possibilities of Television

Television, the infant of dramatic arts, became a medium in its own right during the late forties and early fifties. At the outset it seemed to promise fresh opportunities for bringing drama to large numbers of people. The new art opened its welcoming doors to fresh young talents, who did not demand or receive the fortunes which Broadway or Hollywood could offer. Reginald Rose, Rod Serling, and Paddy Chayevsky are a few of the exciting playwrights who were eager to experiment with telling stories in terms of intimate photography that could be experienced by Americans in the comfort of their living rooms. For a number of those early years television was a novelty and could be as serious as it wanted. The movies were on the wane and had to prove themselves once more. Television gained immediate and wide acceptance.

Cramped studio space, the non-existence of video taping, and relatively low budgeting were helpful to the new medium. Though "The Ed Sullivan Show" was around as early as 1948, the day of the super variety show had not yet arrived. Whatever was presented had to be performed "live," making constant and elaborate costume changes impossible and production numbers difficult to bring off with the polish that Broadway and Hollywood audiences had come to demand. There was a great deal of live drama, stories involving small casts and one or two modest sets.

"Playhouse 90," "The Robert Montgomery Theater," "The U.S. Steel Hour," and the "Philco-Goodyear Playhouse" all had moments of genuine glory but have since been discarded by sponsors who keep trying season after season to maintain pace with the rapidly changing whims of television audiences.

Today, when television is no longer a novelty and a whole generation has grown up with it, the movies are meeting the challenge of competition with multi-million-dollar extravaganzas that play road-show engagements at increased prices. Sponsors try to keep their fingers on the pulse of the American public by spending vast sums on rating surveys and honoring the results of those surveys by almost immediately killing programs that do not win instant acceptance.

Today, the production of a distinguished original drama is rare. The atmosphere is one of constant tension in which script writers (rather than dramatists) work with a copy of the ratings before them. Plot ideas, character types, sometimes even individual lines that are known to have worked are imitated until the public becomes tired and demands a change, a phenomenon that now occurs twice a year.

In its youth television concentrated on what the camera alone could reveal. In "live" drama, the emphasis was on mood and character expression. Without color, large casts, or lavish scenery to display in the manner of its large-screened relative, television concentrated on the personal. The camera close-up magnified an actor's reactions in a special way, unequaled on stage or screen.

Loring Mandell's *Project Immortality*, presented on "Playhouse 90" in 1959, was a particularly impressive example of television drama as an art form. The story concerned a team of young electronics engineers who were programming a computer so that it became a mechanical reproduction of the mind of a scientific genius who had only a short time to live. By presenting a sequence of brief scenes, such as cannot be done on the stage without awkwardness and disturbing the rhythm of the production, the drama created an intimate portrait of a great man in a way that was completely convincing. He was shown singing songs, playing the piano, telling jokes — in short, doing and being interested in the many kinds of activities one would expect of genius. Each scene lasted only as long as it had to, to show the character in a new way. On the stage each scene would have required greater elaboration, because, though time can be believed to have elapsed *between* scenes in the theater, there cannot be the telescoping of time which the screen allows. The result is that the stage can offer more imposing plot structures, while television can bring character into sharper focus.

The author of *Project Immortality* had very little to say about the man's genius other than that he *was* a genius and, consequently, that human greatness cannot be rivalled by a machine. The point has been made before in other forms, of course — in science-fiction novels and in church sermons. From the beginning of the drama — even in the title *Project Immortality* — it was very obviously going to be made again, but anticipation of a familiar theme added to the pleasures of watching.

After the death of the scientist, the narrator makes the comment that he and his colleagues could never be certain that their electronic brain was in fact a duplication of the original: "We only knew that he was gone." As this simple and flat statement was made, the camera slowly panned from object to object in the great man's study. The multiplicity of his interests and complexity of his talents hit home with greater impact than ever and so did the sense of the man's absence. A stage can be empty, to be sure, and this can be used to great advantage, as in Mary Chase's *Harvey* (1945), in which a door opens but no one enters — to suggest the presence of the invisible six-foot rabbit who may or may not be an hallucination. Yet one empty stage is pretty much like another. While it can mean that rabbits or ghosts are around, it cannot so clearly mean that a genius has gone. There is no guarantee that the audience will look from object to object, as the camera forces it to do. Having to look at the entire study all at once, some members of the audience might have thought of a cluttered room rather than of the irreplaceable life of a genius.

A recent development in television is the success of the original musical comedy, a good example of which is *Jack and the Beanstalk* (1966). Several factors contributed to its success; the first is time. Ordinarily Broadway musicals run about three hours, but *Jack and the Beanstalk* lasted only fifty-two minutes. This brevity, necessitated by the expense of television time, had the merit of condensing and heightening a plot which on Broadway is too often unbelievable and rambling.

Secondly, a fairy tale is as good a starting place for a musical as anything else, but it almost *has* to turn into a spoof on the musical form — otherwise it runs the risk of becoming too sentimental for mature audiences. Broadway has tried many spoofs on musicals but usually failed; there is something self-defeating about a Broadway show's making fun of a Broadway show. But television, a totally different medium, can satirize the stage. Seeing the foolishness so close up gave the audience insight into the sort of show it generally has to pay high prices to see.

Furthermore, the director made use of certain techniques available only to the medium. The characters spoke directly to the camera (as they did in the movie *Tom Jones*). This is a convention unique to camera art. Rather than pretend that the camera is the missing fourth wall that the proscenium arch in a theater usually represents, the camera totally reconstructs time and space.

Finally, as in *Project Immortality*, the scenes in *Jack and the Beanstalk* were only as long as they had to be. Since rapid movement and bouncy high spirits are outstanding traits of the musical, this particular production suggested that television, if it wanted to, could have no peer as the very temple of musical comedy. Dialogue was held to an absolute minimum, there existing no need to create elaborate transitions from one scene to another. All the camera had to do was fade out and fade in. Moreover, the frequent fade-outs gave climactic importance to lines that, in a theater, might have fallen limply to the floor.

Most important of all — to enjoy *Jack and the Beanstalk* one did not have to leave home. A critical viewer dislikes the elaborate and time-consuming theater-going ritual for a plot which has not been worth the effort.

The lavishness of a stage production can even make the nonsense more evident, whereas in the television musical, which was much shorter, expense seemed less important than imagination. One can enjoy an hour's relaxation with a television musical because when it is over, the return to the real world is controlled by a flick of the switch marked "off."

Big Screen, Little Screen

Since both movies and television are comparatively new forms of dramatic art, and since neither medium has yet to create a long-standing tradition of pictorial literature or artists whose work has been studied and re-studied by scholars, comparisons between the two *as* media are not yet definitive. Television has proved an appropriate medium for musical comedies, whether original as in the Jackie Gleason-Art Carney Honeymooners shows or in a new version of a fairy tale. With the right story and performers, magically combined to have maximum appeal for the whole family, television does what no other medium can do. The early promise of works like *Project Immortality* suggested a use of the medium which would eventually lead to favorable comparisons with movies made by the freest, most non-commercial directors.

It is doubtful, however, that television will ever do precisely what a motion picture can do. The magnification of imagery on a movie screen seems obviously better suited to audience involvement than the shrinking of imagery on television. Even a favorite movie can be disappointing when it reappears on the late show, and all the blame cannot fall on the perpetual distraction of ill-timed commercials. One still misses the intimacy which the larger screen lends to the experience of movie-going.

The artistic success of *Project Immortality* offers a further clue to what may become the aesthetics of television: the play had a narrow pictorial scope. The final scene, showing the scientist's room, forced the attention of the viewer into a nineteen-inch tube. Moreover, the presentation as a whole had a documentary quality about it and suggests that television is wise when it allows purely imaginative works to resemble on-the-spot coverage.

This "you-are-there" function of television is going to have to be a concern of any future Aristotle of the medium who takes upon himself the job of deciding what its limits are. The director of a live telecast of a football game, a pageant, or a meeting of the United Nations General Assembly is an artist in his own right; for he is exercising selectivity of details. He must anticipate the kind of football play which may be coming up next. He has the "isolated camera" ready to follow the pass receiver down the field or the quarterback as he bootlegs the ball. While the game is in progress, he is analyzing and interpreting and — when he is successful in his predictions — has channeled the experience for the viewer. Watching from the stands never permits so intimate a knowledge of the anatomy of a particular game.

Similarly, when a singer does a song on a variety show, the live audience watching the taping sees him in only one light — tall, short, overly expressive with his hands, fidgeting with his feet, struggling with the microphone cord. The director in the control booth has two or three cameras focused on the performer from different angles. On his monitors he is able to observe different images of the singer, which offer different perspectives. As the song proceeds, he keeps changing the image, changing the mood which is communicated. The result for the viewer is more than simply having seen somebody sing a song. He has had a close glimpse at an artist in the process of *being* an artist. He has looked at the right things.

When the United States delegate to the United Nations makes a speech accusing a nation of aggression, the television camera can focus on the reactions of delegations from that country, and from allied and neutral powers. There have been many times in the relatively brief history of television when the viewer has had the distinct and gratifying sensation of being present while history is being made. Moreover, no other medium has ever been capable of such hyper-authenticity, has ever been able to function as the viewer's third eye, enlarging his entire scope of experience; and thus the small-scale image on the television screen does not become a hindrance. It is by now the condition under which we expect to receive the image of a reality which is being analyzed as it takes place.

The motion pictures will never be able to equal this hyper-authenticity, even though they can outdo the stage in offering realism. Many of the major film directors in Europe have made their reputations by specializing in stark realism, made to seem as undistorted as possible. They tell their stories in the bleakest possible terms and without glamorizing their players. But Ingmar Bergman's symbolism and use of medieval settings in such films as *The Seventh Seal* (1956) and *Virgin Spring* (1960) (see Chapter Twelve) is in itself significant. In wishing to express himself poetically through film, in wishing to use the camera to do far more than photograph, Bergman likes his pictorial images to be removed from a sense of contemporaneity. Thus, Bergman is trying to reach a more universal level of achievement by not allowing his works to be too firmly rooted in the era during which each was filmed.

The most limiting factor in both screen media is this difficult-to-dissolve marriage to their historical contexts. The nature of photography itself tends to discourage the imitation of the past. In films about the flapper era, actresses seldom appear in extremely fashionable clothes; in the Western the heroine normally has a chic hair-do presently in style; and Biblical and Roman epics use "history" as an excuse to reveal feminine anatomy. Each screen Cleopatra has inevitably represented the standards of beauty current at the time of production. Even the most painstaking productions of costume drama become dated very quickly. When we are immediate contemporaries of the pictorial style, it is difficult to assess the degree to which everything about the film will seem old-fashioned ten or twenty years from now. And it is hard to overlook dated elements when they are directly seen, not imagined. (One can read a novel from the past and see its actions and characters in any way one desires.) The bus on which Claudette Colbert and Clark Gable meet in *It Happened One Night* was probably the streamlined special of 1934, but it hinders the modern viewer's acceptance of the whole film. Even the unstylish clothes worn by Miss Colbert take their toll of viewer enthusiasm, because the whole point of the film had been that love for Clark Gable was worth more than being wealthy and living in the height of fashion.

One can regard the necessary aging of films as one of the conventions

of the medium. It takes, however, a powerful plot and strong performances to make this convention acceptable, for just as photography inevitably records a reality too soon turned history, film stories and the values
they embody tend to reflect so much of their times that few ever reach
the universal level for which Ingmar Bergman continually strives.

Another possibility remains for consideration in this regard, and it is
one that may be somewhat frightening in its implications. The time may
possibly come when the staying power of a work will no longer be a prime
critical concern, when universality will mean less than immediate effectiveness. The film medium may bring about a complete revolution in
critical standards, a trend toward pragmatic aesthetics, whereby what
matters most is the power that a work has in its own time. If Sophocles
or Shakespeare had been able to use the pictorial media, who is to say
that their themes would not have been directly contemporary? that
instead of Oedipus, film archives of libraries would be allowing a movie
called *Summer in Athens* to collect dust on a shelf? or one called *Con-
fessions of a Sonneteer* to amuse antique collectors with its quaintness?

Page and Stage

Reading a play is not a simple task. Most plays were written for live
performance quite as much as a screenplay or television script is a blueprint for a specific production. A play in print is to a play on the stage as
the orchestral score is to the performed symphony. There are people who
can enjoy reading a printed score for its own sake. There are a greater
number who hear more in the music when they have studied the score.
Since language is so crucial to the life of the theater, great drama also
possesses a life of its own as literature, and making a predominantly
literary study of a play can enhance the viewer's perception.

A film is a complete, irreducible entity in itself. It is the visual experience of its director, not its original author. For this reason the name of
the director appears most prominently in the screen credits, while the
author of the screenplay is usually given relatively minor stature.

Since live theater is mainly a linguistic medium, no matter what additional help may come from the director's use of spectacle or background
music, the dramatist naturally assumes a more important role, one that
has to be considered on its own ground. A play can have a bad production — or no production at all — but it maintains an independent reality.

Responding to the play as literature makes one acutely aware of the
work of skillful directors and deft performers. Critical viewers who are
adept readers can make the separation of script from production in the
theater. On the spot they can imagine the script and can re-cast a part
which is being badly performed. This added dimension of viewing might
seem to make one more demanding and less satisfied with the product
being offered on the stage. But the logical counter-argument is that,

when a play seems to be flunking its literary test, when it seems to be unimportant and unlikely to survive beyond next Thursday, chances are that it is lacking in real entertainment value. For the critical viewer the sense that what he is seeing is not trivial is in itself a source of pleasure. To give up the casual enjoyment of a silly work that has been given violent pacing and a generally loud production to gloss over its emptiness is to heighten one's appreciation of works that have greater substance.

The theaters of the Greeks and of Shakespeare produced great drama despite, not because of, the physical conditions. It is important to know the staging methods of this era, and these will be dealt with in Part Two of this book; yet possessing historical background is not the same thing as believing that the great dramas of the past were marvelous in performance. A Greek actor *might* have looked awkward in his mask and padded clothes (regardless of how much one tries to understand differing theatrical conventions); the boy who played Juliet surely was acceptable only because Elizabethans did not yet have the advantage of actresses in female roles. Sir Laurence Olivier's memorable screen version of *Henry V* in 1944 began by presenting the first scene as it might have looked in its original production at the Globe. The groundlings in the pit were boisterous, the noblemen seated on the stage distracting. This portion of the movie offered remarkable insight into what could have been the distinctly unglamorous side of Elizabethan theater. Then the film rewarded the viewer by offering his eyes the feast of color and scenery as the play became a film and came to life at last. The point is that the masterpieces of the theater might not have survived had they been tied down to their original productions in the way that movies are preserved in their original state. They might not have survived if it had not been for the medium of the printed word which makes a drama accessible to the imagination of all future ages and to people who, for reasons of geography or economy, are seldom able to attend live theater.

Reading for the Play Itself

Going to a movie or turning on the television set means that one pays his money and takes his director. Whatever purely personal use one might wish to make of a film, he is inhibited by the boundaries of the camera eye which have been imposed by the director. Native Floridians who saw the film version of Maxwell Anderson's *Key Largo* (1948) might have been dismayed to see that the opening image was a vista not of Key Largo, which has a larger land mass than do the lower Keys, but of Knight's Key, which is more picturesque. This discrepancy did not matter in the least to the majority of film-goers, but it bothered the natives.

The play as literature invites a highly personal response, just as a novel or a short story does. If language is its primary element, the language must do the communicating. It should be possible to read (initially anyway) with no regard for the playwright's biography or to the play's historical context, but to respond simply — as a human being reading the words of another human being.

The first advantage of this approach is *spontaneity.* The reader is in complete charge, with none of the burden that accompanies more scholarly reading. For, aside from the usual rigors of scholarship, the scholar must ignore many little things — lines here, a short scene there, a character who makes a brief appearance. But these very elements can offer sudden and inexplicable delights to the "free" reader, who also does not run the risk of having his opinions pre-influenced by his reading about the play.

Second, there is the reward of *free association,* or personal identification. Perhaps one of the characters resembles an old acquaintance, or somebody's mother. The reader may concentrate on whatever character interests him the most. If the play is a tragedy and he feels no pity for the protagonist, he may prefer to follow the fortunes of a different character whose life more nearly parallels his own. If there is a love affair in the play and if the reader is peculiarly responsive to the theme of love at this point in his life, it is legitimate for him to enjoy reading the language of the lovers. Love is love to him, whether it be in the heart of Sophocles' Antigone or Tennessee Williams' Blanche du Bois, two women separated by a gulf of twenty-five hundred years and living in societies with widely differing attitudes toward love.

The potential of any drama for inspiring free association is an important criterion to use in determining its enduring value. *Hamlet* is thought to be among the most personal works ever written, even as it is the richest single mine for scholarly investigation and interpretation in all the theater. Any reader, no matter what his background, can sympathize with Hamlet's anguish over his mother's remarriage or the quick passing of his father's memory or his despair stemming from his own situation in the world. Especially can young readers in college or just starting out in life identify with Hamlet's torment as the prince recognizes the tremendous gap between reality and his former idealism. Aside from anything else, *Hamlet* is a play about strained, tortured, destructive family relationships, and any reader can bring to the first reading an understanding of how family ties can at times form a net from which escape is impossible.

Knowledge of how a certain play came to be written can even inhibit the pleasures of free association. If one learned, for example, that a work was composed during the Nazi occupation of France, he might be forced to consider a certain character in it as a symbol of oppression, a character who would otherwise have held only *pleasant* connotations. Or the discovery is later made that the playwright is a homosexual and that he has

used the play to express his feeling of isolation from society; yet, in looking back, the reader finds that he had seen no sexual connotations in any
of the actions. The mother in a play may be an exact replica of the
author's, but the reader need not know this; the reader may see his own
mother or his first-grade teacher or a composite of different people in his
past.

On this level there is almost no such thing as misreading a play. But
there is the danger of failing to recognize personalism in one's reactions
to a play. There is a considerable difference between "That play is worth
nothing" and "My own memories of military school are so painful that
I can never enjoy a play about service life."

Finding More than the Play Itself

Personal reading of the drama has the same limitations of the uncritical
approach to any other form of literature: it can be fun, but it is not the
highest kind of pleasure. A cheeseburger at a roadside stand will serve
the purpose and is certainly better than starving, but it is not chateau-
briand prepared by a gifted chef and served in the height of style.

Critical perception in the reading of a play begins with an historical
perspective and is enhanced by a knowledge of the playwright himself.
Of the Greeks little is known, and the details which have been gathered
together of Shakespeare's life are sketchy to non-existent; but this does
not mean that scholars of the theater do not regret this important void.

Knowledge of the playwright can be misapplied. A student of theater
is not a scandal-monger or an intellectual peeping Tom, turning the
dramatist's own career into a fiction more exciting than any he ever
devised for the stage. Modern playwrights are especially vulnerable to
this "confidential" approach. The proper use of biography is to investigate
a playwright's known working habits or statements regarding his dramatic
theory. This information substantially increases an understanding of the
nature of his work and the conventions he employs.

Because Ibsen's plays, for example, are frequently concerned with the
quarrel between the artist and the values of middle-class respectability,
it is significant to learn that his own life offers evidence of the same
struggle. For one year he would systematically gather material; the
following year he would write and polish the play. At his peak he offered
a new play at two-year intervals with clockwork regularity. Yet in his
plays he often strongly criticized the kind of people who believed in order
and discipline of this very kind. In other words, an investigation into the
life of Ibsen brings to light certain tendencies in himself which he attributed to others and denounced as being bourgeois. For example, one
of Ibsen's characters, George Tesman, Hedda Gabler's husband, is a petty
academic specialist with an unimportant sense of order — both the direct
opposite of the spontaneity and adventurous immersion in the life of one's

time that Ibsen appears to prescribe. Knowing that there is much of the author in a certain character can indeed guide the proper reading of a play.

Ernest R. Hilgard *on Writing as Self-expression**

1. For *some* artists and writers, the themes that haunt them and form the content of their creative efforts are in a large measure autobiographical, and in that sense may reflect their own unresolved conflicts. This was apparently the case with Eugene O'Neill, whose "conscious" autobiography appears in the play *Long Day's Journey Into Night*, whereas his "unconscious" autobiography is perhaps revealed in *Desire Under the Elms* (Weissman, 1957).

2. Such writers are not necessarily narcissistic or egoistic; that is, they do not write just for themselves, out of inner compulsion, but they generalize their experiences to meet a larger audience. In such a case, the purposes served and the satisfactions achieved are not of the kind to be destroyed by psychotherapy. (It is doubtful if many such writers would even accept the psychotherapeutic relationship.)

3. A writer or an artist who comes for psychotherapy usually does so because his conflicts, far from serving his creativity, are making it impossible for him to create. For him, successful therapy makes it possible for him to *return* to his typewriter or his canvas.

4. A writer or an artist who comes for psychotherapy and as a consequence *gives up* his artistic pursuit was probably not a very gifted person in the first place and so, in giving up his pretense to great originality, was becoming more realistic, and in a sense, less fraudulent.

* Reprinted from *Creativity and its Cultivation*, edited by Harold H. Anderson, by permission of Harper & Row, Inc.

Yet even after having found what appear to be significant characters, events and ideas in the playwright's life, one must exercise caution in making a definite statement of cause and effect. A dramatist may even write a certain play or create a certain character despite rather than because of a personal experience. He may have suffered a crushing rejection of his love and then risen above his feelings to write a work which has nothing to do with love or even is a soaring affirmation of love. As a matter of fact, learning the relationship between a playwright's biography and his play is a way of seeing how much the source has changed. It reveals much about the creative process as a whole.

It is legitimate and necessary to know enough about a playwright's background to recognize the limitations which this has placed upon his work. The reader should be able to tell when he has attempted to depict unfamiliar material or a character foreign to his experience, as in drawing the lives of wealthy people from his imagination alone or trying to describe a place or event when he lacked sufficient information. But one should beware of reading their plays as evidence of intense personal expression.

It can also be illuminating to compare two or more works by the same author and to find answers for a number of pertinent questions:

> Do the same subjects appear from play to play?
> Does the author dwell upon certain kinds of characters? situations?
> Are there any objects or events which, through their frequent use, appear to be symbols?
> By putting a number of plays together, does one form a clear picture of the age which produced them?
> Does there seem to be a development or a regression in the author's artistic ability as he moved from play to play?

When a reader reaches a point at which he is able to make such comparisons, he can begin to share the enjoyment of the intellectual acts of critical investigation and speculation which scholars of the drama seek. The ultimate profit can be measured in so many subtle ways that no single reason can be given to justify such an approach.

The play as literature can be found to offer a fresh view of an event in history that has the added benefit of the artist's insight. Maxwell Anderson's play *Winterset* (1935) may well become one of the principal sources molding the attitude of future generations toward the case which inspired it, that involving two immigrants tried for and found guilty of a payroll-robbery murder. The viewpoint behind the play is that the men were not guilty but were sent to the electric chair out of prejudice. To a great extent this play has helped to mold the popular memory of Sacco and Vanzetti; their execution will continue to be restudied because the idea of the injustice that may have been committed is by now a deeply imbedded one. No one has yet measured the extent to which the popular images of events have derived from all forms of literature, not merely theater.

Drama as a Myth-Making Force

Since the drama can foster the illusion that a story was really an historical event, it is clear that the theater has played a major part in the creation and perpetuation of the myths that underlie our culture. Approaching the drama as a literary medium and acquiring a broad reading background in plays cause the reader to understand better what myth is and the power it wields in influencing the unconscious assumptions on which most people base their lives. Anderson's handling of the Sacco-Vanzetti case, in this respect, takes on mythical status.

A myth is a fictional story which embodies fundamental and enduring truths of existence as well as men's hopes, fears, and attitudes and which remains so vivid in the imagination that it is often mistaken for history itself. An example of an enduring truth embodied in the form of myth would be the cycle of the seasons, for which modern man has scientific explanations but which ancient man dramatized in terms of a story. Thus one Greek myth accounted for winter as the grief of Demeter, the earth mother, for the loss of her daughter Persephone, and for spring as the mother's joy in being reunited with her child.

Myth in the beginning had the effect of making mysterious forces seem human and therefore not so dark, not so uncontrollable as they might otherwise have seemed. Myth represents man's earliest (and in many respects still his most admirable) act of self-assertion in the universe. And the drama, because of its immediacy and because it is a social art, has been important in making myth seem a reality.

What is surprising about a study of myth in drama is that the number of separate and distinct myths is so small. One finds that there are a handful of ancient stories and character types which seem to sum up the case for and against man, which have deeply affected the understanding of man. Orestes, Oedipus, Hamlet, Joseph, and Christ are perhaps the most prominent figures about whom so much fact and fancy are woven that the separation of truth from falsehood no longer seems necessary. The fact remains that all of them continue to have meaning, and their stories continue to find embodiment in modern drama as well as in other forms of literature.

The story of Orestes, given its most famous expression by Aeschylus, is that of a man caught between two fires and having to make a choice between alternatives that are both undesirable. In Aeschylus' tragedy, Orestes had to choose between murdering his mother or allowing the honor of his father's name to go unavenged; but his story could also be that of an atomic scientist of today who had to make a choice between love of country and the realization that unleashing the destructive force of atomic energy could be a disservice to all mankind.

The story of Oedipus, given its greatest treatment by Sophocles, is very complex, embodying the ancient fear of incest as well as the broader, more contemporary subject of man's search for identity. It also has to do with guilt; though it is neither Hebrew nor Christian in origin, it has remained the major story of man's tragic struggle to rid himself of the accumulated evils of humanity and achieve the dignity of true freedom.

The present-day existential playwrights are still using the Oedipus myth as a way of examining the problem of guilt and redemption in a world they believe to be no longer governed by the gods of antiquity or the Judeo-Christian God.

Shakespeare has the honor of being the only originator of a story that has taken on the stature of a universal and enduring myth: that of Hamlet, the idealist who passes from the illusions of youth into the disillusionment of maturity. The theme of the awakening, the initiation into the harsh realities of life, is absolutely central in modern literature.

The figure of Joseph continues to have meaning in our egalitarian age. Ever since his appearance in the Old Testament, Joseph has been a symbol of the inevitable triumph of the underdog over his oppressors. The pattern is particularly common in popular plots because of the basic appeal of the rags-to-riches theme. Works are widely separated in mood and technique as Brecht's *The Caucasian Chalk Circle,* in which a peasant girl defeats a noblewoman in a child-custody suit, and the musical *My Fair Lady,* in which a ragged flower girl becomes the toast of London society, testify to the continuing force of the Joseph story.

Little has to be said about the power over men's minds of the idea of Christ — that is, the story of the man himself over and above its application to particular religions. Writers of no religious persuasion at all have continued to re-write the story of the idealist whose kingdom is not of this world, who remains true to his own principles despite the misunderstanding of society or persecution from the authorities. In some respects, the Christ figure is the opposite of the Hamlet figure, for the latter is forced to renounce his ideals and to face life on its own terms. In literature, Christ has frequently been a symbol of the uncompromising stand, a position with which the artist is naturally in sympathy. Shaw in *Saint Joan* (1923), for example, identifies himself with the Maid of Orleans and with Christ to form a modern-day trinity which faces imminent destruction at the hands of the unimaginative.

There are so many Christ figures in modern plays and movies, including Jean Genet, who sings the glories of the criminal existence as an admirable and hence religious non-conformism, and Gary Cooper as the noble sheriff in the 1952 Western classic *High Noon,* that it is considered quite fashionable to find them, particularly in unlikely quarters, though discovering an apparent relationship does not necessarily have the significance sometimes claimed for it. Often a poor drama will take on undeserved stature simply because it is a new handling of an old myth. The modern theater, with few contemporary myths on which to draw, keeps going back to the same few basic stories. It is more exciting to find fresh and original material that is distinctly of our time but that has a kind of mythological quality to it. This quality is usually a characteristic

of an extremely simple story that seems to invest it with multiple possibilities of meaning.

One notable example is furnished by Samuel Beckett's *Waiting for Godot* (see Chapter Twelve), in which two tramps in a park are anticipating a meeting with a mysterious man named Godot who may or may
not exist. Their whole being derives solely from the necessity of waiting,
but they cannot swear to what they are waiting for. Beckett in a simple
little fable has summed up the modern predicament. The world waits
(for peace? for the Great Society? for a return to religion?) without any
assurance that Godot will ever come; at the same time life without waiting seems unthinkable. One might say that Beckett has provided the
myth of "waiting" itself.

Closet Drama as a Medium

There exists a peculiar species of play known as closet drama, which is
specifically not written for production at all and therefore need not pass
an audience test, real or potential. Some of the greatest works of literature belong to this genre, such as Goethe's *Faust* (1808) or Shelley's
Prometheus Unbound (1820). While they are not intended to qualify
as live theater, they employ many dramatic techniques. They are dramas
of ideal, rather than real, proportions, such as could not be realized on a
stage but belong to the theater of the mind.

John Milton wrote to "justify the ways of God to man." In *Paradise Lost*
(1667), he chose the epic form; in *Samson Agonistes* (1671), closet
drama. Samson is shown at the opening of the play in a pitiful, defeated
state. He has been blinded by the Philistines, who have also shaved off
his hair, the secret of his strength. He feels that, since he has betrayed
God, God has deserted him. But after he is ordered to appear in the
arena to perform feats of strength before the Philistines, he sees at once
a way to use that strength in the cause of his God. To the Chorus he says:

> Be of good courage, I begin to feel
> Some rousing motions in me which dispose
> To something extraordinary my thoughts.

What this "something" is to be we do not learn until a Messenger enters
and describes to the Chorus how Samson pulled down the massive pillars
supporting the arena and brought it crashing down upon himself and
all of the Philistines as well.

In this poem Milton delivers essentially the same thought as in *Paradise
Lost;* obviously God's ways to Samson have been vindicated by the fact
that Samson became the primary agent in God's destruction of the pagan
Philistines. But the truth is wrung out of the depths of human despair;

it grows directly out of the experience of Samson, out of the conflict within him. It emerges from drama, not narrative.

Why then is the poem a closet drama? Actually live productions have been attempted. Unlike Goethe's *Faust* — which does have many epic elements in it — it is consciously modeled after the Greek tragedies, takes place in one location, has few characters, and no violent action on stage at all. But these productions are usually confined to ambitious university drama departments and, while no doubt interesting, they do not appear to have convinced anyone that *Samson Agonistes* is a "must" for all theater-goers.

First, there is the matter of Samson himself, his prodigious, legendary strength, which cannot be adequately suggested by any actor. A mature audience might accept the convention of an ordinary man's posing as Samson, but little is gained by having to play this game when one can read the play and imagine a figure of gigantic proportions. Second, the play is essentially static or actionless — more static than even the Greek tragedies, which usually showed *on* stage the immediate effects of disasters wrought off stage. The pattern of having a prisoner who is visited by one person after another is fine for the drama of ideas but not that of emotions.

Essentially that is what closet drama is: a static play about ideas, which leads to a recognition about something. While the element of thought is an important aspect of the theater (so much so that Chapter Six is entirely devoted to considering it), performable drama is *not a philosophical medium.* Closet dramas are important to read as works of literature in themselves, but also for the awareness they encourage within the critical viewer that he ought to be suspicious of those elements (such as lengthy philosophical speeches) in live performance which might be better read than seen. A closet drama, though related to theater, is a different medium. It is not a play, for an unactable play is a contradiction in terms.

The unique qualities of the film as a medium are central to these essays by Dwight MacDonald, formerly the film critic for *Esquire,* and Father John Culkin, S.J., director of the Center for Communications at Fordham University.

❀ **Dwight MacDonald** *on "Lord of the Flies" as book and film**

> As if to prove no generalizations about art are valid, every few years a British director makes a good movie. (Last time it happened was Jack Clayton's *Room at the Top,* which survived

***

* Reprinted by permission of *Esquire Magazine* © 1964 by Esquire, Inc.

even Laurence Harvey.) Peter Brook is primarily a stage director, but in *Lord of the Flies* he shows a most un-British visual sense; he can actually see what's in front of his camera and he can organize the results into a cinematic structure. From beginning to end, the film has the consistency of a work of art. The grainy still photographs under the titles establish the school and war background, static and remote, which is shattered by the first shot, vivid in tropical sunshine, of a boy walking up the beach looking for survivors. The end is equally well-contrived: the tracking shots of Ralph as he runs through the underbrush, stumbling and gasping, as the yells of his pursuers grow louder; then, as the camera eye becomes his eye taking in from ground level each clump of sea grass as he crawls along the beach desperately, the sudden appearance at the top of the sand-filled screen of two white shoes and the very slow raising up of his eyes to take in socks, bare legs, immaculate shorts, snowy shirt, binoculars, and finally a perplexed, bearded young face topped by a naval officer's cap. The problem was to picture the return of the boys to civilization without either bathos or anticlimax. It is solved by understatement: Ralph's panic as the hunters close in is rendered by their cries swelling closer on the sound track, more ominous than shots of their war-painted faces would have been; and the confrontation of the barbarized boys with civilized authority is all the more poignant by being limited to a few glimpses of Ralph's tearful relief, of the bewildered stares of the other boys (as if they were awakening from a nightmare) and of the even more bewildered faces of the officer and the boat crew. Peter Brook, in fact, solved the problem better than William Golding did.

This is one of those rare instances in which the movie is better than the book, like *The Birth of a Nation,* which D. W. Griffith somehow extracted from Thomas Dixon's *The Clansman.* Not that Brook is not much more indebted to the original than was Griffith and not that Golding is not several cuts above Dixon as a novelist. Still, I've never understood the literary reputation of *Lord of the Flies,* which seems to me a dry schematization that drains the life from its characters to make a political fable that is just an inversion of the Rousseauistic "noble savage" theory, and equally fallacious. The movie puts the life back into the characters; it is dramatic rather than didactic, a story rather than a treatise, and the boys are boys rather than mere vectors of force. They are also, as Jonathan Miller noted in his *New Yorker* review, firmly limited, in time and place, to English schoolboys, as against the dubious paradigm of The Human Condition that Golding gives us:

"The picture's final burst of anarchy, for all its fierceness, is the hum-buzz of insects that is used as an ominous theme throughout the sound track."

🏵 **Reverend John M. Culkin, S.J.:** *The Psychology of Film Viewing**

Free-flow discussion is built into the nature of the film medium. Wrapped in "the narcotic shadow" of the film, viewers are normally swept along by the pace of the film. During the screening there is no time for critical reflection. Each new image and sequence stimulates immediate emotional responses. Unless the projector breaks down, you can't call time out.

Film is literally an other-directed medium. The succession and pace of the images are determined by the director. With a book, the reader can pace himself. He can begin slowly in order to imbibe the atmosphere of the story and to familiarize himself with the characters and plot. He can check back in his reading. He can pause for minutes or days between chapters. He is in charge of the flow of the story. Not so with a film. The director establishes both the sequence and the pace. There is little opportunity for the viewer to stop and analyze, to refer backwards and to project forward, to establish relationships. He is swept along by the succession of images which impinge on his ear and eye.

This steady stream of images produces an experience which is primarily sensory rather than intellectual. The immediate influence has been on the senses and on the emotions, and the pacing of the film has precluded any extended analysis of this progression of images. At the end of the film the viewer has accumulated a stack of images which has piled up within him chronologically in the course of the film. This crude psychological description points to the necessity for the viewer to sort out these images, to interpret and relate them, and to impose, or rather discover, the structure which links them together into a fully human experience.

Seeing a great film produces reactions. To understand a great film, these reactions must be transformed into reflections — "emotion recollected in tranquillity." In retrospect, the individual or group can use the total film for analysis so that the ending feeds back and gives meaning to the parts with which it is related causally or dramatically. For some films it will be advisable to see the picture two or three times, especially in the earlier stages of serious film study. But even after the individual viewer

* Reprinted from *Film Study in the High School*, published by Fordham Film Study Center, 1965, by permission of the author.

has reached a fairly mature level of film understanding, this process of retrospective analysis will be needed because it is dictated by the psychological pacing of the medium itself.

Sister Bede Sullivan, a teacher at Bishop Lillis High School, Kansas City, Missouri, comments pointedly on this phenomenon:

> It is comparatively easy, from the very nature of the medium, to involve students deeply by showing them motion pictures. There is an almost hypnotic power achieved by the isolation in darkness, the constant playing of light and shadow, the compelling absorption of all the senses. What one needs to remember is that just as non-involvement precludes the experience of art, too great an involvement can destroy the experience of art. Our students need to proceed from the emotional involvement, from identification with what they see, to an awareness of the artistic truth about human beings that is inherent in the film.
>
> Where motion pictures are concerned, if one is to avoid the debilitating effect of too great a surrender to emotion, one must deliberately withdraw a little, either by way of an element of intellectual restraint during the motion picture, or a recovery of the element after the viewing of the picture.

Except in the uncommon case of a highly manipulative and dishonest film, I think that the post-screening period of analysis and discussion should be the normal rhythm. See the film and then "see" the film. Experience it and then reflect on that experience. Both are necessary for the total film experience.

William Edward has analyzed the physical and psychological elements which create the total film effect. Seating, lighting, temperature, and all the physical paraphernalia of the theater are programmed to produce a sensory environment in which only sight and sound are allowed to stimulate. In this atmosphere of sense involvement we accept the premises of the film, and during the screening there is a suspension of disbelief. Although we are physically detached from the action of the screen and are only participating vicariously in the drama, psychologically we are frequently quite active in interacting with the emotions expressed on the screen. Movies have a way of getting past our rational and analytic barriers to stir us deeply and in a very personal way. It is one of the few places in our culture where many people experience strong emotional release.

This physical and psychological context explains why the same film can affect different individuals in different ways. Each person sees his own film. This paradox is merely the reaffirmation in a new context of the thesis of individual differences and selective perception. The same film on the screen washes over each viewer as an individual, with individual past experiences, hopes, loves, fears, needs, and intelligence. The psychological mechanisms of identification and projection come into play and further individualize the experience. We empathize with some character on the screen. For a while we become who he is, and we will fill out the experience by reading our own emotions into the character. The result is a variety of responses to the same stimulus. It is normally not a solipsistic kind of irresponsible and indeterminate variety, but usually a range of responses hovering around the central theme of the film.

The strong tone of the above plea for free-winging discussion is not based on optimism alone nor on an innate love of anarchy. The type of communication between human beings which involves an exchange of ideas in an honest and personal way is too important a value to be squeezed out of the schools by a love of efficiency or machine-scored test results. Discussion, with films, is hardly the only way to achieve this value, but it happens to work. The writer has used this method with teachers and students in colleges and high schools and with patients in mental hospitals; he has used it in juniorates and seminaries and even during religious retreats. Espousal Retreat House in Waltham, Massachusetts, now uses feature films as an integral part of all its retreats. The name of the game is "People."

Every film that uses a stand-up fight as a solution accepts the idea of violence and wraps the audience yet more cosily in all its preconceptions. Preconceptions build almost impregnable prisons.*

5 ❀ ❀ ❀

Morality in Drama

Theater as a Moral Force

Drama seldom expresses philosophy in any systematic way, but one traditional concern of philosophy — morality or the question of what constitutes the "good life" — is involved in almost any play, movie or television show. By definition, a drama involves conflict. The source of conflict is usually the playwright's estimation of which actions are good and which are not, or else it is his conscious or unconscious wish to please his audience by having his story reflect the moral values that are currently in fashion.

Behind the plot in nearly every drama is some set of moral or ethical beliefs and a prescription for living. The Cinderella story assumes that: 1) true love is better than marriage for material gain; 2) hard work and perseverance will eventually be rewarded; 3) cream will always rise to the top.

In Miller's *Death of a Salesman,* a serious drama through which it is evident the playwright means to make a statement of moral convictions, one of the basic conflicts exists between Willy Loman's unrealistic ambitions for his son Biff and the latter's intense desire to make his father understand that he is a hopeless failure. Willy cannot be reached; he commits suicide in the ironic certainty that his insurance money will give his son the chance he needs. This resolution embodies a moral conviction: the American dream of success is misguided and irresponsible. This in turn raises a host of possibilities for a better way of life. Perhaps Americans should become more realistic and less materialistic; perhaps

* Reprinted from *Film: Book 2, Films of Peace and War,* edited by Robert Hughes, by permission of Grove Press, Inc. Copyright © 1962.

an alternative to business values would help to discourage people like Willy from destroying themselves in the desperate pursuit of money.

Arthur Miller has articulated his political and social ideals in other plays and through other media besides the theater, but this play is an example of making the theater play a direct role in the molding of ethical opinion. Indeed, an involvement with morality, with values of right and wrong, is, according to Miller, part of the dramatist's obligation to society.

Twenty-five hundred years ago, in the time of Sophocles, the Greeks were accustomed to the moral function of theater. From the choral odes of the great tragedies to the biting satire of Aristophanes, Greek drama is never divorced from the problem of the good life. Dramatists ever since — whether intentionally, like Arthur Miller, or unintentionally — reveal, upon investigation, a moral bias.

And since the drama is a highly social art, its moral outlook has on many occasions been the source of controversy, condemnation, and even of censorship. No part of the history of theater is more exciting and thought-provoking than conflicts about the moral content or supposed moral implications of plays and films.

Roadblocks to Critical Perception

Everyone carries his own values into the theater with him, and it is difficult to forget them even temporarily in favor of the new world on stage. Even the most critical viewer has a tendency to like a play which appears to endorse his own prejudices; it is almost impossible to pronounce fair judgment on a drama that appears to hold the "wrong" viewpoint. Every theater-goer must alert himself to the six roadblocks to proper viewing: emotional, occupational, ethnic, political, sexual, and psychological.

The emotional block can be the most innocuous as well as the most dangerous one of all. This is set up by the viewer who responds so strongly to what he is watching that he fails to remember that a drama is not reality, that it is governed by different laws. The main virtue of theater-going, a willingness to believe, becomes for this viewer a source of confusion as he becomes so involved he sees every work as a true slice of life. "Why," he asks, "did Othello kill his wife without any real evidence? Why didn't he wait until he actually caught her being unfaithful to him? That's what I would have done." But "I" was not married to Desdemona.

The occupational roadblock is erected by the theater-goer with a special knowledge of a profession or trade, in particular, and a way of life, in general, and who fails to notice anything else in the drama. If he is literal-minded or if he feels safe only when he talks about a subject on which he is an expert, he may dismiss a scene or an entire work on the grounds that the dramatist had insufficient knowledge of the subject.

Everyone has heard this kind of criticism: "I have to ride trains all the time in my work, and I know that the hero couldn't have gotten an express for Cleveland at that time of night. Besides, they wouldn't have given him the refund on the unused portion of his ticket unless . . ." A more serious occupational roadblock is sensitivity to the treatment in the play of a particular kind of work. Enjoyment is impossible if the viewer is too busy concentrating on his resentment that a fellow wholesale meat dealer was accused of crime or did not win the girl.

It is difficult for a dramatist to identify a major character as a member of a minority group without giving offense to someone. Dialect, for example, has all but disappeared from the stage and screen, though it once served as quick characterization, often evoking humor and a stock audience response. One knew what to expect the moment he heard, "Here comes Miss Flannery, Dr. Goldberg, Uncle Tom, or Fifi La Fleur."

The existence of an ethnic stereotype for any length of time is enough to alienate the sympathy of the viewer with an ethnic block, and he need not be a member of the group portrayed to be turned against the whole work. It is doubtful that *Gone with the Wind* will ever be as widely admired as it was in its original showing in 1939, when the civil rights issue had not risen to its present importance and when even Negro theater-goers were probably accustomed to watching the almost unending stream of Hollywood's happy slaves from the non-existent long ago of the fairy-tale South. It would take an exceptional viewer of today to overlook Scarlett O'Hara's faithful, fat Mammy and concentrate on those aspects of the film which might still retain some artistic merit.

Another kind of ethnic roadblock prevents some viewers from disliking a bad drama because they naïvely praise any story with a saintly hero from a minority group. To exchange a new stereotype for an old one is not necessarily progress. In the theater "discrimination" is used in its artistic, not racial, sense.

> The cinematic ballad is a curiously Russian form, a sprawling song of the Slavic soul — unashamedly sentimental, proud, naïve and fiercely nationalistic. It will violate the most obvious truths to stir its viewers, or die trying. *FATHER OF A SOLDIER* dies trying.
>
> Its hero is cut whole cloth from the glorified peasant portraiture of Socialist realism. An awkward, aging Georgian farmer with the strength of ten, he journeys to an army hospital bearing family greetings for his wounded son. But the boy has returned to his tank unit. His father follows as part of an infantry outfit that drives the Hun off sacred Russian soil. Sergo Zakhariadze is affecting as the old peasant, his drooping mustache in mourning for all lost sons.
>
> But, for those who do not believe in the sainthood of the peasantry, the farmer from Georgia is but another demigod of Soviet propaganda. He slays Germans with his bare hands, gallops bulletproof into machine-gun

nets and even persuades a Russian tank corps to skirt the ripe German vineyards. Since every Russian soldier on the screen is something of a saint, the tanks spare the crops. At the end, Zakhariadze rejoices in the discovery that his dead son drove the first Russian tank across the German border, a greater fraud still. Only on screen do fathers find their sons' heroic deaths invigorating.*

The politically oriented viewer normally has even more trouble overcoming his prejudices. If he has fixed views about the dangers of the status quo, the Establishment, liberals, capitalists, communist domination, or reactionaries, he finds everything in a drama that can be remotely political. The victory of true love is interpreted as a disguised allegory predicting the eventual ascendancy of the true political party. A soldier's desertion, capture, trial, and imprisonment become the road to the liberal's martyrdom. The foreclosure on an unpaid mortgage or any such exploitation of a poor family might be signs of the domination of capital over labor, while, to another viewer, a speech denouncing the foreclosure is interpreted as dangerous propaganda. During the American 1930's the political sentiment ran so high for so many viewers that both Hollywood and Broadway had no choice but to recognize it.

Thus financiers were not allowed to enjoy their wealth but had to be broken or at all events reach a charitable state of mind. A popular movie of the times, *Mr. Deeds Goes to Town* (1936) was praised in liberal papers and magazines because the conclusion showed Gary Cooper giving away his wealth to the poor. The play *You Can't Take it With You* opened on Broadway that same year and showed delighted audiences that the wealthy had ulcers and were lacking in humor or the capacity for finding any pleasures in living.

The question of sex poses another delicate problem. Changes within the family unit itself as well as an increasingly liberal attitude in society toward the frank discussion of sex suggest that viewers can be displeased if the physical facts of life are ignored in drama. On the other hand, there remain those who are easily offended, sometimes by the slightest word which could be given a sexual connotation. The kind of audience and the area of the country in which a drama is seen are factors influencing decisions in the handling of sex and the language of sex. The confusion which has persistently resulted from this roadblock reached its *reductio ad absurdum* a few years ago when a member of the drama faculty in a sectarian college was given permission to present *The Moon Is Blue* (a comedy of 1951 vintage whose subject was the safety of the heroine in the hero's bachelor apartment) so long as "offending" words like "virgin" were omitted.

The psychological block is personal and irrational. Something about a

* Reprinted from "Saints in Tanks" in *Newsweek*, March 7, 1966 by permission. Copyright, Newsweek, Inc., March, 1966.

performer — his hair perhaps or the way he smiles — so much resembles someone almost forgotten that it is impossible to like the drama in which he appears. A related personal bias is one against a portion of a play which reminds the viewer of an irritation in his own life. If he is quarreling with his own father, no matter what else has filled an evening in the theater he will come away remembering the bitter words of the actor father and son early in the first act.

Recognizing Historical Context

Closely allied to the roadblocks which interfere with a fair appraisal of a play or film is the historical context in which it was originally written or produced. No matter how personal or impersonal a writer may think he is, his work can be counted on to reflect in innumerable ways the times in which it came into being. It is true that any drama, in order to survive its age, needs enduring relevance; its themes and characters should continue to have meaning for future audiences. But it cannot be held accountable for the moral values of those audiences. The critical viewer understands that his first obligation in approaching a drama from the past is to accept *its* moral values as one of the conventions under which it operates.

A good example is offered in the case of British stylized comedy from the seventeenth century, with its cuckolds, fops, sparks, and country girls willing to learn about vice in the city. The court of Charles II, enjoying its freedom after a two-decade domination of London by the Puritans, enjoyed licentious comedies. Modern viewers who snicker at the ornate clothing and graceful movements of the men of the period need to realize that even something which seems so basic and universal as what constitutes manly behavior changes according to historical context.

The old movie re-runs on television are unparalleled specimens for context-observers. Are "glamor girls" with long hair, balloon skirts, and ankle-strap shoes off to a rhumba-packed vacation in Havana? Does the American agent searching for a band of dope-peddlers find his best friends in China and the most evil desperadoes in Japan? Does someone use the term "gold-digger" and are there tax-free fortunes to enjoy? The viewer at home can get some added pleasure even from a forgettable film if he tests his knowledge of recent history by trying to guess the date of production. If the films are from the early forties, he will find references to V-mail, "A" stickers for gas rationing of non-essential automobiles, Ernie Pyle, the USO rule against dating servicemen, to "jailbait," and to Tokyo Rose.

Nothing dates a drama or film (or the viewer himself) faster than an outmoded war. The Nazis in dramas of the last war are consistently brutal and sadistic, while today, if they are depicted at all it is as fumbling, misdirected and uninformed. One can readily imagine what

GRIN AND BEAR IT   BY LICHTY

*"I'm surprised so many young people are opposed to war,
when they can see by the TV programs what a
riot of laughs the last one was!"*

George Lichty's GRIN AND BEAR IT cartoon as published in The
Miami Herald, December 28, 1965, courtesy Publishers Newspaper
Syndicate.

the reaction might have been had a film like *Dr. Strangelove* (1963) been
produced just after World War II. Certainly its vigorous protest against
war for any cause whatever would have been denounced, as would its
wildly satirical portrait of the insane high-ranking military official whose
job it is to press the fatal button that will send the world into nuclear
extinction.

Already the high-vaunted faith in international understanding which
was prevalent during the immediate post-war years is beginning to seem
dated. Serious contemporary dramas and films are paying attention to
the breakdown of such understanding, to the failure of all people to reach
and communicate with each other. No matter what scene and time may
be listed in the program of a play, it is likely to reflect the underlying
pessimism of an age existing under the threat of total annihilation.

Popular drama, in startling contrast, stresses the value of money and education and the importance of continual optimism. The all-time movie box office champion has become *The Sound of Music* (1965) with its uplifting advice to all viewers to climb every mountain until they find their dream. The warmth, the love of life, and the re-affirmation of true love and the sacredness of the family which have endeared the film to millions are nonetheless products of their time, and it may well be that its cheerful whistling of happy tunes in the face of disaster will one day require a footnote to explain the bomb threat under which the audience lived.

Despite the politically oriented viewer, despite the continuing sympathy for the underdog which is a mark of our democratic society, abject poverty has become a dated subject for drama. Movies and television show people of even the most modest circumstances living extremely well. With wages going up every year, with the victory of unions so complete that a man's being fired from his job would not be taken seriously as the premise of a plot, viewers of today have a difficult time enjoying, for example, *The Grapes of Wrath* (1940). Like the little rich girl who wrote a paper on a poor family — "The mother was poor, the daddy was poor, the maid was poor, the chauffeur was poor, the gardener was poor . . ." — audiences now are likely to find the migration of the Oakies to California hard to believe. College students who are required to read Steinbeck's novel dutifully watch showings of the movie but seem relatively unmoved by some of its more bitter episodes. One such student, leaving the auditorium after having seen the film, commented cynically, "They just didn't want to work." Changing context had limited his understanding and had perhaps threatened the survival of that film as art.

Time has made many changes in the drama, so that even works which have survived are considerably altered. Molière's *The Would-Be Gentleman* (1670), for example, dealt with a middle-class dolt with aristocratic pretensions, but the bias that would have strongly ridiculed him in his own day seems cruel to most of today's firm believers in the right of every man to better himself. The comedy continues to be enjoyed, but the humor is more good-natured than Molière would have understood.

In fact, our greater sense of compassion for all has imposed great limitations on contemporary comedy as well as the interpretation of laughter from the past. Even Shakespeare's greatest comic creation, Sir John Falstaff, with his vigorous hedonistic philosophy, seems to be talking our language. The humor of the famous soliloquy on honor might escape the viewer who, like Falstaff, finds it hard to justify death on the battlefield:

> Well, 'tis no matter; honour pricks me on. Yea, but how if honour prick me off when I came on? How then? Can honour set to a leg? No. Or an arm? No. Or take away the grief of a wound? No. Honour hath no skill in surgery, then? No. What is honour? a word. What is in that word honour? What is that honour? Air; a trim reckoning! Who hath

it? He that died o' Wednesday. Doth he feel it? No. Doth he hear it? No. 'Tis insensible, then? Yea, to the dead. But will it not live with the living? No. Why? Detraction will not suffer it. Therefore I'll none of it. Honour is a mere scutcheon: and so ends my catechism.

Falstaff throughout the *Henry IV* plays is subjected to a stream of insults from Hal, his princely playmate, insults to which modern, egalitarian audiences might well object, though Shakespeare's would never have expected equality to exist between the two characters. Near the conclusion of *Henry IV, Part I,* (1597) the prince stands over the body of Hotspur, whom he has just killed in battle, and delivers the kind of long, generous eulogy that was thought to befit a man of rank and honor. Then he turns to the body of the apparently dead Falstaff — presumably his best friend — and says:

> What, old acquaintance! could not all this flesh
> Keep in a little life? Poor Jack, farewell!
> I could have better spar'd a better man.
> O, I should have a heavy miss of thee
> If I were much in love with vanity!
> Death hath not struck so fat a deer to-day,
> Though many dearer, in this bloody fray.

Even more difficult to accept in the context of our age is the famous "rejection" scene which takes place in *Henry IV, Part II* (1597). The prince, newly crowned Henry V, emerges from Westminster Abbey to find his old friend among the cheering bystanders, but he puts an abrupt halt to their companionship by publicly denouncing Falstaff and his way of life.

> I know thee not, old man; fall to thy prayers.
> How ill white hairs become a fool and jester!

One must therefore learn to respond to works from the past in two ways: one, with the eyes of the original audience; and the other, with one's own eyes as an enlightened citizen of the modern world. It is perfectly legitimate to say, "I see why Falstaff was the butt of ridicule, but I think it was unfair of the prince to laugh at him." But it is not legitimate to say, "The king should not have rejected Falstaff because he was the underdog, and Shakespeare should have known better." *This* attitude is also dated within the context of our time.

It is difficult to reconcile historical context with the demand that great dramas possess universality — versatility in story and characters. Obviously to learn the assumptions under which a certain drama was created is not to share them. When the gap in time is too great, the viewer may have to relax his hold and let something go — a speech, a scene, a character, a whole play or movie.

The following questions can be asked of any work from the past and may serve as a guide in helping to form intelligent critical opinions in the present:

1) What seem to be the underlying assumptions?

For example, after reading the *Henry IV* plays, the reader might list as one of these assumptions, "A newly crowned king has the right to reject an old friend."

2) Which assumptions are completely unacceptable to our time?

Unless the reader is a citizen of a country in which royalty is more than a figurehead, he might well consider the above assumption to be unacceptable. Others could be "A divorced woman cannot be invited into a decent home" or "It is folly for a mere mortal to disbelieve in the prophecies of Apollo."

3) To what extent is a sympathetic projection of oneself into the play's context possible?

4) To what extent is enjoyment of the play impeded by its dated values?

One can see at a glance that what is involved in questions 3 and 4 above is an intense look at oneself and the rigidity or flexibility of his own values. A person of broad tastes and wide acquaintance with the literature of many periods is bound to have a perspective in such matters and can adjust himself to differing contexts, just as he can to differing conventions.

5) Is there anything about the play that appears to raise it above the limitations of its context?

Regardless of how flexible one might be, the fact remains that the greatest plays must pass the test of this last question, and they do. The important theme in the *Henry IV* plays is not after all the rejection of Falstaff, but rather the maturation of a king from an energetic youth with divided loyalties to a responsible monarch. Prince Hal's problem — how much he owes to himself, how much to his duties as monarch — is a problem shared by all persons in high position, monarchs or not.

Reading in context is thus an indispensable step in approaching the drama of the past, because it can help to overcome unfavorable first impressions, to interpret with greater accuracy, and to recognize what is truly lasting in any work.

Censorship: Indirect and Direct

Roadblocks to viewing and inability to understand historical context pose huge problems, but the peculiar position of the drama as a social art has offered another continuing complication: external controls over the kind of moral influence that drama might exert. In the case of totalitarian nations the theater and the films are under the direct supervision of the state. Nothing is allowed that can be interpreted as criticism of the regime. But even in the free world there is censorship.

Dramatists have probably been suppressing statements of their deepest convictions since ancient times. The tragedies of Aeschylus and Sophocles appear to uphold the gods and suggest that it is folly for man to go against the traditional religions. But theater in ancient Athens *was* a public entertainment, performed as part of the worship of the god Dionysus. Whatever the dramatists' personal convictions may have been, their work usually accorded well with the spirit of religious worship.

Shakespeare also labored under certain unwritten censorship laws. English royalty of the Tudor line could not be treated unsympathetically, while the enemies of Elizabeth's ancestors had to be. While it was possible to depict the tragic consequences of royal misdeeds (those of other countries preferably), a play had to conclude with the kingdom's being restored to order and in the hands of a responsible member of the nobility. The character of Fortinbras in *Hamlet* serves no other purpose than to take the reins of Denmark at the final curtain. Nothing is known of him except that he is royal; nothing more had to be known.

In contemporary drama the amount of censorship depends upon the medium and the kind of audience for which it is intended. By way of a clarification of the subject, here is a categorical breakdown:

1) Hollywood films designed for a general audience are still subject to the articles of the Motion Picture Production Code, in its revised (1956) form.

2) Hollywood "art" films, such as *Who's Afraid of Virginia Woolf?* or *The Pawnbroker,* which are not for a general audience, are allowed considerable license especially in the handling of sex. (Note that some directors and producers whose eyes are more on the cash register than the artistic integrity of the film think that any frank treatment of sex warrants the label of "art" film.)

3) Foreign films, particularly from England, Sweden, Italy, and France, are normally regarded as art movies and freed from the restrictions imposed upon commercially designed entertainment.

4) Television, with the largest audience, is subject to the most rigid control. Popular Hollywood films easily find loopholes in the Code, but television operates in terror of losing sponsors, who read and act upon the millions of letters which are written every year from viewers expressing indignation over the handling of all possible issues.

5) The Broadway theater, operating for a fairly limited audience, has been for years free of the restrictions placed upon the mass media,

but of late producers themselves tend to be reacting against unnecessary exploitation of sex and the use of profanity, while keeping
a wary eye on the soaring box office receipts of wholesome musicals
like *Sound of Music* and *Hello, Dolly!*

6) The "off-Broadway" and "off-off-Broadway" theaters generally
operate under the obligation of having to deal explicitly with explosive civil rights issues and every form of sexual experience. There
exists in this quarter a kind of "reverse" censorship.

One of the most subtle and insidious forms of contemporary censorship
is the suppression of certain themes or forms of drama on the grounds
that they are not "what the public wants." This is a dodge common in
the movie and television industry, which all too often believes it has
reduced audience mentality and expectations to a science. Yet audiences
cannot dislike what they have never heard of, and dramas which should
build audiences may never get the chance if they are denied production
and distribution. Thus censorship is also imposed, not by public taste,
but by the interpretation of that taste within the entertainment industry
itself.

The Motion Picture Production Code

In 1922 the motion pictures, then the youngest of dramatic media, faced
a grave crisis: the threat of being buried under an avalanche of protest
and boycotted by an aroused citizenry. In rapid succession there had
been sensational scandals involving some of the biggest movie stars; the
legend of Hollywood as sin city was born. To protect itself from imminent dissolution the film industry organized the Motion Picture Producers and Distributors of America, a unique union comprised of representatives from each of the Hollywood studios, whose job it became to
impose censorship on their own products. The studios knew that, if they
did not set up regulations for themselves, the federal government would
step in. The first chief of the M.P.P.D.A. was Will H. Hays, a man with
a politically conservative and religiously respectable background. The
organization became world famous as the "Hays office," bastion of all
that was good, true, and beautiful in the movie business.

To stop the rising tide of filth and violence in the movies, the Hays
office drew up the Motion Picture Production Code, which — with modifications made in 1956 — continues to set the moral standards of the
popular cinema in America, but not in the way that was originally intended. Almost immediately film-makers found that it was easy to get
around the letter of the Code, to allow the audience to enjoy sin on the
screen so long as the forces of righteousness were vindicated at the fadeout. Far from safeguarding the nation's morals, the Code has through the
years been effective mainly as a challenge to the ingenuity of those who
have labored continually to outwit it.

The three General Principles of the Code are:

1. No picture shall be produced which will lower the moral standards of those who see it. The sympathy of the audience shall never be thrown to the side of crime, wrong-doing, evil, or sin.

2. Correct standards of life, subject only to the requirements of drama and entertainment, shall be presented.

3. Law — divine, natural or human — shall not be ridiculed, nor shall sympathy be created for its violation.

The first principle has not been consistently adhered to. Movies would have gone out of business long ago if they had not been able to exploit the unbeatable plot: evil protagonist plotting clever crime and almost succeeding. Suspense is achieved by the threat of the law, which — despite the third principle — is seldom an object of sympathy.

The most popular lawmen in films have usually been the gun-toting Western marshals, who, though representing the right, are rough and rugged and quite skillful with a gun themselves. Other subterfuges include "our side" in war movies, in which we are given the opportunity to identify with grenade throwers, bayonet experts, and wizards with machine guns, to delight in brutality and carnage so long as these are carried out in an acceptable cause.

The second principle affords the biggest loophole of all, for the "requirements of drama and entertainment" can be defined in a multitude of ways. Since the Code received its present wording, movie audiences have been treated to an almost unending parade of films which have decided that a standard of life which is "correct" for the West Aurelia Ladies Sunday School Sodality is not necessarily conducive to drama and entertainment and therefore does not meet the requirements of those stern taskmasters.

Here are a few of the current restrictions, and the reader may decide for himself the extent to which they are skillfully out-maneuvered in current films:

There shall be no scenes of law-enforcing officers dying at the hands of criminals, unless such scenes are absolutely necessary to the plot.

Brutal killings are not to be presented in detail.

The sanctity of the institution of marriage and the home shall be upheld. No film shall infer [*sic*] that casual or promiscuous sex relationships are the accepted or common thing.

Dances suggesting or representing sexual actions or emphasizing indecent movements are to be regarded as obscene.

Complete nudity, in fact or in silhouette, is never permitted, nor shall there be any licentious notice by characters in the film of suggested nudity.

No film or episode shall throw ridicule on any religious faith.

No one will deny that policemen have been getting shot in gangster movies with regularity, and that scenes of brutality have been given lingering close-ups. The sanctity of marriage has been threatened if not devastated by the many triangle plots in which the unsympathetic wife dies at the eleventh hour, finally grants her suffering spouse a friendly divorce, or conveniently changes character for the better as the other woman changes hers for the worse.

The last three restrictions — on dance, nudity, and making mockery of religion — have frequently been violated altogether in movies with an ostensibly religious theme. The evasion of the Code in the Biblical epic seems to have hypnotized millions of movie fans and has become one of

❀ **Murray Schumach** *on The Moral Effect of Movies**

Who shall say whether a movie about crime will "inspire others with desire for imitation"? A classic example is on file at the offices of the movie censors. There one can find a clipping about a youth who murdered his teenage date while they were necking in a car shortly after seeing a movie. The film was Walt Disney's *Snow White and the Seven Dwarfs*. The censors shudder at what might have been the public reaction if the picture had been something like *Anatomy of a Murder*, in which both rape and murder figured so prominently.

* Reprinted from *The Face on the Cutting Room Floor* by Murray Schumach by permission of William Morrow and Company, Inc., Publisher. Copyright 1964 by Murray Schumach.

Hollywood's most profitable ventures, featuring: all manner of fiendish and sadistic acts perpetrated by pagans before conversion; many production numbers involving scantily clad dancers gyrating sensuously before the feasting eyes of thrill-mad Roman emperors (before conversion); and the inevitable finale with its crucifixion scene or lion-devoured Christians ascending to heaven in a blaze of light, purporting to be inspirational, justifying all of the vulgarity that has preceded it, and pretending it has not thrown ridicule on religious faith. To their credit, the major religions have usually refrained from either endorsing or condemning the Hollywood Biblical spectacles, apparently regarding them as beneath their notice.

On the other hand, Hollywood has been attacked just at the very times when it has tried to raise itself from the slough of hypocrisy and offer something sincere and not insulting to the critical viewer. Elia Kazan's memorable production of Tennessee Williams' *Baby Doll* (1956) was denounced from the pulpit of Saint Patrick's Cathedral by Cardinal Spellman who suggested that Roman Catholics would incur sin by attending the film. When the film version of the Broadway success *Inherit the Wind* appeared in 1960, a number of Southern religious groups banded together to protest the sympathetic treatment of Clarence Darrow and attempt to suppress his stirring defense of the right of an educator to teach the theory of evolution. Such attacks, through the years, have tended to give the film industry an unnecessary advantage by making it appear a martyr in the cause of truth.

To please the public without noticeably giving offense has thus remained, in general, the artistic principle by which Hollywood has guided itself. The fact that *Baby Doll* was not a resounding financial success would have been another indication that it did not profit a studio to suffer the gain of its soul if it lost the whole world by doing so. Sympathetic treatment of adultery, drug addiction, or murder were all right so long as they appeared in the long run to have caused the wrongdoers to suffer. The public did not seem to want the truth any more than it wanted purity *as* purity.

During the late 1940's and early 1950's, on the heels of Senate investigation of unAmerican activities in all prominent areas, Hollywood's fear of giving offense by harboring radicals became yet another form of censorship from within the industry itself. The "blacklist" was drawn up — a document kept by each studio containing the names of people in the business who were thought to be too far to the political left — and added to systematically as more and more accusations or suspicions were hurled by patriotic organizations.

Like Willy Loman, Miller's tragically doomed salesman, Hollywood has always wanted to be well-liked. The competition of television has forced it to counter with unprecedented spectaculars like the fifty-million-dollar *Cleopatra*, (1963) and to increase the license taken with the Code. Yet the public opposition to this license has in turn created the trend toward wholesome entertainment which the whole family can see and enjoy together, a trend which Walt Disney Productions has parlayed into a powerful empire. Small wonder that the confirmed and dedicated popcorn eater of today is confused.

On Monday he observes the effects of undetectable poison, silenced bullets, and flame-throwers as James Bond disperses a variety of deaths for good cause. On Tuesday he sees a romantic heroine coyly inviting a young man to her apartment, turning down the lights, offering him a martini, and righteously slapping his face as he tries to kiss her. On

Wednesday the sheriff comes to clean up Dodge City, though it takes a blood bath to do it. On Thursday, an upstanding citizen, father of three, falls under the spell of Hollywood's latest sex symbol, who plays his secretary; he forgets his family until the last few minutes when he pleads forgiveness and/or dies after recognizing the error of the first 80 minutes of his story. On Friday the film-fanatic is treated to a religious renaissance, this time delighting in all the orgiastic festivities around the Golden Calf before Moses comes down from the mountain to spoil the fun. On Saturday night he stays home with his own family and watches old movies on television, featuring gangsters, gold-diggers, and unwed mothers.

The desire to please, paramount in the thinking of not only Hollywood but the television industry and the Broadway stage as well has, of course, led to the inevitable perpetuation of these dependable characters and situations. These are not harmful if they are properly approached; to the popcorn eater for whom the screen image is just as real as the person sitting in the seat next to him, the stereotype can be a source of error, can permanently hamper his understanding of reality. In some respects, the blatant sensuality of the Biblical epics is more honorable. At least the night club chorus girls who are imported to portray the handmaidens of Herod never seem to be anything more (or less) than exotic dancers. But those characters closer to home — the absent-minded professors, wise immigrant patriarchs, flinty New Englanders, vulgar Texans, and problem teen-agers — have over the years insinuated themselves into the expectations carried outside the theater.

Does anyone really believe in that often-seen supposedly typical American family of the situation dramas — well-dressed, free of strife and economically affluent from a mysterious source? Will the newer stereotypes being fashioned out of the new possibilities for frankness be any more real — or simply a distortion as extreme in its gloom as the older ones were in their cheer?

Winners and Losers

Popular drama in America tends to revolve around the classic American alternatives of success and failure. Some characters make it, while others do not. When the success is on the side of prevailing moral standards, the Code is appeased — as though it were the morality, not the fact of success that mattered most. But sometimes the success is just barely covered by the Code by stretching it to the utmost, as when, for convenience, the unsympathetic wife and not the philandering husband is allowed to die. Even the moss-encrusted moral tag "Crime does not pay" has a fiscal ring to it: not "Crime is against the law of God" or "Crime is a flagrant example of man's irresponsibility to his fellow man," but, rather, "The percentages are really against making consistent profit by

HOME-SWEET-HO-HUM DEPT.

The "Great American Dream" is to live in peace and harmony with an ideal wife and well-mannered children in an atmosphere that's free from worry and tension. It can't be done, you say? You know of no one who has ever achieved such a euphoric existence? Well, you're wrong! There's a family that lives in bliss week after week! And what's more, it's been doing so for 14 years! We're talking about that happy group of innocents who live completely and hermetically sealed off from reality. We're talking about . . .

THE
NILSON
FAMILY

ARTIST: MORT DRUCKER   WRITER: STAN HART

Hello, dear. How did things go today?	Terrible. Just **terrible.** First, I pulled the wrong cord on the Venetian blind and the slats went up instead of **down.** Then, Art Linkletter's House Party was preempted by a Space Shot. And then, a button worked loose from my cardigan sweater. It's been one thing after another.	Harried, why are there **holes** in Oozie's newspaper?	I cut out all the articles that might **disturb** him. If he ever learned about **REAL** problems, he'd **crack** up.	Gee, that's a very good idea.	Not **always.** This year, he's planning a vacation in the **Dominican** Republic!

I don't mean to be "catty," but what is Oozie doing at **home** on a **Tuesday** afternoon? In fact, **every** afternoon? I mean, like he's **always** home! Just what does he do for a **living** exactly?

Oh, Cara, **every** family has its little secrets. What Oozie does for a living is **his** little secret. I wouldn't **dream** of asking him.

Gee, I got myself into a real bind. I'm supposed to referee the **Little League Chinese Checker Tournament,** but I also made a date with some **Cub Scouts** to work on a **kite** for the **Kite-Flying Contest!**

Oh? You're helping them make their kite?

No, they're helping me make mine! You know what an adorable incompetent I am.

leading a life of crime." In other words, crime is bad because criminals are often caught.

For the criminal who is especially charming, there are tricks to make it appear that he has paid his "debt to society." He may win a pardon by aiding the lawmen toward the last, escape to exile in South America — without the loot — or even go cheerfully to jail while his faithful wife (or mistress) promises to be waiting at the gate on the day, in the near future, when he is released. The winner remains a winner.

All forms of popular drama, no matter what the medium, by very definition must end in a manner that is acceptable to the audience. By analyzing the conditions existing at curtain or fadeout — who gets the girl, who repents, who pays for neglecting her child, who dies, who lives, who is forgiven, who wins a fortune — the viewer can learn much about the real (as opposed to the apparent) mores of his own and other times.

Sometimes innocuous entertainment glosses over fundamental moral assumptions which warrant closer scrutiny. For example, when the aging collie dog rescues a duckling from the jaws of a hungry wolf, justice has triumphed once more. No one supposed it would not or supposed the wolf would be dining sumptuously at the fadeout. But why?

> Should not wolves eat?
> Are small animals necessarily better than large animals?
> Is a duck superior to a wolf?
> Is not the wolf really hungry?
> How does such a rescue affect the balance of nature?

The issue is moral honesty and moral dishonesty. It is cheating to imply that what we know to be untrue, actually *is* and *must be* true. One turns off the television set, secure in the lie that one can always count on help, that just as the super-dog will leap to the aid of stricken animaldom, so will there always be powerful help for stricken people. Most viewers would scoff at the mere suggestion that they really believe such evident nonsense. Besides, ducks are saved from wolves only in children's shows. Yet the universe whose basic structure is made to favor the duck is the same one whose basic structure allows the nasty wife to die.

Thus, the Code notwithstanding, the winner-loser dichotomy is the real censorship bureau, and the paradox of mass entertainment is that the censorship bureau is at the same time the source of the greatest moral harm. Here is a partial list of some assumptions which can be found deep under the most innocent play or film:

> It is better to be poor and sweet than rich and conceited.
>
> Rich and conceited people had better change their ways, or they will be losers.

Bucolic common sense always wins out over urban intellectualism.

Artists are all right for amusement, but conventional people know how to live better and are happier.

People in tight bluejeans and beards are sick members of a sick society that the viewer is happily not a member of.

A girl who pursues a man will never win him.

The nations of the world are just like members of a family; they may have their misunderstandings, but love will eventually bring them together.

Members of the clergy — especially priests and nuns — are absolutely adorable (like children) and have entrancing little weaknesses.

And, finally, the major moral assumption which has had a stranglehold on popular drama ever since the eighteenth century: THINGS LOOK BAD, BUT SOMEHOW THEY ALWAYS WORK OUT ALL RIGHT IN THE END.

The Musical Play as Inspiration

The necessity for subjecting deep-rooted assumptions to intense scrutiny is not intended to suggest that moral idealism in itself is questionable. There is a kind of popular entertainment — today found mainly in the form of the stage musical — which pretends to be nothing more than a glorified fairy-tale and which cannot be said to inflict moral harm upon the viewer. For one thing, the lack of verisimilitude which is central to this kind of theater prevents it from sharing the guilt of movies and television, which have the technology for making a fairy-tale world seem authentic.

The reservations which the critical viewer may have about *The Sound of Music* as a movie do not necessarily apply to the same work in its original stage form. During the forties and fifties its authors, Richard Rodgers and Oscar Hammerstein II, dominated the Broadway musical stage with a home-grown style of music drama that cannot be lightly dismissed. Shows like *Oklahoma!* (1943), *Carousel* (1945), *The King and I* (1951) played an important role in keeping up the morale of America during the insecure post-war years, the Korean war years, and throughout the atom-threatened fifties.

A study of their plays by future scholars of the theater will not show a direct reflection of the troubled era in which they sang the assurance that a golden sky awaited at the end of the storm. But it will show that there *was* a storm and that the very vagueness of the promise made was perhaps the only condition under which it could have been made in the first place. Theatrical optimism expressed in song is infectious and helps to promote a temporary feeling of well-being within the audience.

The almost unbeatable approach of the musical experts on Broadway is to center their stories about someone fresh and wholesome, morally rather than physically beautiful, who evokes a strong protective feeling within the audience and who both survives and prevails because of her wholesomeness. It is the winner-loser, duckling-wolf pattern again, but made so obviously hokey that it becomes a welcome pause in the day's occupation. The American musical, sometimes called a truly native "art form" by perhaps over-zealous devotees, functions as a *morale* force, and there are times when this is important.

Drama as a Source of Idealism

The uplifting quality of some drama is not original with the Broadway hit show. Taken in small doses, the affirmation of life and the essential goodness of people, which are enduring ingredients of popular success, can have the effect of reminding us of goals that are worth striving for. To doubt the moral honesty of a film which revels in bloodshed and cruelty but ends on a plea for universal brotherhood is not to reject the ideal. Some few works of drama, which endure from age to age by virtue of their irresistible Utopianism, have merited the respect of drama historians and critics and deserve to be called "idealistic" rather than "morally dishonest."

Such a play is *Cyrano de Bergerac.* The reason it has become a stage classic instead of an example of fraudulence in moral assumptions is that the hero, with all his beauty of soul and nobility of spirit, actually exists within the world of the play only. The whole play was an anachronism even in 1897 when it first appeared. Cyrano is a myth, and nobody who saw the play now would expect to meet him outside the theater. The work has all the theatrical brilliance of a great musical, with Rostand's sensuous verse acting as the orchestral accompaniment.

Some of the traditional ideals of our society, to which the theater periodically returns, are:

The capacity for sacrifice is one of the most beautiful of human traits. Many of the great heroes, since the advent of Christianity, have been willing to sacrifice: Joan of Arc, Cyrano, and recently Sir Thomas More, hero of *A Man for All Seasons* (1962). Ultimately related to the crucifixion, the love of sacrifice for its own sake has become a trait of the noblest protagonists. Shakespeare glorifies the greatest of the English monarchs, Henry V, and turns him into a King Arthur-Christ figure, subordinating his personal interests to those of his subjects.

There is personal responsibility for evil. This is quite different from the "Crime does not pay" hypocrisy of the Motion Picture Production Code. The traditional attitude, beginning with the Bible, has been that there is such a thing as sin and that evil-doers suffer. Some of the world's greatest dramas, among them *Hamlet,* are founded on the assumption that good and evil exist as antithetical, warring qualities; that this warfare is intrinsic to the universe. What is significant, however, is that, in the major works founded on this ideal, the force of good is likely to be destroyed as well as that of evil. Hamlet's efforts to purify Denmark succeed, but he must give his own life. Denmark has lost a potentially great ruler. The regularity with which good conquers evil is almost exclusively the property of the popular drama.

Idealized love is best. In *Romeo and Juliet* Shakespeare idealizes the sexual attraction to the point at which it loses almost all traces of its physical basis. Both the lovers, we assume, are physically attractive. But whatever drew them to each other initially is so transcended as their relationship grows that no sexual union can possibly take place between them. They are created to be together only in the next life, just as Cyrano longed only for the sound of Roxane's voice and derived pleasure from the secret knowledge that she was reading the poetic letters he ghost-wrote for the physically handsome but unworthy Christian.

The Christianized and Platonized version of relationships between the sexes has such a long-standing tradition behind it that it cannot be linked to the popular drama. As a matter of fact, popular films often suggest that illicit physical actions will take place only to evade what had seemed inevitable and be resolved in a morally blameless fadeout.

The difference between theatrical idealism and movie dishonesty is further illustrated in two different versions of Robert Andreson's *Tea and Sympathy* (1953), a drama in which a sensitive young boy in a prep school is suspected of homosexuality, only to have an opportunity at the conclusion to prove his manhood with the housemaster's wife. The final few moments of the play made the work successful and famous because of the fusion of sex and idealism. There will be physical relations between the two, the author makes no attempt to deny, but he also insists that the sexual act can be pure and spiritual even, on this one isolated occasion, outside the bounds of marriage.

The movie adaptation at first seemed to be punishing the wife for her adulterous act. She was revealed to have lived on in lonely isolation, feeling guilty and paying for her sin through the dissolution of her marriage. But on closer inspection, her loss turned out to be a disguised gain, since the husband was ultimately revealed as someone who had persecuted the boy out of hidden doubts concerning his own masculinity. By being divorced from so clearly undesirable a mate, the wife became a winner.

Marriage and Death in Drama

The film version of *Tea and Sympathy* really treated the affair between the older woman and the young boy as a stolen moment of forbidden love. And in so doing it not only fulfilled the requirements of the popular drama but it joined forces with yet another ancient tradition — that of making marriage seem less desirable and exciting than illicit love. Though modern plays and films are criticized for failing to hold up good marriages as models, few important dramas have ever done so. Romeo and Juliet and Cyrano and Roxane are never shown married. Nor is there even a hint of the later life of Cinderella and Prince Charming. Almost up to the present century, marriage was not necessarily connected with love. Matters like titles and estates were more important than love, and as a result playwrights were faced with ready-made audiences for themes of back-street romances.

The use of drama to provide audiences with vicarious escapes from their own marital problems has a parallel in the use of drama to evade the reality of death. In the film *Never on Sunday* (1960), a warm-hearted modern Greek woman attends a performance of Euripides' *Medea* and argues with her escort that the children have not really been killed, that no mother would murder her offspring. The companion tries to convince her to face the fact of death in the tragic action but comes to defeat when the play ends and the children leap onto the stage for their curtain calls. In triumph the woman cries, "You see? I told you!"

In one sense, the woman was right. The children were not really dead. The curtain calls should have been anticipated by the man as well. The woman was not finding fault with the fictional handling of death on the stage, but only with the suggestion that she really believe it was taking place. In this respect, she was wiser than her companion. The cheerful optimism with which she watched tragedy infuriated him, but she was absorbing from her theater-going what audiences have been absorbing for centuries — the recognition that death is make-believe.

The Greeks have their characters die off-stage or at some distant time in the future. Shakespeare's audiences tolerated, even liked, death in wholesale quantities, quick, violent, and manly. Modern drama dwells so much on the morbid aspects of death and the actual process of dying that it perhaps reflects a deep-rooted need of our age to make death seem less terrible by facing it head-on.

Recently past its crest but still marketable on screen and television is the doctor drama in which viewers are exposed to one terminal illness after another, to say nothing of the marathon operating room scenes, featuring close-ups of worried doctors and confused nurses glancing from surgeon to surgeon and then back to a rather unpleasant-looking rubber bag breathing apparatus that inflates and deflates and finally stops. Such a protracted and intense preoccupation with tumors and white corpuscles serves only to sentimentalize death even more. Audiences are not more prone to face it realistically but are simply so frightened of it that they cannot resist it. Besides, the doctor drama offers it with an added bonus: the nobility and altruism of doctors who care — as if to tell us that we are not abandoned after all, that, when death does indeed come, a soft-spoken young M.D. with gentle eyes will carry the news.

Perhaps it can be said that the theater has always done a service in rendering death unreal. At any rate, what seems undeniable is that the fictionalizing of death becomes more offensive to the critical viewer when it is played off against a background of otherwise total verisimilitude. The nobility of a doctor in an authentic hospital bedroom is harder to accept than the spectacle of the four bloody corpses at the conclusion of *Hamlet*; for *Hamlet* is a poetic tragedy existing in its own theatrical world, one that is not meant to look and sound like real life. Stage death belongs in a stage world. Real death belongs in a real world, and except for the theater of cruelty with its super-real assault on the senses, dying in realistic drama is best handled with *aesthetic distance* — that is, not directly shown or dwelled upon.

Death as it often occurs in real life — like happy marriage — does not lend itself to exciting drama. The sober young doctor with the gentle eyes might pull down the lids of the deceased and slowly draw the sheet up to cover the face, but then the corpse does not exist any more — not even as a corpse. Do we follow it to the morgue? Do we attend an autopsy? Above all, do we really come to understand the complex thoughts and feelings which come and go in the minds of the bereaved? In drama, they have their moment of proper grief; the curtain falls or the scene fades out, and then we move on to something else.

The Real Moral Issue

The critical viewer, understanding that all drama is make-believe, is not likely to object to a work's standing for the "wrong" kind of values. But he is very likely to be offended by not knowing what he is expected to believe — being asked to believe one thing at the outset (perhaps that a character is petty and inarticulate) and something else at the conclusion (that the same character is noble and eloquent). He will accept the poetic view of death, so long as it is not offered up against a background of very authentic hospital paraphernalia. He will accept the fact that people who commit adultery are made to pay a price, so long as he does not suspect the author or director of cheating and exploiting the sensationalism before the moral is finally reached which will justify everything. He will even believe that crime does not pay, so long as he has not been asked to exult with the lawbreakers in the commission of the crime. Or he will gladly sympathize with the criminals, so long as he is not asked to be happy that they have been caught or to believe that a purely illogical chain of circumstances has led to their apprehension.

He does not go to the theater mainly for moral instruction. Though his serious thinking about what constitutes the good life can be profoundly influenced by serious drama, he must always measure the likelihood of such influence against a constant recognition that drama embodies truths without being literally true. The drama has certain requirements of form — intensification, for example — that sharply distinguish it from real life.

The great tragedies may resolve themselves with bitter observations on universal injustice or the meaninglessness of life or even the perversity of God who allows evil to exist and the innocent to be hurt. No change in the viewer's life is expected — beyond the beneficial change always wrought by emotional release. A person who walks out of a theater after seeing *Othello,* deciding that he can never again trust his wife or that he can never again have a close friend because both will betray him, is just as deluded as one who has seen so many ducklings saved by so many kindly dogs that he will never again lift a finger to help himself. The mature attitude to bring to the theater is the knowledge that one is being asked to make a contract with the drama, to accept certain conventions and certain moral values that operate within the theatrical conditions which are said to exist. This mature critical reaction begins with the consideration of whether these conventions and values have been consistently maintained, whether the play or film has obeyed its own moral rules. Not to do so is the major moral offense of drama.

6 ❀ ❀ ❀

Thought in Drama

The marquee on the theater announces that the film is Federico Fellini's 8½, "Winner of ten grand prizes." It is time for the last show to let out. The doors open; the people spill through the lobby out onto the sidewalk — some with bewildered faces. All around are low whispers of "What did it mean?" "What did it mean?"

It has become traditional to ask this question, primarily because it is almost impossible for a serious dramatist, working in either of the two major theater media, to tell a story without meaning something. Dramatists are human beings, after all, and human beings reveal meaning in everything they say or do.

In its basic sense — that is, in the fundamental way the word should be used in connection with drama — meaning involves *values* — the assumptions and premises which underlie the story.

In its secondary (not necessarily higher) sense, meaning is more consciously intended, but its presence in or behind the drama cannot be detected in just one specific manner. The statement "Here is a play that seems to have something to say," so often found in critical reviews, is one that always needs, but does not always receive, further documentation. The question "What is the author trying to tell us?" remembered by everyone who has ever studied a play in school, does not contain any hint of the method by which it can be answered.

Meanings vs. Moments

In any case, plays and movies *mean* mainly on the printed page or in retrospect. After the members of the audience have left the theater and begin to mull over certain characters, situations, lines, they make applications of these things to current issues in society, the "global situation," or, on the largest possible level, to the nature of man, his existence, his purpose, his destiny. A great drama cannot fail to make such applications inevitable. To say this is to say only that the great writers possess profound minds and the habit of thinking.

But in the theater itself, during the immediate act of viewing a play or film, what is initially experienced is not the understanding of ideas but the response to the action. A dramatic event on the stage can be compared

119

to the burning of a building in real life. Both are exciting events before they are anything else. A dull incident on stage or screen can mean all it wants to, but the attendance of the audience will not have proved justified, and when others hear that it is "worthwhile" but "slow," there will be no audience at all. Drama in the theater must have its burning building first, its meanings second. When the protagonist of Euripides' *Medea* stands on the steps of her house, her face distorted in her anguish, the blood of her murdered children dripping from her hands, the hush that overspreads the darkened theater indicates that an act of communication is taking place — the transference to the viewer of the playwright's own excitement at the initial creation of the moment and the actress' excitement in recreating the moment on the stage.

But while he is watching events that excite him, the viewer in the theater can also experience the sense that these are trivial, intended solely for diversion, or else significant of things beyond the immediate moment. Even in real life the burning building can come to "mean." If someone rushes to the scene of the fire, attracted by the sirens and the general atmosphere, he may respond to the frenzy, only to have his feelings change by the sudden recognition that the building is also the new home of close friends who have invested all of their life savings in it and who have not yet insured their property.

The onlooker to whom the homeowners are strangers may find other kinds of meaning in the event: an act of God, a proof that the universe is governed by chance only, or a manifestation of obvious greed in that the fire must have been deliberately set. All of these possible interpretations involve the values of the interpreter. In the theater, however, while it is always possible that we are reading our own beliefs into a drama, an awareness usually develops that the events of the plot, the kinds of characters created, and the dialogue they speak make a pattern of values. This general pattern may be called the "overview" within which the plot functions. In the plays of Chekhov, for example, many incidents occur which show the frustration of characters when reality rudely contradicts their expectations, even as there are many speeches in which characters express their fervent and optimistic faith that life will somehow justify one's ideals. It is impossible not to recognize that Chekhov probably believes that life is not going to reward the dreamer, that things do not happen for the best, and, above all, that man's longings are worthy of compassion. Indeed, if the latter value were not intrinsic to Chekhov's plays, it is hard to imagine why they were ever written.

Dramatists on the whole are not deliberate teachers, using the stage or screen as their particular manner of developing theories. Plato, for example, used the dialogue form because the question and answer method worked best for him as the means of analyzing problems and coming to certain conclusions; but nobody would find a performance of a Platonic dialogue invigorating theater. With very few exceptions, playwrights are not philosophers. Ideas and concepts preoccupy the philosopher; his world is one of abstraction; he would be just as happy to sit in a dark room with his eyes closed, with the sights and sounds of the world at large locked out. People may interest him; he may love or hate like other men; he may want a raise in salary or a new car. But he is not involved directly with the world at the same time that he is practicing his profession as philosopher. His experiences in that world may ultimately have little to do with what he writes; for what concerns him is causation, relationship, classification.

The playwright, conversely, is very much immersed in the world. When people are most interesting to him, he is most at work in his profession. When experience is affecting him in a certain way, he is laying the foundations for the work we will eventually watch. And when his play finally reaches us, the audience, the first consideration is whether we have been affected by it. If we wish to become more proficient critics of the drama, we may look back at the play and try to determine how and why we were affected and whether we would be affected on second or third viewing. Even Ibsen and Shaw, who are more determined to communicate meaning through their plots than most dramatists are, must earn the right to be interpreted; if their works are to survive as theater, they must be capable of holding the interest of the audience during the act of meaning.

How Does it End?

The basic meaning of any work of theater (and here the term includes television as well as movies) lies, then, in the values or assumptions which the author seems to hold. The final scene is the best place to look for them, since the manner in which an author resolves his plot generally tells us what he thinks would happen or ought to happen. If, however, the work contains the standard boy-girl plot, right down to the final embrace and the suggestion of a happy-ever-after relationship, it is justifiable to assume that the real values behind the thing in this instance are not in the plot but rather in the cash drawer of the box office.

But when, for example, a play like Ibsen's *A Doll's House* culminates in a wife's leaving her husband — a drastic decision which most women in 1879 would never have dared reach — Ibsen is clearly assuming that women are human and have their rights. We know how he feels about the double standard, the unwritten law which allowed a husband to enjoy liberties and privileges not granted to a wife.

When the protagonist of Williams' *A Streetcar Named Desire* (1947), Blanche Du Bois, is led from her sister's house in the last scene by strangers who will place her in a mental institution, and when the author has a roughhouse poker game going on in the same room, we know he believes the world belongs to the insensitive. Yet the last statement, as such, cannot be said to constitute the meaning of *Streetcar*. As one of the great plays of the twentieth century, *Streetcar* shares the fundamental attribute of all theatrical greatness: its meaning(s) cannot be stewed down to one sentence. Nor can one insist that *A Doll's House* says "The double standard must go" or "Women deserve the right to vote." Both plays are complex and offer other values to think about. Finding the assumptions behind the last scene of a notable work of drama marks the barest beginnings of the search for meaning.

Still, there are many works of stage and screen which offer no meaning other than the assumptions evident in the final curtain or fadeout; and the recognition that this is so can be sufficient to merit a "Reject!" stamp — particularly when the values strike a thinking viewer as being grounded in falsehood. In light comedy, most musicals, and melodramas, justice has triumphed with the victory of the deserving and the defeat of the wicked. Lovers are paired off, murderers apprehended, battles won, and money bestowed through coincidence. The underdog becomes top dog; the wrong side of the tracks always turns out to be the right side. Since the viewer knows the world is manifestly not like that, he must also know he is being deceived. The perception that a play or movie has been and continues to be truthful right up to the final moment is itself a keen source of pleasure.

"Truth" in the Theater

"Truthful" is not always the easiest word to define in a critical response to a drama, but in general it has to do with the realization that the assumptions about life which the play appears to show are plausible, in keeping with the probabilities of human experience. Observations like "I doubt that she would really take him back" can be apt and just if they are related to the characters and situation presented.

But all too often the awareness of a play's values turns into a checklist whereby the viewer approves or disapproves according to his own attitudes. "I liked it because I think true love should find a way" or "It's an extremely fine movie because it shows how unhappy married people really are" reveal the viewer's values, not those of the playwright.

The mature critical response is recognition of a drama's primary meanings, its values, without personal prejudice. A play about marriage written by a homosexual playwright might be unacceptable on any number of grounds, but not because, automatically, it can have no meaning for the viewer. If it is the dramatist's deepest conviction that marriage would be an unpleasant experience, if he tends to interpret the marriages of his friends in a certain light, the story of marriage he will finally dramatize will be resolved unhappily, but the resolution will be appropriate to what has gone before. The truthfulness of the work can then be applauded, and its basic meaning can be understood.

What is most maddening to the viewer, what is most "untruthful" about a drama is confusion. When a character does something that appears impossible *for him* within the context in which he has been created, there is a violation of meaning. The character is implausible, not because what he did is impossible but because he was not likely to do it. An example would be a sudden ability shown by a character who previously had shown no special ability at all. Suddenly he is dancing, discovering a formula, or showing special wisdom, and these talents seem to have been engineered for the sake of solving a problem in the script, or aiding the fantasies of the audience. It is not necessarily confusing for these things to happen in a drama if the author wants to make fun of reality, but the mixture of the real and the farcical makes no sense. If a serious theme is out of place in a musical, so is a close-up of a corpse in a romance.

Sometimes a scene is allowed to take place that seems to be a flagrant intrusion upon the forward motion of the plot. Everyone is racing to a certain destination, and there is time out for observing a native fiesta. Nothing happens to the main characters because of the fiesta; it seems to have been shown for the sake of the colorful costumes. Perhaps someone thought frenzied movement would look like "action," but to the audience it has been an irrelevant few minutes. Similar spectacles for their own sake are fashion shows and superfluous side trips in a movie with a foreign setting. Sometimes there is a scene between two characters who turn out at the end of the drama to have served no purpose at all, although at the time something tender or exciting seems to have been happening. This is not to say that "meaning" is restricted to a well-made play, in which there is "use" for every item mentioned.

Finally, there is no meaning and hence no enjoyment when the resolution of the plot violates the promise made earlier. If the story from the beginning has pointed to the arrival of an important stranger, there would be a violation if everyone started talking about something else; if he does not arrive, then the effect of this disappointment — or unexpected joy — must be evident.

The "Right" Ending

In the film *White Mane* (1957), a group of ranchers captures a wild stallion and attempt to break his spirit by restraining him with ropes. After a great struggle, observed by a young boy who dreams of befriending the horse, White Mane breaks free and escapes. The ranchers make an effort to recapture him, but the horse lashes out so vigorously that in disgust the men tell the boy White Mane belongs to him — if he can catch him.

The boy relentlessly stalks the object of his adoration and finally manages to hurl a rope over his neck. There follows a fierce ordeal, as, clinging to the rope, the boy is dragged through sand and water until the horse stops, learns to trust the boy, and allows him to ride. But when the ranchers see that the horse can be captured, they break their promise to the boy and imprison White Mane once again.

The stallion, wilder than ever in captivity, becomes wounded in a desperate showdown of strength with his captors but still manages to escape a second time. The men are now obsessed with the desire to prove to an animal that human beings are his masters, and so they set a ring of fire around the field to which they have pursued him. The boy braves the danger and is able to lead his horse through the smoke to the freedom of the plains beyond. He and White Mane enjoy a brief time of idyllic happiness, but the ranchers soon appear — a determined, grim posse, desiring one thing only: the capture of the white horse.

There is a long chase scene, which ends when the pursuing men realize that the river is just ahead. The boy will surely never be able to cross it. Boy and horse, driven on by the momentum of the chase, plunge wildly into the raging current, while the men on shore call out, "Come back. The horse is yours to keep."

If the film had ended at this point, no viewer could possibly be satisfied. One final moment is needed: the resolution of the plot. The following is a partial list of possible endings:

1) The boy turns around not too far from the shore and decides against running the risk of drowning. The men take the horse away.
2) Boy and horse are shown, struggling against the raging current and eventually make it to the other side and freedom.
3) Boy and horse are shown struggling, but they lose the battle and go under.
4) Boy and horse are shown swimming in the current, and we never know their fate.

Each instance involves certain values, and the basic meaningfulness of the film would depend upon which resolution was used.

Ending number one offers a cynical view of existence. The boy, trusting the men once more, would find himself totally defeated. This would be meaningful but perhaps not truthful, in that the whole character of the boy makes it seem evident that the horse has come to be more to him than life itself. Besides, the viewer might well suspect that this solution was chosen in order to keep the child alive — on the grounds that, ultimately, audiences believe children — even fictitious ones — to be more important than art. In that case, the assumptions would be about audience expectations, not about life. The work would fail to have meaning.

Ending number two is the most blatant lie of the four suggested resolutions. This is the sort of audience wish-fulfillment that we have come to expect, familiar as we are with movie and television formula plots. The apparent values behind such an ending involve a universe so moral that things always manage to turn out for the best. Since we know that no writer could seriously believe such a thing, we recognize that we are being lied to. Again, the film fails to have meaning.

Ending number three is the most tragic of the possibilities, but not necessarily the right one. Just as contrived happy endings are based on falsehood, so too may contrived catastrophes represent a deliberate perversion of probability. The view of life apparent behind a disastrous resolution to the story would be that this is a world in which the good and the innocent are likely to suffer bad fortune. But this would not be any truer than the apparent belief that the world is inevitably moral. An unhappy ending, which need *not* have taken place, tends to diminish the meaning of the work.

The fourth ending is, therefore, the one which should have been used. The boy loves the horse, and besides, he would not be mature enough to make rational decisions; hence the plunge into the river and the desperate swimming away. The river is wild, but the horse is strong. They might make it across. Or perhaps they will not. In this instance ambiguity is the only resolution possible. The fact that the boy may die for his horse offers, indirectly, a comment about childhood innocence that belongs to a time-honored, established literary tradition. The world is a vast and bewildering place to the young; they cannot always cope with it, and sometimes they are destroyed by it.

This ending also involves a comment about the vast gap between the world of adults and that of the child. The men are self-centered, concerned more about their "property" than they are about understanding a boy's heart. These two forces, the child and the adult, inevitably work towards a climactic meeting. To have insisted upon the cruel destruction of the child would have been dishonest on the author's part, and so would the turning of the boy into a young superman who tames a raging river. The indefiniteness of resolution number four embodies the assumption that the world is a hard place in which things do not happen as we would wish, but as they must. The nature of the men, of the boy, of animal instinct all lead to the river's edge, but beyond that, only chance rules. This ending appears to be the most honest, the most in accord with the probabilities of human experience, and, above all, it makes sense relative to the story that has gone before.

White Mane did, in fact, employ this resolution and can therefore be said to be a meaningful film. Its ending was "right," except for an unnecessary comment by the narrator about boy and horse being together for eternity. It was as if the film-maker feared that the picture had not spoken for itself.

Theme, Thesis, and Message

Whether the values behind a play or movie seem questionable or not, every work of theater contains a theme — that is, the general subject around which the characters and the plot revolve. The theme of *White Mane* can be variously stated: childhood innocence, man's inhumanity to man, or the need for love. When a given drama is recognized as containing a strong set of values, its theme is usually capable of being expressed in more abstract terms than a drama which is obviously intended to be an afternoon's diversion. In fact, one of the major tests of meaningfulness is the broad applicability or universality of theme.

The determination of the real subject matter is reached through trial and error. We ought always to see just how high we can go. If a drama seems to be about a "man who turns to crime because he could not get a raise," it may actually concern "the causes of crime" or perhaps even "social injustice, which drives men to crime." The playwright need not even be conscious of *having* a theme. Perhaps he merely wants to make money with a formula plot. Yet, if he is a sensitive artist, if he is given to thought, he may transcend his own narrow aims.

A large theme, of course, does not guarantee that a work will be skillfully written or that its resolution will appear plausible. A movie could be about "imminent nuclear extinction" and remain a banal, trite piece of third-rate science fiction. The primary reason for seeking out the theme at all is that the suspicion that what is viewed has significance beyond itself tends to enhance its potential for pleasure. After seeing or reading enough plays and movies, one learns not to waste time on trivial plots and characters unless he is in an extremely uncritical frame of mind.

Momentarily narrowing a total work down to its theme can also aid more effective judgment of its worth. For example, there may seem to be "something wrong" with a movie but what was wrong is not clear. The acting seemed believable and the dialogue relatively free from the usual clichés. Only in looking for them do we realize that the subject of the film, which promised to be the futility of war, was actually the effort of an American soldier to win the love of a Japanese girl. Or perhaps the subject was the problem of interracial marriage. Or was it the conduct of the armed forces in foreign lands? The trouble was that the movie started out to be one thing, then seemed to become another, then another. There were a few sententious speeches about war; later there were some about the way Americans behave while abroad and what a bad impression of our country they leave. Perhaps the original author, who was secretly a pacifist, kept returning to the idea that all of these problems stemmed from the fact of war itself; but the producer, who wanted to introduce a new star, insisted on having the girl's part "built." The dedicated and confirmed popcorn eater may have no difficulty adjusting to the devious twists and turns of a themeless drama, but everyone else should demand thematic integrity from what he sees, even if he is willing to devote time to silly subjects.

Sometimes in conversations people have about works they have seen, or even in critical reviews, the theme of a drama is confused with *the* meaning and often expressed in a complete sentence, beginning "The play says . . ." No important dramatic work can be so simplified, but some contain a thesis — a strong, underlying conviction which determines the kind of characters and plot incidents that will be used by the dramatist. The thesis, unlike the theme, can be expressed in a complete sentence. It might be directly stated, but, in serious works, it is usually the inescapable conclusion which the audience is supposed to reach when the final curtain falls or after the final fadeout.

"Capital punishment should be abolished" is one example of a thesis. Another is "Only bad can come of bad environment; therefore it is high time slum conditions were improved." Thesis dramas are also known as "problem" or social plays, since dramatists normally have strong sentiments to communicate when a particular evil in society needs to be eradicated. A thesis play does not demonstrate that God is love or that all men are brothers.

In the history of the theater there are not many notable problem dramatists or thesis plays that have survived. It stands to reason that the more specific the conviction, the more readily dated it becomes. (Of course the playwright may be less interested in his own future reputation than he is in bringing about an important change in opinion or legislation.) Ibsen and Shaw remain the two major social playwrights, and their works contain some elements that are outmoded and some that still hold the stage. When *A Doll's House* is regarded as a play containing the thesis that the double standard is wrong, it has little to offer our times. But a re-reading of the play, especially from the husband's point of view, might bring to the surface the neglected tragedy of a bad marriage in which both parties are victims of a social code. Even if the code is no longer the same as it was during the Victorian age when the play was first written, the story of a man who acts from motives which he considers thoroughly blameless and who loses everything can still be moving.

Shaw, on his part, is even less narrowly a problem playwright than Ibsen. It is true that he seldom misses an opportunity to sermonize, both directly and indirectly, but his greatest works strike at so many targets and survey the social scene so thoroughly that they ultimately transcend the fate of becoming anachronisms. What most arouses the anger of Shaw is human stupidity — a social frailty which, unfortunately, still exists to lend support to his convictions.

The chances are that, when a thesis play is reduced to one thesis, it is being badly treated and probably means more than a one-sentence statement. What is sometimes confusing about play analysis is that such simplification is often hailed as critical discernment, when it *should* be a last resort and — at that — an indication of a weak play or film. A further deterrent to such analysis should be the recognition that problem plays are not continually being written, but are the products of special social conditions. They flourished in England and on the continent during the latter quarter of the nineteenth century, when the rigidity of Victorian morality gave fresh young voices in the theater something to want to say, and during the American thirties, when the labor movement was still exciting to young imaginations. Recently, strong convictions about civil rights have inspired the writing of problem plays.

On the other hand, undesirable as narrowing the possibilities of meaning may be, there is surely nothing more deplorable than looking for a moral — unless it might be actually finding one! The moral or "message" of commercial plays and films is a convenient little tag easily attached to the conclusion, telling the audience "Crime doesn't pay," "No one who commits adultery can be happy," or "We are all brothers, regardless of race, color, or creed." The Aesopian method may be effective for the ethical education of the young, but it does not make for enthralling theater. It does not really lend meaning to the theater. What so often happens is that the excitement of crime and the pleasures of adultery are exploited, and then the moral is added to justify what has gone before.

The Narrator as Spokesman

When a play *means* consciously — that is, when meaning involves something more specific than underlying values or general theme, when it contains one or more definite theses that the author insists upon communicating — it generally does so in a specific place or by means of a specific character, sometimes the narrator. Though he may act as a character in the play, the narrator also acts outside it, as someone who represents the author's thoughts. He has special insight which allows him to see more significance in the events of the play than the other characters do. His speeches can be underlined as representing the thought of the play; as a matter of fact, they are so frequently separated from the events that they seem to call attention to themselves.

One of the most famous narrators in the theater is the Stage Manager in Thornton Wilder's *Our Town* (1940), who speaks directly to the audience, setting the time and place and introducing the characters, announces the intermission, and even acts several roles in the play itself. But above all he is a philosopher with a total perspective outside the action of the play, and Wilder handles him with less obviousness than many other dramatists would be tempted to use. His direct utterances to the audience are not so much philosophical articulations as they are embodiments of a tone of stoic calm which encourages acceptance of the phenomenon of existence even with its uncertainties. Instead of speaking the author's beliefs personally, he makes it possible for one of the characters to come to a recognition of life's goodness:

> Oh, earth, you're too wonderful for anybody to realize you . . . Do any human beings ever realize life while they live it — every, every minute?

The Stage Manager's reply is simply, "No. . . . . The Saints and poets, maybe — they do some."

Many modern playwrights feel they have no right to use the device of a narrator. The Greek dramatists had used the convention of a chorus to explain the background of the story and to guide understanding of the meaning of the events, but playwrights today usually consider the choral device to be clumsy and old-fashioned. They struggle, sometimes unsuccessfully, to communicate background and meaning in some more imaginative fashion.

Miller's *A View from the Bridge* (1955), like *Our Town*, is a play that imitates Greek conventions by using a one-man chorus, the figure of the Lawyer, who sits on the side of the stage and gives further meaning and perspective to the movement of the play. His presence helps to prevent the work from becoming just another story of love and violence; that is, his presence automatically insures the fact that there will be understanding from what is witnessed.

Nonetheless, Miller's narrator is less successful than Wilder's Stage Manager, who has a clearly supernatural function in the play and stays consistently within this framework. The Lawyer acts a realistic role within the story and speaks realistic dialogue; the trouble is that he carries the realism with him to his outside-the-play post and so imposes a limitation on our belief. The narrator as spokesman works better when the play makes liberal use of fantasy.

Even more successful is the device of the Story Teller which Bertolt Brecht uses for *The Caucasian Chalk Circle*. In addition to performing the choral functions noted above, he speaks in verse and, since the main story is a fable, he can directly steer audience understanding of the events, even to the point of using simple moral labels, as in the question, "How will this human child escape the bloodhounds, the trap-setters?" At the end of the story, he sums up very explicitly what we are to derive from it:

> Take note what men of old concluded:
> That what there is shall go to those who are good for it,
> Children to the motherly, that they prosper,
> Carts to good drivers, that they be driven well,
> The valley to the waterers, that it yield fruit.

A Character as Spokesman

In some plays — especially those of Shaw — not the narrator but some character in the play seems wiser than the rest; he comments on the foolishness of the others. Frequently he is in the play as an obvious spokesman for the playwright, and his occupation — judge, minister, physician — provides a reason for frequent visits within the realistic framework of a conventional play and an opportunity to make these pronouncements.

It is hard to make such an all-wise person seem convincing, flawless as he is.

The character as spokesman therefore needs special handling by the playwright, but he need not be clumsy. One test for the device is to see whether one is aware of preaching as he watches or reads. Shaw was sometimes aware of how to sugarcoat a thesis with humor and even allowed wry admissions from his spokesman — the kind a confident man might make, such as "I'm not as young as I used to be" or "My rival believes in romantic nonsense, and he gets the girl."

In his deliberate efforts to guide the intellectual responses of his readers and audiences into the proper channels, Shaw also revives a major figure in the history of British comedy — the rogue hero. Dominating the London theater in the latter half of the seventeenth century and appearing at infrequent intervals from then on, the rogue hero is a man of aristocratic mien, exquisite tastes, a genius for eating, drinking, and loving in the high Roman fashion, a man so intelligent, witty and perceptive that he utterly transcends the rigid moral code which the middle class appears to require. He is a dramatic imitation of the figure Lord Byron cut for himself in real life or that has at least been cut *for* him by romantic critics of romantic poetry. He is the Nietzschean superman with a sense of humor and humanized through his capacity for understanding that even supermen can sometimes go too far. Besides, his aim is not to conquer the world but to save it from itself.

The outrageous snobbishness of many of Shaw's best spokesmen, combined with our realization that humanity does indeed make as many mistakes as they say and that at least one person does exist in real life — namely, Shaw himself — who is wiser than most people, makes them far more acceptable to an audience than Wilder's gentle Stage Manager. For *him* there seems no real-life parallel, and therefore what he has to tell us about the world seems less authoritative.

The leader of the chorus in a Greek tragedy was often given the major share of philosophical utterances to make. A figure of no specific character or personality, the leader represented to the Greek audiences the common man, raised by the playwright to a level of equality with the aristocratic characters of the plays. In other words, it was meaningful in fifth-century Athens for the spokesman character to be uninvolved personally in the action. It was like having the rulers falter and the people remain stable. But modern dramatists cannot use such a figure as effectively as did the Greeks because modern drama has no rulers; it has mainly those very common people whose function in a play was so elevated at the dawn of the theater. Shaw turns the whole thing around and creates a stable figure of ruling intellect to act as the voice of reason when the common man falters.

Still another device for the communication of meaning is the use of the unexpected spokesman, as in Albert Camus' *Caligula* (1960). In this play Camus' protagonist and spokesman are the same person. It is usually unsatisfactory to have one person in both roles, since a protagonist is too involved in conflict to be believable as the speaker of undistorted truths. Caligula, however, has become known in history as the mad emperor. Two Hollywood films, *The Robe* (1952) and *Demetrius and the Gladiators* (1954), used him to represent extreme villainy, irresponsible dictatorship, power run wild. Knowing that his protagonist came to him with all the credentials of the perfect cliché Roman despot, Camus unexpectedly turned Caligula into an object of sympathy. He is a Shavian spokesman character, highly reminiscent of Shaw's own unexpected treatment of such historical personalities as Caesar, Napoleon, and Saint Joan. Far from being irrational, he is more perceptive than any other character in the play; the others are made so much less intelligent than he that the audience is forced to view the play from his point of view. He is also the prime mover of the plot even to the point of deliberately planning his own assassination by allowing the conspirators enough rope to hang him with. In *The Robe*, on the other hand, Caligula, though the antagonist, is not the prime mover. He is merely the excuse for setting the Christians to work undermining his pagan, orgiastic empire. By representing all that is good, *they* become spokesmen, while every word that comes from Caligula is automatically denounced.

Camus turns the emperor into a fascinating vehicle for existential thought by showing that his madness is really sanity when measured against the absurdity of existence itself. As the assassins close in on him and draw their daggers, Caligula smiles and makes a final existential assertion of deliberate individuality by reminding them that he, not they, will live in history. Thus dies a powerful man who has known all along — better than his conspirators — that his unlimited power was dangerous, to others as well as to himself. No one else had the right to decide when it was time for him to die. Camus' mad emperor is so different from the cliché Roman rulers that the thought is communicated efficiently because of, not despite, the difference.

The Recognizer as Spokesman

More common than the intellectuals of Shaw and Camus is the character who comes to see the truth after suffering some great loss, and this truth is what the author wants the audience to remember after the final curtain. Arthur Miller's *All My Sons* (1947) is a notable example of a thesis play with an unmistakable thesis. The protagonist has made money in the war by manufacturing airplanes with defective materials and has justified his deeds on the grounds that he was taking care of his own family, a natural thing for any man to do. When he discovers that his own son has killed himself after learning of his father's crime, he reaches a moment of truth:

> Sure, he was my son. But I think to him they were all my sons. And I guess they were, I guess they were.

Then he commits suicide.

Considering the play's title, we know there is no room for argument as to the author's thesis. While encountering so neatly stated a message on the final page is satisfying — as understanding what an author is driving at is almost always satisfying — it must be said once again that the greater the play, the more meanings it suggests and the less simple its solutions to life's innumerable problems. With the works of Shaw, the thinking of the character-spokesman is complex and really takes the whole play to absorb and comprehend, so that a generalization might be that *sudden realizations of the truth are often superficial.*

The generalization does not necessarily hold true in the case of Greek tragedy, which usually culminates in a recognition speech of the protagonist. At the conclusion of Sophocles' *Antigone* the central character, Creon, having suffered the loss of his son and his wife because of his stubborn pride, is able to speak a truth to which he has been blind:

> Lead me away. I have been rash and foolish.
> I have killed my son and my wife.
> I look for comfort; my comfort lies here dead.
> Whatever my hands have touched has come to nothing.
> Fate has brought all my pride to a thought of dust.

There is no reason to suppose Creon is not echoing the beliefs of his creator. The Greeks are direct in their plays. When Creon, in conflict with his son, cries, "And the City proposes to teach me how to rule?" we know that he is in error and that he will be destroyed for his haughtiness. This is the pattern of the tragedies, and the recognition speeches are intended to make the meaning quite clear.

What makes the thought derived from *Antigone* less superficial than that of *All My Sons* is that what Creon says comes from the more intense *personal* suffering; his philosophical recognition is related only to himself. Miller's spokesman reaches a very broad, universal kind of understanding involving human brotherhood. His realization is perilously close to being a moral tag. Although both Creon and the father in Miller's play discover that their sons have committed suicide, in both cases a disaster attributable to the father, Creon is warned by his son that the suicide is going to take place unless he changes his ways. Miller simply allows the suicide to happen. It is extraneous to the integrity of the plot development, especially since the dead son has never been a character in the play at all. In other words, it seems that the death of the son has been an obvious contrivance on the author's part in order to punish the father and to bring about his necessary realization. Above all, the implication is that such a realization is important in itself regardless of the means that are used to effect it. Unfortunately this is not the case.

In 1952 John Steinbeck's poetic and memorable film *Viva Zapata!* was released just as the Stevenson-Eisenhower presidential campaign was in high gear. Steinbeck, a well known supporter of the Democratic candidate, may or may not have had politics in mind when he wrote the screen play. At one point, however, Zapata is offered the presidency of Mexico by Pancho Villa, who simply wants to enjoy life now that the revolution is apparently over. Zapata is forced to accept the responsibility but later gives up the job when he realizes that a military man can become dangerous as a political leader. One critic hailed the movie on the grounds that it *said* former generals (i.e. Mr. Eisenhower) make bad presidents. But even if Steinbeck were being allegorical at this point in the film, Zapata's recognition does not make the movie the better or worse for it. Surely the critic who praised the "meaning" must have known in advance that he was not going to vote for Mr. Eisenhower.

In order to justify the use of the dramatic medium for propagating an idea, we have to be moved by the play itself and by the plight of the character who reaches the idea. The sentiments reached by the father in *All My Sons* represent too big a leap from his habitual preoccupation with himself and with his family. It would be far more plausible to have had the father, discovering the true motive for his son's suicide, realize that his intense desire to provide handsomely for his family has been a misguided one, that his family had wanted him to be a father, not merely a rich man.

There is one further consideration. The simplicity of the Greeks is, unhappily, one of the lost treasures of the classical world. It is indeed true that such uncomplicated directness as is found in *Antigone* is difficult to accept in modern plays. One reason is that the conventions in *All My Sons* are far more realistic than those used in *Antigone*. Direct expression of recognition is less believable in a very real-looking suburban backyard than it is in a poetic drama performed against a very stylized background, while the poetry itself in *Antigone* is a factor which helps to make philosophical utterances more characteristic of persons who speak in nothing but verse throughout the play.

Names, Symbols, Titles

Other aids to interpretation of dramatic meaning are names and symbols which may not seem worth noticing on first reading, but to which reflection gives greater importance. These clues are not, of course, of equal significance. The test of their significance is their appropriateness to the apparent purpose of the play.

Except for allegorical plays in which characters have names like Goodness or Vice, it should be possible to enjoy the action without concern for the names of the characters. But the author may have selected names to add extra fun and sometimes suggestions of further meaning, and recognizing them provides pleasure for its own sake. Comic figures with names as obvious as Lady Wishfort, Mrs. Loveit, Lady Squeamish, Mr. Pinchwife, Sir Fopling Flutter, Sir Backbite, Lady Sneerwell, and Mr. Surface, are partly characterized before they have uttered a word. They offer themselves for humor without asking to have the subtleties of their personalities explained. In a similar tradition is the governess of *The Importance of Being Earnest.* Miss Prism comes very close to exemplifying her name as if it were spelled without the *s.*

While the gossips, fops, and aging romantics of comedy are appropriately named, serious characters provide a more sensitive problem when they go beyond Jim, Tom, and Sally to significance lurking beneath! The family name "Loman" may not really add to the significance of Miller's salesman protagonist. His state might seem even lower without the explicit name. Tennessee Williams is fond of emphasizing the personal traits of the heroines with names which mean something else in their language of origin, such as Blanche, Rosa, or Alma.

Williams is also fond of using objects, places, and settings as *symbols,* which have in drama a function somewhat similar to that in literature: that is, they do what Shakespeare says poets do — they give "a local habitation and a name" to what would otherwise be inexpressible. In addition, a dramatic symbol should not possess an A-to-B correspondence with a definite idea, but should emerge from the logic of situation and plot development and slowly radiate delicately colored lights. The "glass menagerie," for example, is at once a real collection of glass animals which the daughter in the story might reasonably be expected to have for a hobby and a constant reminder of the fragile world of illusions in which all four of the play's characters live and in which all of us spend much of our time.

The pleasure of recognizing a symbol is greater than understanding its exact meaning. Dramatic symbolism in a play or movie gives fleeting glimpses into hidden worlds which can be taken home and thought about, and in this way the joys of theater-going are perpetuated beyond eleven o'clock. Unfortunately viewers often incur the danger of assuming that a play or film is better than it really is simply because they are able to locate some symbols.

The crucial factor is whether the symbolizing element is over-intrusive or not. A symbol does not earn its right to exist merely because it *is* one. The title of the play *A Streetcar Named Desire* is so striking, for example, that Tennessee Williams was probably justified in using the fact that in New Orleans there really was a streetcar to a place called Desire and that one of the stops was really Elysian Fields. But one of Blanche Du Bois' first speeches contains too-obvious a description of her streetcar ride and her destination. Reality has become symbolism that seems to stand out too boldly from the action. The characterization of Blanche as well as the overall structure of the tragedy is so superb that the symbols throughout the play are often superfluous.

In *Summer and Smoke* (1948), a play that is for many reasons less successful than either *The Glass Menagerie* or *Streetcar,* little help is given by an extremely obvious use of dramatic symbolism. The story deals with the conflict between flesh and the spirit, and the play has a setting which shows simultaneously a doctor's office with a huge chart of anatomy and the garden of a minister's house with a huge statue of an angel.

In striking contrast is the sound effect which Chekhov describes in the stage directions during Act Two and at the final moment of *The Cherry Orchard* (1904) — a sound which seems, as he says, to come from the sky "as of a breaking harpstring, which fades mournfully away." No precise explanation of the sound's meaning is possible or even necessary. The drama is about the dying away of an era and the coming of another; it is about the fading of a way of life and a kind of people which may never again exist on the earth; it is about the losses everyone must suffer — childhood, youth, innocence, love, happiness. *The Cherry Orchard* is, in fact, about so many elusive things that can be felt but not spoken that Chekhov cannot find the dialogue which will express enough about all of them. Instead he allows the dramatic symbol to capture his fragile meanings and freeze them once and for all, making it possible for his complex emotions to be shared by future audiences.

Nobody can really explain the haunting effects of true stage symbols, except that the human need for symbolizing is deep-rooted and constant. Perhaps one way of trying to understand the phenomenon of response to symbols is to recognize that people would probably not know why they should admire a superlative performance by a track star if motion were not a universal instinct. In childhood, the dawning signs of human intelligence are known when an insatiable interest is shown in the names of things. It is always a pleasure for the child to find that something *has* a name and that it is strangely and excitingly possible for a sound to stand for an object. Communication through symbols can be done only by human beings, and perhaps, as we mature, it is increasingly gratifying to respond to subtle and unexpected symbolism. But the fact remains that the thought which comes through the medium of a dramatic symbol can rarely be adequately expressed in words.

It sometimes happens, especially in thesis dramas, that authors are so ambitious for the audience to understand the central thought behind their plays that they announce it in the title. Miller's *All My Sons* is an example. It is embarrassing when the title of the play or film turns up in some line that is pointedly meaningful. When the name is taken from a poem, chances are that the audience will not be given credit for recognizing the allusion. At some moment a character is bound to say, "You know, this all reminds me of that old poem I used to know when I was young. . ." And usually the connotations behind the poem will spell out in neon the main idea of the drama.

A generalization that can be made is that obvious titles are less praiseworthy than those which are either not explained at all in the play or else mean more than they superficially appear to mean. A fine example of a title which is not insisted upon is Edward Albee's title *Who's Afraid of Virginia Woolf?* (1962). It is true that both George and Martha sing the little song which they have heard at the party and which parodies an old nursery rhyme, but Albee's characters are intelligent beings, members of an academic community. They would not need to tell each other who Virginia Woolf is, and therefore they do not tell the audience. It actually increases our total enjoyment of the play to recognize that the author is paying us the compliment of not explaining his title.

Albee's *The Zoo Story* (1959) offers an example of the second kind of title. On the most basic plot level the play is about one man's efforts to tell another a story about his trip to the zoo. But inevitably the title turns our thinking in the direction of people's isolation from each other and to even further possibilities which are not insisted upon by the author.

Similarly, Carson McCullers' *The Member of the Wedding* (1950) is basically the story of a lonely young girl whose burning desire is to accompany her brother and his bride on their honeymoon; yet, quite obviously, since the word "member" is not immediately appropriate for a wedding party, we are compelled to consider the story as a whole in broader terms — to see the real subject as that of the need to belong, to identify with something beyond the self.

Ibsen's *Ghosts* (1881) has a metaphoric title in which the application to the events of the play is not literal and which therefore definitely invites a search for meaning. The ghosts are the dead traditions which unrealistic people continue to believe in, even as they are the repercussions of past errors which continue to haunt our lives. The use of a metaphor thus makes it possible for an author's sphere of meaning to cover more territory.

If Miller was unsubtle in his use of *All My Sons* as a thought title, he was not in the case of *Death of a Salesman*. The phrase is introduced with apparent casualness in a speech in which Willy Loman describes the vanished dignity of the salesman's profession. Alluding to a fine old gentleman whose life had symbolized this dignity, Willy adds ". . . and by the way he died the death of a salesman, in his green velvet slippers in the smoker of the New York, New Haven, and Hartford, going to Boston . . ." It would seem at first that one ought to cringe once more and say, "Here comes the title"; but when Willy finally meets his own death in a self-inflicted car smashup and for the deluded reason that his son Biff, a hopeless failure in life, will do wonders with his insurance money, we see that Willy has *not* died the true death of a salesman at all. The dignity he has sought in life is denied him in death, and thus the title takes on connotation after connotation. The word "salesman" itself comes to mean more than Willy Loman, more than even all salesmen; it comes to mean, perhaps, the common man himself, the average citizen who wants only to be free of debt, to be respected by both his peers and his superiors, and to raise his family in peace and honor.

Great Plays Have Many Meanings

Since most of the examples given in this discussion of thought in the theater have been drawn from modern drama, it begins to be clear that the newer writers mean much more in a sense than the classical tragedies of ancient Greece or the works of Shakespeare — that is, they are likely to communicate more pointed thoughts. But they can also be said to mean less when "meaning" refers to enduring value to the human race or universal relevance. In short, the phenomenon of thought in the theater has to be put into proper perspective. The discovery of ideas and the rich suggestions of a symbol can be gratifying and perfectly legitimate responses to drama, but they can also obscure the fact that a play may fail as theater for many other reasons. Thought alone does not guarantee excellence.

The great works of the theater tend not to be limited to certain ideas. They have great characters, memorable situations, magnificent dialogue; they create some kind of reality in which we can believe. They *are* experience; they become a part of our lives; they can be relived, remembered, re-interpreted just as our lives can be; they enrich us in the thousand different ways that all experiences do.

As far as thought specifically is concerned, great dramas can be seen in retrospect to have dealt in some fashion with some — usually all — of these four basic questions ultimately posed by any of the humanities:

What is the nature of man?
What is man's purpose in living?
What is man's destiny?
What is the good life?

These questions are encompassing and enduring. For example, a book on government has to take a stand in the issue of man's basic nature, and all forms of society contain an underlying philosophy derived from a theory of man's purpose on earth. Similarly, the great dramas of the past and the present contain stories and characters that pertain to the big problems, and our awareness that a play has an important theme or culminates in a major realization about existence definitely enhances our respect for it and adds to the pleasure it affords. Great plays, because they have relevance to major issues, are more permanently valuable, will endure longer; we enjoy awareness that a drama either has lived through the centuries or very likely will do so, not because of the questions themselves or the answers proposed, but by virtue of its complexity.

This account of a search by a famous theater personality for the "right" sound illustrates the difficulty of transferring great dramatic symbols to practical stage terms.

 Aline Bernstein: *Off Stage Noises**

"They sit thoughtfully. It is quiet. Suddenly a distant sound is heard like the breaking of a harp string."

That was the stage direction in the script: the Cherry Orchard. They wait, and Lubov says, "What was that?"

It was the warning to their souls of disaster, making the quiet more quiet than it was, in that sad nostalgic scene. You knew as soon as you heard that sound, that fate was marching and would soon be on them, as they waited in the long Russian twilight; all of them so foolish, so loving, so tender, so weak, and so beautifully portrayed.

"Too bad we got no harp in the orchestra no more," said Pete, "we might try it out how it sounds to break a harp string."

Off stage noises were not my business, they were Pete's or the stage manager's; but down in that theatre in those days we all worked together. So I said I had to go round to the pawnshop anyway to get some heavy gold chains for the men to wear draped across their vests and a watch hanging from a fleur-de-lis to pin on Mme. Ranevsky's shirtwaist. So I got a harp string, we tied it to the iron rail of the stairs, and broke it. But it only sounded like opening a parcel in a hurry. I knew what the sound should be, it should have a distant twang, and a long diminishing resonance, so gradual that you did not know at the end whether there was sound, or just a feeling left in your own heart.

I finished checking up the prop list with Pete, and he said seeing I had to go uptown to pick up those odds and ends, would I drop around to the Booth and ask Baldy did he ever have such an effect.

"I got the droshky door slamming," he said, "and the bells on

* Reprinted from *Vogue's First Reader*, 1942, a Condé Nast publication, by permission.

the harness and the horses going off and the wheels on the cobblestones, but this here is the toughest thing since we rigged up the bell for Mrs. Leslie Carter to swing from way back in Civil War days at the Herald Square."

I had an awful lot to do, scenery was coming in day after to-morrow, but as I said we all worked together. The odds and ends I had to get were the darling little cupboard and the dear little table of Lubov's childhood. I knew what I wanted; a little melancholy cupboard with rosewood doors, not more than two foot nine inches wide so it would fit in between the door stage left and the window, and a mahogany table small and shabby enough to make you think of your own childhood and want to cry. Those things must be somewhere in New York, I only had to find them, and find the rest of my list; one of those old "S"-shaped settees to use in the party scene, a china punch bowl thick enough not to break, some pictures to hang in the hall over the staircase, two pairs of Nottingham lace curtains, a harness and leash for the dog, a lot of old luggage that had to look as though it had been elegant when new, some period pocketbooks for the ladies to carry, and four yards of chiffon for a veil. It only needed footwork, the headwork had been done. But that sound, that was something super, something in another realm.

I hopped onto the Sixth Avenue car. I thought I'd go straight up to the Booth. But at Thirty-fourth Street there was a stop in the traffic and I saw a nice empty cross-town car waiting with its doors open. So I got in and went on over to Second Avenue. It was not a matinee day and Baldy might not be there yet. I walked up Second Avenue one side and down the other, then over and up Third one side and down the other, then over to Fourth up one side and down the other. I got some curtains and the chiffon at a remnant store on Fifty-ninth Street. I had the whole list rounded up except the dear little cupboard and it had got to be five o'clock. I was pretty weary, but I went on over to the Booth.

Joe was standing at the stage door watching a crap game across the alley in front of the bus station. "Baldy? He just stepped out for a cuppa cawffy, back in a half hour, say three-quarters and make it safe."

"Half an hour's a lot of time in my business, Joe," I said, and Joe said, "Well, when you figger on going all the way downtown and maybe coming up again, I'd say drop around to the Palace, B. Lillie, and by that time he'll be back."

I dropped around. I was in luck, a singer was just finishing and B. Lillie was the next but one on the bill. A lady dressed in not quite enough goods for her size was singing about somebody feeling terrible way down south. Then the cards changed, but I did not notice. It felt good to rest my feet and stop thinking. The curtain went up on a farmyard scene, and a couple of fellows came on dressed up like hicks in overalls, red check shirts, boots and peanut straw hats. They had little tool chests they kept dropping to be funny, they each had a saw tucked under their arm, and a sort of milking stool in their other hand. They came down to the orchestra, stomped their feet, threw off their hats, and sat down on the little stools.

"Ready, Hiram?"

"Ready, Silas?"

Each took the handle of his saw in his left hand, and with his right bent the blade into a shining arc, then let go gently. There was a sound; a distant twang, and a long thrilling resonance. It sounded me out of the theatre and onto the sidewalk, and vibrated in the bones of my head all the way downtown in the taxi. I ran through the stage door and it banged behind me. Whitey held up a finger to his lips and tiptoed to show me I must be quiet. He spoke to me in dumb show with exaggerated motions of his mouth.

"Rehearsal most over, last act."

I tiptoed down the passage, and there behind the back drop was a fellow in a Russian blouse slamming a door in a door frame that stood stark alone in space. A tall chap was pulling a child's toy express wagon, the wooden wheels were carved into teeth, he was rolling it over a strip of flooring made of half-round bits of wood. A dreamy fellow was softly hitting two coconut shells against the seat of an old kitchen chair, and the boy who used to play Slightly in Peter Pan was walking away, gently shaking a string of beautiful bells mounted on a long handle. It all grew fainter and fainter, then Pete took his axe and gave a volley of terrific blows to a log on the floor.

On the stage old Fiers had dropped his cane and settled down to his last sleep. There was silence.

The stage manager came running back. "She says what's this, a lunatic asylum?"

"That's what it looks like," I said.

"It sounds like the Sixth Avenue El coming down," he shouted prophetically, "Now take that log way back in the passage almost to the door and hit it as though you were sorry this orchard is coming down."

I waited until they tried that log chopping all over the house before I told them I had found the sound of the breaking of a harp string.

'Tis hard to say, if greater want of skill
Appear in writing or in judging ill.

Alexander Pope

7 ❀ ❀ ❀

The Pleasures of Criticism

Criticism provides two kinds of pleasure, active and passive. Active criticism is thoughtful judgment of a drama based on one's own knowledge and previous experience, and it occurs during and after a performance. Passive criticism is reading and responding to the judgments of others. Most viewers pay some attention to the professional critic, even if only to check the reviews before buying tickets. Those who do not are forced to rely on advertisements or the opinion of a friend. Neither of these sources is as reliable as that of a good, responsible critic whose evaluations have proven trustworthy in the past.

The problem is to find the right one; for critics come in a wide variety of purpose, intelligence, and style, ranging from an always-cheerful newspaper reviewer who apparently believes that finding fault with anything is bad manners, to the most remote theoretician who seems permanently disappointed with everything written since 1904.

Criticism for its own sake is a pleasure to read, and the critic is as much an essayist as a shield between bad drama and the public. The reader can share his enthusiasm that a worthwhile play has been performed well somewhere, even if the production will not reach the city in which the reader lives. In reading the review, he can compare it in his own mind with a performance he had once seen of the same play — or even of an ideal performance he had envisioned. The reader can also derive pleasure from the critic's response to a bad play by sharing the critic's reasons for the cause of failure as well as his wit in expressing dissatisfaction.

The Cosmopolitan Critic

Not all critics offer pleasure to the reader; not all criticism is significant expression for its own sake. Some of it is merely the garden variety which is found in local newspapers and which functions for movies and plays as the "Where to Dine" listings do for food. The kind of dramatic criticism which can be considered one of the humanities in its own right, which is actually a form of theater art, is the kind which can be labeled "cosmopolitan"; this comes mainly from New York.

The most influential drama and film critics write for a few New York papers such as *The New York Times* and *The Village Voice* and for *Time, Newsweek,* the *Saturday Review,* and *The New Yorker.* Even *Vogue,* which specializes in women's fashions, and *Playboy,* which specializes in women, often provide high-level criticism of the theater. Critics who write for these publications have a fully developed philosophy of drama and a consistent viewpoint that comes to be known and even predicted by their followers.

Their subject matter is almost always topical: reviews of recent offerings and personal statements on the depiction of a minority stereotype or the element in a playwright's own life which may affect his writing; occasionally, however, something approaching a general comment on aesthetics appears. Some critics, late in life, begin to take stock of themselves and the theatrical era through which they have lived and so publish collections of essays on dramatic art.

Because their writing is widely available, in publications with large circulations, cosmopolitan critics are continually offending and bewildering readers. They sometimes publish angry letters, and the issue generally becomes the old battle between the highbrow and the lowbrow. While *The Village Voice* is not likely to be read by the casual reader, it *is* possible for a magazine such as *Time* to be picked up by someone who was seeking information about a new tennis champion whose picture is on the cover. In flipping toward the back of the magazine, the tennis fan notices reviews of new films. One movie is dismissed as being sickeningly wholesome, so goody-goody "it would have driven Joan of Arc to a life of crime." But instead of crossing the film off his list — as the critic assuredly hoped he would — the reader sees, from the accompanying picture, that one of his favorite stars is in it and that it also has children and dogs. The reader decides to take his family and loves the picture; the next day he may write an indignant letter, beginning "I wonder who you people think you are . . ." The gulf between cosmopolitan criticism and the general reader widens even more.

It is perhaps unfortunate that such a gulf exists, for the cosmopolitan critic is in an ideal spot to provide leadership. He has read and seen more plays and movies than most of us ever can, his opinions are respected by theater people, and the publication for which he writes reaches many people. All too often, however, the critic himself does little to narrow the gap. The need to write in a very limited space under the pressure of time makes it very tempting for him to seek the clever remark and let it go at that. He is confident that his followers will immediately perceive what he is driving at, will understand his veiled allusions to other works, and will sympathize with his quips and witticisms. Moreover, the war breaks out anew every time a drama or film scores a tremendous box-office success despite adverse reviews. Then the anti-intellectual contingent points out as usual, "Nobody liked it but the public!"

But when the reader does become a week-by-week follower of a cosmopolitan critic, he is aware of a larger framework within which daily reviews are written. Thus the good critics need to be defended from several recurring charges.

The first charge is that the critic is a vindictive persecutor of talent, that he is perpetually dissatisfied at being an analyst after the fact rather than the originator. For this reason he is made to appear doubly guilty when he criticizes a play he could not have written himself. Some critics have been able to write plays and still remain detached enough to judge the work of others, but being able to create drama is hardly the prime requisite for a critic. George Jean Nathan once said that, while the theater and theater people were lovers, criticism was a chaperone. He believed that the best critics improved the theater by keeping it from going out of bounds.

The second charge against critics is that they prevent the playgoer from making up his own mind. Perhaps there are a few insecure readers of criticism who dare not give an opinion without prior consultation of a master whom they can then quote verbatim, but even so the critic declares himself not at fault. For most people the critic is a source of unbiased judgment, a more reliable, better trained source than any other. He is to be read and his comments enjoyed and perhaps used as a guide to playgoing. But no one is required to come under his influence, nor even to agree with him all the time.

Examples of the gulf which sometimes exists between the critic and the general public are the following reviews of one of the most popular films ever made.

✿ **Pauline Kael** *on The Sound of Music**

The success of a movie like *The Sound of Music* makes it even more difficult for anyone to try to do anything worth doing, anything relevant to the modern world, anything inventive or expressive. The banks, the studios, the producers will want to give the public what it seems to crave. The more money these "wholesome" movies make, the less wholesome will the state of American movies be. "The opium of the audience," Luis Buñuel, the Spanish director, once said, "is conformity." And nothing is more degrading and ultimately destructive to artists than supplying the narcotic.

What is it that makes millions of people buy and like *The Sound of Music* — a tribute to "freshness" that is so mechanically

* Reprinted from *McCall's*, May 1966, by permission of Pauline Kael and the editors of *McCall's*.

engineered, so shrewdly calculated that the background music rises, the already soft focus blurs and melts, and, upon the instant, you can hear all those noses blowing in the theater? Of course, it's well done for what it is: that is to say, those who made it are experts at manipulating responses. They're the Pavlovs of moviemaking: they turn us into dogs that salivate on signal. When the cruel father sees the light and says, "You've brought music back into the house," who can resist the pull at the emotions? It's that same tug at the heartstrings we feel when Lassie comes home or when the blind heroine sees for the first time; it is a simple variant of that surge of warmth we feel when a child is reunited with his parents. It's basic, and there are probably few of us who don't respond. But it is the easiest and perhaps the most primitive kind of emotion that we are made to feel. The worst despots in history, the most cynical purveyors of mass culture respond at *this* level and may feel pleased at how tenderhearted they *really* are because they do. This kind of response has as little to do with generosity of feeling as being stirred when you hear a band has to do with patriotism.

I think it is not going too far to say that when an expensive product of modern technology like *The Sound of Music* uses this sort of "universal" appeal, it is because nothing could be safer, nothing could be surer. Whom could it offend? Only those of us who, *despite the fact that we may respond,* loathe being manipulated in this way and are aware of how self-indulgent and cheap and ready-made are the responses we are made to feel. And we may become even more aware of the way we have been *used* and turned into emotional and esthetic imbeciles when we hear ourselves humming those sickly, goody-goody songs. The audience for a movie of this kind becomes the lowest common denominator of feeling: a sponge. The heroine leaves the nuns at the fence as she enters the cathedral to be married. Squeezed again, and the moisture comes out of thousands — millions — of eyes and noses.

And the phenomenon at the center of the monetary phenomenon? Julie Andrews, with the clean, scrubbed look and the unyieldingly high spirits; the good sport who makes the best of everything; the girl who's so unquestionably good that she carries this one dimension like a shield. The perfect, perky schoolgirl, the adorable tomboy, the gawky colt. Sexless, inhumanly happy, the sparkling maid, a mind as clean and well brushed as her teeth. What is she? Merely the ideal heroine for the best of all possible worlds. And that's what *The Sound of Music* pretends we live in.

Audiences are transported into a world of operetta cheerfulness and calendar art. You begin to feel as if you've never got out of school. Up there on the screen, they're all in their places with bright, shining faces. Wasn't there perhaps one little Von Trapp who didn't want to sing his head off, or who screamed that he wouldn't act out little glockenspiel routines for Papa's party guests, or who got nervous and threw up if he had to get on a stage? No, nothing that mars this celebration of togetherness. Not only does this family sing together; they play ball together. This is the world teachers used to pretend (and maybe still pretend?) was the real world. It's the world in which the governess conquers all. It's the big lie, the sugarcoated lie that people seem to want to eat. They even seem to think they should feed it to their kids, that it's healthy, wonderful "family entertainment."

And this is the sort of attitude that makes a critic feel that maybe it's all hopeless. Why not just send the director, Robert Wise, a wire: "You win, I give up," or, rather, "We both lose, we all lose."

Lawrence DeVine: *But Don't Knock "The Sound of Music"**

The job security of a critic is generally somewhat less than beginning bomb demolition students, parachute testers or Balkan kings, if better than certain sheriffs, Gabor husbands or left-handed third-basemen.

In some places, the only thing that will displace a critic — for better or worse — is the earth opening up and swallowing him whole, or a successful assassination plot carried out stealthily in a darkened theater.

In less estimable situations, however, it takes but a little mail and the hapless critic is out of his attuned ear. Such a case reached prominence last week in that worthy organ devoted to the molding and shaping of the public taste, McCall's magazine.

McCall's was paying legal tender to one Pauline Kael to write its film reviews. This she did to the best, it is presumed, of her ability. Then it happened. Mrs. Kael, a wife and homemaker herself, wrote that the wholesome and lovable movie "The Sound of Music," was really sort of icky.

That did it. Call Dr. Spock a Bolshevik, condemn The Pill, but do not tread lightly on "The Sound of Music." Mrs. Kael was instantly deprived of her salary check and her place on the masthead as the letters poured in in defense of the Trapp family film.

Now Mrs. Kael is a published author (of "I Lost It at the Movies,"

* Reprinted from *The Miami Herald*, May 24, 1966, by permission of Lawrence DeVine.

a book of film criticism) and former reviewer for Film Quarterly and Sight and Sound magazine. It seems safe to speculate she perhaps knew more about whether "The Sound of Music" was purest marshmallow than did the folks back at the office writing about prettier feet, the teenager and the telephone and timely warnings about Captain Kangaroo.

That, of course, is secondary. Primarily, it seems that grounds for cashiering one of your troops, company pride aside, ought to be something stronger than letters from Julie Andrews fans.

About mail: H. L. Mencken used to inscribe his angry mail with the words "You may be right" — and sent it back from whence it came. A sensible and altogether gentlemanly approach.

Mrs. Kael, however, may be better off looking for work elsewhere. Plato phrased it as succinctly as anyone: "If men should order their counselors to pander to their wishes . . . I should consider as unmanly one who accepts the duty of giving such forms of advice and one who refused it to be a true man" Or, in this case, a true woman.

Oh well, McCall's back to the recipes and foot care.

A third charge is that the Broadway critics ruin the theater by failing to give proper encouragement to the mere fact of theatrical activity itself. This is a more serious accusation, one that is not always easy to dismiss. Theater people weary of making the constant complaint that the expenditure of hundreds of thousands of dollars and months of preparation ought not to be made futile by the reactions to one performance of a very limited number of people, who never make the slightest effort to be entertained if the drama does not force them to. They argue that film criticism, on the other hand, does little damage since movie reviews are not read simultaneously on the same morning and therefore that the peculiar kind of attention given to stage criticism should offer a margin of compassion.

The principal argument advanced by the critics against this charge is that packing the theater at bad plays will simply alienate people from live theater and send them straight to the movies. The hyper-critics of movies for their part insist that bad films already make enough money without requiring assistance and that some voices of sanity are necessary to counterbalance poor taste, poor acting, and rich producers. Almost every cosmopolitan critic believes that the critical function lies beyond considerations of commerce. He judges for the ages, in terms of the ideal, and expects to see few great plays in his lifetime. On the other hand, since he does have less opportunity to praise than to pan, it is always a delight to find enthusiasm in his columns. He has waited so long!

Pauline Kael's critique of *The Sound of Music,* which caused her to lose her job, is only one example of the martyrdom suffered by the cosmopolitan critic in his war against mediocrity and banality.   In another case, the critic Robert Brustein encountered vigorous reader protest for an unenthusiastic review in *The New Republic* of a revival of Goldsmith's comedy *She Stoops to Conquer*. Though the angry reader had on his side the acknowledged worth of the play itself and the praise of another responsible critic, Mr. Brustein defended the position and the rights of the critic in a significant essay.

Robert Brustein: *Why I Write**

A few weeks ago, an indignant subscriber wrote a letter to this magazine, hotly protesting my "uninformed comments" on the theatre, which he proceeded to characterize, in a flamboyant Augustan manner, as "unadulterated tripe." The stimulus for this wholly unsolicited flattery was a negative notice I had written of the Phoenix's *She Stoops to Conquer*. Observing that most of the "competent" drama critics on the newspapers had confirmed him in his enthusiasm for the production, this correspondent enclosed a rave review from the *Times* as incontrovertible proof of my professional "incompetence." After stating that all who love the theatre should support ambitious groups like the Phoenix, he concluded his note with a demand for an "apology" or, at least, a "reasonable explanation" of my outrageous conduct.

Confound your infernal impudence, I roared, eagerly dipping my pen in formaldehyde and framing a reply in my most poisonous style — but as I paused to consider the implications of this letter my belligerency vaporized into astonishment. Clearly, this correspondent had assumed 1) that I am accountable for correctly anticipating *his* response to a play, 2) that critical "competence" is measured by the writings of newspaper reporters, and 3) that a drama critic has a duty to love the theatre! Where had he picked up such outlandish notions? Had I inadvertently put them into his head? Quailing at the thought that others might be nourishing similar delusions, I determined to make my critical purposes — clear enough to me — explicit to the more benighted of my readers. So here, in lieu of an apology, is an explanation of why I do and do not write.

First, dear reader, let me assure you that I do not write in order to arbitrate your theatregoing activities. I confess to the darkest ignorance about who you are, how much you know, or what you consider a good play, so it would be the sheerest impertinence for me to try to guide your taste. I have a further confession to

* Reprinted from *Seasons of Discontent*, copyrights © 1959–1965 by Robert Brustein, by permission of Simon and Schuster, Inc.

make — I am not even sure that you exist. So to be perfectly safe, I imagine you as an ideal spectator, one who responds only to the best in the theatre, and who therefore visits it very seldom, generally with a profound distaste for what you see. If it depended on you and me, the Broadway box office would close tomorrow, and all the producers would go back into the real estate business — if, indeed, they ever left it. For while we share a fanatical devotion to dramatic art, we suspect the "theatre" is very rarely a place where this is displayed.

Now if you find this character fits you, then we shall be friends and communicants; but I grant that you may wish to dissociate yourself from such a rigid description. Perhaps you are a "common" spectator, and for the sake of a few hours of relaxation are willing to accept considerably less than perfection. If so, depart from me, along with your brethren the "common" reader and the "common" man, and go consult a "common" reviewer. You will find him in your newspaper, especially hired to cater to your taste, his virtue being that he knows just as little as you, and sometimes even less, having qualified for his present job by his supreme averageness. What he practices is called journalism, a technique created in the eighteenth century with the rise of democracy, the lowering of standards, and the growth of a large lay public which wanted to be informed quickly without troubling its brains too much. He is your man, if your demands are not too severe, for he is much more eager than I to proclaim new masterpieces — inflating reputations, publicizing personalities, and boosting the economy of the theatre along the way. But do not, like our indignant Augustan, confuse his work with criticism, which was invented by Aristotle, designed for experts, dedicated to absolute standards, and practiced today by very few.

For the function of criticism does not lie in the designation of some trumpery piece as "the best damn show I've seen in years." It is, in the language of a modern Aristotelian named T. S. Eliot, "the commentation and analysis of works of art . . . for the elucidation of art and the correction of taste." By this definition, to be sure, we all stand condemned of non-critical, if not journalistic, practices, because in an age of bad literature like our own there is little else to be written on a regular basis — unless you would prefer a depth analysis of *Under the Yum Yum Tree*. A drama critic working in a journalistic capacity, unwilling to lower his standards, and continually confronted with the spurious, the mediocre, and the false, can become a social philosopher like Bernard Shaw, an aesthetician of the stage like Stark Young, or an analyst of dramatic technique like Eric Bentley — if he works for a mass magazine, he is more likely to become an entertaining stylist like Kenneth Tynan. But he establishes his claim to serious criticism when discussing a genuine work of art, bringing his whole experience and expertise into the service of analysis, illumination, and interpretation. And this is why I bite with such obvious relish into the occasional masterpieces that come my way; and why, lacking these, I often choose to belabor you with extracritical lectures on the dismal state of our culture, our theatre, and our national spirit. For if the critic is the humble servant of genuine art, he is the implacable enemy of pseudo art, waging war on all the conditions which produce it, including the writer's cynicism, the producer's greed, the actor's ambition, and the spectator's spiritual emptiness.

As for the correcting of taste, this function every true critic guards as jealously as if it were his own personal property — not for the sake of a contemporary theatregoer's ephemeral pleasure but for the sake of a harsh posterity much less inclined to charitable opinions than our own age. It is under the cold, impersonal eye of the future that the dramatic artist writes, suppressing his natural desire for fame, love, success, and money in order to communicate his vision truly in eternal aesthetic form. And under the glare of this eye, the critic, too, must make his judgments, always conscious that he will ultimately be judged himself. Can you imagine the mordant laughter with which twenty-first-century man, picking up a rotting copy of a play like *J. B.*, will note that someone once considered it "one of the most memorable works of the century"? This laughter is what terrifies us in our sleep, and nudges us forward in the ruthless pursuit of art.

Here are two examples of the cosmopolitan critics' flattering assumptions about readers' familiarity with standard plays and movies and famous performances. The critics expect their readers will recognize allusions and will have some degree of sophistication and a good vocabulary.

❀ **Edith Oliver** *on The Importance of Being Earnest*

A new company, Repertory Theatre, has bravely chosen to begin with Oscar Wilde's "The Importance of Being Earnest" and has brought it off with some style and charm. The play needs no comment from me, so here is a scattering of notes on the production, at the

COMMENTS

bravely: *assumes the reader knows that the play has been performed so often it is difficult to do anything new with it.*

* From "Importance and Unimportance." Reprinted by permission; © 1963 *The New Yorker Magazine, Inc.*

Madison Avenue Playhouse. The minute the curtain goes up on Algernon's flat (upholstery of black velvet and green brocade, golden draperies with ball fringe), it is evident that everything is going to be all right, and everything is. The scenery, by Thea Neu, and the costumes, by Ray Diffen, are decorative and witty, and perfectly set the tone of the piece. The cast doesn't fool around but really plays, though without many of the vocal mannerisms of British high comedy. Ann Shoemaker, as Lady Bracknell, has the hardest assignment of all — to get rid of the voice and the readings of Edith Evans, the all-time Lady B. (in that recent movie with Redgrave, on that phonograph record with Gielgud). Well, it is almost impossible, but Miss Shoemaker does manage some sound readings and modulations of her own. When she quietly asked "A *handbag?*" instead of booming it out, I almost stood up and cheered her. Her Lady Bracknell is no high comic turn; it is a performance — not the most brilliant one on earth, perhaps, but a good one. And Michael Allinson, as Worthing, is quite good, too (again, not brilliant but good). Worthing's woeful entrance, in deep mourning and choked with sobs, in Act II, and his cry of "Mother!" to the fussed Miss Prism, in Act III, are tricky and potentially uncomfortable spots that can send the comedy plopping to the ground, and Mr. Allinson hit both of them just right. When the principals are competent, as these are, but with bravura, something is lost, yet something is gained, too. The secondary characters come into their own, and so, in a way, does the play.

Act I, a set piece, is unavoidably haunted by all the Worthings and Algernons of the past munching away, by the Worthings proposing to the Gwendolens, by the Lady Bracknells' classic queries on the Worthings' suitability. In Acts II and III, the current company takes over. Carrie Nye is the best Cecily, Jean Cameron the best Miss Prism, and Melville

to . . . voice: *The readers have presumably heard Edith Evans' interpretation.*

quietly . . . out: *A reference to the scene revealing Worthing's identity at end of play. Very famous line in theater history. Handbag = Lady Bracknell as door-slamming = Ibsen's Nora.*

woeful . . . uncomfortable: *critic recognizes (and assumes the reader does) difficulty and possible tastelessness of dealing with grief in a comical way. Production style avoided the difficulty.*

munching . . . queries: *mention of these activities is specific and likely to evoke pleasure in the reader who recalls the funny situations and dialogue surrounding them.*

Cooper the best Canon Chasuble I've ever seen. Miss Cameron is the essence of plump, fuzzy spinsterhood, and her innocent, oblivious pleasure at the recovery of her handbag is a delight to watch. Miss Nye, slyly ingenuous and smooth as cream in a peach-colored Kate Greenaway dress, is particularly effective in her diary scene with Algy and in her scene at the tea table with Gwendolen — both girls burning with rage and icily hanging on to the amenities. As for that funny fellow Mr. Cooper, he just plain invented old Chasuble; he sounds as if he had made every word up himself. All the actors, under Douglas Seale's direction, do exactly what they are meant to do. They play together, and they don't miss on a single funny line or notion. How well the jokes do hold up, even the millionth time around! And there are always a few that have just slid by before and suddenly pop out: "I am not in favor of this modern mania for turning bad people into good people at a moment's notice," and "Now that I think of it, I have never heard any man mention his brother." There isn't a bum line in the lot, but I must say that I'm getting tired of those cucumber sandwiches.

Miss Prism . . . Chasuble: enthusiastic praise rare in this kind of review.

Kate Greenaway dress: the readers would know the famous illustrations of nursery rhymes and the children's fashions named in her honor.

The rest of the review is almost pure rapture, in praise of originality of characterization and the seemingly eternal comic value of the play as written. Even the last line, with its reference to the cucumber sandwiches, is not an accusation so much as a reminder of the fact that reader and critic share some happy memories of an often performed and much admired play.

❀ **Arthur Schlesinger, Jr.:** The Appaloosa, *"Something Has Gone Sour"**

Spengler may have anticipated a little when he wrote about the decline of the West. But the decline of the Western would have been another matter. The Western used to be the noblest tradition of the American film. Purists regarded it as the essence of cinema itself. For decades those splendid images haunted our consciousness: the riders silhouetted against the sky, the clattering chase across the

Note the broad viewpoint, which sees the film in relation to a whole genre, the Western, not as an isolated case.

* Reprinted from *Vogue*, November 1, 1966, by permission. Copyright © 1966 by the Condé Nast Publications, Inc.

cactus-dotted landscape, the wild brawl in the saloon, the long walkdown in the silent street, and always the Western hero, diffident, laconic, slow to violence but, once committed, invincible. How superb it all was! Yet, watching Marlon Brando in *The Appaloosa*, as filmed with respectful care by Sidney J. Furie, one can only conclude with Emerson: "Every hero becomes a bore at last."

Mr. Brando plays an exhausted cowboy in the contemporary vein. In earlier days William S. Hart, the young Gary Cooper, even John Wayne declined to talk, it seemed, out of deliberate choice. But Brando and his generation appear to have been forced into silence by unutterable fatigue. Brando's only possession is his horse ("I got a horse up there that's the best damn stallion in the whole Southwest"); his only ambition, to redeem a life of murder and sin by settling down with some peace-loving Mexicans as a horse breeder. Unfortunately a non-peace-loving Mexican steals the stallion and humiliates the cowboy by lassoing him and dragging him across a mountain stream. This scene, with its flashy crosscutting of spray, rock, and the anguished Brando, is Furie at his best. Then the cowboy sets out in pursuit of the horse, tracks the bad Mexican down, is captured by him, escapes, and finally, in an oddly anti-climactic climax, disposes of his enemy and rides off to begin his new life.

The old conventions of the Western are as weary as Brando's cowboy. But in recent years the trick has been to give them a new charge: make them existential (*High Noon, Shane*); transpose them from the Japanese (*The Magnificent Seven, The Outrage*); parody them (*Cat Ballou*); film them in Spain, Italy, or even Czechoslovakia. It would be too easy to say that Mr. Furie, the gifted director of that brilliant and ingenious film *The Ipcress File*, has tried in *The Appaloosa* to cross the Western with the spy thriller. But he does use many of the

The Western hero historically viewed, so that the failure of the present hero has larger significance.

Note the assumption that the superficial division of good and bad is deplorable to all persons of taste.

An indication of what can be done, artistically, in the Western, so that the condemnation of the movie gains more authority.

devices which worked so well in his earlier film, especially the very tight close-up, above all of eyes and feet, and the Op Art effects, as of a match flaring spectographically in the dark. They work less well here. One ends with the feeling, indeed, that Mr. Furie's clichés have been superimposed on the clichés of the Western without much stimulus to either.

As for Mr. Brando, he remains a puzzle. He has radiated reserve strength so long without ever calling it up that one begins to wonder whether there is anything left behind that façade of powerful languor. He is still a stylish player but an increasingly apathetic and monotonous one. His supporting cast — John Saxon, Anjanette Comer, Emilio Fernandez — emerges intact as if from a hundred previous films.

The reviewer is against star worship and requires that famous personalities continually earn their right to our respect.

The fact that *The Appaloosa* has defeated the combined talents of Messrs. Furie and Brando does not mean, of course, that the Western is through. But surely something has gone sour. One would like to think that this country is tiring of the ethos of the simple solution — of the theory that humanity is neatly divided between the white hats and the black hats and that the toughest problem can be solved by a revolver shot. But then one reflects on Viet Nam and concludes that *The Appaloosa* is probably just a bore on its own.

The Indulgent Critic

The critic who is different from the cosmopolitan critic in almost every way is the reviewer of movies and occasionally plays who appears on the amusement page of the local newspaper throughout the country. He does not have the national reputation of the cosmopolitan critic, but the local man is likely to influence as many people, all those who check the reviews before going to a show.

This reviewer tends to like everything he sees. His lack of discrimination may be caused by his mistaken belief that one should say something nice or keep quiet; it is more likely, however, that he was moved to his position of critic from some other job on the paper and that because of a general lack of knowledge about drama he has a heart too soon made glad.

The indulgent critic pays little attention to plot, except to suggest what the story is about. But he likes adjectives of praise, some of them sounding as if they were reprinted intact from advertisements and publicity releases: "fun-filled," "sparkling," "delightful" are frequently in the headline or lead paragraph of this kind of review. It is, of course, totally irresponsible criticism with no sense behind it. Rather than clarify, the words obscure the meaning with flossy generalizations which substitute for knowledge. For example, this kind of review may use the term "monumental" to describe a movie long enough to require an intermission.

"Classic" is another misleading term, used very loosely to mean either the adaptation of a novel admired as literature, or a drama which has been revived some years after its first run. According to this latter definition, the comedy *You Can't Take It With You* must be called a "classic" each time it is played these days.

There are other terms — "significant," "frothy," "lusty," etc., and one of the incentives of reading such criticism is trying to locate the sense lurking behind the language.

The Didactic Critic

Far more serious than the indulgent critic is the critic for a publication with special readership, who judges a work for its involvement in a special cause. Art is subordinated to issues according to the philosophy of this kind of criticism. If the work supports a certain idea favored by the editorial policy, it is praised. If not, it is condemned, though other reasons are sometimes given. A work called "boring" or "tasteless" by the didactic critic may simply be guilty of not being sympathetic enough to the religious, political, or other special-interest point of view of the critic. Didactic criticism is not a recent phenomenon. At one time it was the only acceptable approach. Samuel Johnson, in the Preface to the 1765 edition of Shakespeare's Works, was disapproving of Shakespeare's casual attitude toward morality. In Dr. Johnson's view, the instruction of the reader was one of the most important characteristics of a great work of art, and he considered Shakespeare theatrical rather than moral:

> ... he makes no just distribution of good or evil, nor is always careful to show in the virtuous a disapprobation of the wicked; he carries his persons indifferently through right and wrong and at the close dismisses them without further care and leaves their examples to operate by chance ... it is always a writer's duty to make the world better, and justice is a virtue independent of time or place . . . He omits opportunities of instructing or delighting which the train of his story seems to force upon him, and apparently rejects those exhibitions which would be more affecting, for the sake of those which are more easy.

Similarly, modern didactic critics are eager for drama to help "make the world better" and take "opportunities of instructing," though all would not agree on the means. A religious magazine, in the didactic tradition, calls *Who's Afraid of Virginia Woolf?* "a moral nightmare." A political magazine, just as didactic, objects to the same play because of its "lack of significant thematic content." The suggested improvements from each source would be quite different, but the critical approach is the same. The didactic critic is always conscious of expected public reaction for the cause as depicted in a drama, and even an isolated fragment involving an unflattering treatment of a sensitive subject is discussed to the neglect of the rest of the drama. The result is unbalanced criticism, with praise and blame distributed according to sociological and moral principles, and broad tolerance for content which critics less devoted to the cause would not admire. The didactic critic, like the didactic playwright, bases his attitude on the imperfection of the world and the importance of a particular way of improving it. According to this view, then, it would be the obligation of the didactic critic to alert his readers to the unflattering presentation of a person or argument in a play and to warn them against supporting it, sometimes to the point of encouraging censorship. Yet he does not resent a stereotype which reflects his own views. The didactic critic notices not only what was in a drama but what was not, and often makes disparaging comments on the basis of what might have been done if the play had been carried on to what appears to him to be a logical conclusion — perhaps revolution or mass conversion.

The Literary Critic

The purely literary approach is not for everyone. It is found in academic quarterlies, scholarly books, and certain high-level magazines of comparatively small circulation. Writers assume a readership familiar with traditional criticism dating back to Aristotle and with the ability to understand allusions to a great many, sometimes obscure, dramas from different eras. Literary criticism covers a wide range of topics, though it concentrates on the play in printed form. It is broad enough to seek general principles, yet narrow enough to concentrate on detailed emendations of a play manuscript. The literary critic is accustomed to the accusation that he prefers scholarship on the accurate wording of a line of dialogue to the enjoyment of a live performance. His retort is that he would rather stay in his ivory tower where he can enjoy an ideal visualization than be forced to endure what is available downtown.

In leisurely debates with other critics, he may argue the classification of an important or obscure drama, each man quoting lines to prove his assertion. He is skilled in interpretation, and his comments on character and meaning are usually pertinent and well documented. The director and the actor should occasionally read literary criticism for the depth of analysis which is the result of years of close reading. In addition, the work of the literary critic is of interest to students, who will find explication of a specific work, a comparison of it with others, and a sensitive treatment of the relation of the work to the author.

In the time allowed for the preparation of scholarly articles and the space allowed for their publication, literary criticism is unlike any other. Moreover, the conviction that their readers are interested in timeless standards frees literary critics from the distractions of the marketplace. They furnish the kind of thoughtful analysis unavailable anywhere else.

Here is an example of literary criticism applied to films. The critic has the responsibility of commenting not only on character and conflict but on the significant use of the camera as well.

Alan Casty, *from "The Films of Robert Rossen"**

But it wasn't until *The Hustler* (1961) that [Robert] Rossen achieved a full breakthrough in technique, not by applying extraneous conventions to his material, but by extending the range and limits of social realism. In it the surface terms are much the same as *Body and Soul,* but the significance of the terms has changed and so has their treatment. Rossen has pushed beyond the usual classifications of American films, the usual neatly patterned boundaries for our responses, the pat socio-economic allegory of his earlier films. Certainly the picture is still about the corrupting influences of money, but even on that level it has a greater complexity. We no longer have the empty symbol of the corruption of capitalism in the gambler-promoter. For as George C. Scott captures the complexity of his satanic power and human weaknesses, the gambler's professional lust for money is only a part of a syndrome of illusory symbols of identity: lust for power in its own right, power over another human being as an object of one's ego; sexual lust on the same terms of domination and destruction — sadistic and perverse, rising from sexual insecurity and ending in sexual failure. In the same way, Eddie, the hustler [Paul Newman]is a more complete version of Rossen's young seeker. His desire for money and status within his "art" is even recognized by him as destructive of other impulses toward identity he feels within himself. The feelings of love surprise his defenses, but in the hemmed-in, trapped tightness of the girl's small apartment, the possibilities of

* © 1966 by The Regents of the University of California. Reprinted from *Film Quarterly*, Vol. XX, No. 2, pp. 8–10, by permission of The Regents. Used also by permission of Robert Casty.

love are overrun by the distortions of aggression (the counterpart of his need to be the top man of the world of the pool hall). Only in one scene in the open air, in which Rossen uses the wide screen to set up the strikingly contrasting sense of the openness of possibilities of tenderness and creativity, can Eddie verbalize his sense of his skill as more than a tool of conquest — as, rather, a creative and fulfilling artistry — and his sense of love as more than a battle for victory of the self. But Eddie is not strong enough to carry out these possibilities. The girl [Piper Laurie] — physically crippled, emotionally warped — is not yet destroyed, not yet without love. She is insightful enough to know what is happening — "We are all crippled," she says — but too weak, too wounded herself, to forestall it.

The film, then, is not merely the realistic depiction of the milieu and tricks of the trade of the pool hall and pool shark. It does not merely depict a battle between the old pool player and the young — within the reflex convention of old doctor and young, old gangster and young, old lawyer and young, old cowboy and young. It depicts, rather, the struggle between the gambler and the girl for the unformed soul and the unshaped energies of the pool-playing young American, the wanderer, skilled but isolated, without purpose, mission or connection. The triangle of conflict is much the same as that of *Body and Soul,* but this time made more complex, more meaningful, more fully human.

The sequence that forms the climax of this struggle for and final destruction of the possibilities of love is one of the most effective extended metaphors I can recall seeing in an American film. Derby Week at Louisville — gambling, money-making and spending, and their attendant pleasures — is the background for the final power struggle. The girl's isolation and inevitable doom is captured strikingly (again taking full advantage of the wide screen) in a long, dollying shot that follows her uneven, unnoticed path down a stairway and through a lobby and bar crowded mainly with men who pay no attention to her, until she stops at a doorway at the screen's right and is eyed, briefly but completely, by an objectifying glance of disinterested lust.

A bright, hot, cloistered downstairs billiards room (an expensive sophisticated hell) is the final battlefield. The hustler's broken thumbs have healed, but not his spirit. He needs more than money now from the gambler; he needs an almost sexual reflection of fulfillment from the gambler's taunting eyes, an OK that will prove his manhood even as he is destroying it, even as he turns from the girl and thus seals her destruction. The game's "sucker" is obviously a homosexual, and no mean pool player himself. His excitement builds with the budding sweat on their faces as he struggles expertly and daringly before succumbing, with obvious masochistic pleasure in his inevitable submission before the hustler and the power of men. But who is the "sucker," finally, who the half-man who submits as it appears he might (and in Eddie's case does) win? Eddie can only flee from this twisted triumph, and return too late to prevent the gambler's final twisted triumph over the girl, who in a tormented act of "crippled" self-destruction has submitted to him and then killed herself.

The subsequent resolution of the film is not the equal of its climactic sequence. Although it is certainly likely that Eddie would have learned something from the girl's death, the details of his regeneration (much like those of Rossen's boxer and bull fighter) do not convince. The dialogue is weak, the motivation sticky, but most important the vehicle used to dramatize his new awareness damages the tenor of the statement. We know that what is important is the way that he is playing pool now, the way he is winning and why; but still what we have is the final sports-movie triumph, and it is just too distracting. Possibly such things as fights and pool games can best be employed as negative symbols of imperfect humanity; the realistic data and the concern for who wins seem to get in the way of would-be spiritual phoenixes.

Uncritical Critics

Two minor kinds of comment on drama are worthy of note because of their prevalence. Both represent irresponsible criticism. One is that of the sensationalist, generally a columnist, who focuses on notoriety in the lives of the performers and on such peripheral matters as salaries, the breaking of contracts, threats of censorship, picketing, box office figures, etc. These are of great interest to the public, and publication of such matters in turn has an effect on the attendance records. Needless to say, the pseudo-critic who encourages patronage or avoidance of a drama on the basis of accompanying scandal performs no service to the public.

The other kind of pseudo-critic is the person who writes his (usually her) personal feelings about some topic barely suggested by the drama he pretends to review. This kind of reviewing begins and ends with self; and since feeling is the only standard of judgment, no one can argue with it — except to say that it is inconsistent and unreliable and that it reveals far more about the reviewer than about the work ostensibly being reviewed. In this kind of impressionistic criticism, any drama becomes an excuse for personal reminiscence: "This movie took place in a small town in the twenties. Boy, a lot of us will never forget what it used to be like to live in a small town, without crowds and smoke and. . . ." Or "This movie has a scene in an expensive hotel on the Riviera, with some of the best-looking clothes and sports cars you ever. . . ." Or "The hero's girl friend was the only thing wrong with the movie. I never liked the kind of girl who. . . ."

With slight exaggeration this is the general tone of such reviewers, some of whom are regularly found on the women's page of the newspaper. They are chatty sounding; they avoid difficult words which might frighten their readers, for they pride themselves on representing the common man. If they are read at all it should be for their enthusiasm and ability to communicate feelings. But responsible criticism begins where the impressionistic critic ends.

PART TWO ❀ ❀ ❀

Background
and Backstage

PROGRAM NOTES

The cosmopolitan critics of the drama continually allude to playwrights and theatrical eras of the past and assume on the part of their readers a familiarity with the important periods in theater history and with the movements and trends which helped to shape its course. The viewer who would like to become even more perceptive in his theater-going will therefore need a fundamental knowledge of how the drama reached its current status.

He will also need at least a passing acquaintance with what goes on behind the scenes: with the function of the director, with the various styles of acting appropriate to the different kinds of productions encountered on stage and screen today, and with the contributions of setting, lighting, and costume.

8 ❈ ❈ ❈

Classical Tragedy

If the ancient Greeks had had a choice of what drama to attend, how many would have cared if they were to miss the world premiere of *Oedipus the King?* If musical comedy had been invented, who knows how many Greeks would have thronged to a performance of *The Apollo Follies,* leaving the foolhardy producer of Euripides' *Medea* to gnash his teeth at the stupidity of the masses? Originally, when theater was developed by the Greeks, there was nothing but tragedy, a religious exercise as well as entertainment. All theater was tragedy.

It is important to realize that tragedy is the parent genre, just as most modern languages can be traced back to a parent tongue, the Indo-European language. The ancient Greek audiences loved and supported tragedy because they had no choice other than the comic afterpiece which concluded a day's drama program. The experience of going to the theater and becoming emotionally involved in a given series of events, of being carried along on the crest of tumultuous passion to a climactic moment, of leaving the theater purged of pent-up tensions — this was the experience of seeing tragedy on the stage.

But audiences and social conditions changed, and many other factors caused a variety of theatrical experiences; tragedy, the parent genre, broke down into different kinds of productions or production styles. *Forms of drama, other than tragedy, would probably never have existed if the conditions favorable to the preservation and development of tragedy had remained stable.*

Today, the production styles that are still capable of holding audiences have survived; those which have lost their usefulness have not. One may consider the greatness of tragic drama and the other forms he may choose from and then make his decision accordingly. Fortunately, we are in a position that the ancient Greeks might have envied but could not have paralleled. Although we did not originate the theater, we live in an age in which we can profit from the accumulated contributions of the past.

Tragedy and the Killer Instinct

The driver who passes a bad accident on the highway, one which has brought a number of red-flashing police cars, an ambulance, and countless spectators, is very strongly tempted to pull over to the side of the road and run over to the scene of the disaster. Many cannot resist such temptation; and, when asked why, they are likely to say, "We just wanted to see if we could help."

Every year on Memorial Day thousands of people watch the Indianapolis Speedway five-hundred-mile auto race. Is every one a devoted auto-racing fan? Can every one of these spectators see all of the course? Are there some who can see very little of the actual race? Still they come to Indianapolis, where, if statistics hold up, a number of crashes are almost guaranteed to occur. Do some appear despite the probability of an accident? Do some appear *because* of it?

What constitutes a bad prizefight? A poor display of pugilistic skill? Or the fact that nobody has been seriously hurt? All one has to do is listen objectively the next time a major fight is aired over the radio. The bloodier it becomes, the more excited the sportscaster sounds as he enthusiastically describes broken noses, swollen eyes, bleeding faces.

The fact is that, while we talk condescendingly of "ancient Rome" and its barbaric practices, of the chariot races, the gladiatorial combats to the death, and the Colosseum with its lion acts, we have many entertainment preferences which are basically no more civilized. The big crowd-pleasers of the circus, the high-paying acts, are those with the greatest element of danger — the daring young men on the flying trapeze or the reckless few who ride bicycles across high wires. The suspense engendered by their performances is what constitutes the real pleasure of watching them, and the suspense basically is the delay of their possible doom. Putting a net under the trapeze tends to diminish the enjoyment of the act.

Yet those who sigh at the circus do not attend because they hoped to see somebody killed, and the thousands who throng to Indianapolis would not be titillated by the reality of a car's careening from the track, crashing through a fence, and exploding into flame. The silence that would follow, the acrid odor of death everywhere, would horrify. There would be no release of the emotions. Death in real life is not a theatrical entertainment.

The *idea* of disaster strikes our fancies, not the fact of it. It is always to be enjoyed when it remains a comfortable distance away. People accept death, can even be entertained by it, after the embalmer has done his job and the funeral director has created his artistic setting of floral scenery, slumber room, music, and theatrical lighting. But the deceased has to be someone not too very close to us. He cannot be too real. And no matter how frequently corpse-watchers say, "He looks just as though he were asleep," there *is* an essential artificiality about the whole occasion. It is deliberately made false; the people responsible for it are in a very real and very respectable sense showmen.

A funeral can offer a total theatrical experience. There is an audience, of course. They sit in rows of seats either in a funeral parlor or in a church. They watch a definite ritual which has familiar conventions. Above all, there is a protagonist — a central figure, around whom the entire ritual revolves. It cannot be anybody else's show; as a matter of fact, no actual drama in the theater can possibly have so central a character. The funeral therefore has intense focus on one character and one subject, and the demise of that character.

There is no possibility for any emotion other than sorrow. One who would laugh must suffer ostracism. If the thought of loss, of the waste of great talent, or of the futility of life cannot stir, then the candles and the organ music and the unearthly silence *will*. And, once having been stirred, once having all of the emotions channeled into one object of attention, one general field of focus, the onlookers must reach a point at which they are temporarily out of emotional response. This is a state which theater-goers know and understand very well. It is what Aristotle calls *catharsis*, the condition which all of drama aims to produce in us, but which tragedy — *great* tragedy — comes closest to doing most completely.

Now, two things must be understood about catharsis: first, it is most effectively set in motion by solemn events, and second, those events must be divorced from reality. At the Speedway, the actual sight of disaster disturbs but does not purge the emotions. How could it? No one ever knows when a crash will occur and so cannot be really prepared for it. It is the same with funerals. The reality of death has already been experienced by the time of the funeral; the brutal shock has already had its impact.

Such unreality has multiple uses. Psychologists have shown that people can enjoy funerals when they have not known the deceased because they experience a secret sense of superiority to him. After all, *they* are still alive. They have won a victory in a little side drama not even on the program — their own battle with life. No matter what troubles one may have weighing heavily on his mind, all he has to do is attend a funeral, and the troubles seem to shrink in importance. When all is said and done, one says to himself, I am still here; *he* isn't, and that in itself is a lot.

People gang up on each other all the time. They rush to hear of someone else's misfortunes. For these they have always a willing ear. There must surely be people who read the obituary section of the newspaper to see whether they have ever known any of those who have passed on. Perhaps, as people grow older, the temptation to do this becomes even stronger, not weaker; "We are still in the race — hallelujah! the inevitable has not yet caught up with us." After a natural disaster, such as a destructive storm or a tornado, people stand around the next day, for hours, excitedly gabbing away about it. It is over; it is not real any more.

Some of them even exaggerate the element of danger in which they found themselves. And especially does everyone show interest in somebody else's damage and experience a secret disappointment when there is no damage.

This all too universal tendency is the *killer instinct,* and it can be much rougher than has been described. It can be manifested in outright cruelty, such as the enjoyment of somebody's being fired, losing his home, wrecking his new and uninsured car, failing in a business venture. People display it when they gather together in three's and then become two's. Nobody likes the sinking feeling that comes when he walks away from a group and senses an ominous silence behind him or imagines that he hears faint whisperings and snickers. Everybody has had this feeling, and practically everybody has caused it. It is human; it is normal; it is not dangerous, because it does not involve real malice.

The person who has been fired is not real. We do not allow ourselves to think of him dragging his feet slowly homeward, opening the front door so unexpectedly in the middle of the day, and having to confront a surprised wife whose smile vanishes by degrees. The man who has wrecked his car will somehow get another one, credit being what it is these days. (Just as, incidentally, the cartoon cat whose tail is plugged into an electrical socket by the crafty mouse will become whole and well again in the next panel.)

We are ill-wishers, then, only in private — that is, only subconsciously; the fact is nothing to be ashamed of: humanity shares it equally. And anything so universal, so deep-rooted, so ancient in the race undoubtedly has its uses. It did even with primitive man who was not quite so private about his destructive impulses. He believed in realism and did away with his own flesh and blood, but still he called it "sacrifice." It helped him to believe he was placating the powers of darkness and also gave him an outlet for pent-up tensions. Without theaters or television or boxing matches or football games, what else was there to do?

The "Pretend-Sacrifice"

The dividing line between primitive man and modern man may well be the point at which ritual became the play. The earliest plot known to man was hunter vs. hunted, and the earliest form of suspense was the pleasurable delay before the kill. The tribe was directly involved in sacrificial rites when real blood was spilled: as hunters, everybody participated in ritualistic dances and songs which culminated in the destruction of the victim or animal chosen as the hunted. The tribe, the "audience," *was,* in fact, the show.

According to this theory of the origin of drama, theater evolved from these primitive rituals and sacrifices. As man became more civilized, his killer instinct was controlled and channeled by the forces of society. By imitating ritualistic killings in a "pretend-sacrifice," man discovered that he could experience the same release of emotion that he had in the authentic sacrifices. In effect, he had the benefit of letting out his submerged aggressions without the pangs of conscience that followed the spilling of real blood. It was gore without guilt, brutality without bodies. The art of acting was born.

The pretend games continue to manifest in symbolic form the same essential dramatic plot: hunter vs. hunted. Whether they are called cowboysanindians or copsanrobbers, the pattern is that some kids chase other kids, and then they change sides (except the neighborhood creep who is usually forced to play the heavy). Of course, children *are* exposed to civilizing forces, such as the fairy-tales told by parents, about how the big bad wolf learned a lesson from Little Red Riding Hood and was never wicked again; and in recent years, there has been television to take over the parents' role. Thus on any given block in any given city one can find gangs of kids playing Lone Ranger or Zorro or Batman; but the name scarcely matters nor does the fact that the good guys get the bad guys.

The parents themselves are not the bastions of law and order they would like to have children believe. It is an unhappy fact, but a true one nevertheless, that even nursery rhymes can be secret hiding places for the killer instinct. In fact, the sweeter the surface, the greater is the likelihood that the serpent will seek it as a camouflage. A lullaby says it is full of a parent's infinite love, even though it may go like this:

> Rock-a-bye, baby, on the tree top.
> When the wind blows, the cradle will rock.
> When the bough breaks, the cradle will fall.
> Down will come baby, cradle and all.

There is no point speculating on the fate of babies who fall from trees — not from the lower branches, at that, but from the absolute, the very top.

This is by no means to suggest that parents who sing "Rock-a-bye baby" are to be investigated by the local police or that the doting aunt who continually gurgles, "I'm going to eat you up!" is really reverting to cannibalism. These are all only additional instances of the survival of the savage destructive tendencies which have been diverted by symbolism and siphoned off harmlessly. It is not to man's everlasting discredit, but rather to his glory that such symbolic games are possible. And atop the heap of the glorious games sits drama, the most organized and most completely satisfying of the pretend re-creations of the old hunter-hunted ritual.

Tragedy must then be considered the parent genre of the theater. If theater is a civilized version of the ritual, an intensely *human* method of releasing our tensions where they cannot do anybody any harm, tragedy is its most logical condition; for tragedy in any form is about somebody's being destroyed.

The Audience as Hunter

The theater has a secret use, as the means of a rebellion against the social restrictions by which people live. One of the most unbeatable of all plots in popular drama is the one which creates instantaneous sympathy and involvement for an evil-doer in his evil. Nobody is ever interested in the police; indeed, the police are rarely treated as heroes. No writer can miss if he begins with a crafty jewel thief, plotting the perfect robbery, or even the skillful murderer, aiming to be the first man in history ever to commit the perfect crime. The suspense is derived from only one source: fear lest the evil-doer be caught.

The memorable French film *Rififi* (1956) centered about the efforts of four totally unscrupulous, but engaging, crooks to break into a reputedly invincible jewelry company and take off with a million francs in diamonds. The movie achieved its major fame on the strength of one particular sequence, lasting over thirty minutes, in which the thieves gain access to the diamonds by making a hole in the ceiling and lowering themselves into the store by means of a rope. What made the suspense compelling, absolutely a marvel of its kind, was the ever-present possibility that the burglar alarm might go off. The store, we were to believe, had the most sensitive alarm system ever devised. A mere cough might trigger the complex mechanism, the wires of which were everywhere. Throughout the long sequence in the film not a word was spoken by the thieves; not a sound could be made; the slightest whisper might mean disaster. The silence became enthralling. Had one syllable escaped the lips of one character, the entire audience would have screamed.

There exists, to be sure, a somewhat paradoxical code in popular drama, especially on the screen. The evil-doer must eventually pay, not always for his crime, but as a sign of some mythical sense of universal justice. If someone commits murder, somewhere, sometime, even if no one ever finds out, he is bound to step off a subway platform into the path of an onrushing express. Hence the diamond thieves, after successfully engineering their *coup* and winning the eternal admiration of the audience, are shown to lose not only the fortune but their lives, one by one. In a pretense at morality, "justice" prevails, but only after each wrong-doer is killed, either by one of his own men or by other wrong-doers. One has his throat cut; another is tied to a post and shot in cold blood. Both of these instances of justice were performed like rituals, with great solemnity, the victim fully aware of his doom. In a sense, the audience was made the hunter of the thieves. The film remains, however, a masterpiece of popular drama, a thoroughly respectable, fully legitimate pandering to the universal love of pretend sacrifice.

Unfortunately, American moviemakers appear to lack either the opportunity or the courage to handle such "ruthless" and entertaining plots. A British film, *Kind Hearts and Coronets* (1949), was about an unscrupulous and engaging scoundrel who, discovering that he was tenth in succession to a dukedom, decided that the only logical expedient was to murder everyone standing in his way. The whole plot consisted of nothing more than a series of delightful, original, and amusing homicides. The powers behind this film satisfied the moral code rather ingeniously, if cynically, by having their hero, who has been condemned to death for a murder he did not happen to commit, obtain a pardon at the eleventh hour only to leave behind in his cell a copy of his memoirs, boasting of all the crimes for which he really *has* been responsible. For distribution to American audiences, however, the producers were required to tack on a final scene in which a prison guard discovers the manuscript and rushes out to apprehend the "villain."

The History of Compassion

Plots such as those just outlined are modern forms of the most primitive tribal empathy: the identification with those who are performing the sacrifice. The victim is very distant. Who, after all, thought about the man who owned the million francs' worth of diamonds? Who considered the murdering heir to the remote dukedom as being unkind to any real person? The phenomenon also applies to real-life catastrophes in which victims are at considerable remove from us. Sensational murder trials delight newspaper publishers because the ordinary, law-abiding citizen rushes for his morning paper, eager to see what will happen next and whether the death penalty will be invoked.

The death penalty and execution are interesting real-life evidences of the hunter-vs.-hunted ritual. The very word "execution" suggests the rather bureaucratic manner of the approach of death. Usually there is an audience; in fact, electric chair executions have a theatrical arrangement, with the onlookers seated in rows which face the front of the room — or stage — with its sole article of furniture and its single actor.

This is scarcely a commentary for or against capital punishment or the method of execution. The moral question is irrelevant here; what throws some light on the nature of theater is the essentially dramatic structure of executions. It is as though, if one were given a choice between ways of performing a perhaps necessary bit of unpleasantness, one must inevitably select the theatrical method. Is it that the theatricality itself protects the watchers from the reality of what is happening? It would be just as efficient to shoot the condemned man on the spot, as soon as the sentence had been passed, but one cannot imagine the judge removing a gun from under his robe, aiming and firing, then rising and announcing, "This court stands adjourned." Society would rebel against such brutal tactics.

Whether capital punishment is morally defensible or deplorable, the fact remains that it has always weighed heavily on the civilized conscience. Human sacrifice can no longer be entered into lightly or enjoyed openly. The sense of guilt — or at least the possibility of guilt — must often conflict with the rational conviction that *some* way must exist to punish those who kill. The ritualized execution has the virtue that high tragedy always provides: catharsis. The step-by-step solemnity, the mounting anticipation of doom, the approach of the inevitable moment, the attainment of the climax, and then the aftermath, then the silence and the sober acceptance of the fact that the ways of civilization are often hard and that it is the lot of man to be faced always with such cruel decisions.

The human race assuredly took a giant step forward when it transferred its involvement from the delights of the kill to compassion for those who *are* killed. This meant a change from the pleasures of the stalking and torture of prey to a sober reflection on man's inhumanity to man and to the place of evil and suffering in the universal order of things. And then to the even broader question of whether such order exists at all.

Tragic drama contains at its best two aspects, not necessarily harmonious with each other but nonetheless essential: first, a plot which contains the pretend-sacrifice in disguised form; and second, a resolution which forces attention on the cruelty of existence, the sorrow of being human, and the rightfulness of the disaster in an ordered world. Dramatic works which merely exploit the sacrifice itself are deliberate hokum perpetrated in the interests of sensational entertainment and making money. Sensitive theater-goers can take them or leave them as they wish; but they see through the hoax. They know that what it means to be truly human is to care about the hunted.

The Beginning of Formal Tragedy

Not knowing who is responsible for the transition from killing-as-play to *the* play *about* killing, we are tempted to attribute this milestone in human progress to the Greeks. Since they are responsible for the first formal theater in the Western world and since we know that their theater evolved from an ancient ritual, we may assume that the Greeks were precociously concerned about the meaning and value of the pretend sacrifice.

The ritual which became drama was associated with the god Dionysus, who ruled over the domain of the earth's vegetation. It celebrated an old myth which bears a striking parallel to the Christian story of Easter; it maintained that winter resulted from the annual death of Dionysus and his descent into the nether world and the earth was reborn with his resurrection in the early spring. A comparison of this tale with similar stories in other societies strongly indicates that to ancient man the growth of the crops and the fertility of the earth, depended upon supernatural activities; and one of the most prevalent means of insuring the rebirth of vegetation was sacrifice.

But all of this occurred before recorded history. When we find evidences of old Athenian religious celebrations as the forerunners of Greek tragedy, they are those of the spring fertility rite, some form of which existed with every people dependent upon agriculture for survival, as well as rites held in early winter. As with other religious rites, the outward forms remained long after the original meaning had vanished. It is still the case that very civilized people can do things that are in reality the pretend sacrifice in symbolic form. Athenians came together in winter and spring to perform over and over again a ceremony of death, a death that had been real long ago, a death that had been necessary for the survival of everyone. And they also recreated symbolically the intense pleasures that were traditionally associated with the sacrifice — not only the joy of feeling secure now that the earth would bear fruit, but also that of the ancient act of killing. What may once have been a violent tribal orgy became a social revelry, an institution of civilized living.

The outer forms, then, remained for the Athenians: the tradition of the all-out feast, together with the religious sanctions that made everything decent and respectable. In like manner is the Mardi Gras celebration in New Orleans with all of its famous high-spirited fun capable of philosophical justification because it will be followed by the lean and austere days of Lent.

Another vestige of the earlier rites was a chorus of men who sang and danced and who wore masks, as most primitive tribes had done in committing sacrifices. It is traditional to say that the drama developed out of the odes of praise to Dionysus sung by the chorus and called *dithyrambs*. How these came to have plots is hard to determine, but the nature of the earliest extant plays certainly provides a clue. The stories are tragic stories involving the death — or at all events the destruction — of one central figure; in other words, the figure of the *hunted*.

Since the sacrificial rite had necessarily centered about this main "character," it is not surprising that the first recorded kind of dramatic performance as such finds the chorus alternating with a solo actor to present its hymns of praise and perhaps to tell a rudimentary story as in present-day responsive readings between clergyman and congregation. In 534 B.C. Thespis (from whom we derive the word *thespian*, meaning dramatic or tragic) is known to have been the winner of a contest held in connection with the spring festival for the best tragedy performed. The play is not known, but Thespis himself played all of the characters — apart from the chorus — a phenomenon made possible by the continued use of masks. This means, however, that the earliest recorded play was a series of scenes between the chorus and only one other figure.

The existence of a competition for the best tragedy indicates the popularity of this new kind of pleasure. The Greeks had, in short, found the entertainment value of tragedy. There was the pretend sacrifice element (hunter vs. hunted), while at the same time there was the more civilized aspect of religion. The choral odes continued to be hymns to the gods, and the huge amphitheaters in which the plays were performed had stone seats in the front row for the priests of Dionysus.

Aeschylus, Sophocles, Euripides

The great achievement of Athenian fifth-century tragedy must be regarded as one of the milestones in human civilization. The forty-two plays which survive are evidence of the astonishing development of great themes and perfect structure after primitive beginnings. For anyone whose interest in drama is confined to plays of his own time, it is still important to know the Greeks, for tragedy in its purest form is Greek.

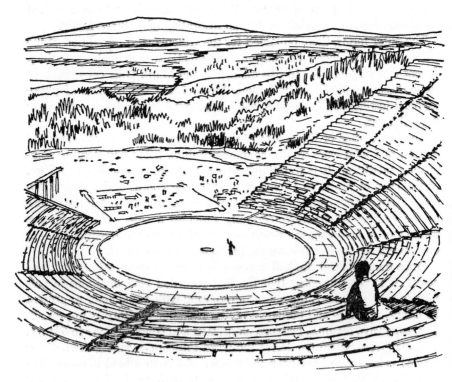

Greek amphitheater, emphasizing distance from actor to audience.

To know what theater can be and can do, it is necessary to know what the Greeks did in their theater.

Before formal drama, audiences were apparently content in listening to the choral odes and watching the dances that were part of a religious tribute to Dionysus. But after Thespis introduced a solo performer, dialogue could be written to be spoken by the leader of the chorus, the chorus, and one actor, who could take more than one part.

When, later, a second actor was added by Aeschylus (525–456 B.C.), much greater variety and flexibility in story enactment became possible. Aeschylus wrote scenes for two actors without the chorus, and also provided for the interaction of character and chorus. The Aeschylean dramatic pattern made possible the first true plays because it introduced conflict. The works of Thespis must have been little more than expanded and more complex rituals. But the chorus had traditionally worked as a single body and so could not be involved in real conflict. The chorus had no personality and, for a period even during the fifth century, retained its basically religious function in the drama. With two individual performers, however, Aeschylus was able to use real plots, to turn the ritual into an altogether new way of telling a story by having it acted out.

He also originated and developed the pyramidal structure. But Aeschylus was more than an innovator whose contributions would later be improved upon. His *Oresteia* trilogy (458 B.C.) is a powerful work in its own right and ranks among the greatest works in dramatic history.

Each dramatist, to compete in the annual contest, had to submit a trilogy, three tragedies which might or might not be on an inter-related theme, and one comic afterpiece called a "satyr" play. The *Oresteia* is the only surviving complete trilogy. Its three parts — *Agamemnon, The Libation Bearers,* and *The Furies* — tell the story of the murder of Agamemnon by his wife and her lover, the revenge of the son Orestes by the killing of his mother and the lover, and, finally, the persecution of Orestes for the crime and his eventual acquittal by the goddess Athena after the theater's first courtroom scene. Though the work as a whole reaches a happy ending, the plight of Orestes is essentially a tragic one: first he is torn between two forces, the love for his mother and the need to avenge his father, and then he is cruelly punished for committing a crime that was expected of him by the moral laws of society.

The first play of the trilogy, *Agamemnon,* is an almost perfect tragedy in itself. The prologue, spoken by the Watchman on the castle tower as he sights Agamemnon's ship returning from Troy, would have been saturated with irony for the Greek audience, for they had heard the savage tale over and over. Each scene intensifies the action and leads inexorably toward the hero's doom.

The play illustrates that the structure of the pretend sacrifice had not been buried in antiquity, that it was to become the structure of tragic drama. *Agamemnon* is the pretend sacrifice in its most naked form. It builds suspense as it works toward the obligatory moment — the horrendous off-stage cry of the warrior as he is slaughtered. Its resolution solves nothing. The queen and her lover appear and justify their crime; the Leader of the Chorus denounces them but is told that he will pay for his insubordination.

Agamemnon can be enjoyed for its own sake, apart from the rest of the trilogy; indeed it is the most dramatic of the three plays. But Aeschylus, the most philosophical of the great fifth-century tragedians, inevitably poses questions on the nature of a moral universe. If the play had ended after *Agamemnon,* a murderer would have escaped justice. The three-play form allows for a long-range perspective which shows retribution, as Agamemnon's son Orestes kills the murderers, then is tormented himself until at the end Athena's rational and fair dispensation of justice in favor of the hero reaffirms Aeschylus' faith in the moral fitness of things.

Not so sure was Sophocles (496–406 B.C.), who seems to doubt, not that the gods know what they are doing, but that they are paternally interested in mankind. Sophocles concentrates on the tragedy of being human, on the sufferings of man, rather than on the relationship between man and gods. In his masterpieces *Antigone* (440 B.C.) and *Oedipus the King* (430 B.C.) the gods function as movers of the plot instead of the agents through which it is resolved fairly. Both Oedipus and Creon, the hero of *Antigone,* are destroyed through their pride and arrogance, Oedipus because he insisted that there was no truth in prophecy and Creon because he placed his own will above that of the gods; but the ultimate affirmation of a moral universe, one in which human pride invites certain disaster, is one of the harsh facts of existence, not a source of rejoicing as it is at the conclusion of *The Furies.*

Besides, Sophocles is the dramatist, the perfector of the pyramidal structure, not the philosopher in the theater, and he subordinated thought to both plot and character. Years later, when Aristotle came to formulate his famous theory of tragedy, he cited *Oedipus* as the perfect play and listed thought as the third most important of the six elements of tragedy.

Sophocles added the third actor to a dramatic scene and made possible a greater plot complexity. At one point in *Oedipus,* for example, the messenger from Corinth has come to inform the king that his supposed father has died. Jocasta, also on stage, hails the news with great relief and points out to Oedipus that he should now be convinced that there is no truth in prophecy. But, as the scene progresses, the messenger tells Oedipus that the king of Corinth was not his true father and begins to reveal the circumstances through which he was originally brought to Corinth, a recital of events which causes Jocasta to realize that she is indeed married to her own son. There are thus three levels of consciousness represented on the stage: the messenger's limited knowledge of the past, Oedipus' aroused curiosity but ignorance of the full horror of his situation, and Jocasta's complete recognition of the cruel truth. No scene in any play could take more complexity than that. The Sophoclean third actor is thus a triumph in stage art, not merely a step forward.

Finally, it is the continual use of irony that causes the Sophoclean structure to be as tight as it is, that makes each scene work within that structure. Nor is this irony a mere dramatic contrivance. It is a happy result (for the theater) of something Sophocles is still able to cling to — the Greek recognition of an ordered universe, one in which the punishment of the ancient sin of Labdacus, grandfather of Oedipus, must renew itself in each generation, in which the real tragedy lies in the fact that human pride, a source of admiration and greatness in itself, is forever fated for destruction.

The vision of both Aeschylus and Sophocles is that of a world governed by forces beyond the control and understanding of man, but Sophocles does give man a greater degree of moral responsibility for his own actions. Oedipus does not plead for mercy on the grounds that he has been a mere puppet of fate, even though it is precisely that belief in fate which allows Sophocles to use irony so effectively. On the other hand, Sophocles seems not to want the inevitable consequence of placing all of the blame on the gods — the loss of human dignity. His final play, *Oedipus at Colonus* (406 B.C.), written during his last days, is extremely mystic and attempts to reconcile the contradictory positions of accepting fate and asserting freedom of the will. Yet whatever final truth of things Oedipus sees as he disappears from earth into a blinding heavenly light is not for us to understand.

Euripides (484–406 B.C.), though almost an exact contemporary of Sophocles, seems to have been entirely caught up in the liberal spirit of free inquiry that dominated fifth-century Athens. Sophocles remained almost dead center in the struggle between the dying forces of conservatism and the rising forces of scientific investigation and atheistic thought. Euripides' famous use of the *deus ex machina* as well as the peculiar kind of bitter irony he invented indicate that he was far more cynical than either of his great predecessors. The careless manner in which he resolved his plots, often with a happy ending, suggests a faint trace of mockery, not a sunny optimism. The fact that Medea goes free after murdering her children tells us only that this is *not* an orderly world; perversity is the rule, justice an accident.

As a result of his pessimistic outlook, Euripides' themes are not those of human pride locked in a hopeless struggle against fate. His three greatest works, *Medea* (431 B.C.), *Hippolytus* (428 B.C.), and *The Trojan Women* (415 B.C.), show man against the background of an alien, unfriendly, and inscrutable universe. In such a context pride is less admirable than it is ridiculous or pathetic. And in such a context the Sophoclean perfection of plot structure makes less sense.

Instead, Euripides concentrates on the intense tragedy of character and inner conflict. Both *Medea* and *Hippolytus* offer heroines who are overcome by passions they cannot control. Medea's natural love for her children wars against her hatred of her husband. In *Hippolytus* Phaedra's sexual passion for her stepson wars against her better sense. Euripides made the greatest innovations in the art of dramatic conflict, turning the pretend sacrifice into an even more terrifying drama in which the hunter is also the hunted. In such circumstances, there can be no satisfying moral resolution, but there is still catharsis. At the conclusion of *Medea* the audience is drained of emotion because of the terrible things that have happened, but there is also that distinctly Euripidean sense of frustrating incompleteness. The catharsis is wrung from the suffering of the heroine, which the audience shares, but which simply must be accepted for itself; it is not that of a woman in the act of sinning. The tragedy is that of a woman in the act of suffering.

In the Euripidean vision of life the innocent suffer as much as the guilty. Merely to be human at all is to be susceptible to destruction; merely to be human at all is to be a potential hero of a tragedy. Life *is* tragedy, and the theater is the means of showing it. It is therefore not surprising that Aristotle referred to Euripides as the most tragic of the three great playwrights which the Athenian theater had produced. And it is little wonder that Euripides seems as modern as tomorrow's headlines; for we who live under a continual threat from ever deadlier weapons of destruction have no difficulty understanding the cruelties and terrors which characterize his dark landscape.

The Shadow of Greek Tragedy

The first critic of the theater was Aristotle (384–322 B.C.), who wrote *The Poetics,* famous as an essay on tragedy long after the great period of Athenian drama had passed. Surveying the accomplishments of Aeschylus, Sophocles and Euripides as a whole and from the perspective of a century's distance, Aristotle arrived at his famous definition of tragedy as a play that is "serious, complete, and of a certain magnitude; in language embellished with artistic ornaments . . . in the form of action, not narrative; with incidents arousing pity and fear, wherewith to bring about a catharsis of the emotions." Aristotle's theory that catharsis is the aim of tragedy could well extend to the entire range of theater. It could be said that tragedy is theater at its best.

Tragedy is to drama what the symphony is to music. As composers dream of creating great symphonies that may one day stand beside those of Beethoven or Brahms, young playwrights long to compose a great modern tragedy. It is almost impossible for a serious contemporary dramatist not to be intimidated by Aristotle's summary of the Athenian achievement and his abstraction from it of the universal, enduring principles of theatrical art at its greatest. Aristotle listed the main ingredients as six: *plot, character, thought, diction, music,* and *spectacle.* The last two, which he considered the most superficially theatrical and the most dispensable, are too often the main ingredients of modern popular theater. The most important element according to Aristotle was *plot,* which gives a play completeness and without which catharsis is difficult to achieve.

The vitality of the Greeks is nowhere better evidenced than in the continuing critical measurement of drama according to the excellence of classical plotting. Thus it is usually said of Shakespeare that he reached the heights despite the fact that most of his plots have not the simplicity and the intensity of Greek tragedy. The shapeless plot, which has become a standard fixture in modern theater, has always to vindicate itself, to offer something to compensate for its lack of form. Careful plotting has saved many an otherwise empty piece of dramaturgy. Writers of successful thrillers are apt to swear by Aristotelian construction because they recognize the enduring success in the theater achieved by the traditional scheme of exposition-intensification-obligatory moment ("Surely you knew, inspector, that the jewels were in the watch fob all the time.") — and resolution.

The Greeks may have been fortunate that they knew less about character than we do today. Euripides was precocious about character, but his heroines like Medea and Phaedra act and react with that same economy which marks all the major Athenian masterpieces. Euripides came up with a new version of a plot, but he did not delve into intimate details of personality the way modern playwrights do.

Psychiatrists are indebted to the Greeks for labels such as "narcissism" and "Oedipus complex," but the playwrights were not psychiatric in their approach to personality. Oedipus himself had no Oedipus complex for all the jokes that have been made about him and his plight. He was definitely *not* a man in love with his mother. The story of Oedipus actually could have happened in ancient Greece: that is to say, a man might well have married a woman twice his age if it meant a throne.

The same plot today would take longer to tell because a modern dramatist would feel obligated to investigate the erotic ramifications of the story. One can imagine Oedipus' discussing his feelings about his queen both before and after he learns the truth of their relationship, saying, perhaps, "I see, darling, why I used to feel strangely about you," as they decide to seek guidance of a psychiatrist! If Sophocles had had to be burdened with any of this, he should certainly never have created the world's most perfect plot: unified, compelling, inexorable in its movement to a logical and significant conclusion. Sophocles' hero is noble and proud, as a king should be, but beyond that we know little about him.

It is not fair to say that *character* in Greek tragedy is unimportant. Rather, it should be said that Greek characters are usually generalized; they are types in the highest sense of the word. Oedipus is a strong and arrogant ruler; his failing is his deluded conviction that he cannot be wrong. Other leaders fit the description, whereas characters in modern tragedies tend to be more particularized. The great advantage the Greeks had is that their characters do not easily become dated. If Medea is not representative of a broad segment of motherhood, she is drawn so broadly as to be a prototype of jealous hate. She has not become trapped in the rubble of a decayed civilization waiting to be unearthed by archeologists.

Modern attempts at tragedy sometimes relate too closely to their times. Will Arthur Miller's salesman be as meaningful under a different economic system? Will Tennessee Williams' Blanche Du Bois have as much to tell a future that has become even more remote from her Old South heritage? Oedipus and Creon and Phaedra were born from imaginations that inhabited for a moment a time and place that never were and so always can be.

It is through character, however, that the Greeks achieve the magnitude of which Aristotle speaks; and here again the modern tragedian is haunted by a ghost from the past — Aristotle's famous dictum concerning the proper hero for a tragedy. The protagonist should be, he states, a man of noble background who is mainly virtuous but who is brought to destruction by one basic weakness in his character. This flaw, at least in the plays of Aeschylus and Sophocles, is pride (*hubris*).

When Aristotle speaks of virtue, however, he means it in his sense, not ours. There is no understanding that the hero must be sympathetic because he is fundamentally "nice." (See the discussion of "The Protagonist" in Chapter Three). The classical hero makes no appeal other than that of his greatness. But the modern author, looking for a substitute hero, invariably settles for a person who is distinguished from others, not by rank or built-in nobility, but by a real goodness which is warped by some kind of psychological disturbance. The mother in Eugene O'Neill's *Long Day's Journey into Night* is addicted to dope, while both Willy Loman and Blanche Du Bois are really insane by the conclusions of their respective plays, but all three — and this is significant — are shown to have been concerned for the welfare of their families; in other words, they are made to *deserve* our sympathy. The classical hero *demands* it. Nonetheless, the contemporary tragic dramatist is well aware that in the modern world, nobody waits around long enough to see what happens to anyone. The doom of one individual does not have that much to say about the kind of universe in which we live — unless the author is able, as Arthur Miller is, to make his hero seem representative of a large segment of the population.

Aristotle relegates *thought* to the position of third in importance, but many modern dramatists put it first. Perhaps the reason is that the age of relativity poses its greatest challenge to the intellect. With nothing sure, all things are possible; and a man's main hope of being heard is to have something important to say. Though the days are gone when a character can command instant respect by saying "I am world-famous Oedipus," he may force us to listen to remarks which sound wise. The audience grants him the benefit of the doubt: he is worthy of respect because he sounds profound, even when his meaning is shrouded in ambiguities. To Aristotle, thought in a play is "the faculty of saying what is possible and appropriate." It is making a general observation whenever the situation calls for it, but he makes it clear that the aim of theater — catharsis — is best served by the interaction of plot and character. He even specifies that thought "is found in the dialogue and speeches of a tragedy." Thus he excludes it from the domain of the chorus, which is the principal conveyor of philosophy in a Greek play. It seems to be understood that philosophizing extensively retards the forward progress of the action, that general observations are to be made by the characters only when they arise logically from the situation. Thus, in *Antigone*, Creon's son Haimon makes use of thought as an argument against his tyrannical father: "It is no City if it takes orders from one voice." This is a moral truth to which Creon is blind and is thus vital to the conflict of the play. What Aristotle did *not* envision was the muddy intellectualism of much contemporary drama which requires constant interpretation during the act of viewing because neither plot nor characters have any impact in themselves. Indeed, if the Greeks had bogged themselves down in excessive philosophizing, it is unlikely that so many of their tragedies would still hold the stage.

The last of Aristotle's indispensable elements is *diction,* which is the convention of using elevated and dignified poetry as the means of communication between the characters. One reason is surely that the ritualistic origins of Greek tragedy made the use of a solemn, highly unrealistic idiom imperative, but at the same time Aristotle's definition of diction is interesting; it is "the metrical arrangement of words." Rhythm seems to be the main factor, and what is rhythm but the principle whereby sounds *move?* Rhythm, in short, is linguistic plotting. The emphasis is not on the absolute literary values of poetry, such as imagery and metaphor. These were made into elements of dramatic language by Shakespeare. In the Greek theater it is the solemnity as well as the rhythm of the language that most matters. Even in translation the idiom of a Greek tragedy can be hypnotic, as in the Tyrone Guthrie production of *Oedipus* in 1955 in which both choral and character speeches had a chanting, incantatory quality. It may not have been authentically Greek, but it certainly suggested what Aristotle might have meant by "metrical arrangement." The words were intoned in a manner which clearly separated them from any connection with the language of real life. For tragedy must be larger than life if it is to impress us with its awe and majesty.

Many modern writers are concerned about the dying institution of poetry as the basic language of the theater. Criticism after criticism of contemporary drama bemoans the dearth of noble language. Unfortunately, those who have attempted to fill the vacuum — T. S. Eliot, for one notable example — have been literary, not stage, poets and have given us dialogue that reads beautifully but does not always move us when spoken in performance. One difficulty is that modern poetry "means" more than classical poetry, because it is more personal than classical poetry was supposed to be; and the theater simply is not the place in which a man can bare the most subtle depths of his soul and expect to communicate. Probably more significant and moving is the visual poetry which film directors like Fellini and Bergman achieve with the camera.

The monopoly which the Greek tragedians, through the interpretation of their work by Aristotle, have maintained on the art of tragedy may seem unwarranted after so many centuries; but the fact remains that their influence goes on and on. Even when Arthur Miller writes an essay called "Tragedy and the Common Man," to defend Willy Loman's humble stature, the spirit of Aristotle is being invoked. The theory of alienation held by certain proponents of the avant-garde drama is a conscious rejection of Aristotle's theory of catharsis.

Yet alienation may possibly not exist at all, and when one reads or sees a play like Miller's *The Crucible* (1953), one wonders whether its power comes from its message-laden speeches reminding the viewer of modern parallels to the persecution of witches in Salem or from the fact that it is carefully plotted with a simplicity and a precision that Aristotle himself would have applauded.

The Long-Running Greeks

The Greek tragedians, however, most deserve study because they still provide great theater. The subject matter of their plays would assuredly not prevent their being enjoyed by uncritical audiences today; murder, suicide, madness, incest, jealousy, hatred are among the most universally workable subjects for dramas. All that is necessary is a willingness to accept conventions different from those of the theater of today.

In reading a Greek tragedy, one is likely to be discouraged by the choral odes, which interrupt the orderly flow of the plot, allusions by myths and mythological characters which may not be familiar, and by the elevated language, which at first may seem cold and remote. Modern readers also tend to expect verisimilitude from every play regardless of its period and are bewildered by the sparseness of a Greek tragedy and the fact that little or nothing is indicated concerning the way of life of the characters. A preliminary reading, which ignores the choral odes and the obscure allusions, can be reassuring, however, by bringing to light the classic simplicity of the plot and the stark intensity of the conflicts. In subsequent readings the function of the chorus becomes clear, so that the odes and the diction of the characters go together and the ritualistic character of the play is evident. Obscure references, particularly to names used more than once, are then worth tracking down, if for no reason other than to help narrow the gulf of time.

Seeing actual productions affords fewer problems. Normally a Greek tragedy is attempted only by university theaters or by professional repertory companies such as those of Tyrone Guthrie in Minneapolis and the Actor's Workshop in San Francisco, and therefore the viewer is in the hands of directors and actors who have carefully studied the conventions of Greek staging.

Merely reading the plays does not give the best idea, for example, of the spell that is cast upon an audience by the chorus, a number of voices all chanting together in unison. Originally used as the voice of the private citizen or as the "ideal spectator" of the action, the Greek chorus remains an astonishing dimension of drama — the constant presence of a stable, unshakeable rationality against which the gradual disintegration of the major figure looms even more terrifyingly.

Another convention of Greek staging was the masks worn by the original actors and the chorus in the Athenian theater. By means of these one performer was able to appear in more than one role, and characters in plays could be female, even though only men were able to act on the stage. The original need for the masks no longer exists, but the 1955 Guthrie production indicated that they could enhance the power of the tragedy as well as suggest the barbaric splendor of a period much closer to the sacrificial origins of theater. Besides, seeing a masked production eliminates the distractions of the physical characteristics of the actor. Since Greek characters were not individualized, facial expressions are far less important than sonority of voice and vocal rhythms.

The convention of the messenger is likely to be harder to accept and seem more dated than either the chorus or the use of masks. The messenger's function was to report off-stage action. For a number of reasons, one of which may have been the problem of staging itself, the Greeks never showed any violence on the stage; rather, they concentrated on showing the reactions of the characters to off-stage action. A Greek play is not static to view, even though long speeches by messengers are always involved. The device of the messenger, especially as refined by Sophocles and Euripides, makes the off-stage action so vivid that it seems to be enacted as part of what happens on stage rather than merely being recounted after the fact. Moreover, theatrical "action" is capable of a broad definition that does not necessarily include motion or observed violence. The final entrance of Oedipus, his face stained with gore, his eyes empty black sockets, has impact precisely because we do not see him tear out his eyes. Similarly, the cry of the children of Medea, as they are being slaughtered within the palace, is more chilling than fake murder committed in full view of the audience.

A consequence of the convention of the messenger is aesthetic distance, the classical suggestion of horror instead of the bloody depiction of it. The modern penchant for exhibiting violence and bald emotion, especially in film close-ups, usually does little to make the classical convention seem dated and unwise. The viewer made uncomfortable by being carried too close to the action in plays and films of today has no trouble adjusting to the messenger, who can have the effect of causing what is not seen to yield more terror than anything that could be shown.

The final convention of Greek tragedy is unity of time, place, and action. Resembling a modern football stadium more than a playhouse, the Greek theater made scene changes unnecessary since no illusion of place was possible to begin with. The action took place there, either in the *orchestra*, where the chorus danced, or on the steps of the stage building, where the episodes of the plot occurred. Time as such was not telescoped; rather it was non-existent. And the relative shortness of Greek tragedies made subplots impossible; nor would they have made much sense to the Greek love of simplicity.

Greek unity is disconcerting at first to the theater- or movie-goer who has been weaned on a diet of multiple scenes and artificial time sequences which often allow years to pass in the space of two hours. Not that shifts in place and the shortening or lengthening of time are difficult to accept, but something can yet be said for the theatrical value of unity. The box set, which is comprised of painted flats joined together and made to look like a solid room, is still the major scenic convention of Broadway; and it can help to promote a Greek intensity that is usually shattered when Hollywood "makes the movie" and destroys the sense of unity. Compression of time can achieve an intensity of build towards the obligatory moment, whereas liberties taken with both time and place are often characteristics of episodic plotting. Likewise, the failure of a modern play or movie to develop a single plot action is often a sign that the dramatist could find no situation or character interesting enough to go the distance. Instead, he has resorted to the safety of numbers.

The subsequent history of drama offers many innovations from many hands. Shakespeare is not classical, while the modern giant Chekhov is just about as far from the Greeks as anyone can be. Yet the achievement of the Greek tragedians remains the foundation of all drama. It is so considerable as enduring entertainment in itself and as the standard-setter for the ages that it remains the point of reference by which all theater practices are analyzed and evaluated.

9 ❁ ❁ ❁

Elizabethan and Seventeenth-Century Tragedy

Tragedy and Humanism

Two thousand years separate the Athens of Sophocles and the London of Shakespeare. In the intervening time no great tragedy was written, and it has not been written since. The certain conditions which promote the development of tragedy existed in the fifth century B.C. and in the early part of the seventeenth century, both ages of belief in the greatness of man. Most of the writers who have attempted to imitate that belief without living in an era which accepted it have been able to write only imitations of the form but not the spirit of great tragedy. The seventeenth century was one such age, better suited to the more social art of comedy. The modern age with its relativistic values is ill suited to the moral preoccupations of the Greeks; and the helpless "common man" of today can only look with nostalgia on the giant heroes of Shakespeare.

Sophocles' Athens and Shakespeare's London had much in common. Both were becoming important centers of trade and cosmopolitan centers of learning. Both were becoming highly proficient in the urban arts — including theater attendance. And both were immersed in a tremendous revolution, as old beliefs were being questioned by new, more liberal viewpoints. The result of all this activity was, in each case, the emergence of the basic condition favorable to tragedy, humanism.

Humanism can be defined as the belief in the perfectibility of man. Sometimes called the religion of man, humanism, as it flourished in Greek civilization and in the Renaissance, held that man by his own intellectual resources could master the world in which he lived, that man had the power to observe and the ability to reason. The conclusions that he draws are based on his making the proper rational connections based on what he sees more than what authority requires him to believe on faith.

The humanistic attitude towards man is reflected in the famous statement made by the philosopher Protagoras (481–411 B.C.), "Man is the measure of all things." Disagreeing with older religious interpretations of existence, Protagoras maintained that human reason was not distinct from sensory perception. All man knew was what he experienced, and thus man's perception of an apparent order in nature actually put that order there. Whatever ultimate truth might be, man need be concerned only with his version of it. It is thought that Protagoras is the author of a lost book of which only the opening sentence survives: "Concerning the gods I do not know whether they exist or do not exist."

Humanism generates tragedy because it demands so much of man and makes human fallibility disastrous. The daring man pays a high price for error. Thus Sophocles' Creon and Oedipus can be seen as embodiments of a fantastic pride which invites its own destruction. Both insist, like Protagoras, that their versions of the truth are the "measure of all things." Euripides' irrationally-driven heroes and heroines are powerful rejoinders to those who boast of man's perfectibility and his chances of mastering nature. Inhabiting a world operating on blind chance and ignorant of man altogether, his characters realize only the pain, not the achievements, of being human.

Yet in the long run tragedy elevates, rather than downgrades, the image of man. Whatever evils men do, whatever disastrous fates they suffer, one fact remains: man has made his presence felt. What he does, matters. For Aeschylus and Sophocles the protagonist's arrogance has disturbed a universal order that, in destroying him, reasserts itself. His doom, in short, is the necessary condition of universal order. For Euripides man's plight is so full of anguish that scarcely anything else matters. It was still to be many centuries before the infinitude of space began to shrink the human image.

The Renaissance Superman

The Elizabethan England which produced Shakespeare as well as great explorers and philosophers was at last sharing in the Renaissance. Though Italy as early as the fourteenth century had begun to emerge from the Middle Ages, finding in art and political theories revolutionary assertions of humanism, the Renaissance did not reach England until the time of Queen Elizabeth's father, Henry VIII. When it finally did, there burst a flood of exuberance for terrestrial life and the unlimited potential of man that had already become immortalized in the dome of St. Peter's. Even on the Vatican, dedicated to the spiritual life of Western man, Michelangelo had unmistakably imprinted the stamp of humanity. It enshrined the golden cry, "Here, to the glory of God, is the monumental work of a human being." The characters of Shakespeare were to be as strident.

One of the consequences of Renaissance enthusiasm for this world and for man as its master was the emergence of the superman figure, sometimes called Renaissance Man. Urged on by the realization that there was no after-life and that one ought to do as much, be as much, and know as much as possible in one lifetime, the age created the dream of the all-around man, marvelously proficient in a variety of skills, ever perfecting himself. Renaissance Man epitomized the whole concept of humanism.

The prototype of this figure in Elizabethan drama was the hero of *Tamburlaine the Great,* by Christopher Marlowe (1564–1593), setting forth the ideal in its simplest, most fairy-tale form. The superman has remained one of the most enduring and popular of all heroes; modern counterparts are Superman himself and the Lone Ranger. But Marlowe's version is of his time and is entirely self-centered. There is no pretense at altruism. The superman is the measure of all things. Unlike Clark Kent, who hides his true identity and derives his principal satisfaction from the knowledge that he is serving mankind, Tamburlaine wants everyone to know who he is and what he can do. Unlike Clark Kent, who sees to it that the law is upheld, Tamburlaine makes his own laws. Self-assertion is his basic drive, something the German philosopher Nietzsche was to call the "will to power." He was the wish-fulfillment of the Renaissance and seemed to say, "I am here only once and for a very short time and will therefore be everything I can. Whoever gets in my way must be crushed."

Two examples from Shakespeare will serve to suggest the dimensions of his superman figures. The first is the chorus's description of King Henry, from *Henry V* and the second from *Antony and Cleopatra:*

> Upon his royal face there is no note
> How dread an army hath enrounded him;
> Nor doth he dedicate one jot of colour
> Unto the weary and all-watched night,
> But freshly looks, and over-bears attaint
> With cheerful semblance and sweet majesty;
> That every wretch, pining and pale before,
> Beholding him, plucks comfort from his looks.
> A largess universal like the sun
> His liberal eye doth give to every one,
> Thawing cold fear, that mean and gentle all
> Behold, as may unworthiness define,
> A little touch of Harry in the night.

Cleopatra's description of Antony is even more extravagant:

> His legs bestrid the ocean; his rear'd arm
> Crested the world; his voice was propertied
> As all the tuned spheres, and that to friends;
> But when he meant to quail and shake the orb,
> He was as rattling thunder. For his bounty,
> There was no winter in't; an autumn 'twas

> That grew the more by reaping. His delights
> Were dolphin-like: they show'd his back above
> The element they liv'd in. In his livery
> Walk'd crowns and crownets; realms and islands were
> As plates dropp'd from his pocket.

It seemed as though, when the Renaissance threw off the shackles of medieval religion, it turned man himself into the very deity that had been denied.

Universal Order, a Legacy from the Middle Ages

The humanism of the Renaissance, unlike that of the Greeks, drew its sustenance from a religious view of the universe. "What is man that thou art mindful of him?" was the question in the Biblical psalm, and the answer had been, "Man is a little lower than the angels." The Renaissance ignored the angels to insist that man was central in creation.

The Middle Ages, largely influenced by the Aristotelian and Ptolemaic view of the universe, believed that the earth was in the center of everything, and that around it revolved seven heavenly bodies, including the sun and moon, as well as the stars. Each body that moved around the earth had an orbit, which was a perfectly circular wheel; and each wheel fitted inside the other. Encasing all of them was the outer wheel, called the *Primum Mobile* or "First Mover," which, set in motion by God Himself, was responsible for the movements of all the others. The heavenly bodies on their wheels moved in such exquisite fashion that one aprocryphal belief was that they gave forth rhapsodic sounds in their turning — the "music of the spheres" — harmonies such as no mortal had ever heard.

One of the most famous statements of this universal order is that which Shakespeare gives to Ulysses in *Troilus* and *Cressida:*

> The heavens themselves, the planets, and this centre
> Observe degree, priority, and place,
> Insisture, course, proportion, season, form,
> Office, and custom, in all line of order;
> And therefore is the glorious planet Sol
> In noble eminence enthron'd and spher'd
> Amidst the other; whose med'cinable eye
> Corrects the ill aspects of planets evil,
> And posts, like the commandment of a king,
> Sans check, to good and bad. But when the planets
> In evil mixture to disorder wander,
> What plague and what portents! what mutiny!
> What raging of the sea! shaking of earth!
> Commotion in the winds! Frights, changes, horrors
> Divert and crack, rend and deracinate

The unity and married calm of states
Quite from their fixture! O, when degree is shak'd,
Which is the ladder to all high designs,
Then enterprise is sick.

Such a cosmos can be either the product of God's deliberate creation or a vast machine, operating eternally according to fixed laws. The Middle Ages had accepted the former theory, while the age of Newton, the seventeenth century, was to accept the latter. The Elizabethan period falls between the two.

It was not, in short, ready to accept the full consequences of a universe of pure chance, in which chaos was the law of existence and order the dream of man; but science had not yet reached a vision of pure mechanism — rational order without the necessary doctrine of deliberate creation. Copernicus had already put forth the idea that the sun, not the earth, was the logical center of existence, and in 1610 — virtually the year in which Shakespeare's major period ended — Galileo invented the telescope, which revealed a miniature model of the universe in Jupiter and its system of satellites.

The Renaissance clung tenaciously to the dream of order without the mechanistic rationality which science would soon impart to the universe. Many minds of the age sought to find acceptable substitutes for concepts sanctioned by the Christian interpretation of everything. For example, monarchy, once taken for granted as the "divine right" of an earthly kingdom to imitate the heavenly one, was now justified by Machiavelli's *The Prince* (1532) on logical, not religious, grounds; and Thomas Hobbes supported monarchy in *The Leviathan* (1651) as the inevitable consequence of natural human evil. Neither man would have based his belief on Scripture alone.

The Quintessence of Dust

But the real stumbling block was the medieval belief in order within the mind of man. The faculty of reason was God-given and put there for man to nurture and refine or else allow to dissipate. Emotions were to be controlled, as was bondage to the life of the senses. The beauty of the world was created for man's aesthetic enjoyment, but even this should not be indulged in beyond reasonable bounds. The sensuous music of Dante's verse in *The Divine Comedy* (1321) is somewhat antithetical to his supposedly moral purpose in writing the poem.

The Renaissance, however, accepted Dante as its child; his work accorded with new views of art and literature which made aesthetic rapture the goal of the humanities. Emotion was no longer suspect: "enthusiasm" and "vitality" came to be more highly regarded than "self-control" and "discipline." Renaissance man laughed and loved and responded to stimuli with freedom and delight.

This all-too-evident contradiction — that is, between the dream of order and the ideal of unrestrained living — evoked a cynical reaction in many quarters. The French philosopher Montaigne (1533–1592), whose works were translated into English by John Florio and published in 1607, expressed the view that man was basically irrational, driven by passions he could not comprehend or control except with the strongest and most deliberate effort of will.

> I would have a man to be doing, and to prolong his lives offices, as much as lieth in him, and let death seize upon me, whilst I am setting my cabiges, carelesse of her dart, but more of my unperfect garden.

Hamlet, which echoes much of Montaigne's pessimism, can be interpreted as the tragedy of a disillusioned idealist, of a young man who once believed in universal order, in the logic of monarchy and the sense of responsibility which power gave to people in high places, and in the possibility of a man's achieving self-mastery, suiting his actions to his rational thinking.

But the prince of Denmark experiences a number of startling setbacks early in the play. He learns that his uncle, the king, is an usurper and the murderer of Hamlet's father; that his mother may have been an adulteress; that the supposed universal order apparently destroys the innocent as well as the guilty; and finally, that he himself is a victim of scrupulous efforts to understand a world which may not be understandable. All of his talents (he is a scholar, a courtier, a soldier, a swordsman, and a poet) go for naught. What is it to be a magnificent individual if one cannot serve meaningfully in the scheme of things? What is it to be great if it means being consumed by the very fire that should light up the heavens?

At one point in the play, Hamlet sums up the warring sides of the Renaissance attitude towards man:

> What a piece of work is a man! How noble in reason! How infinite in faculty, in form and moving! How express and admirable in action! How like an angel in apprehension! How like a god! The beauty of the world! The paragon of animals! And yet, to me, what is this quintessence of dust?

Romantic vs. Classical Tragedy

Elizabethan tragedy is "romantic" when measured against the simplicity and structural perfection of the Greeks. It shares both the virtues and the problems of the Renaissance: it is vast, colorful, many-sided, sometimes orderly, sometimes too majestic for classical simplicity (the intricacy of the Vatican, for example, compared with the stark clarity of the Parthenon), and sometimes noisy, profuse, and chaotic.

To understand fully how undisciplined and complicated Elizabethan drama can be, one need only read a few of the works of Shakespeare's lesser contemporaries. To appreciate Shakespeare's own greatness, one needs only a handful of facts about the Elizabethan public theater and its audience. Shakespeare absorbed the bigness of his time and managed to transcend its chaos.

None of the London theaters of Shakespeare's time is still standing, and the familiar models and diagrams of the Globe are based upon a drawing made in 1596 of the newly built Swan Theater. Recent scholarship tends to cast doubt on the authenticity of such models and to consider other architectural possibilities. Whatever the details of design, there seem to be a few safe assumptions about the influence of the Elizabethan theater and its audiences on the kind of plays created during that time.

First, the audience was heterogeneous, comprised of all ages and levels of society, and Shakespeare catered to the tastes of his audience in a way that Aeschylus, Sophocles, and Euripides — writing for a different purpose — had not. For the rude and unsophisticated — the groundlings who stood in the pit as well as those in expensive seats — Shakespeare provided on-stage violence: the cutting off of a hand, the gorging out of eyes, and multiple deaths; and there were ghosts, witches, and ribald comedy, sometimes in the middle of a tense and very somber part of the play. Just before Cleopatra's awesome death scene, she has an encounter with a clown that would not be out of place in a musical comedy. Even Ophelia's tragic "mad scene" is not entirely above suspicion, as the pathetic heroine enters, singing songs that include some earthy references to human sexuality.

The platform on which the actors played jutted out into the middle of the pit and was surrounded on three sides by audience. This made two things impossible that were mainstays of the Greek theater: the somewhat static dignity of classical tragedy, necessitated by its distance from the audience, and the clear unity which this distance allowed. The closer one is to the action of a play, the more one wants to see and to know. Hence romantic tragedy capitalizes on intimacy with the audience and, at its greatest, achieves depths of characterization not even attempted by the Greeks.

Two Elizabethan conventions aid in the creation of individuals rather than types: the *aside* and the *soliloquy*. The former is a short speech delivered to the audience while other characters are on the stage who are not supposed to hear it. The most famous aside in the theater is the first line spoken by Hamlet; when the king, showing great outward fondness for his nephew, invites him to explain why he has been so sorrowful lately, the prince says for no one in the court to hear, "A little more than kin, and less than kind." In nine words Shakespeare is able to tell us much about the king, about Hamlet, the relationship between the two, and the probable direction of the plot.

A soliloquy is a speech of some length spoken directly to the audience while the character is alone on stage. Its purpose is to express the inner workings of his mind so that the audience will clearly understand his motives. Prince Hal's reassurance that his consorting with thieves and drunks is only temporary and that he will one day be ready to assume the responsibilities of kingship is a straightforward explanation, while Prospero's farewell to his magical powers has been interpreted as having a meaning beyond the play as if it were a personal statement by Shakespeare himself in his last play. The four soliloquies in *Hamlet* are notable examples of introspective soliloquies, and through them Shakespeare was able to delineate a complex inner life more fully than any dramatist has ever been able to do. Some Shakespearean scholars have even gone so far as to trace the development of Hamlet's character through an analysis of the soliloquies, thereby attributing a high degree of sophistication to Shakespeare's use of a common Elizabethan device, one that became almost inevitable because of the closeness of actor to audience.

Modern playwrights undoubtedly regret the loss of the soliloquy more than that of any other single convention. Eugene O'Neill, who was a tireless experimenter, had the daring to use it in his long drama *Strange Interlude* (1928), written directly under the influence of Freudian psychology. In O'Neill's hands the soliloquy became a means of baring the unconscious mind, but it succeeded in making the play more novelistic than theatrical. It requires nine acts and six hours of playing time for O'Neill to tell his story. The reason is obvious. When does the subconscious mind stop working? In such a drama spoken dialogue between characters becomes the real convention, a brief interruption to the flow of soliloquies. No dramatist has been willing to sacrifice as much theatricality as O'Neill did, and the demands of verisimilitude in contemporary drama have tended to relegate the soliloquy to oblivion. One finds traces of the convention in movies and on television, as the camera offers a close-up of a face and the sound track offers the inner thoughts of the character, and also in musical comedy, whenever a character sings a song that is supposed to objectify his feelings.

The soliloquy is a highly conscious ordering of thoughts. It cannot realistically embody the subconscious life any more than it is believable that a character could speak so extensively aloud. It remains the child of the Elizabethan playhouse, of a time when the labyrinth of the ego had not yet been delineated. Even so, psychiatrists themselves have studied and written about Hamlet and have expressed astonishment over Shakespeare's intuitive knowledge of human behavior and the workings of the human mind. Perhaps the unscientific framework from which Shakespeare worked was an advantage. The influence of modern psychology on the drama has too often resulted in unique characters, special cases, interesting clinical studies, rather than in a total awareness of man and his world. The most famous soliloquy in *Hamlet* begins "To be, or not to be: that is the question." It is doubtful that anyone will improve upon that as *"the* question."

If each soliloquy in *Hamlet* is taken by itself, it offers a rich poetic experience and dramatic intensity relative to its position in the play. But though many scholars have attempted to show a psychological continuity, *Hamlet* will always remain the least "understood," as well as the most popular, play of all time. It holds the stage because almost every scene works. If its ultimate meaning is obscure, its separate parts contain everything. The main plot — Hamlet's stalking of Claudius to avenge his father's murder — makes the play basically the greatest "thriller" in stage history.

The Elizabethan playhouse, with its bare stage, gave playwrights the opportunity to present a limitless number of scenes. In this respect the technique it inspired is similar to that of the movies, a medium for which Shakespeare might well be writing if he were living today. Since the platform represented nothing in itself, it could, through imagination, be transformed into any place and every place, battlefield, throne room, forest or moonlit garden. The Elizabethan playwright had to satisfy his audience's insatiable thirst for variety, so different from the limited subject matter and adherence to the unities of Greek drama. It is no coincidence that the same age which saw the birth of *Hamlet* also produced the world's first novels — such as Cervantes' *Don Quixote* (1605), written in the "picaresque" tradition of loosely connected adventures — the very opposite of classical structuring.

The Wheel of Fortune

Shakespeare's thirty-seven plays fall into three periods of his life, and it is customary to call the middle phase his "tragic" period. Though the problem of assigning precise dates to all of the plays constitutes a perennial challenge to Shakespearean scholarship, it is generally agreed that the decade from 1601 to 1610 saw the productions of *Hamlet, Othello, King Lear, Macbeth,* and *Antony and Cleopatra.* If this is the case, Shakespeare exploited and exhausted all of the resources of his playhouse and of his audiences in a very short time.

Though *Hamlet* remains the world's most intriguing tragedy, its creator did not stop there. He seems unacquainted with Greek tragedy, but nonetheless *Othello* has a more pyramidal plot than *Hamlet.* The reason is undoubtedly the story itself: Iago's diabolic scheme to destroy Othello by causing him to suspect his wife of adultery and finally to murder her. The death of the wife becomes a natural obligatory moment, unlike Hamlet's eventual killing of the king, since marriage itself eliminates most of the possible alternatives to the action. When Othello orders Desdemona to prepare for bed, she has a premonition of doom but cannot disobey her lord and master.

Confinement to the tightness of the classical plot was not something Shakespeare strove for. His next play, *King Lear,* has even been called the greatest work of man, for it combines form with Renaissance magnitude. Perhaps the least producible of all the plays because of its dimensions that do not fit easily into the boundaries of a stage, *Lear* has a vast theme and a vast structure that unites for once the warring aspects of the Renaissance.

Its hero is an old monarch who has been ruling for so long that he thinks of himself as infallible, immortal, and universally adored, a representative Renaissance Man. Little by little he comes to know that he is only human and that to be human means to be vulnerable to the blind cruelties of a universe which does not operate for the benefit of man. During a storm scene — a magnificent piece of writing — the old king, lashed by wind and rain and driven to pitiful madness, takes shelter in a cave along with his faithful court jester, who huddles against him for warmth. It is then that he, in his madness, reaches an enormous moment of recognition which became the conscience of the Renaissance and has reverberated through the centuries:

> Poor naked wretches, whereso'er you are,
> That bide the pelting of this pitiless storm,
> How shall your houseless heads and unfed sides,
> Your loop'd and window'd raggedness, defend you
> From seasons such as these? O, I have ta'en
> Too little care of this!

But the world which so punishes King Lear for his selfishness is not the world of blind chance which Euripides envisioned. It seems to proceed according to a vast principle of cosmic irony, ultimately as moral as the medieval view of creation. Perverseness rather than mercy is its central attribute, but paradox is based on order rather than chaos. For example, Lear reaches a sane view of his true unimportance only when mad; another character in the play learns to see things as they are only when blind. Lear's initial mistake was to regard his two evil daughters as being good and his only devoted daughter as being evil. The world of *King Lear* is one in which the apparent and the real cannot be distinguished; man is too limited in his capacities. He cannot presume to place himself in a central position, since his inner disorder is not a reflection of universal order.

The world of *King Lear* revolves endlessly with the clockwork precision in which the Middle Ages believed, except that its purpose is incomprehensible. It is as though the Renaissance had retained the image of the vast wheel and lost the identity of the mover. It is as though one were to ride a ferris wheel in an amusement park of today, enjoying the pleasant sensation of going around and around, only to look down suddenly and realize that the operator of the ride had abandoned his post. In Shakespeare's next play, the hero Macbeth was to express the terrifying image of order-without-purpose:

> To-morrow, and to-morrow, and to-morrow
> Creeps in this petty pace from day to day
> To the last syllable of recorded time;
> And all our yesterdays have lighted fools
> The way to dusty death.

If any theme can be said to emerge from Shakespeare's great middle period and to characterize his work, it is indeed that of the inevitable destruction which attends all those in high places. The turning wheel becomes the Wheel of Fortune, raising some to the top, while necessarily consigning others to the bottom — only to reverse itself at any time. Such a universe is not wholly without its morality, for the Machiavellians, those who deliberately perpetrate evil and those who become corrupted by their own power, can also look forward to a fall from the heights. Edmund, the villain of *Lear*, doffs his hat in respect to the mysterious governing forces of existence which have dwarfed him: "The wheel is come full circle; I am here."

When one thinks in terms of the Einsteinian universe with its unending yet bounded, its limitless yet curving, space, one must respect Shakespeare's vision of the Wheel as being worthy of the often misapplied term "universal."

"A local habitation and a name"

Though it is difficult to pin Shakespeare down, intellectually, and to say that a certain system of ideas definitely constitutes his "philosophy," it has become traditional to identify certain recurrent themes — such as that of The Wheel — by means of a close study of the imagery in his plays. An image is a group of words which create in the mind of the reader or listener a concrete picture whereby an abstract idea is made accessible to the understanding. A simple example is provided by *Romeo and Juliet*, when the heroine, expressing an ominous feeling of doom because of the intensity of her love, says:

> It is too rash, to unadvis'd, too sudden,
> Too like the lightning, which doth cease to be
> Ere one can say it lightens.

But Shakespeare's use of imagery is more than merely decorative and reveals a great deal about the ideas that were most frequently in his mind.

One was the idea of the theater itself. Apparently fascinated by what the human imagination could do to transform a bare stage into the forest of Arden or an island full of magic spirits, Shakespeare referred over and over again to the world of the theater. He found in it, it seems, a compensation for the instability of real life. The playwright does what is attributed in *A Midsummer-Night's Dream* to the poet. He

> Doth glance from heaven to earth, from earth to heaven;
> And as imagination bodies forth
> The forms of things unknown, the poet's pen
> Turns them to shapes and gives to airy nothing
> A local habitation and a name.

The "naming" function of the theatrical poet has remained one of Shakespeare's most important services to humanity. Much of our inherited wisdom comes down to us in the form which he gave it. It is not the wisdom of the great philosophers; it is sudden, piercing insight that comes, not from systematic reflection, but from the uncanny sharing of every man's experiences.

Yet even over and above the positive value of the insight is the enjoyment of the *way* things are said. The beginning reader of Shakespeare often robs himself of this pleasure because he is anxious to get on with the story; the language seems an encumbrance rather than something that should be paused over and responded to for its own sake.

There are, to be sure, many aspects of Shakespearean language that can be overlooked at first reading. Elizabethan audiences, with far greater toleration for intricate word play than audiences of today, no doubt enjoyed elaborate punning; and there are countless slang terms to slow down the reading process. In addition, the names for Elizabethan articles of clothing, food, sports and other items of everyday living are unfamiliar to today's readers, who may well be confounded by "And is not a buff jerkin a most sweet robe of durance?" Editors provide help in side-by-side or bottom-of-page glossaries, but it is annoying to read with such uncustomary impediments. It is just as grievous a mistake to assume that everything Shakespeare wrote is sacred as it is to suppose that he has little to offer us today. Perhaps too much, for example, has been made of the humor of the clowns in Shakespeare — particularly the gravediggers in *Hamlet*. Academic directors of the play are sometimes overly scrupulous and refuse to cut a word of the graveyard scene, even as they generally resort to many visual comic tricks in an effort to make the scene lively.

Then too, the grammatical complexity of Shakespearean poetry can be discouraging to an age raised on play and movie language that is largely monosyllabic and rudimentary in sentence structure. The reader who manages to understand what the words are saying should go back and enjoy the richness of sound, the majesty of rhythm, as well as the profusion of images which come billowing up from the page in never-ending plenty.

Shakespeare mainly employs blank verse — that is, unrhymed iambic pentameter (five repetitions per line of poetry of an unaccented followed by a stressed syllable), and it is always extraordinary to read a few lines for their pronounced rhythm and then to realize Shakespeare sacrifices neither meaning nor drama for the rhythm. During the famous prayer scene in *Hamlet*, the hero comes upon the king, kneeling in his chapel; he senses that here is his opportunity to murder him and so avenge his father.

> Now might I do it pat, now he is praying;
> And now I'll do't. And so he goes to heaven . . .

The second line is perfect iambic pentameter. Every other syllable is stressed, as is the case with these lines from Alexander Pope's *An Essay on Criticism* (1711):

> Unerring NATURE, still divinely bright,
> One clear, unchanged, and universal light.

Pope's lines boldly announce the rhythm. One reads each unit of verse consecutively after the other. The meaning is perfectly parallel to the rhythm. In Shakespeare's lines, on the other hand, the actor is forced to pause dramatically after "do't." Obviously a great deal of reflection precedes the second part of the line. Hamlet goes from determination to hesitation, as he realizes that the death of the villain in the state of grace would not be revenge for his father. Many writers have been able to achieve iambic pentameter. One might say

> Ah, now the king's at prayer and I can kill
> To get revenge for blood that he did spill!

But this would merely serve to indicate the peculiar genius Shakespeare had for keeping to the rhythm and yet making the poetry seem to be what the character would and should say, not what the verse allows him to say.

In addition to the dramatic pause and the image, other characteristics of Shakespearean language include verbal dynamics and listing. The former is a linguistic counterpart of what Beethoven does in music: moving from loud to soft and soft to loud or changing the pace without warning. For example, in the same speech Hamlet continues:

> Why, this is hire and salary, not revenge!
> He took my father grossly, full of bread,
> With all his crimes full blown, as flush as May;
> And how his audit stands, who knows save heaven?
> But in our circumstance and course of thought,

> 'Tis heavy with him; and am I then revenged,
> To take him in the purging of his soul,
> When he is fit and seasoned for his passage?
> No.

It can readily be seen that the "No" follows a sustained passage of mounting anger; it is sudden simplicity that works because great artists always seem to know the value of contrast.

Later in the speech Hamlet lists the various places or actions in which it would be better to catch the king.

> When he is drunk asleep; or in his rage;
> Or in the incestuous pleasure of his bed;
> At gaming, swearing, or about some act
> That has no relish of salvation in't . . .

Shakespeare likes to give the actor more to say than is absolutely necessary for the sense. There are always enough syllables there to take care of the emotions with a thoroughness no other dramatist offers. Modern audiences are sometimes embarrassed by the torrential passions which pour forth from the stage, because modern actors are forced into underplaying by the sparseness of prose that attempts to duplicate the real language of real people. Thus the complex of thought and feeling in these lines might, in a contemporary version, emerge something like this:

> HAMLET (grimly): I'll get him when he and Mom are —
> well, together. That'd be the best time.

The impoverishment of language, which is one of the main characteristics of modern drama, always reveals itself with greater intensity and shocking clarity whenever one reads Shakespeare for more than plot or listens carefully enough in the theater to discover the deepest, broadest treasure mine in all of civilization.

The Neo-Classical Audience

The theater audiences of London and Paris in the last half of the seventeenth century are almost as interesting as the plays they attended. They were special audiences of similar backgrounds — dressy, rich, well-educated, ostensibly reverent toward the classics, and embarrassed at any display of emotion which did not also teach. Their period, called "neo-classical" because of a conscious imitation of Greek and Roman models, lasted from about 1650–1750, and was the last time in history when the aristocracy dominated drama, though long before the middle of the eighteenth century, middle-class hostility to tragedy had halted its development. For an audience so much concerned with correct rules of social behavior, comedy was superior to tragedy, but while comedy taught by ridicule of the rule-breaker, tragedy taught by showing his unhappy plight. Neo-classical tragedy was orderly, careful about the unities, neat in its poetry, restrained in its depiction of emotions. There are few memorable characters, and even the universal laws they express sound today like platitudes.

Still, the plays of Racine survive to this day not merely as historical curiosities but for their own power. Most of the other neo-classical tragedies, however, serve as warnings of the danger of attempting to pour old wine into new bottles.

Modeling themselves on the ancient Romans, neo-classical audiences refined and cultivated the art of living well in one of the cultural capitals of the Western world. The exuberance of the Renaissance was simmering down to a stabilized class system. The groundlings who had paid their penny to see *Hamlet,* whose tastes had been so influential in Elizabethan drama, no longer had the right to an evening's entertainment, any more than they might have given parties or gone calling in the afternoons for tea and a round of gossip.

The Puritans in England had closed the public theaters down in 1642 because of what they considered rampant immorality and the altogether uncalled-for attraction of entertainment to iniquitous mankind, which might better occupy itself with working toward salvation. In 1660, with the restoration of monarchy, theater in England became one of the major upper-class amusements. In Paris the reign of Louiv XIV began a century of glittering cosmopolitan life with theater a major source of culture; French drama entered its classic period, reaching heights of articulation and elegance it has not equaled since.

Theaters became far more glamorous places of entertainment than they had been before. The chandelier, lit by candlelight, made it possible to have the stage lighted artificially. Theater-going became a night-time entertainment, from which the lower classes were totally excluded. One dressed extravagantly; one expected to be seen as well as to see. The new plays became the topic of conversation at all the "best" tables.

The change in theater architecture aided the new ostentation in the audiences. The Elizabethan playhouse had been round or octagonal, open in the center for purposes of lighting, and audiences stood or sat informally close to the actors. Seventeenth-century theater was a long, rectangular structure with a proscenium arch stage and the audience sitting only in front, separated from the stage by the frame which is familiar to all theater-goers of today. Curtains, which had been used in the Roman theater, were re-introduced and drawn between acts. The institution of the intermission became a social high point; even if the play were bad, there was always the mingling with friends in the lobby.

The frame stage permitted the introduction of perspective scenery, which had been the innovation of Italian architects and scene designers before 1650. Scene changes, possible for the first time, were exploited by super-showmen quick to see the commercial possibilities of the new medium. As a result, opera and other extravaganzas burst upon the stage.

The period had a new toy, and, like all spoiled children, audiences frequently were not able to get enough of a good thing. As a result, the "neo-classical" period saw the beginning of the theater's long decline, one which some cynical observers claim is still in process.

Neo-Classical Tragedy

Though the pleasure-loving aristocrats preferred tragedy, they had been taught about the glories of the classical past, and tragedy, as one of the glories, had reputable connotations. Tragedy became what opera is today: a cultural grace, nurtured because it was time-honored. The greatest tragedies of the period were, of course, not as popular as the more spectacular entertainments, which were usually quite the opposite of the controlled and polished behavior of high society.

Many of the neo-classical tragedies did not deserve warm audience support. All too often they were pale imitations, "rewrites" of old masterpieces by academic hacks who knew the rules but lacked the fire of genius. The impetus for copying Greek and Roman originals was provided by a literary philosophy which dominated the entire period: the belief that the "ancients" had already done everything worth doing and had said everything worth saying. For some the endlessly revolving Wheel which the Renaissance envisioned was clearly running out of momentum. Without a supernatural hand to guide it, any wheel would eventually come to a stop. Sir William Temple, employer and mentor of Jonathan Swift, was a proponent of the theory of the "Decay of Nature," which saw the entire universe running down and therefore the entire human race as being without a future.

In his *Essay on Criticism* Pope praises originality, when it is the product of genius, but not as something to be cultivated for its own sake. Most writers, he felt, would do better to concentrate on structure and the well-turned phrase — "What oft was thought but ne'er so well expressed." Theater neo-classicism, however, stressed the three unities of time, place, and action more than it did the Sophoclean pyramidal structure, which made a total assault upon the emotions. The social ideal of controlling one's emotions, of never allowing others to know the extent of one's feelings gave to serious drama the one original quality which the age was in a position to bestow; hyper-restraint, sometimes to the point of dullness.

The Roman influence became much stronger than the Greek. The Roman theater had had two antithetical sides, as did its seventeenth-century counterpart. One exploited the love for on-stage violence and massive spectacle, while the other (perhaps out of a solemn sense of duty) appealed to the dignity and sobriety of the audience. One characteristic of the chief Roman playwright Seneca (4 B.C.–65 A.D.) had been exhibited to Elizabethan audiences through such episodes as the blood-spattered fifth act of *Hamlet*. But Shakespeare had not imitated the other side of the Roman theater, also found in Seneca and in Neo-classical tragedies: long, sententious, didactic scenes. Moral problems were introduced, analyzed, talked about, the actors would change positions slightly, and more talk and moralizing followed. Among the many charges levied against Elizabethan drama by its snobbish descendants was its failure to provide sufficient moral instruction. Whether neo-classical audiences loved every last analytical moment of their tragedies, moral enlightenment they did indeed receive.

England's Indoor Tragedy and Show Biz

During this period England produced no tragedian of major stature, though in John Dryden (1631–1700) it had a skilled craftsman who was capable of writing every kind of play. In politics Dryden could be liberal or conservative, depending upon what was fashionable; in religion he embraced both Protestant and Catholic beliefs. His verse was meticulous; it scanned precisely and was filled with brilliant witticisms. In the theater he was adept in writing both audience-pleasing claptrap and academically reputable imitations of the classics.

As an example of the difference between authentic tragedy and its mannered imitation, one need only compare Shakespeare's *Antony and Cleopatra* and Dryden's *All for Love*, or *The World Well Lost* (1678), a unified play that deals with most of the same surface events that are found in Shakespeare; but instead of the Renaissance tragedy of the superman, Dryden's version offers the tragedy of the social *faux pas*. The lovers are guilty of a social indiscretion more than an outrageous assault upon the universe. They are egotists, but in a more limited sense. They belong to the neo-classical indoors not to the vastness of the Roman and Egyptian empires. They can be reasoned with, as in the famous scene in which Antony's wife, Octavia, brings her two little daughters to make a womanly appeal to Cleopatra's finer sensibilities. The issues which Dryden considered most important come to the surface unmistakably. In response to Cleopatra's assertion "I love him better and deserve him more" Octavia announces the high price Antony has had to pay for such love:

> You do not; cannot: You have been his ruin.
> Who made him cheap at Rome, but Cleopatra?

Whereupon Cleopatra's defense of her position is a classic statement of the case for the other woman in drawing-room drama:

> If you have suffered, I have suffered more.
> You bear the specious title of a wife,
> To gild your cause, and draw the pitying world
> To favour it: the world condemns poor me.
> For I have lost my honour, lost my fame,
> And stained the glory of my royal house,
> And all to bear the branded name of mistress.

All for Love is a well-wrought imitation tragedy of shimmering surface, precise pentameter, and carefully articulated problems. And it
clearly belongs to an age that cared a good deal about social reputation.
Its theme, the conflict between love and honor, is the best the period had
to offer; but the basis for the tragedy — the revenge of society on those
who transgress its code — is one that also would have served as the basis
for comedy. It is a highly specialized and sophisticated kind of tragedy,
one with subtle flavors, requiring a rarefied background or highly trained
tastes.

In addition to its narrow range as tragedy, *All for Love* might have
been guilty of what its audience was capable of doing: pretending a
belief in the "right things" without necessarily being honest. Dryden's
epilogue is symptomatic. In it he anticipates some of the objections that
might be raised against his work and concludes

> For should you raise such numerous hosts of foes,
> Young wits and sparks he to his aid must call;
> Tis more than one man's work to please you all.

In so many words Dryden has written the manifesto of show biz; nor
is it surprising since he was himself one of the major showmen of the
entire age. The neo-classical period often imitated the Greeks but invariably lived like the Romans, observing the same inconsistencies. A
Roman might have finished reading a treatise on the pleasures of sobriety
and then left for the Circus Maximus. The aristocrats of London, like
their Parisian counterparts, had their own occasional arenas of slaughter:
the theaters. And Dryden could please the tastes of the blood-thirsty as
well.

One of the most popular dramas on the London stage in the seventeenth century was, not *All for Love,* but rather Dryden's marathon ten-
act extravaganza, *The Conquest of Granada* (1670), an example of a
specious genre called "heroic tragedy." Its hero, Almanzor, is the familiar
Superman figure but rendered even more implausible than Marlowe's
Tamburlaine — so implausible, indeed, that, were Dryden writing now,
it is probable that he would have peddled the creature to the animated
cartoons. Almanzor is Achilles and Sir Galahad and Hercules all rolled
into one flamboyant package, destroying whole armies with one mighty
blow, yet speaking perfectly scanning verse. One critic has referred to the
heroic tragedy protagonist as the "libido" of the neo-classical age — a
reckless fighter and lover who transcends the social norms in a way that
the members of the audience could not. He is a distant ancestor of the
Byronic hero of the nineteenth century.

Dryden and the others who worked in the genre exploited the technical
potential of the new theaters. The scenery was lavish, scene changes
many. The art of costuming was developed to an all-time peak. Women,

allowed to play female roles for the first time, were exquisitely gowned and coiffeured and paraded before admiring and envying eyes. The classical unities, so scrupulously adhered to in the drawing room tragedies, were completely disregarded. Music and dance were liberally interpolated, whether their presence was dramatically meaningful or not.

Most egregious of all was the *tragi-comedy*, another genre unique to the period and common in Dryden's repertoire. This was a play containing two plots, one completely serious, the other completely comic, which normally had not the remotest connection with each other. In fact, the characters central to each plot were not related even casually. The genre represented a virtual admission that audiences of the period were hard to entertain, that writers had a better chance of appealing to them by alternating funny and sad scenes.

If this commercialization of the theater is regarded as the beginnings of show biz, the natural question arises: why cannot the Greeks or Shakespeare be included in the category? Surely the Greek amphitheater, with its seating capacity of up to seventeen thousand, and the Elizabethan playhouse, with its undisciplined groundlings noisily eating their lunch during one of Hamlet's soliloquies, were closer to public taste than an off-Broadway theater of today. There are even scholars who take the most cynical possible view of Shakespeare, seeking to account for every element in the plays in terms of audience requirements.

Yet show biz nonetheless has its proper beginnings in the seventeenth century. The difference is that at last the theater-goer had a legitimate choice to make. One cannot have show biz, or commercial theater, without having its opposite. Drama in Athens or in Elizabethan London could be as great as it wished, or as bad as it might happen to be. Not every surviving Greek tragedy scales the same heights as *Oedipus,* and Shakespeare was quite capable of having a major character in *King Lear,* ask, in response to a blood-curdling cry for help, "What kind of help?" There were, to be sure, private theaters in Shakespeare's day and university performances not open to the groundlings, but it is enough to know that the public theater tradition produced *Hamlet.* If one is to apply the show biz label to *Hamlet,* then the commercial institution is blighted forevermore by a former greatness which it will probably never come close to equalling. Show biz most meaningfully exists when it has a definite dedication to provide a certain level of entertainment to a public that can go elsewhere if it wants to.

In our time the movies and television are the dwelling places for show biz. It is hard for the live theater to rival the artificial but sensuously impressive hoop-la of a film like *Ben-Hur.* It is snobbish and altogether unrealistic to condemn such spectacles — at least for the reason that they *are* spectacles. Surely there are times when we want nothing more than to sit back and be amused, when we are not interested in a total emotional experience. There is nothing wrong with the showmanship of show biz provided it is the best around. When the story will not bear close scrutiny and the dialogue must be glossed over to hide the clichés, the audience has a right to expect nothing but perfection in all the technical departments.

Show biz, however, has become big business to such an unprecedented degree that it has some basic fallacies of which Dryden was innocent. It often tries to palm itself off as something else. Nothing is more disconcerting than to find a social message suddenly leering out from the middle of a noisy, fast-moving musical. Suddenly the whole thing is supposed to have a point. One has every right to question the integrity of a show such as *South Pacific* (1949) which begins by revelling in the uninhibited animal joys of Marines as they sing "There is Nothing Like a Dame" and ends by treating race prejudice in quasi-profound music and dialogue. Dryden at least left no doubt as to his intentions when he had somebody named Almanzor come stomping out on the stage.

French Classicism

In Jean Racine (1639–1699) the Parisian theater produced the foremost tragedian of the entire period. His masterpiece is unquestionably *Phaedra* (1677), which is by common critical consent the greatest single work on the French stage. All French actresses want to play Phaedra just as English-speaking actors keep Hamlet as their ultimate goal. Both plays, with their sensitive protagonists whose minds are tortured by introspection, offer the utmost challenges to performers.

As might be expected, *Phaedra* is a re-telling of a classical story — Euripides' *Hippolytus*. Like the original, Racine's version concerns a queen who falls in love with her handsome and honorable stepson. Struggling to control her passion, she is finally driven to confess her true feelings and to beg him to return her love. Out of Phaedra's inner conflict between love and honor emerges the major treatment of the characteristic theme of the neo-classical drama.

The work is deeply married to its age in one respect. In offering herself to her stepson, Phaedra commits the sin of immoderation; she behaves badly; she fails to exhibit the good sense that a lady of breeding should have. But it differs from *All for Love* in that Phaedra's problem is her own. She is trapped by an antagonism which is not the trapping of the social code, but that code transmuted into a personal ethic. Dryden's tragedy finally is reduced to a woman-to-woman basis; its tragic pattern is triangular, but in Racine's the conflict is internal. *Phaedra*, in common with the theater's greatest works, rises above its time.

The theme becomes reason against passion, which is broader than love and honor, because, while it belongs to the drawing room, it is characteristic of only certain of its occupants. Phaedra is a woman of inordinate sensibility, of exquisite self-knowledge — in truth the feminine counterpart of Hamlet. Though the Euripidean myth is followed almost to the letter, the force which destroys is *unreason* in an age *of* reason. Racine's heroine does not belong to Euripides' stormy and bleak world with its jagged rocks looming ominously against the sky. She is the product of a more advanced stage of civilization. She represents a period in which women possessed an equality with men unprecedented in Western society, in which they could be capable of as much self-control as men. Phaedra is educated and derives her queenliness from deserving it. She is expected to be the model of deportment.

The neo-classical period is at its best in the works of Racine. Borrowing more than mere stories from the ancients, his tragedies express that same stoic ideal, that admiration for self-mastery, which can be found in the teachings of Aristotle, Zeno, and Marcus Aurelius. Its contemporary child is existentialism, with its belief in the possibilities of personal salvation through the disciplining of the self and the personal acceptance of responsibility toward one's fellow man regardless of religious or social sanctions. Phaedra's inner conflict grows out of the social context, but one has the feeling that her standards for herself would be unchanged even if the context were altered. She does not need a book of etiquette to inform her of the value of self-restraint. Her suicide at the end of the play is the only recourse, since no possibility of happiness can exist for someone so hypersensitive to her own weaknesses.

Phaedra is not as big as Shakespeare's greatest tragedies. The doomed queen fights a quieter losing battle than does King Lear, who is brutally punished on the vast Wheel which turns all of existence. But Racine, knowing that the sky had been replaced by the drawing-room ceiling in his time, chose to develop in fine detail the stoic tragedy of the failure of the self-image. Its classicism — that is, its precise unity — keeps it from incurring the danger of excessive character analysis; but though it is undeniably the epitome of neo-classical tragedy, it also anticipates one of the problems with which contemporary dramatists continually have to contend — the loss of dramatic impact through a preoccupation with psychology. To appreciate *Phaedra* one must possess a highly cultivated theater-going habit and a willingness to listen very carefully. Most of the dramatic action of the play is imbedded in talk — elegant, dignified, beautiful talk — but not in surface excitement.

10 ❀ ❀ ❀

Comedy — Pure and Simple

Popcorn Fun and Critical Smiles

The Athenians invented the tragic theater but gave the world almost at the same time its first theatrical comedy. The first audiences, sitting on hard stone seats from sunup to sundown on any given day during the drama festivals, watched three tragedies and a comic afterpiece known as the "satyr" play. Little is known about this earliest form of comedy except that it was presumably very funny and very bawdy. The satyr, a mythological creature, half-man and half-goat, who chased and then deflowered pretty wood nymphs, was probably the ancestor of the playboy hero of a much later age of comedy. The ancient and honorable producers of the Greater Dionysia felt that their patrons, who had spent most of the day on tragedy, were entitled to go home laughing.

Comedy is more difficult to describe than tragedy, for it has a number of forms which work best under different circumstances and with different audiences. It is not, however, as the uninformed sometimes assert, the alternative to "serious" drama. All too often comedy seems to be exempt from the critical scrutiny given to other theatrical arts. In this area more than in any of the others the popcorn eater is likely to object, on the grounds that his one remaining safe haven has been invaded by the destructive forces of intellectualism. It is further argued that the analysis of the comic is likely to make it seem forever after unfunny. The student who had to read Max Eastman's *Enjoyment of Laughter* (1936) commented that, now that he knew how to enjoy it, he never would again. Freud has analyzed jokes right down to their erotic little souls and made it risky business for his readers ever to tell any.

But the value of being critically aware of whether comedy in the theater is *working* or not is to enlarge the sphere of one's potential to laugh. With comedy as with other forms of drama one can be involved and detached at the same time. One can laugh and also catch himself in the act of laughing. If he is sitting in a nightclub and roaring with the others at the silly vulgarities of a stand-up comic, he can realize the silliness without even breaking the rhythm of his guffaws. The difference is that the thoughtful person is able to go straight home and read George Bernard Shaw and find pleasure in what has been called "laughter of the

204

mind," while the popcorn eater is likely to persist in the delusion that comedy has no intellectual aspects whatever and is off limits to the highbrow.

The fundamental fact of theatrical comedy is that at its best it is not merely an escape from the cares and travails of existence. Historically it has not been altogether unintellectual; it has not been the opposite of morbid or a rose-colored plastic sheet thrown over the world. Very often it is more serious even than tragedy itself, the product of a brilliant and ironical observer of the follies of humanity who finds the human situation too sad for tears.

The immediate effect of the comic in the theater is to make us feel better about things. The experience of being in the theater with others, laughing with them, creates an undeniable sense of high spirits. Personal problems tend to seem less pressing than they might the next morning.

But there is a profound difference between being made happy and receiving a fresh perspective. To run to comedy as a means of "forgetting" is to ask for a false happiness that resembles intoxication — fun for a while but pain when it wears off. Each time one returns from a laughing holiday one is likely to find his personal problems seeming a little bit worse, much as the poet A. E. Housman describes the disadvantages of drink:

> Oh, I have been to Ludlow fair
> And left my necktie God knows where,
> And carried half way home, or near,
> Pints and quarts of Ludlow beer:
> Then the world seemed none so bad,
> And I myself a sterling lad;
> And down in lovely muck I've lain,
> Happy till I woke again.
> Then I saw the morning sky:
> Heigho, the tale was all a lie;
> The world, it was the old world yet,
> I was I, my things were wet,
> And nothing now remained to do
> But begin the game anew.*

Incongruity, the Essence of the Comic

All good comedy then has for its basic function to give us a fresh perspective by making us, at least for the time being, saner. Henri Bergson, the French philosopher, says in *Laughter* (1900) that we always laugh at

---

*From " 'Terence, this is stupid stuff;' " from "A Shropshire Lad" — Authorized Edition — from *The Collected Poems of A. E. Housman.* Copyright 1939, 1940, © 1959 by Holt, Rinehart and Winston, Inc. Copyright © 1967 by Robert E. Symons. Reprinted by permission of Holt, Rinehart and Winston, Inc. Used also with the permission of The Society of Authors as the literary representative of the Estate of the late A. E. Housman, and Messrs. Jonathan Cape Ltd., publishers of A. E. Housman's *Collected Poems.*

the same thing — incongruity or irrationality. From the clown slipping on the banana peel to the subtlest form of verbal wit, the comic offers something that violates our reason. It turns the world topsy-turvy for the moment and, in so doing, shocks us. The tension we experience from this shock finds its release in laughter. Laughing is the victory of reason over unreason.

But it does not have to be a guffaw; sometimes the release is an inward smile that is scarcely perceptible on the face. The value of the comic is to be measured not by the volume of the laugh but by the extent to which the incongruity offered is believable.

For example, having someone trip and fall when he makes his appearance on the stage could easily elicit audience laughter, because it is unexpected; anything we are not prepared for can be called an incongruity. But great comedy is a vision of the incongruities that really exist. Once we laugh at the tripper, we forget about him. Some people trip; most do not. But a pompous fool who affects an erudition he does not in fact possess *is* universal. Everyone has met such a person. Laughing at *him* is a richer, more satisfying experience because it protects one from being victimized by him in the future.

A sense of humor is perhaps a person's most valuable asset. People who lack it are likely to be susceptible to extreme fits of depression or to find themselves tied up in emotional knots. Knowing when not to take something seriously, because it is ridiculous, does not deny its presence, but it does promote a sane evaluation of it. Uncritical laughter — popcorn fun — encourages one to ignore and light-heartedly tear up one's overdue bills. A true sense of humor can help one to see the absurdity of being so heavily in debt, can encourage one to stay out of debt in the future; it does not suggest that one should forget the debts altogether.

The critical laugher is moved to laugh, then, when his sense of values is upset, when he sees or hears something that contradicts his notions of what should be. Queens should not sneeze in the middle of a dignified address to their subjects; people should not take literally a statement that is meant figuratively.

The important laughter of the theater can best be understood through this concept of *incongruity,* which runs through the works of the greatest comic writers, from Aristophanes to the contemporary satirists.

Satire, Classic and Modern

Theater began as tragedy, and comedy began as satire. Both have their formal origins in Athens. Out of the satyr play with its probably crude situations and lines emerged the work of the world's first satiric playwright — Aristophanes (445–385 B.C.).

Aristophanes was an angry young man of ancient Athens, a rebel who used the theater as a means of venting his dissatisfaction with the social and political trends of his time. In his lifetime the whole Athenian democratic experiment was beginning to come apart.

After years of enjoying her superior rank among the cultures of the known world, Athens began to suffer from the disease which inevitably catches up with all great societies — inner dissatisfaction. The philosophy of Socrates and Plato, for example, reflects an increasingly critical attitude toward the principle of democracy itself. And the comedies of Aristophanes reflect the disapproval by the young Athenian intellectuals of the long years of war — war with Persia, war with Sparta — of the blindness of the government, of the moral decay of society, and even of the deterioration of the arts, including the theater itself.

The word "satire," derived from the "satyr," can be applied to the plays of Aristophanes, who believed that the best way to make people conscious of what was wrong was to make fun of it. Bergson tells us that comedy is distinctly social; it is the revenge of society on all those forces which threaten its stability. People "laugh out of existence" the dangers to them and in this sense are made to feel better. He might have been describing the function of Aristophanic comedy. Satire is the classic condition of theatrical comedy, an art through which a critic of society communicates his wrath to his audience. It is one of the most devastating weapons ever invented. There is almost no defense against it, because it can make us laugh even at those things we normally respect.

Aristophanes' masterpiece is *Lysistrata*, (411 B.C.) which has remained one of the most effective anti-war dramas in theater history. Its plot revolves around the efforts of an aggressive female to stop the war against Sparta by committing the women of Athens to a no-sex policy until their warrior husbands call a truce. The purpose of the play is a classically satiric one: war is foolish, and a comedy can make everyone stop taking it seriously.

So simple is the plot, so convincing is Aristophanes' underlying condemnation of war as inhuman — because it is sheer nonsense for human beings to kill each other over things nobody really understands — that the play continues to serve in its original satirical capacity. The test of a great satire is obviously whether it continues to be relevant. *Lysistrata* will be performed so long as men find war appalling. On the whole, however, satire is not one of the livelier theater arts of today. It flourished only twice in all of theater history: once under Aristophanes and once more in the neo-classical theaters of London and Paris in the seventeenth century.

The art of satire has declined in our era for two main reasons: one, the effect of middle-class taste on values expressed in the theater; and two, the difficulty of getting enough people together who share the same viewpoint. Ever since the late eighteenth century middle-class audiences have condemned satiric comedy as being cruel and unfeeling. Theatrical comedy should be buoyant, full of high spirits, and unfailingly romantic. The modern "romantic comedy" as well as the musical comedy are both children of this attitude.

Moreover there is the danger of giving offense, a problem which especially plagues the American theater. What is amusing in Manhattan is tasteless in Iowa. Catholics tell jokes about Protestants, Protestants about Catholics, and Jews about each other. We live in a period of "in-group humor" which scarcely leads to universal satire.

Tensions are so great in our time that the satirist runs the risk of offending as many people as he influences. Even war has to be handled delicately as a theme in this Cold War era. *Lysistrata* may be enjoyed because of the remoteness of the Peloponnesian War, but some people were made decidedly uncomfortable by Terry Southern's *Dr. Strangelove*, a modern film satire on war. Although most audiences could no doubt have laughed at obvious incongruities like the opening shot of the loading of a giant nuclear bomb while a chorus sweetly sang "Try a Little Tenderness," politics colored one's acceptance of the burlesque portrait of an American president and the absurdity of competition in nuclear arms as a method of achieving peace. The sexual exploits of a prominent member of the Atomic Energy Commission seemed to be fair game for comedy, with lines such as "I told you never to call me here" spoken *sotto voce* into a telephone during a conference to decide the fate of the world; but characterizing the general responsible for dropping The Bomb as a dangerous lunatic might have caused high-level eyebrows to go even higher. While *Dr. Strangelove* did not horrify the civilized world, it was accused of enough tastelessness to indicate that the contemporary satirist must tread more lightly than did his ancestors.

During the thirties, for example, satiric criticism of big business was acceptable to huge segments of the population, but such criticism is now offensive to many ticket buyers with large incomes. Poking fun at labor and at the "little man" was — and still is — taboo. Nowadays, a critical treatment of American politics, such as the famous Gershwin musical comedy *Of Thee I Sing* (1931), would probably not be written or produced. There is increasing reluctance at least in popular drama to attempt the kind of outrageous treatment given to the political figures of that show.

The sharpest barbs at present are being hurled not from the Hollywood screen or the Broadway stage, but from the foreign cinema and the small theaters and coffee houses in Greenwich Village, San Francisco, and London. Groups such as New York's "Second City" have developed a kind of theater known as the intimate revue, featuring young, enthusiastic casts who work with improvised material and who, nightly, change their routines in order to keep up with any new developments that might need their "treatment." They present wildly funny sketches and sing witty songs about such topical subjects as barriers to civil rights, war, The Bomb, the draft, air pollution, and sexual prudery.

Much contemporary satire is labeled "sick," a term which has become increasingly honorable in theater circles. Sick humor proceeds on the assumption that it is going to be condemned by many and might as well be as shocking as it can. As a result it delves into subjects that once were reserved for serious drama, such as sexual promiscuity, drug addiction, even death.

The Loved One (1965), a movie version of Evelyn Waugh's novel, one of the first satiric exposés of the undertaking business, was not a box-office success, mainly because it dwelt incessantly on death. The film was a legitimate triumph of satire, nonetheless, for it found subjects that needed to be criticized: the conniving that goes on behind the somber façade of undertaking institutions and the generally unrealistic attitude towards death held by most Americans. The appeal of *The Loved One* to a limited audience indicated once more that satire cannot flourish without a homogeneous, urbane public.

The Principle of Comic Irony

It is possible for a comedy to evoke laughter without being pointedly satiric, and even satire must contain ingredients other than criticism. People do not laugh at criticism by itself. The comedies that have lived through the years possess basically funny premises: that is, the very idea which is central to the plot represents a fundamental incongruity. All comic ideas embody the principle of comic irony, a counterpart of Sophoclean tragic irony.

The comic idea must be more than merely the subject itself. Much of the wild comedy of *The Loved One* came from the unlikely theme of death, but the movie did indeed lack the simplicity of a classically funny story line such as that of *Lysistrata*. In the history of the theater there are few outstanding comic plots, revolving around a situation and a character that, even on the face of it, cannot fail to be irresistibly funny; and all of them are rooted in comic irony.

If we see a woman leaving a fancy dress ball and then turning around to wave goodbye to her hostess; if, furthermore, we see an open manhole behind her, directly in her line of movement, we begin to laugh. Should she say something like "I'll drop in one of these days," the intensity of laughter increases sharply.

Now, obviously there is nothing funny about saying that one will "drop in" — except in relationship to a handy place nearby just made for dropping in. The situation is a ridiculous counterpart to the opening moments of *Oedipus the King,* in which the ruler comes forth from the palace and proudly speaks his own name. There is nothing potentially tragic about a man's name — except in relationship to our knowledge of his inevitable fate. Both comic and tragic irony involve the making of a promise to the audience.

The Loved One has innumerable targets to its satire and offers no promise of its eventual outcome. The scene in which the young girl mortician, an ethereal creature who cannot bear the harshness of reality, embalms herself is bitterly funny and thought-provoking; but its principal dramatic value is that of shock, since we have not been prepared for it. Similarly, the conclusion of *Dr. Strangelove* finds The Bomb being dropped, as predicted, but the humor of the scene comes from the fact that the bombardier is a Communist-hating Texan who rides the bomb to earth giving the Texas yell. Modern comedy, satiric or otherwise, generally has to depend upon such outrageous surprises.

Aristophanes' *Lysistrata* makes the promise at the outset that the heroine will herself be unable to live up to the terms of her own bargain. All a character has to say is that life without physical love-making is possible, and she has committed herself to her undoing. The audience knows that the remainder of the play will test her ideals and looks forward with pleasure to her eventual commission of the same breach of contract for which she censures other women. The plot also demonstrates that suspense is as intrinsic to comic as to tragic plotting.

Every moment in *Lysistrata* is not hilarious, but it does not have to be. The controlling idea is deliciously funny. Its situations are rooted in the basic absurdity of the whole structure. Each scene shows a new development in the growing inability of the men and women of Athens to live without sex.

The distinctly uneasy sensation that everyone is trying too hard ruins many popular comedies of today. Gag line follows gag line almost without pause; targets are chosen at random, and instead of satire there is a parody of something already too trivial to be worth further attention. But the intent is movement for its own sake. Often it all resembles the sudden entrance of a gang of noisy gluttons into a room full of gourmet food. The pace is violent, the activity incessant, and the aftermath over-stuffed.

Especially on the screen, today's comedy often tries to do what the narrator of *The Glass Menagerie* did: it seeks to find in motion what is lost in space. Many films are trying to recapture the lost delights of the old Mack Sennett-Keystone Cop days — in which the outlandish speed in an automobile chase *was* an incongruity. Today excessive speed is so much a part of our lives that its exploitation for comedy usually falls wide of the mark. Cars whiz the length of enormous screens, their tires squealing from all sixteen stereophonic speakers, with guns blasting, tailpipes exploding, music crashing.

On the stage we are given rapidfire wisecracks and the physical racing around of the characters. Few plays of recent vintage have been able to achieve a totally comic structure or even a premise rooted in a fundamental absurdity. They have to keep providing new sources of humor.

Comedy based on sex has been popular since *Lysistrata,* but it concerns promiscuity more often than abstinence. Because there is no incongruity inherent in surrendering to one's desires the author is forced to contrive situations that will stretch out his plot and keep the audience amused. Stuffy parents arrive unexpectedly to visit daughter in her New York apartment — only, what to do with the young man who is shaving in the bathroom?

The British seem to have reached (and passed) a golden age of screen comedy. During the fifties Sir Alec Guinness appeared in a series of films almost certain to be classics of their kind: All were based upon a plot premise that embodied a definite form of incongruity. *The Lavender Hill Mob* (1950) concerned the attempted theft of millions of dollars worth of gold from the Bank of England by a ridiculous and unlikely set of thieves, while *The Ladykillers* (1956) featured a murderous quartet who pretend to be classical musicians, renting rooms from a sweet old lady who never seems to notice that they are thugs.

But there is still a difference between these films and the greatest, most enduring comedies of the theater. The principle of comic irony must be complemented by the presence of at least one memorable character whose traits are comic but at the same time typical of large segments of humanity.

The Comic Character — Single-Mindedness

Lysistrata is not a fool. Rather she is a dynamic, intelligent woman with the kind of awareness that is also suitable for tragic figures. What makes her comic is a single-mindedness in her outlook which detracts from the respect she should command from us. We are able to laugh when, at the eleventh hour, she fails the test because of her limitation. It is incongruity that a person should be obsessed; the human norm is still the one we have inherited from the Greeks themselves — the ideal of seeing things steadily and seeing them whole.

We find ourselves using this very principle in the evaluation of the people we meet. We say of this one, "He'd be so much better off if only he would . . ."; of that one, "It's impossible to talk to him on the subject of . . ." Whatever may be true of our own characters, we tend to admire most those persons who display total awareness, who never allow themselves to be trapped. If someone is not mechanically skilled, he should not try to fix a television set. Nobody irritates us more than a person who pretends to be an authority in a certain area in which he is incompetent.

It has been suggested that the Greeks, who invented the stoic ideal, did so because they needed to; that is, they admired moderation because they could so easily become immoderate. They respected self-control above anything else because it was not easy to attain. Perhaps this explains why they awarded prizes to thinkers and athletes, controlled minds and controlled bodies. This also explains why they invented tragedy — an art form that shows the consequences of immoderation and leads to a restoration of self-control within the viewer by purging him of emotion. The Aristophanic principle of comic characterization rests on the same foundation.

The seventeenth century, which was richer in comedy than in tragedy, applied a concept known as the *ruling passion* to human nature and considered this to be the root of man's troubles. Borrowing most of its standards from the Greeks and Romans, the age — at least in theory — strove to reach the stoic ideal, which was self-mastery, moderation in all things, the emotions securely under the hold of reason.

If the tragic protagonist possesses a tragic flaw, a blind spot which leads him to destruction, the comic figure therefore possesses a comic flaw which leads to his undoing, if not disaster. The most common tragic flaw is that of pride, while the usual comic flaw is that of single-mindedness. When pride is also involved, the comedy is even more delicious.

To take a simple example: the rotund social lioness with the huge stomach and the plunging neckline stands at the foot of the staircase and is heard declaiming in strident tones about something she does not like, "I won't have it. I tell you I won't have it." High above her, a clownish servant is trying desperately to balance a tray loaded with dishes of ice cream. We are laughing already. The woman is simply inviting a sudden visitation from one of those dishes. Her blind spot is not recognizing the danger. People should not say "I won't have it!" without checking to see if they are about to get it.

Nobody can be aware of everything all the time. Each of us has five senses, all operating simultaneously. It is simply not possible to be equally conscious of all five at once, so that a good deal of life is passing us by at every moment. Blindness is such a universal human failing that comedy was bound to survive. In other words, ever since it has been possible for men to say "We know better," there has been comedy, and there will continue to be comedy until it is possible for men to say either "We have reached perfection" or "We've stopped knowing better."

For all the difficulties it is having today, comedy has still outlived tragedy, perhaps because man secretly recognizes that his imperfections do not truly warrant the exalted stature to which tragedy once elevated him. Aristotle maintained that tragedy "aims to represent men as superior" and comedy "as inferior to their actual condition." This brief statement provides the clue to an understanding of comedy and its enduring popularity, for the exaggeration of single-mindedness which lies at the base of comic characterization helps us to feel better about ourselves than we normally would. It is as though one were to think, "I'm pretty bad about those things too — *but not that bad.*"

Comedy — even when it is not specifically satiric of something — is at its best when it embarrasses us by its insight into our own blind spots. The laughter we experience releases the tension of the embarrassment; hence we say that we enjoy laughing. Actually what we are enjoying is being saved from the embarrassment.

Henri Bergson calls this single-mindedness the mechanical element in human character. His contention is that we all recognize instinctively that nature is an evolving, dynamic force and that man in nature should be capable of constantly readjusting to new situations. The person who has a serious blind spot is really resisting change; he is not moving forward with the rest of nature. Thus he becomes a social menace — and comedy teaches the dangers of resisting change. Since nobody is able to be infinitely attuned to new things, everybody shares to some extent this basic human inadequacy.

Single-mindedness is the very evident foundation for the humor of this famous anecdote made popular by Myron Cohen:

> Two men, Henry and Joe, partners in a women's dress business, discover that they are nearly bankrupt. They have one more season in which to become solvent again. One day their dress designer comes up with a particularly striking new fashion; Henry and Joe, frantically eager to test its marketability, set their dressmakers to work. In their enthusiasm, however, the two partners give the dressmakers the impression that all of the existing stock of material should be used to make this one kind of dress.

> Accordingly, Henry and Joe are presented with fourteen thousand garments — all exact replicas of each other.

> The wretched men now hold their fall fashion show, with one model wearing the one dress; and, naturally, the potential buyers leave in amusement upon learning that no other styles exist. Just as all seems lost, however, an elderly lady, hobbling on a cane, enters and demands to see their fashions. The model is brought forth once again, and, to the delight of the partners, this last buyer becomes very enthusiastic about the dress. "The only trouble," she adds, "is that I am employed by the largest chain of department stores in the world. I would need at least fourteen thousand copies of the same dress."

> Well, of course, it so happens that Henry and Joe are able to fill this impossible order. But there is one remaining reservation. The buyer must fly back to the central office with the designer's sketch in order to receive a final okay from the store owners. "If you hear nothing from me to the contrary by Friday afternoon at five o'clock, you may ship the dresses to us," are the old lady's ominous parting words.

> All day Thursday Henry and Joe show signs of their gradual deterioration. They lose weight — even some hair. Their nerves become so tight that the employees are terrified to ask the simplest question.

By Friday morning a pall of doom hangs over the factory. Each time the telephone rings the partners become frozen with terror. Every knock on the door might be a messenger of disaster. By three o'clock they have walled themselves in their office, refusing all calls, unable to speak even to each other.

At five minutes to five, their heart beats wildly accelerating, Henry and Joe begin the countdown — out loud. The end, the absolute end, of their agony is approaching.

But at one minute to five, there is heard a loud knocking at the door. "Who is it?" asks Henry in a croaking whisper. "Western Union," is the efficient reply. The partners, the blood gone from their faces, exchange dead glances. Obviously there is nothing to be done but open the door; there is no holding off the inevitable defeat.

With the clock solemnly striking the hour, each man stares at the manila-colored envelope lying on the desk. Neither wants to be the one to open it. Finally they toss a coin, and it falls to Henry's unhappy lot to have to read the fatal words.

He looks at what is written on the telegram, and then suddenly a broad smile bursts across his face. With tears of joy welling up in his eyes, he exclaims: "Joe, it's good news. Your brother is dead."

This little story is a classic of its kind. The tension has driven Henry into the single-minded position of having only one frame of reference left; the news that half the world had just been destroyed would doubtless have found him as joyful.

But there is more to it than merely the blindness of the partners. The situation is not incredible. The passionate longing of the men for business success has its parallels in the life of everyone. Their hopes and fears are human and understandable and far from unsympathetic. The reaction of the telegram reader is an incongruity, but a logical one. We are really laughing from the embarrassment of understanding just how Henry feels.

The question might arise: why then is there not as much tragedy in the story as comedy? Does not tragedy deal with universal human failings? The answer is that laughter is possible because we do not have to face Joe's reaction to Henry's joyful news. It is probable that Joe would not share his partner's enthusiasm — since, after all, it is not Henry's brother who is dead. If he *did*, the story would lose most of its humor. Joe would then be heartless; instead of incongruity we should have perverseness. It might be human, but few listeners to the story would be willing to admit it.

The great comic figures all share a fundamental humanity; this is one of the reasons, for example, that Jack Benny has amused Americans for decades. The characterization he has created for himself is both incongruous and believable. He is tight with his money and afraid of growing older — both understandable weaknesses, shared by many, yet funny because of the extremes to which Benny carries them. The man who has been thirty-nine for about as many years used to delight radio-listening America on Sunday nights by his visits to the subterranean vault in which he kept his money, a vault guarded by a pallid creature who would usually greet his employer with a question like, "How is President Roosevelt getting along, sir?" When informed that FDR was just fine, he was likely to add, "FDR? Isn't his name Teddy?"

Single-mindedness is the comic essence of almost all the great characters created by Molière (1622–1673), the great French dramatist who was perhaps less of a satirist than Aristophanes, but who has given the stage more memorable single figures. It might be said that Molière is to comedy what Shakespeare is to tragedy. Each of his major works contains a protagonist whose ruling passion represents some universal comic weakness: miserliness, religious hypocrisy, misanthropy, hypochondria, affectation, Philistinism.

One of his masterpieces, *The Miser* (1668), revolves around the figure of Harpagon, an aging middle-class merchant, who cares only for his treasure of gold hidden in the backyard. No matter how much money he has, he keeps thinking of ways to get more or at least to spend nothing — even in the matter of marrying off his only daughter. At one point in the play there occurs a famous scene in which Harpagon describes to his son a man who is willing to marry the girl without a dowry. The son-in-law-to-be is nearly as old as Harpagon himself, but

   without a dowry?
He is mean and ugly — but
   without a dowry?
He is not really in love with the girl — but
   without a dowry?

Each objection posed by the son is given the same answer by the father — the extreme in single-mindedness. Later in the play, Harpagon's daughter elopes with her lover, and, when the old man is informed that his "treasure has been stolen," he nearly goes mad with grief. Then — very much like Henry who was so happy that Joe's brother was dead — Harpagon shows elation when he realizes that it is *only* his daughter that is missing.

Cruelty and Distance in Comedy

More than any other dramatist, Molière has immortalized the characteristic of affection or self-delusion as a comic trait. *The High-Brow Ladies* (1659) is a satire on women of high society who spend their lives systematically trying to be what they are not; and *The Would-Be Gentleman* is the classic story of the Philistine — that is, a person with money but with no innate breeding and taste, who aspires to these things but inevitably makes a fool of himself.

Monsieur Jourdain, the protagonist, is a likeable enough fellow, but Molière allows him to be maltreated in the play, allows him to be the butt of seemingly cruel ridicule. For example, at one point he is given a false title by his daughter's fiancé who, disguised as a Turkish nobleman, has decided to have a little fun with the man that thought him too lowborn to have as a son-in-law. The gullible merchant not only is forced to go through a preposterous ceremony but is beaten soundly by the fiancé's friends, who pretend to be his Turkish retinue.

One theory of comedy has it that laughter is possible only when our humanitarian sentiments are chilled. It is true that we cannot allow ourselves to see the comic figure as being *too* human. The comic flaw may be a universally human one, one that embarrasses us, but if we are to laugh at all, certain real aspects of the total situation have to be kept in the shadows:

> Even though Monsieur Jourdain is beaten, we do not believe that he is truly experiencing pain; he suffers no fractures or bleeding, requiring a physician.

> We do not feel that the ridicule of him is excessive or cruel because he is still richer than we are.

> Finally, it seems justifiable for Molière to have allowed him to become a fool because of his pomposity, his pretensions to a dignity he does not really possess.

Actual cruelty in comedy is not funny. In *Kind Hearts and Coronets* the charming murderer and his ten victims were such exaggerations of probability that the premise of the plot was acceptably comic. For the most part, the murdered people are not allowed to become our friends in the progress of the story. Neither they nor the method of death is close enough or real enough to make believable the painful agony of being killed. One character is a dull and doddering minister who takes the murderer on a brief tour of his churchyard, pointing out an example of "early perpendicular" in the architecture. Another is a lady who goes up in a balloon and is shot down by a bow and arrow. But the tenth and final victim is an intelligent country squire who is done away with in a fashion that is neither plainly ridiculous nor distant. The writer allows him to be caught in a bear trap during a hunting trip and shot in cold blood by the protagonist. It is not funny. It is necessitated by the plot and the fact that the author seemed to have run out of ways for murdering people with comic finesse.

Pathos in Comedy

The death of the squire is not tragic, even though it keeps the sequence from being comic. The business partners in the telegram anecdote are not tragic because we are kept at a respectful distance from the reality of the brother's death. But there *are* times when only a very thin dividing line exists between a comic moment and a tragic one, a comic figure and a tragic one.

A number of years ago there was a Charlie Chaplin revival in colleges and universities — not primarily because of the comic techniques of his films but because a great deal was made of the character made world famous by Chaplin: the little tramp, dwarfed by a confusing and perverse world, trying to hold on to his dignity. New interpretations sprang up, and the tramp became a tragic personality, sometimes the victim of capitalistic economy, but always the social misfit, the loner with whom the post World War II college generation could identify.

The presence of the tragic possibility behind the comic façade appears to have been almost certainly put there by Chaplin as he developed and refined his art. It can be an enriching experience — a double experience, in fact — for an audience to be moved to laughter and tears simultaneously. Few dramatists and performers in the history of the theater have managed to offer it.

Chaplin's situations are not silly. They are exaggerations, as all comic situations are, but they are rooted in some underlying sense of plausibility. It is hilarious when, during a howling wind storm in *The Gold Rush* (1925), Charlie's cabin is blown to the edge of a cliff. There is the comic irony of his preparations for going out, little knowing that he may plunge to his doom. The teetering cabin provides a firm basis for comedy, because there *are* howling wind storms in Alaska. Out of such respect for reality Chaplin went on to create the deeper comedy of *Modern Times* (1936), the bitter and cynical comedy of *Monsieur Verdoux* (1947), and finally the haunting sadness of *Limelight* (1952). By the twilight of his career Chaplin had passed far beyond the simple absurdities of his original walk and the rapid motion of the silent movies.

On the other hand, many have tried to be as deliberately tragi-comic as Chaplin without success. A close-up of the face of world-famous circus clown Emmett Kelly is an experience that is funny and sad and poetic. Kelly is a universal type: the pathetic creature who is forced to earn a living by being a freak. But many imitators have thought that the mere donning of a clown costume is enough to insure instant pathos.

The tragic overtones of a comic situation or character cannot be overly emphasized without losing the comedy altogether. When this happens, we have a right to expect the fullness of tragedy but usually do not get it. If we have to worry about whether Charlie Chaplin will really be killed as he steps from the door of his cabin, we might as well not see the film in the first place.

Comedy can be, should be rooted in the truths of human nature and experience, but the method of presentation must not be that of truth. The closer it is to stark reality, the more difficult it is not to become emotionally involved. A general law, then, is that a certain distance must always be maintained in comedy between the audience and the characters. Comedy fails to do its job when it forgets what it is and shows us too much to make sufficient detachment possible. There is a famous scene from Molière's *The Miser* in which the old man's gold treasure is at last actually stolen. Throughout the earlier portions of the play Harpagon has reacted so violently even to the faintest suspicion that he might have been robbed that when the dreaded event does indeed take place, he is given by his creator a soliloquy in which he addresses his stolen money as though it were a dead friend he was apostrophizing:

> my dearest friend, they have deprived me of you; and as you are taken from me, I have lost my support, my consolation, my joy: everything is at an end for me, and I have nothing more to do in this world.

If the money *were* a real person, Harpagon would be completely pitiful. But we suddenly realize that carrying on so about money is ridiculous. Harpagon reveals his extravagant single-mindedness when he demands that "magistrates, police officers, provosts, judges" be sent for to provide "instruments of torture, gibbets, and executioners"; and he adds "I will have the whole world hanged; and if I do not recover my money, I will hang myself afterwards." Molière safely maintains the distance between the audience and the miser, as he does between the audience and Monsieur Jourdain, the Philistine. It is always a source of pleasure to encounter an unexpected bit of pathos in the midst of an otherwise pure comedy, but the brief recognition of pathos should not be allowed to spoil our fun.

The Vanishing Comedy of Manners

Satire declined in the theater as the characters became humanized to the point of pathos. Neither Aristophanes nor Molière would have approved the practice of confusing the issue by promising the audience laughter and then adding tears, but the middle-class audiences which began to control the theater in the eighteenth century found satire cruel and vicious. While there are those today who dislike satire for the same reason, others believe that this change of heart has resulted in a disintegration of the art of comedy altogether.

Regardless of which side one prefers to take, there is a variety of comic theater which *has* all but disappeared: the comedy of manners. Depending upon an extremely homogeneous audience that was upper-class and aristocratic, the form flourished during the latter half of the seventeenth century in London and Paris. It is a play that holds up for admiration the way of life of its audience and reserves its most severe ridicule for those who do not belong. In its time it provided not only an evening of comic entertainment but an endorsement of the stratification and codification of society. Certain features of upper-class living might have been gently satirized, but the all-out Aristophanic war on everything would have been considered vulgar and hardly conducive to social stability.

While this period had Racine and the rarefied neo-classical tragic drama, it was best suited for comedy. Tragedy was, after all, demanding; it assaulted the emotions, and this was the golden age of high society with its emphasis on genealogy, etiquette, and the control of the emotions. It was also an age that had nowhere to go (except, eventually, into two revolutions) and probably did not wish to be reminded of the fact. Tragedy in the Greek and Elizabethan sense was unattractive; stories of deposed royalty and of noblemen who reach disaster were, naturally enough, not its idea of entertainment.

London and Paris in the seventeenth century admired and respected Greek art and philosophy, but they tended to imitate the Roman manner of living. Even as Rome during the Augustan period (27 B.C.–14 A.D.) had cultivated the art of civilized existence beyond anything the world had known before, so too did London and Paris reach the zenith of urbanity. Excessive leisure time made social events and social visits "productions" which were carefully planned and meticulously enjoyed. It was the time of the country estate in the summer and the town house for the "season," which was measured in terms not of agriculture but of parties, balls, opera, the theater, and the daily afternoon round of scandal-gathering.

The manners of the period were at an all-time peak of perfection. The term "refinement" developed the meaning it still carries, and aristocratic young ladies and gentlemen were educated in the social graces more than in practical "subjects." If one could execute a dance with stately elegance, if one could develop a reputation for being witty in conversation, if one's house were a little more elaborate than the others' and his manner of dress a little more ostentatious, then one ascended to the top of the list of preferred acquaintances.

But if one were a trifle awkward in the dance, or slow on the uptake in a fast-moving repartee, if one pretended to tastes that he did not innately possess, then he was a legitimate target for ridicule. Laughed at most, because secretly feared the most, were the Philistines (like Molière's Monsieur Jourdain) who had a great deal of money but lacked urbanity and who, by multiplying their kind, endangered the purity of society.

In short, the neo-classical period in London and Paris was the heyday of snobbery, and the comedy of manners was its official voice. In its purest form this kind of drama is characterized by a silly, complicated plot revolving around the theme of *pursuit* — the endless round-robin of the game of love, in which husbands chase other women, sex-starved widows chase young men, and goutish country squires chase scullery maids. But the plot action is only an excuse for the part of the play that the audience loved best, the part that is most difficult for modern audiences to enjoy: long sections of witty dialogue, introduced for their own sake rather than for the advancement of the story.

The enjoyment of wit demands a cultivation of taste, but so does the love of high tragedy. A theater-goer of today who can project himself into the age of the comedy of manners can find pleasure in the fact that he perceives the witticisms; he can enjoy the sprightly and elegant dances that are interpolated into the plot and which have a charm that transcends their historical period.

However, Molière has survived this time better than most of the other comedy writers of the period, probably because his humor is less intellectual than that of his contemporaries, particularly in England, where the standardization of English grammar was beginning to create that "verbal class distinction" of which Henry Higgins sings in *My Fair Lady.* Both in situation and in language Molière's art is rooted in universal incongruities. His single-minded heroes all represent characteristics that are still amusing to audiences today as much as they were to the court of Louis XIV.

Audiences in a democracy may sympathize with a character who, to the aristocrats, would have been simply a target of ridicule, while the affectations and cruelty of the aristocratic characters, acceptable to like-minded audiences of their own time, are not seen in as favorable a light today. In *The Would-Be Gentleman,* for example, a pair of lovers, a count and a marquise, are important in one of the subplots. Viewers or readers of the play who are unfamiliar with the comedy-of-manners tradition might find the treatment of these figures somewhat confusing. The count borrows money constantly from the merchant and does so by adroit double-talking which has Monsieur Jourdain actually feeling grateful for the privilege of being swindled out of a small fortune. At one point the count buys an expensive ring for the marquise with Jourdain's money on the pretense that it is to be a gift from the merchant himself, whereupon he gives the ring to the lady as his own present and admonishes Jourdain that it would be bad taste to ask the marquise whether she was pleased with the gift. As a result, the lady never knows that she is wearing an offering from the heart of one who is sick with love for her and who will never have the opportunity to reveal it. Such a hoax strikes the modern theater-goer as cruelty and the count an unprincipled fraud. But in Molière's own time the audience would have concurred that Monsieur Jourdain deserves whatever treatment he receives for even having the presumption to be in love with a noblewoman.

In London Molière's count would no doubt have become the protagonist of the play, for the British comedy of manners featured a playboy hero, an upper-class scoundrel who continually escapes from bankruptcy by extorting money by any means at his disposal. He has no scruples whatever and — to the middle-class audiences of later centuries — was even more reprehensible than the count because the rogue hero employed his body as well as his mind in order to get what he wanted. The typical plot deals with his efforts to support himself in the extravagant manner which he believes to be his natural right. The idea is that someone who is clever enough to survive handsomely without a fortune deserves the spoils of his conquest; for he is a marvelous conversationalist, a connoisseur of the arts, a gourmet, and, above all, a superb lover. To him every moment of every day must be lived as though it were an art form. He would rather be poor and have to live by his wits than be rich in a routine job; it is the game, after all, that matters.

Today, in slightly different form, the rogue hero is still around. He may even work for a large organization, something his free-and-easy ancestor would not have done, but if he is James Bond or a dozen other exponents of the modern ideal, he has many opportunities to live dangerously, love incessantly, and break most of the rules of middle-class morality. Perhaps he is just as necessary for our sanity as the representatives of human weakness which Molière offered.

But though one of the heroes survives, reborn out of the hedonism of contemporary society, the comedy of manners as a theatrical form is a thing of the past. Since the seventeenth century it has been found only now and then in the plays of a few dramatists. Richard Brinsley Sheridan (1751–1816) created the famous Mrs. Malaprop (in *The Rivals,* 1775) who was comical because she misused and mispronounced impressive-sounding words in her attempt to sound better educated than she actually was. She spoke of having a "supercilious knowledge in accounts" and of the "allegory" that slithers along the banks of the Nile. (Today, when Jimmy Durante does the same thing, we laugh with him rather than at him because he does not really expect us to believe he knows much.)

George Bernard Shaw, usually thought of as a thesis playwright, employed some of the elements of the comedy of manners in *Man and Superman* (1905), in which a forthright upper-class heroine pursued her unconventional hero to the accompaniment of witty dialogue, and in *Candida* (1903), which featured the comic treatment of an earnest clergyman, too busy with his attempts to help the community to recognize that his wife and a young, attractive man were talking of love. It is characteristic of Shaw to go only so far with the frivolity of the comedy of manners; in *The Circle* (1921) some years later, W. Somerset Maugham had a love triangle similar to the one in *Candida* — heroine, lover, and the preoccupied, somewhat pompous husband. But each author chose a different way of solving the heroine's dilemma, and Shaw's choice, characteristically enough, was on the side of morality.

Oscar Wilde (1856–1900) revived the tradition of elegant wit and managed to avoid Victorian sentimentality in *The Importance of Being Earnest,* which remains the most popular example of the comedy of manners. (The tone of the play is illustrated in this characteristic line: "When one is in town one amuses oneself. When one is in the country one amuses other people.")

Noel Coward (b. 1899) is the most recent writer of the genre. His comedies of the 1930's and 1940's were popular largely because they offered nostalgic visits with the British upper classes who were fast becoming anachronisms in a changing world.

Today, only remnants of the comedy of manners are found in the ridiculing of isolated characters in other kinds of plays. It is disappearing, if not dead, because in order to flourish, it needs a rigid class structure and a sense of frivolity that have vanished from the Western world. Moreover, its comedy is mainly of wit rather than situation, and since wit is the comic in language, the most subtle kind of comedy to enjoy, it depends upon the audience's ear for language and suffers from the current linguistic drought.

The Romantic Comedy

During the eighteenth and nineteenth centuries, comedies became increasingly good-natured. "Nice clean fun" became the province of "light" entertainment — as opposed to the wholesale lampooning of satiric comedy and the brittle wit of the comedy of manners. The new audience which filled English, French, American, and German theaters were mainly non-aristocrats who would have found a Monsieur Jourdain someone much too close to themselves to be a target of ridicule.

The favorite subjects of the new brand of comedy — the romantic comedy — were true love, love over money, love over thought, wholesome country people over morally disreputable and educated city people, emotion over intellect, and so on. The specific subjects change from time to time, but the species survives, with and without music. Without romantic comedy both Broadway and Hollywood would go bankrupt. Known in the trade as the "boy meets girl" play or movie, it is usually described by overly tolerant critics as "frothy entertainment," "a madcap romp," or "a delightfully zany evening." Far beyond its actual dramatic value, it has become one of the battlefields in the war between those who insist that the theater should do nothing but entertain and those who insist that the romantic comedy is an insult to intelligence.

A descendant of the medieval romance, which celebrated a Christianized and supposedly non-physical relationship between the sexes, the romantic comedy perpetuates the "made for each other" tradition. While there is nothing wrong with romance itself or with the idea that "some enchanted evening" everyone will find that stranger of his dreams, the endless repetition of the same plot has done little to advance the art of the theater.

The stage has kept alive the genre of the romance, but Hollywood has fed and fattened it. During the 1930's it offered escape from the depression for moist-eyed popcorn sharers, who loved to watch, for example, the trivial amorous entanglements of two adorable roommates who inhabited a rather sumptuous Fifth Avenue apartment and whose only ostensible employment was in the five-and-ten. The plot might eventually focus on a triangle, involving one of the girls, her steady boy friend, and a stranger she meets in an elevator. The man to whom she is engaged is a young executive trainee, a graduate of the Harvard Business School; he wears glasses and lives his life according to a rigid schedule. He does not believe in doing more than holding hands until after marriage. He has nothing to offer but plenty of money. The stranger, of course, is handsome, carelessly clothed, and broke; he has barely made it through high school, albeit with an inexplicable trace of a British accent (since Cary Grant usually played the part). All he has to offer is love. To a populace who had to worry about the next meal, the myth of spurned wealth was no doubt beneficial.

This was the era of Claudette Colbert and Clark Gable and their memorable *It Happened One Night* (1934), which gave high style to the myth and which did about as much as could be done with the romantic comedy. The plot is classic for the genre: wealthy socialite runs away from rich father who wishes to run her life; takes a bus from Miami to New York on which she meets Clark Gable; storm comes up, road is washed out, and the pair are forced to spend night in a motel, registered as man and wife; Gable is gallant in the epic medieval manner and puts up a blanket between the two beds; Colbert is hateful to him for the longest time, resisting his advances, much to the delight of millions of American housewives; the call of romance becomes too strong, and Colbert ultimately spurns a lifetime of security for a lifetime of love. Moral: hardship and privation can be bravely borne by any girl who has Clark Gable for a husband.

The intermediate phase of the Hollywood romantic comedy began in the late forties with the advent of new stars like Doris Day. Movie-goers were no longer so concerned about earning their daily bread, and the new heroine was a sophisticated, but virginal, career girl who neither sought nor spurned wealth. Economics was not as interesting as sex and the romantic comedy moved from the living room to the bedroom, while remaining as innocent as ever. In what purported to be a more grown-up brand of comedy, the Doris Day myth looked squarely at the facts of life and somehow managed to see beyond them. The moral code was satisfied, but the hint of the risqué was enough to sell millions of tickets nightly.

The romantic comedies of the late fifties and sixties, greatly influenced by the New York theater and an increasingly liberal censorship code, moved from the bedroom to the bed; the lie became, paradoxically, bigger than ever. A typical situation was that of *Born Yesterday,* the play (1946) and film (1951), which set the standard. The ingenue was a dumb but captivating blonde "kept" by a rich heel who eventually lost her to a poorer, younger, more marriageable man. The girl was the myth figure of the fifties, immortalized by Marilyn Monroe, who could be a "sex symbol" and satisfy the hunger of audiences for greater and greater frankness but at the same time remain vaguely innocent.

It is difficult to disparage any characterization which reaches mytho-logical stature, and nobody will deny that Marilyn Monroe and Clark Gable possessed an inherent fascination and magnetism that enabled them to transcend inferior scripts. We are fortunate to have in the films an imperishable record of their performances. Indeed there are times when one is forced to admit that, were it not for film, much contemporary drama would by now be forgotten. Yet one wonders whether a movie star can be considered a universal creation, like the comic figures of Molière, who have been interpreted and re-interpreted by many different actors; and one wonders whether the scripts of the popular romantic comedy, whether from Broadway or Hollywood, would hold up under the supreme test of reading.

Wit, Jokes, Gags, and Corn

In evaluating comedy, one must consider the enormous difference be-tween reading and seeing. The test of laughter in the theater is, after all, whether we have in fact laughed, but the test of the comic in read-ing involves recognizing the laugh-provoking potential of certain charac-ters and situations, as well as the comic principle in the language of the play. In the case of language, reading is sometimes more rewarding than listening. Oftentimes a skilled performer can, by vocal inflection, make an unfunny line sound as if it should provoke laughter. But the cold appearance of the printed page absolutely dares us to laugh, even to smile inwardly. When we cannot help ourselves, we know that the author has overcome a major obstacle.

Incongruity is the basis of all verbal humor; and when so much license has been taken that the sense of incongruity is all but missing, we are justified in looking elsewhere for our amusement. It is in the language of comedy that the greatest class distinction exists. Situations have some-thing in common with vocal inflections: that is, they can be made to seem funnier than they are. Even characterization can depend more upon the actor than the writer. A personality like Jack Benny usually transcends his material. But certain lines in comic drama have a classic ring to them;

others are tolerable, evoking mild amusement; while still others elicit groans from the sophisticated viewer. A talent for verbal humor is nearly as rare as a great poetic gift and should be revered almost as much.

The scale of comic language thus runs:

wit — the most subtle kind of incongruity; often fails to identify itself as humorous upon first hearing or first reading; frequently marked by irony

jokes — contains the principle of incongruity in a surprise climax after a build-up to an entirely different ending

gags — telescoped jokes; at their best in the hit-and-run method; will not hold up under analysis

corn — gags whose incongruity is too obvious; insults to the intelligence

From this ladder, it can be seen that the element of thought is a vital factor in verbal humor in that the fundamental appeal is to the mind. Even in the silliest gag, the assumption is made that the listener possesses a certain rationality, a stable set of values.

It has been pointed out that the two principal forms of irony in tragedy are Sophoclean and Euripidean and that comic plotting has its parallels. In the story of Henry and Joe, the dress manufacturers, a definite build-up of mounting intensity was created, moving towards the obvious defeat of the partners, moving assuredly towards disaster. The smile that crossed Henry's face as he read the telegram also has its counterpart in tragic drama. In *Oedipus* it occurs when the messenger from Corinth arrives to tell the king that his father has died of natural causes. Oedipus is greatly relieved to suppose that the prophecy has not been fulfilled. Even though we, the audience, know that the king of Corinth was not the true father of Oedipus, the king's false joy serves to make his eventual ruin even more tragic. With Henry and Joe, we assume from "Good news!" that the victory has been won. The knowledge that in this case victory means the death of Joe's brother is very much like Euripidean irony, which has been defined as a cruel twist of fate. The shock of this knowledge, added to the shock of Henry's altogether unfitting reaction, created the tension whose release is laughter.

On the level of linguistic wit, the same pattern can be noted. Oscar Wilde's *The Importance of Being Earnest*, which might well be the wittiest single play ever written, provides an example. The protagonist Jack Worthing is being interviewed by his fiancée's mother, Lady Bracknell, to determine his eligibility. At one point she asks "Do you smoke?"

JACK: Well, yes, I must admit I smoke.
LADY BRACKNELL: I am glad to hear it. A man should always have an occupation of some sort.

Jack's affirmative answer seems to promise disaster. Obviously one of the most powerful leaders of London society could not tolerate smoking. Lady Bracknell's endorsement, then, much like Henry's smile of triumph, reverses everything and seems to promise victory. But the reason she gives is Euripidean; it is perverse. It does not really mean what it says; it really states, "I recognize that you are an idler, young man, and that smoking is as far as people like you ever go in the direction of being useful" or else, "You and I both know that this class system is a lot of poppycock but that we are supposed to be glad when someone lives a life of nothing but leisure. Let's go along with the nonsense." The true source of the humor is the incongruity between the words spoken and the underlying meaning, but the irony has been made possible by the total structure.

Wit is seldom as effective when it does not emerge from such a structure, and this helps to explain why most of the wit that survives has originated in drama; that is, from the context of dialogue.

To cite another example from the same scene:

LADY BRACKNELL: Are your parents living?
JACK: I have lost both my parents.
LADY BRACKNELL: To lose one parent, Mr. Worthing, may be regarded
as a misfortune; to lose both looks like carelessness.

The knowledge that Jack is an orphan develops an expectation of a sympathetic response from the woman; and indeed her reference to the death of one parent as a misfortune continues to guide us in a definite direction. But when we come to "carelessness," we have reached a Euripidean moment again. In this case, however, the shock is from the outrageousness of her use of the term and her *lack* of sympathy.

The musical play *Fanny*, based on the "Marseilles" trilogy of Marcel Pagnol, has provided one of the most effective single lines in the history of the comic theater. The heroine, it is learned, has committed an act of indiscretion with her boyhood sweetheart, with the usual consequences, except that in this instance the situation is complicated by the young man's having shipped to sea for three years. The problem then becomes that of finding a husband with all due dispatch. When at last a willing taker is found in the person of a wealthy merchant whose only failing is his rather advanced age, Fanny tearfully asks her mother what would happen if she should marry the old man and then discover that she was not really pregnant after all. The mother replies: "You can get married without being pregnant. Many girls do."

Here we are led to think that the mother must be very angry with Fanny for being so ungrateful and will tell her something like, "How dare you put it on such a basis!" Instead her mother, being *very* motherly, wants to reassure her only daughter that marriage without an ulterior motive isn't so bad. We are not prepared for this position on the matter.

But — and here is a crucial point — the mother's position is not without its logic. It is one thing to come up to someone and say, "Did you know that many girls who marry are not pregnant?" There is no wit here; one would be met with a stony stare no doubt. It is only the context of the moment in the play that makes the line witty, and the *logical illogicality* of the line is another reason it is funny. The best forms of wit frequently contain this element. It is the element which usually accounts for the subtlety of wit. Sometimes the mind of the listener must do a double take; it says, "Now wait just a moment. That sounded logical, but . . ." Here, for example, is a remarkable bit of wisdom:

> Since statistics show that most serious railway accidents take place on the last car, why not leave off the last car?

Henri Bergson's favorite example of verbal humor is this little dialogue:

> MOTHER: Why do you always go to the casino to gamble? Don't you realize that you win one night only to lose the next?
> SON: Very well, Mother; in that case I shall go every other night.

The apparent logic of both solutions is like the apparent victory of Oedipus over the oracle of Apollo. In every case the triumph is short-lived. Oedipus is brought to disaster, and our sense of reason tells us that the logic in the anecdotes is a sham.

This particular technique of logical illogicality was a favorite of the great comic, W. C. Fields, who, in one immortal instance, was asked why both of his pockets were bulging. "In this pocket," came Fields' wry drawl, "I carry a bottle of snake bite medicine." He held up a flask of whiskey. "In the other pocket," he added, "I carry a snake."

The difference between wit and jokes is mainly that the former works best in a definite context, *one in which we do not particularly expect humor.* In other words, nobody asked Lady Bracknell to turn ironic in a serious matter like Jack's loss of his parents. In real life the people of wit are those who actually sneak up on us with their humor; it is the subtlety itself that is most gratifying. We enjoy the company of such people; our intelligence has been complimented.

Once during a perfectly serious lecture, a professor of philosophy, discussing circular reasoning, pointed out that this was something like the position held by the young defendant on trial for the ax murder of his parents who pleaded for mercy on the grounds that he was an orphan.

This little analogy could be turned into a joke:

> There was a young man on trial for the ax slaying of his mother and father. After he was found guilty and the sentence of death was about to be passed, he said, "Your honor, I think I am entitled to mercy." "Why?" asked the judge. "Because," said the boy, "I am an orphan."

No one will deny that the joke is funny, but it is *not* as funny as the professor's witticism.

Jokes seldom are as funny as wit because too much is made of them. As soon as someone comes up to us and says, "Have you heard this?" our attention is altered, and our defenses are raised. We think, "This had better be good." The advantage in wit is that the listener or reader is caught off guard; the shock of finding humor where it is not supposed to be creates an instant flare-up of tension. In a joke situation, the basic premise is that what follows is not going to make ultimate sense anyway; there is thus less chance for Euripidean irony.

This may help to explain why the vast majority of all the jokes people tell are rooted in sex. This remains the one subject which is itself an incongruity in polite society, the one subject which is almost guaranteed to make the listener tense before very many words have been uttered. An analysis of such stories is not really necessary since almost any reader may think of his favorites and then apply these tests to them:

1) Is a certain outcome to the story inevitable, only to be reversed at the last?
2) Is the eventual irony all too evident before we reach it?
3) Does the humor really grow out of the fundamental structure of the joke, or does it depend upon the incongruity inherent in the subject itself?

An affirmative answer to this last question may indicate that the joke is a bad one. Clergymen, for example, are notorious favorites for off-color stories, and this constitutes an unfair capitalization on the dignity of the cloth.

Wholesale absurdity should not be rewarded with laughter; greater pleasure stems from the subtle in comic language. The next time the reader laughs at a joke, he might stop and ask himself whether he might not be laughing just to be polite.

With gags there is likely to be even less of a reward for the attention given. Gags are low forms of wit. They represent ironies that are as subtle as a billboard. One hears them in popular comedies and musicals. They differ from true wit in two ways: 1) they are usually very short; and 2) they do not relate meaningfully to a total context, so that there is never any question of possible seriousness. Their only excuse for being is the sudden shock which they create at their best, a brief comic point made and then passed over very quickly.

The comic Bob Hope has for years been the undisputed master of the gag. Unlike the comic actor whose comedy is developed out of a total and consistent characterization, Hope specializes in a rapid-fire monologue with gag succeeding gag in almost breathless fashion. The individual lines seldom stand up under analysis; his success depends upon the quickness of speech.

The stand-up comics, one of whom is to be found on every television variety show, have become a dominant species in show biz today; most of them derive from the Bob Hope tradition. The difference between a good stand-up comic and a poor one is the extent to which the brief absurdity of a true gag becomes the preposterous or the silly. Tom Lehrer usually interpolates gags into his banter between songs, but they appeal to the intellect. When Lehrer, introducing a folk song, comments, "The reason most folk music is bad is that it was written by the people," he is not merely tossing in a gag. He is making a quick, incisive, and critical comment on the folk music craze, which, in his opinion, has gotten distinctly out of hand. Lehrer's method has something in common with that of Bob Hope: both adopt a relatively serious approach. They refuse to admit that they are about to come up with a gag. In this respect, they compensate for what gags are by providing as far as possible a context in which irony can operate — a context of mock seriousness. The comic who deserves our scorn is the one who makes silly faces at us or, even worse, laughs constantly at his own gags, hoping that we will at least laugh at his laughing.

The lowest form of verbal humor is corn. It is simply the joke or the gag that doesn't work. The incongruity is so obvious that no shock develops; there is no tension, and consequently no need for release. Corn was the stock-in-trade of the old vaudeville and burlesque comics, who would come roaring out on the stage to the blare of music and indulge in such low repartee as:

SAM: Do you know how many people are dead in that cemetery?
BILL: No.
SAM: All of them.

Or even lower:

SAM: Say, do you know where bugs go in winter?
BILL: Search me.
SAM: No, thanks, I just wanted to know.

This last example is comic irony in skid row. The trouble is that with "Search me" the twist that is coming has taken place before the words are spoken. Corn is thus a failure of the intellect to go the distance.

On nearly the same level is the pun. Normally it is a distinctly cheap way of begging for a laugh, as, for example, when the drama student was asked to go up to the stage and perform an extemporaneous scene based on the word "Viking" and began his speech with, "Vhy, King, vot iss wrong with you?"

Punning is at its best in the Shakespearean sense—that is, when the possible, but really illegitimate, implications of a word or a group of words are employed to make a certain point.

One of the famous sonnets of Shakespeare begins:

> When my love swears she is made of truth,
> I do believe her, though I know she lies

The first two lines contain about as much thought as there is in the entire poem: the poet is under no illusions but goes on loving his love despite her falseness. Reading further, however, one is rewarded by a marvelous pun in the concluding lines:

> Therefore I lie with her and she with me,
> And in our faults by lies we flattered be.

Since the early portions of the sonnet have dealt with the moral question of fidelity and infidelity, the use of "lie" in the second context is a Euripidean twist, a perversion of the original idea. It also serves to suggest that the continued relationship between the poet and his love is not wholly one of martyrdom, and the incongruity between the poet's pretended nobility and the actual pleasures he is experiencing is a classic source of humor. In addition, the word "therefore" promises a logical sort of conclusion, so that the pun itself is unexpected. Punning is better when it can be introduced in a serious context, so long as it is not too badly *out* of context. Some justification must exist for the distortion of word meaning. Shakespeare's second "lie" is ironic, but nonetheless relevant.

Somewhat akin to punning is the *double entendre* (statement with two possible meanings, one of which is clearly a perversion). The reader is no doubt able to provide examples from his own experience of occasions on which acquaintances have deliberately twisted innocent remarks around to cause them to have other (mainly sexual) applications.

Used judiciously, the *double entendre* can be fun, though it is certainly not as gratifying to the intellect as wit itself. It is a rather obvious linguistic contrivance and has little to do with logic. Molière's *The Miser* — which has provided us with examples of virtually every other kind of comic device — also contains instances of the double meaning. The old man's misunderstanding of "treasure" — supposing it to refer to his money when actually his daughter is meant — is one.

Extended, the *double entendre* becomes the technique of the *cross-purposed conversation* and also suffers from obviousness.

A young man, one of twins, had recently lost his boat in an accident at sea and was out for a walk when he was mistaken for his brother, whose wife had recently died.

"I was sorry to hear of your loss," said the passer-by.

"Oh, I'll get over it," said the young man.

"But not easily," suggested the passer-by.

"I'm on my way now to look for another one."

"What???"

"I was going to in any case; the old tub was rotten from stem to stern."

This little anecdote illustrates that when humor is bought too cheaply, it is like a bargain-basement item that falls apart very easily.

In fact, one theme has run throughout this chapter: the comic must be rooted in rationality. There can be no incongruity, no absurdity that is not measured in relation to what is congruous and not absurd. Humor that strives too hard — far-fetched puns, stand-up comics making funny faces — becomes as tiresome as the movie chase.

Like tragedy, comedy aims to humanize by providing the viewer with an emotional release. Its peculiar province is the exploitation of irrationality. It works because man *is* capable of losing his rational hold on things, just as tragedy works because man *is* secretly a hunter and enjoys vicarious participation in the pretend sacrifice. Tragedy purges us of our more dangerous potential, and comedy purges us of our irrationality, reminds us that it is the purpose of man to be sane and stable.

By exposing the insanity of the world, comedy has contributed immeasurably to making the growth of civilization possible. Above all, comedy has always been necessary to offset the tendency of tragedy to elevate man beyond his capacities. Somewhere between the two major theatrical forms the truth of human existence may be found. It is not likely to be recognized by those who are unacquainted with either form.

11 ❋ ❋ ❋

The Nineteenth Century and The Changing Audience

Three Revolutions

The neo-classical social barriers, the continual search for pleasure, and the aristocratic delight in satirizing Philistines like Monsieur Jourdain and Mrs. Malaprop, could not have lasted indefinitely. The absolute social order was maintained only at a great price: the suppression of the rights and privileges of countless thousands, who eventually asserted themselves in three revolutions: one in the American colonies, one in France, and one in the humanities.

Gilded lordlings of the seventeenth century who kicked street urchins aside for fun believed that the masses of mankind were evil and irresponsible. The street urchin was low, morally as well as socially, and closer to the devil. The people at the top were intrinsically "better" — more rational, more human.

Throughout the eighteenth century there were objections on both sides of the Atlantic to these attitudes of inherited superiority. Greatly influenced by the revolutionary ideas of John Locke (1632–1704), who had likened the human mind at birth to a blank tablet, the democratic philosophers argued that experience was free to everyone. Though differences developed later, it could not be said that the prince would always be better equipped to rule than a common man. Thus the makers of the Declaration of Independence spoke of "natural rights," while the leading intellectual force behind the French Revolution, Jean Jacques Rousseau (1712–1778) advanced the social contract theory, according to which government could be tolerated only for the benefit of all. The revolutionary spirit found great support, too, in *primitivism*, a belief that man in the state of nature was intrinsically good and that the sources of human evil were to be found, not in man at all, but in social institutions. Strong central rule, organized religion, and authoritarian educational theories all shackled the would-be free human spirit.

The word "reason" assumed shifting, sometimes vague meanings. In the neo-classical age "reason" had meant a human faculty for perceiving truth and falsehood — and was made a property of the select few rather than of the multitude. In the new age "reason" was often allied to natural instinct — an inborn faculty for perception which was nature's gift to man. "Reason" virtually became "common sense," a denotation it still carries today in popular usage. Knowledge and understanding, like property and social privileges, became the common possessions of everyone.

A further confusion was made between reason and emotion. Greek and Roman philosophy had made emotion suspect; it was an attribute of the lower or animal self and interfered with the pure operations of the mind, preventing it from seeing things as they really were. But now, emotion as a manifestation of natural instinct was interpreted as being good in itself, as being not divorced from reason but actually a form that reason could take. Thus when a person said, "I have a feeling I should buy this farm," he was not admitting that only impulse was guiding him, but rather that natural understanding had occurred to him in the form of a "hunch."

Faith in the superiority of emotion over thought is usually found in popular literature and popular entertainment. As late as the 1940's Annie Oakley, the heroine of the musical comedy *Annie Get Your Gun* (1946), could sing the praises of the unreflective, uneducated life in "Doin' What Comes Natur'lly."

Characteristic book titles of the eighteenth century were Hugh Mac-Kenzie's *The Man of Feeling* (1771) and Laurence Sterne's *A Sentimental Journey* (1768), both of which extolled the virtues of unabashed emotionalism and the simple life of the city.

The arts in general shared in the new acceptance of sentiment. Neoclassical stress on form gradually shifted to stress on content. The personal feelings of the artist were considered more interesting than the attempt to reach general, universal types and concepts. The new art justified and exploited the particular. In music, precise classical forms were stretched to permit a more extensive expression of emotion. Beethoven's late quartets profoundly probe the depths of a vast mind and are intensely introspective.

But the revolution also was a boon to popular literature and popular drama, since the primitivistic assumptions about the common man were so flattering. The new myth became that of the "noble savage" — the man whose natural habitat was in the depths of the forest or on some exotic island. Defoe's *Robinson Crusoe* (1719) had helped to popularize the myth, which was given a great boost by the emergent American writers of the late eighteenth and early nineteenth century. James Fenimore Cooper (1789–1851) contributed Natty Bumppo alias Hawk Eye alias Deerslayer, and that cat-footed son of nature who spent most of his time running away from marriage and other citified institutions became America's first major addition to the world's gallery of literary types.

Sentimentality and Melodrama

It is not surprising that America, as a child of the revolutionary spirit, should have become a major voice in the new art. American drama as a native form really began at this time. In the beginning — that is, during the seventeenth century — the influence of the Puritans had been too strong to allow much theatrical activity. Just as they had closed the London theaters in 1642, they forbade all formal entertainment in the colonies, though some performances did manage to take place. A performance of *Othello*, for example, was allowed in one community because it was given as a dramatized moral lecture on the evils of jealousy.

The first play written by a native American was Thomas Godfrey's tragedy *The Prince of Parthia* (1767), which was very much like the heroic tragedy popular in London a century earlier. Its themes include the love vs. honor motif as well as the newer, primitivistic concern for the corruption of natural goodness and the joys of emotionalism. The play is tragic in name only; there are gruesome happenings in it, but the conflict is entirely superficial, a contrived struggle between characters.

America's first comedy, *The Contrast* by Royall Tyler (1787), is more significant since it has a contemporary setting and characters who directly reflect the values of the period. The opposition suggested by the title is that of Colonel Manly, who represents the primitivistic hero: good, sentimental, and anti-intellectual; and Dimple, the fop: urbane, educated, and unsympathetic. The women are fragile creatures, capable of fainting at a moment's notice, utterly brainless, and (to a middle-class audience wishing its children to be ladies and gentlemen) entirely exemplary.

American theater, from its inception to the twentieth century, can be taken as representative because its European counterpart is not much better. The nineteenth century for the most part was temperamentally better suited to art forms other than the drama, which to serious artists was far too confining for intense self-expression.

But drama was popular. The middle class, which by now held the balance of economic power on both continents, crowded into the stalls night after night. Theater fell into the hands of the showmen, who were able to cater to the relatively simple demands of the new audience and convert its easily provoked delight into huge fortunes.

One reason for the popularity of the new drama may have been the need to escape from the very social restrictions that the revolutions had denounced. Indeed, far more dramatic than any stage play of the period was the story of how the natural man turned by degrees into the respectable middle-class citizen. The middle class began to impose a code of morality and social deportment which in its own way was as demanding and as snobbish as the aristocratic mores of the neo-classical age. When they went to the theater, the middle-class citizens loved to watch lurid tales of seduction and murder, so long as they ended up by re-affirming the wholesomeness of anti-intellectual folk, the sacredness of marriage and the home, the desirability of being emotional, and the corrupting influences of wealth.

The two necessary ingredients for popular success in nineteenth-century drama were *sentimentality* and *melodrama*. Sentimentality is the dishonest exploitation of "tender" emotions for their own sake — that is, whether motivated by the action or not. Its roots are clearly primitivistic and anti-intellectual. Plots which elicit a tear in the eye, a lump in the throat, a surge of joy in the bosom are unconsciously associated with middle-class virtues and opposed to those which require thought and are depressingly "morbid." Having a good cry at the theater or in the movies is still equated by some with enjoying themselves; and it remains a sign of a basically good person.

Melodrama, a kindred art, is the superficial division of characters into good and bad; it has somewhat more subtle modifications in the work of serious dramatists. It can take the form of a deliberate split between the sympathetic and the unsympathetic, with some important social implications. A modern hero can be a drug addict (as in Michael V. Gazzo's 1955 Broadway success *A Hatful of Rain*), who deserves sympathy because his wife is pregnant and he is the provider for a middle-class home which must be saved at all costs. For dramatic purposes he is a good man opposed by a completely rotten and callous crew.

For the changing audience of the nineteenth century, tragedy in the old sense was unthinkable. Even if it were to be relocated in middle-class settings, there still remained the problem of the tragic hero with his weakness of character that leads him to disaster. There could be no such thing as a sympathetic middle-class figure with a real flaw. If he held values contrary to those of his audience, he became a villain whose destruction was just, because "it served him right." The audience demanded theatrical rewards for those who adhered to its most sacred values. Nonetheless, it did throng to and endorse plays and grand opera that masqueraded as tragedies. *Carmen*, for example, has a heroine who is torn between her pure love for the simple and virtuous Don José and the sophisticated city-slicker, Escamillo the Toreador. She proves unfaithful and is ultimately stabbed to death by her original lover. Sin could be exploited as much as the author wished, so long as it was never shown to have been profitable.

Even more popular were stories such as that of *Emilia Galotti* by the German sentimentalist Gotthold Ephraim Lessing (1729–1781) in which a father murders his daughter rather than see her dishonored. This death scene suggests the tone of the whole play:

EMILIA: Oh, father, if I understood you! But no; you don't want to do that either. Because why did you hesitate? (*In a bitter tone, while plucking the rose*) There was once a father, who, in order to save his daughter from disgrace, stabbed her through the heart with the first dagger he could find — and thus gave her life for the second time. But all such deeds are from an age long past. There are no fathers like this any more!

ODOARDO: But there are, my daughter, there are! (*Stabbing her*) God, what have I done! (*As she's about to fall, he grabs her in his arms.*)

EMILIA: Broken a rose before the storm robbed it of its petals. — Let me kiss this fatherly hand.

Significantly enough, *Emilia Galotti,* like all nineteenth-century "tragedy," culminates in the death of the central character, whereas the Greeks and Shakespeare consider suffering, not death, the actual catastrophe. Violent death was so far from the normal, well-run household that it could safely be enjoyed in the theater without provoking any serious doubts about the everlasting fitness of things.

So appealing did theatrical death become that the melodramas often went out of their way to offer this popular feature. Death was attended by a sweet sadness that proved a high source of pleasure and undoubtedly made the reality seem even more remote. *Uncle Tom's Cabin* (1852) was the biggest hit produced on the American stage in the entire nineteenth century and offered, as one of its main attractions, the exquisite death of little Eva, followed by her ascension to heaven to establish the precedent of suggesting immortality, not death at all, as the reward for a wholesome life.

The deathbed scene offered an opportunity for a kind of wish-fulfillment. In *Cyrano de Bergerac,* the play that summed up the entire nineteenth-century sentimental theater and became its one masterpiece, has the longest death scene in drama, requiring nearly the entire last act. It takes place in the courtyard of a convent amidst the falling petals and the distant sound of singing nuns. Yet so appealing is the hero, so pure and true is his love for Roxane, so pathetic is the disparity between the beauty of his soul and the ugliness of his face that the work can lure anyone into its spell and make the most critical viewer wish that life were as sweet.

Nineteenth-century audiences loved the play of sweet sadness as much as they loved its comic counterpart, the play of pleasantness. They scarcely distinguished between the glow from one and the glow from the other. The play of pleasantness was all the period could muster up for comedy. Since satire in the classical sense was considered cruel, serious criticism of social incongruities was replaced by "gentle humor." Lower-class characters, who had been targets in the seventeenth century, became, at very worst, lovable dolts. In Tyler's *The Contrast,* for example, the hero Colonel Manly has a country bumpkin servant named Jonathan, whose characterization is representative.

On the one hand, Jonathan is not overly bright, and thus the audience has the opportunity to enjoy itself through amused condescension. He cannot perform the simplest act of multiplication.

> Why, as to fortune, I must needs say her father is pretty dumb rich; he went representative for our town last year. He will give her — let me see — four times seven is — seven times four — nought and carry one; — he will give her twenty acres of land —

But on the other hand, in this very scene Jonathan is being favorably contrasted with Jessamy, an English manservant. When the latter, who enters with an affected "Vôtre très — humble serviteur, Monsieur," questions Jonathan about his duties, the American replies, "I am a true blue son of liberty . . . no man shall master me: my father has as good a farm as the colonel." Tyler tries to have both condescending humor and genuine sympathy, a paradox common in the sentimental theater.

The affected foreigners are, however, fair game, as were Americans who had made money and considered themselves better than anyone else. Anna Cora Mowatt's *Fashion* (1845) is typical of the middle-class comedy of manners, in which the wholesome virtues — a modest home, a solid marriage, and thrift — are held up for admiration, while aristocrats and the nouveau riche are ridiculed. The names of the characters virtually tell all. The misguided couple with the acquired wealth are the Tiffanys, while a clerk with delusions of grandeur is named Snobson; the solid hero is Adam Trueman, and the foreign fop is Count Jolimaître.

Economic well being was hardly derided in itself. What the middle-class audiences deplored was extravagance and the gaining of wealth through inheritance, embezzlement, and any other means that did not spell hard work. The one exception — and it is a great one — was the economic reward that normally accompanied sexual purity. The exposure of a villain (illegally wealthy, city-bred, college-educated) by the hero could be counted on to result in the transfer of the ill-gotten gains to the hero and heroine, who fall into each other's arms clutching hundred-dollar bills as the curtain descends.

Hank Truhart, the Melancholy Dakotan

One might sum up the sentimental period in theater history and come to an understanding of why it produced no major play or playwright (with the possible exception of *Cyrano*) by speculating on the fate of *Hamlet* had some enterprising showmen thought to transfer its story and characters to the middle-class playhouses. The plot runs something like this:

> Hank Truhart, the somewhat fragile and bookish son of Farmer Truhart, has been in the East attending Harvard, when he receives a letter from his mother, Grace Truhart, announcing his father's death. Hank

leaves school and returns to the North Dakota homestead to find a very suspicious situation. His mother, whom he remembered as being a frugal, God-fearing woman, has become a "painted lady" and has married a foppish, terribly snobbish foreigner named Claude Eros. Whenever he attempts to ask questions about the nature of Farmer Truhart's passing away, his mother bursts into a kind of forced gayety, suggesting that Hank stop moping around and enjoy life. They have plenty of money, after all; why, he might even go to Europe with them the coming summer.

Hank, who still feels bad, visits the daughter of the hired hand, Olive Pollen, who secretly loves him and who hints that her own father may have some information about the mysterious death.

Hired hand Pollen appears; he is a lovable country bumpkin who loves to prattle on with many pious sentiments that bring a gentle smile to all who hear him. For example, even though he should know that Hank and Olive might want to be alone, he does not take the hint, but instead keeps prattling. Suddenly, however, Hank begins to listen to Pollen's gossip about an argument he heard between Farmer Truhart and his wife over some foreign fellow she was rumored to have taken up with. There was a shot, and Pollen, hiding behind a haystack, had seen the foreigner running from the barn. Shortly after that Grace and Mr. Eros had gotten married.

Hank knows now. He resolves to have it out with the foreigner, but Olive pleads with him not to go. Enraged, Hank throws her to the floor, denouncing her for impurity and declaring all women to be false and fickle. Broken-hearted, Olive goes crazy.

Back at the homestead, Grace and Claude are desperately packing in an effort to escape before Hank returns. But to no avail. The boy bursts in upon them, whereupon Claude — an extremely skillful marksman — produces a pistol from his carpetbag. A scuffle ensues, in the course of which the pistol is discharged, killing Claude. Grace is overcome by shame; she delivers a lengthy sermon on the evils of adultery, affectation, and extravagance, then drinks poison.

At this point Olive and her father arrive, and we discover that Olive was only temporarily insane. Her joy at being reunited with Hank is, however, short-lived; for the young man seizes Claude's pistol and announces that, since he has killed, he must pay his debt to society. Olive reminds him that he killed in self-defense, but Hank is too scrupulously honest to be dissuaded. He then shoots himself and dies in Olive's arms, after admitting that he should never have gone East to college and left the old homestead and the girl he has always loved and will continue to love.

But all is not lost. A handsome strong young man enters and announces that he is Manly Truhart, Hank's older brother, who had long ago left the farm to make his way in the world. Having become disillusioned with the fast life of the big cities, he is now content to be a farmer. Olive — undoubtedly noting how well-dressed he is and how he will have even more money now that he is the sole surviving heir to the Truhart and Eros fortunes — smiles warmly in his direction and takes her leave, hinting that she will see him again. As Manly grins and says, "I wouldn't be surprised, ma'am," the curtain falls.

Ibsen: Craft and Social Reform

If the theater had never risen from the depths of bathos and banality to which it descended in the nineteenth century, there would today be no choice other than sentimentality. But it did rise. And one man was responsible: Henrik Ibsen (1828–1906), who broke with tradition by his insistence on writing about important social issues of his day — no matter what groups he offended.

The extent to which Ibsen was himself the child of nineteenth-century theater cannot be overlooked. He used but did not invent "realism," the imitation of the appearance of reality. The box set, a collection of canvas flats joined together and painted to look like a real interior, was common throughout the nineteenth century, for the melodramas of the time dealt with contemporary people. The actors were idealizations of types one could meet in everyday life.

Ibsen's unorthodox and daring social themes were inhibited by another convention of his time, the well-made play structure, which had been developed by the French dramatist Eugene Scribe (1791–1861). The audiences who were shocked by Ibsen's subject matter were not bewildered by the precise organization of his works. The well-made play had become the triumph of theatrical know-how and was characterized by:

1) tight plots, with one event leading directly to another
2) a few basic character relationships, developed in an almost geometrical fashion
3) definite resolutions in a final scene that leaves no doubt as to the ultimate fate of all characters
4) contrived motivations, contrived situations
5) economy in total structure, so that every allusion eventually becomes significant, as well as every prop (If a jewel is mentioned, a jewel is later lost or stolen)

While not great and lasting, the well-made play was attended by a slick professionalistic competence that helps to explain its enduring popularity. Today, this competence is still found in popular melodramas which are in every respect relics of nineteenth-century sentimentality, but which at the same time represent glittering showmanship.

Ibsen's world, like his plots, is perfectly organized. The life he creates onstage works itself into certain clearcut, understandable patterns, capa-

ble of interpretation and even moral evaluation. Ibsen is the father of
the "problem" or "thesis" play, constructed with careful theatrical craftsmanship. He is the father of "professionalism" as the word is used on
Broadway today to refer to exquisitely crafted dramas which entertain
by their hyper-intensity and which also have something to say.

Modern thesis plays are tight, expert theater pieces, which work meticulously, scene by scene, toward a high point. They are set against
realistic-looking backgrounds and have characters that presumably could
or do exist. But they have become weak in their targets for reform, raising issues that give offense to nobody. Issues are as mild as greed, love-
less marriage, and non-conformity. Few current subjects of thesis plays
have the power to shock any more. But Ibsen was shocking to the conservative factions of his time which were outraged by his attacks on
hypocrisy in church, business, and marriage. He supported the adherents
of science, those who were making optimistic interpretations of Darwin's
theory of evolution, who believed in man's successful interaction with his
environment and man's capacity for introducing significant social changes.
To these proponents of "meliorism" — the belief that man can improve
nature — "science" and "progress" were always linked.

Ibsen and the new dramatists re-evaluated the playwrights of the past,
including Shakespeare, found them lacking in social significance and excessively conservative. While characters like Creon and Oedipus did
reach certain moral conclusions, they but affirmed what had already been
true from the start. The old plays began with certain assumptions about
man and the gods and returned to the same position.

According to Ibsen, drama should not celebrate old established attitudes; it should not be an affirmation of unchanging moral values. Rather
it should begin at one point and end somewhere else. In this respect he
made a more significant use of the well-made play. At its best the Ibsen
plot is a theatrical parallel to the inductive method of science — that is,
it arrives at a conclusion only after the evidence has been presented.

In *A Doll's House* Ibsen attacked the Victorian double standard — the
unwritten social law that gave a husband almost unlimited freedom but
turned the wife into a slave. To Ibsen this law was an *ideal,* which he
defined as a commonly held belief that was not a scientific truth; according to that definition, ideals were enemies of mankind.

Ghosts horrified audiences with its frank attack on religion and its
redefinition of sexual morality. A woman, avoiding scandal at all costs,
jealously guards the image of her dead husband, who had been a philan-
derer, only to learn that her son has inherited venereal disease from his
father. Ibsen's biology was erroneous, but he made his point about the
danger of living according to unrealistic ideals, especially in the famous,
unresolved ending in which the mother is forced to choose between mercy

killing and the torment of living with a feeble-minded son. *Ghosts* is a landmark of nineteenth-century drama.

In some of his plays Ibsen used a special form of irony. It is a device whereby the audience, believing it has comprehended the play's main idea, gradually becomes aware that the author has been driving at something else. The best example of Ibsenian irony emerges from a frequently misinterpreted play, *An Enemy of the People* (1881), which concerns an idealistic doctor and his crusade to close down lucrative mineral baths he believes have become polluted. The work, at first appearing to be the story of the man of integrity holding out against crooked politicians who would wrongfully make a profit by endangering the health of unsuspecting people, is in reality a much subtler study. The doctor accomplishes little in the play except to ruin himself and his family. He becomes a Don Quixote figure, whom we might pity but never admire.

Unconventional ideas require unconventional techniques, and Ibsen came to realize that the subtleties he sought could not be achieved by the inherited vehicle of verisimilitude and the contrived plot. With *The Master Builder* in 1892 he entered upon the final phase of his career, one which the faithful Ibsenites of today regard as his most important period. The last plays are of increasing complexity, heavy with symbolism and mysticism, conceived with the external appearance of reality but representing a total rejection of the convention of verisimilitude and its misleading implications. The theater was *not* supposed to show things as they are to the senses, but rather the underlying meaning of things, such as only the visionary could glimpse. It was for him to light the lamp and lead the audience into the shadows. Had Ibsen lived a little longer, he might have worked his way into the anti-verisimilitude movements which were already springing up by the time of his death.

Shaw and the Theater of Ideas

Because he lived at such a vibrant time and wrote about current issues in the tradition of the thesis play, George Bernard Shaw (1856–1950) reflects in his work the major currents of nineteenth- and twentieth-century thought. He shared Ibsen's belief that the business of the dramatist is primarily to affect the audience's thinking and lead to significant changes in the social scene. He continually whispers to us behind the play, "If you aren't interested in what I'm saying, you are not alive." Shaw dares us not to be concerned with his subjects.

So insistent was he for his ideas to reach as wide an audience as possible that he wrote complex and brilliant prefaces to his plays, which were sometimes longer than the plays themselves. He wrote stage directions that often take up several pages in print, delineating his characters with such precision and subtlety that it is doubtful whether his major creations have ever come to total life on the stage. Each of his masterpieces is dominated by a tremendous central figure who is Shaw's spokesman, and the actor who plays the part would have to match Shaw's own genius in order to do full justice to the role. The plays tax the efforts of most non-professional acting companies. There is still much controversy over whether the theater *should* be a place in which ideas become primary. When the shock value of a play's idea is diminished, when the central issue of a play is no longer current, the play may die along with the issue. What remains lively in Shaw's plays is the wit of his dialogue.

As literature, the works of Shaw remain valuable for the profound thinking which reflects the intellectual climate of their age, including, for example, the influence of Friedrich Nietzsche (1844–1900). Indeed, most of the plays mean more with a basic knowledge of the nineteenth-century thinker who taught that the world was in dire need of the Super-man. No one since his time has proved himself completely worthy of the title (not even Shaw who must have considered himself to be a major candidate!), but educated persons continue to find Nietzsche's ideas pro-vocative. Both the problem of how the masses of people in society should be organized and governed in the best interests of everyone and the proposed solution of the Superman have been of continuing concern to international relations and world peace. The frequently pompous but always intimidating position adopted by Shaw's supermen cannot be dis-missed without investigation. Andrew Undershaft, the superman figure in *Major Barbara* (1905), makes his living as a munitions manufacturer and calmly announces that the only thing to do with society is blow it up periodically and start all over again. Though Shaw does not intend Undershaft to be taken literally, his spokesman's analysis of the middle-class is prophetic and disturbing.

The wry cynicism behind the plays, the subtle twists and turns of Shavian thinking, the further refinement of Ibsenian irony — all of these make rewarding reading and solidify the position of Shaw in the front rank of English writers. What then can be said for Shaw the dramatist? Is he more or less dated than Ibsen as a composer of thesis dramas?

Even as Ibsen contributed his most provocative work to the theater when he rose above the confining convention of verisimilitude, so too is Shaw at his most theatrically vital when *he* abandons verisimilitude.

Shaw on the whole is less dated than Ibsen — despite the heavy literary atmosphere of his plays — because he allowed his imagination consistently freer reign than did Ibsen. Shaw was not averse to a liberal mixture of fancy, wit and realism.

Apart from the long speeches which convey his thought and which are found in all of his works, Shaw's favorite elements are:

1) The use of history and historical characters, re-interpreted by Shaw with more attention to wit than truth; the plays *Caesar* and *Cleopatra* (1898) and *Saint Joan* (1923) belong to this category;
2) The use of fantasy, as in the famous third act of *Man and Superman,* in which the protagonist dreams that he is Don Juan in hell, having a typically Shavian conversation with the devil;
3) Verisimilitude with a difference: no one in real life — that is, except Shaw — could be as crisply articulate and witty for such lengthy amounts of time as the Shavian supermen.

To appreciate Shaw's greatness, one should read a play or two by Sir Arthur Wing Pinero (1855–1934) and Henry Arthur Jones (1851–1929), turn-of-the-century contemporaries of Shaw, who wrote problem plays which are now hopelessly dated. Filled with the themes of social scandal and Victorian hypocrisy, they do not rise above their time because their plays lack the saving grace of Shaw's brilliant wit or Ibsen's irony. Their characters are all involved in the problems of the plays, whereas the Shavian superman stands apart, too superb to have ever lived; he remains a distant goal for humanity to aspire to. Nor do their stories ever reach the level of mysterious symbolism Ibsen attained in his later career. To read Pinero and Jones is to realize that the problem play *can* constitute a minor movement in the theater.

Professionalism Today

The plays of Pinero and Jones, unfortunately, do not mark the end of the nineteenth-century melodrama and sentimentality nor the end of the problem-play movement. Instead, the two traditions have blended together. Broadway and London theaters continue to offer slick, well-made vehicles for competent actors and actresses who know a portent when they see one and who are able to underscore every important moment for the audience; they appease the conscience of the critical viewer by having a little something to say. But the curtain falls; the audience goes off to continue its evening of merriment; nobody loses sleep; and the producer loses no money.

If anything, the tradition of verisimilitude is stronger than ever, having been adopted by movies and television and reared as their very own child. While Ibsen saw its limitations and Shaw refused to allow it to dictate to him, the modern professionalistic theater is now a grandparent from the mating of surface realism with the thesis play. The offspring can be termed "kitchenism" and is found on television soap operas, many commercials, and movies and plays that purport to show a "slice of life." Such dramas as *Dead End* (1936) by Sidney Kingsley and *Street Scene* (1929) by Elmer Rice as well as movies like Paddy Chayevsky's *Marty* (1956) were painstakingly authentic in locale, characters, and dialogue; and all made perfunctory comments on society without compromising their major purpose, which was to entertain and not disturb the audience. The thesis play remains a legitimate art form only so long as it treats a social problem seriously.

Contemporary kitchenism, a descendant of the nineteenth-century melodrama, carries on the honorable family tradition of appealing cheaply to the emotions. It suggests all too often a simple and sentimental cure for very complex ills. Chayevsky's Marty rejects his narrow-minded, dull background to find Cinderella in a dime-a-dance emporium and to prove, once more, that middle-class love is exciting and beautiful and romantic. Professionalism today can almost predict within a fraction of a second when the first glow will begin to nudge the conscience and warm the heart of the audience.

There are many serious viewers of theater today who believe that humanity can be saved, that society can be improved, and that modern social drama should not evade important issues. They are weary of inoffensive social commentary and would like to hear some bold new voices who have found new ways to be shocking, as Ibsen once was.

Masterpieces of the past are good for the past: they are not good for us. We have the right to say what has been said and even what has not been said in a way that belongs to us, a way that is immediate and direct, corresponding to present modes of feeling, and understandable to everyone.

Antonin Artaud

12 ❋ ❋ ❋

Modern Currents

If the trends established by Ibsen and Shaw had prevailed in the modern theater, an essential spirit of optimism would characterize the work of today's important dramatists and film directors. But a theater as they saw it, dominated by the belief that social change is both necessary and possible, has not prevailed. Twentieth-century drama is marked by an underlying vein of pessimism, one that gleams darkly even behind the shining façade of happy Broadway musicals and technicolored romantic comedies.

End-of-Century Despair

The optimistic interpretation of Darwin's theory tended to equate evolution with progress and saw nature as a force that could be developed by man for his own well-being. At the end of the century, English Victorians, for example, dreamed of an expanded British colonialism that would carry the torch of civilization to the remote and backward corners of the globe. Rudyard Kipling's voice spoke out loud and bold, vigorously affirming the glory of Bengal Lancers and gin and tonic. The American democratic experiment seemed to promise a new dawn of greatness for humanity. The eloquent poetry of Walt Whitman and of his disciple Carl Sandburg spoke for the cresting enthusiasm, exemplified in the title of Sandburg's first work, *In Reckless Ectasy* (1904).

According to the melioristic outlook, man had reached a mature state of development and had at last recognized the folly of warfare. The formation of the League of Nations following World War I was hailed as the greatest single achievement in history, proof that a natural instinct had been "corrected by a superior force: human wisdom."

However, much darker interpretations of nature in general and Darwin's theory of natural selection in particular had been advanced even before the first global holocaust, which, to the pessimists, seemed convincing proof that "progress" was merely a word. The American historian Henry Adams had pointed out that chaos was the law of nature and order the "dream of man." The struggle for survival — unending and pointless — was the common lot of all species, including man. Contemporary drama and literature are the products of those who took this darker view.

During the "gay" nineties cynical voices outnumbered the satisfied and optimistic ones. A century which had seen so much social and artistic change, which had witnessed the advance of science to a position of supremacy, which had fostered the epic conflict between science and Christianity, seemed to float down to its terminus with a brooding sense of resignation and despair.

This despair, however, was not always apparent. Rostand's romantic Cyrano brightened the stage as did the tuneful and merry operettas of Gilbert and Sullivan. But the title of one, *Utopia Limited or The Flowers of Progress* (1893), ridiculed British smugness.

Oscar Wilde's *The Importance of Being Earnest* caused theaters to ring with uninhibited laughter, but its gayety was deliberately concocted out of a hyper-conscious and meticulously adhered-to theory of literature: artsakism, or art for the sake of art. Wilde found life meaningless, purposeless and maddeningly dull. As an escape from it one might drink, take opium, read a book, or go to the theater. The value of the artist to society was that he provided the most effective means of escape.

A countryman of Wilde, J. M. Barrie (1860–1937), created "Never-Never Land" in his desperately entertaining escapist play, *Peter Pan* (1904). The impish young man — usually played by a woman — who refuses to grow up and face the world of reality has remained a symbol of the pleasures of evading responsibility and still beckons enchanted audiences into his world of fanciful mushrooms and "fierce" pirates. Barrie's theater is beyond meliorism but unwilling to articulate its pessimism.

The nineties, however, introduced many new writers who were far less evasive in their despair; others were learning their craft and were soon to publish or be produced. In the theater they were to shun the Ibsen-Shaw social crusade and become the founders of the major school of contemporary drama: naturalism.

"Heightened Realism"

According to philosophical naturalism, there is nothing real outside of nature; the laws of every form of life are the laws of nature. In itself naturalism is not pessimistic: it merely states its position. It does not even rule out the possibility of re-interpreting religion so as to place deity as a force within nature. Nor is it incompatible with humanism, for the superior faculties, the distinctly human faculties which the humanists say distinguish man from other forms of life are still within nature. And primitivism, which underlies most nineteenth-century drama, is a naturalistic position.

In the theater, however, naturalism has come to be a label specifically applied to a fundamentally pessimistic school of plays and films that deal with one major conflict: the opposition of man and nature. Nature, which is regarded as indifferent or even hostile to man, proceeds in accordance with its own laws, which do not necessarily coincide with those of human reason. Man himself is driven by natural forces that he imperfectly understands and cannot always control, but, if he *has* a faculty of reason that is special and unrelated to animal instinct, then he is doomed to go one way while nature goes another. Meliorism is a human ideal, for example, not a natural law.

The naturalists disagree with the position taken by the followers of Ibsen and Shaw. They interpret social "evils" as natural phenomena. We may not like everything that happens, but greed, warfare, and murder will persist. The perfectibility of man was an ancient dream from which the race has at last awakened. The theater has no business boring its audiences with social protest and the exposition of problems. There *are* no problems. There is just life, and the playwright is dedicated to showing it without disguising its shadows.

Naturalism in drama has been called "pessimistic realism," since it often seems to be trying to mirror the appearance of reality, in common with Ibsen's use of verisimilitude. But it becomes a confusing issue if such "realism" is insisted upon. Anton Chekhov (1860–1904) certainly deserves to be called a naturalist, but he freely uses symbols, as do Eugene O'Neill and Tennessee Williams, two American naturalists.

The confusion, however, disappears if theatrical naturalism is thought of as an underlying assumption about nature rather than as a specific technique. O'Neill, for example, could be a hyper-realist, often ponderously building up a detailed illusion of reality, as in *Long Day's Journey into Night,* but he could also write *The Great God Brown* (1925) in which the characters have symbolic names like Dion Anthony and sometimes wear masks. The label "heightened realism" is more suited to this kind of drama; for it better suggests what all of the naturalists, regardless of their individual techniques and devices, were doing: probing behind the surface of reality to show the natural forces that are at work.

If it were possible to eliminate the terms realism and naturalism altogether, the study of theater might be able to disperse the fog that ordinarily attends this phase of dramatic history. The fact is that both movements, that led by Ibsen and Shaw and that led by Chekhov, represent a theatrical renaissance and its major artists were primarily concerned with exploring the dimensions of the stage as a serious form of human expres-

A Victorian box set typical of late nineteenth-century verisimilitude in the well-made play.

sion. They were not concerned with staying within firm categories. All of them recognized that the world of the theater was not the real world. If verisimilitude, as the main convention inherited from the nineteenth century, worked, then it was useful; if a dramatist could not stay within its confines, then he did not.

To summarize the differences between these schools, the following guidelines may be useful; they will not be pertinent to every play of every playwright, but they will suggest certain parallels and differences:

Beliefs held by school of "heightened realism" or "naturalism"	*Rejected convention of Ibsen school or "realism"*
The world is not moving toward any recognizable goal. Nature does not keep improving herself.	"Well-made" play, geometric design; maximum use of every word and character to advance plot.
There are irrational forces in the world.	Box-set stage, with its suggestion of neatness and order.
People do not really say what they feel inside.	Clearly motivated dialogue.
The depth of the human mind must be explored; for instance, we can physically be in one place and through memory and day-dreaming be in many others.	Less psychological view of character.
The world is so complex and illogical, happiness cannot come through legislation or change in attitudes.	Definite solutions to the problems of society.

Chekhov's Microcosmic Drama

Chekhov came to the theater late in life, after a career as a physician. This spirit of scientific awareness undoubtedly influenced his revolutionary style of writing drama, for he did away with the play of one central figure in favor of the play which deals with a group of persons, their actions and interactions. Almost every character in a Chekhov drama is at one time or another an object of sympathetic understanding; he is made the hero of a tiny "microcosmic" drama that has a beginning, a middle, and an end in itself but does not become the basis for the total plot. Chekhov's plays are plotless in contrast with almost every form of drama that preceded them. They reflect the dedicated physician's concern for all of his patients, the insight which is gained through listening and observing, and the unwillingness to make moral judgments.

Ibsen, on the other hand, always has a central figure around whom a problem revolves; and the characterization of this figure usually embodies a moral evaluation. The heroine of *A Doll's House* is "right." The double standard which enslaves her is "wrong," and she is justified in leaving her husband. Had Chekhov written *A Doll's House*, he would have given equal time to the husband.

Chekhov's output was small, and his plays are not often performed. But they have great importance in the history of drama. They were responsible for the rise to a position of great eminence of the Moscow Art Theater and its director, Constantin Stanislavsky (1863–1938). The story of the meeting between playwright and director, their misunderstandings, and the eventual creation of an entirely new system of acting and style of directing can almost be taken as the story of theatrical naturalism itself.

Chekhov's first play *The Seagull* (1898) was accepted for production by Stanislavsky; but the director, who had made his reputation primarily from the staging of operettas, simply took the work at face value for his original production of it. That is to say, scripts were doled out, actors memorized their lines, the director instructed them as to when and where to move and gave notes to the cast on line misreadings and general character misinterpretations. But the play did not work in its first performance. To an audience accustomed to theatrical magic, to gayety or to colorful spectacle or to wringing-of-the-hands melodrama, *The Seagull* seemed lifeless, aimless, lacking in fiery characters and explosive situations.

But Stanislavsky refused to give up on a property he considered unusually interesting and rewarding. He re-staged the play and eventually made both Chekhov and his company world-famous. The Moscow Art Theater still has a seagull on its curtain.

What set Stanislavsky thinking in new terms was the extraordinary fact that the characters and situations of *The Seagull* seemed to go on living in his mind. Since there were no heroes and villains, there was no question of endorsing this character's behavior, condemning another's. It was, really, a matter of trying to understand why certain things happened. Stanislavsky found that Chekhov had not spelled anything out. He seemed to have created the broad outlines of characters, set them in motion in certain situations; and then they proceeded according to mysterious laws of their own being.

These laws, Stanislavsky realized, were those governing human nature. In order to understand people in real life, one had to know that when people did anything, the reasons they gave were not necessarily the ones that were acceptable or believable. Not only that, but in real life people seldom behaved as one would expect, because all too often people were observed, not as they were, but in terms of certain preconceived, stereotyped notions. He realized that Chekhov was being true to his own observation and knowledge of human nature, rather than to time-honored clichés that would be instantly understandable to theater audiences.

For example, in the opening scene of *The Seagull* a young writer named Trepleff stages a play he has written that is highly poetic, highly abstract, and highly incomprehensible. His mother and the other guests take it lightly; they refuse to listen but interpolate mocking comments. He stops the performance in an immature rage. We realize that he is both idealistic and untalented as a playwright. His leading lady, Nina, whom he adores, falls in love with a successful commercial dramatist who is present for the performance and runs away with him to Moscow in the hopes of becoming a great actress. Time passes. Nina, abandoned by the playwright, returns to the country and once again meets Trepleff, who has become a published author of respectable but commercially unsuccessful literary stories. In recalling old times, the wildly romantic Nina begins to recite the opening speech from the ill-fated performance of long ago. Trepleff leaves the stage abruptly, goes inside the house, and shoots himself. *The Seagull* ends.

Stanislavsky feared that presenting this play scene by scene would be bewildering for his audience, who knew *what* was happening but not *why*. Taken at face value, the suicide of Trepleff is without clear motive. He *has* become a writer, and he has the satisfaction of seeing that the girl who left him for someone else has come back to him. In almost any drama from the Greeks to Shaw, an action in a play is given a definite cause. Modern psychological interpretations of *Hamlet* may suggest that Ophelia's insanity is motivated by her frustrated desire for the prince, but the reason Shakespeare gives is the death of the girl's father. There is no justification for believing otherwise. The difference is that Chekhov often gives no reasons at all for what his characters do.

It became necessary for Stanislavsky to apply real-life criteria to the attempted understanding of all of the actions in the play as well as all of the dialogue. If in real life a person were seen sitting by himself at a party, speaking to no one, someone might say of him, "He is anti-social." Someone else might say, "He is an introvert." Someone else might say, "He feels guilty about something." The only way one could reach the truth would be to observe the same person in many situations and to determine what kind of behavioral pattern seemed characteristic of him.

Thus Stanislavsky reasoned that the characters in *The Seagull* did not cease to exist when they left the stage. There was a continuity to their inner life which he later, in constructing the elements of his famous "System" of acting, was to call the *channel*. He found that it was possible to take each character as a separate entity and construct a psychological pattern which would then serve to explain not only his overt deeds but also the comments he makes to other characters including those which seem irrelevant. Trepleff kills himself because Nina's recitation of the speech, intended as a tender reminder of the past, has the opposite effect. Nina does not know that Trepleff secretly considers himself a failure, regardless of his literary reputability. Nor does Trepleff know that Nina is herself a tragic failure. He has remembered her as she was to his youthful, idealistic self — beautiful, fragile, with a poetic mist about her. He tells her:

> You've found your way, you know where you are going, but I still move in a chaos of images and dreams, not knowing why or who it's for. I have no faith, and I don't know where my calling lies.

Nina, of course, does not believe this. But she does not tell him so, nor does she tell him how empty *she* is. Inadvertently she is the cause of his death.

In his monumental work *My Life in Art* (1924) Stanislavsky explains that his System is based on nature. Just as Chekhov followed the laws of nature in conceiving and realizing his characters, just as he allowed his insights to guide the course of his "plots," so too must the actor, by becoming a student of life, sharpen his own powers of observation and insight so that he may put himself in place of the character. He does not ask, "What did the author intend by this?" but rather, "Why must I, as this character, do this?" His guide becomes his own knowledge of the laws of nature. He is, in effect, asking, "What would *I* do in such a situation?" Sometimes Stanislavsky referred to his System as the "As if" method, while the contemporary theater, especially in America, has labeled it simply "the method." It has become the fundamental approach taken by a large number of directors and actors to almost any script.

The assumption behind both Chekhov's plays and Stanislavsky's System is that there is a common bond of humanity that links author to director, director to actors, and actors to audience. But much depends upon the performance. In the hands of amateur actors, who have not experienced enough of life to give them insight into Chekhov's characters, *The Seagull*, as well as the other three major works — *Uncle Vanya* (1899), *Three Sisters* (1901), and *The Cherry Orchard* (1904) — can be baffling to audiences. This is particularly the case when the plays are performed so as to try to tell a story. The typical response is, "What happened?" Only a few directors have achieved any success with Chekhov.

Chekhov himself was presumably unhappy with Stanislavsky's production of *The Cherry Orchard*, which saw in the general theme — the passing of the white Russian bourgeoisie — the basis for a modern tragedy. The author insisted that the play was not intended to be as somber as the Moscow Art Theater played it; and, in truth, as one makes a careful study of the play, one finds many microcosmic dramas in it that could be amusing or at least are tinged with irony. Chekhov's dissatisfaction underscores one of the prime difficulties with naturalistic drama: the problem of whose version of natural law a production is going to follow. "Method" actors and directors since the time of Stanislavsky have become notorious for being charged with a failure to realize what the dramatist wanted.

It may be that Stanislavsky was wise in making the definite decision to give *The Cherry Orchard* a tragic tone. The momentary dramas of this and the other plays are more enjoyable when they are seen in a total context that gives them meaning. It is, after all, not "pure life." No playwright can create this much on the stage. Chekhov's work has one major theme: the lack of parallelism between man's desires and nature's movements. But, specifically, nature takes the form of sociological and political changes. Over and over Chekhov returns to the idea, prevalent in his time, that a better future was on the way; and he sees the tragedy of the meliorist, who is deluding himself by supposing that nature works towards definite ends and that these are in accord with human desire. While all of his plays reveal that man is helpless in his environment, Chekhov's kind of naturalism works better with his bourgeois characters, who have no place to go but down. They are passive in nature because the changes coming in society discourage dynamic activity. They take refuge in memories of the past and in spinning illusions about the present.

There is a distinct "atmosphere" to a Chekhov play that is unique and inimitable. It is at once a permanent record of a particular way of life that has passed from the world and a melancholy dying echo of that life. At the very last moment of *The Cherry Orchard* comes the sound of the snapped string in a distant sky. What stays with the reader and viewer of Chekhov is the lyricism and the broad humanity of the playwright. His work offers an experience in compassion; as much cannot be said for every naturalist who followed him.

Deterministic Tragedy

The Cherry Orchard cannot be classified as tragedy — at least in the established sense of the term. It does not center about one strong hero, who is brought to destruction by a flaw in his character; and, because it does not, it helps to illuminate the problem of modern tragedy as a whole.

There has yet to be a modern hero who is a worthy opponent of nature, who seeks to battle her on her own terms, only to be destroyed at the last. Naturalism in general tends to subordinate man to nature and thus eliminates the possibility of having a dynamic hero. Chekhov's characters, for example, lack the freedom of choice which the heroes of both Greek and Elizabethan drama possessed. They are all inextricably bound up in a social network; the well-being of each depends upon someone else, who usually is unaware of it. Many of them withdraw into themselves at some point, only to take refuge in illusions. The withdrawal is a further symptom of the loss of will. Tennessee Williams' Blanche Du Bois, the heroine of *A Streetcar Named Desire*, sums up the case for the naturalistic protagonist when she says to the people who have come to take her to a mental institution, "I have always depended on the kindness of strangers." We are to pity her, as we pity the ill-fated bourgeoisie in Chekhov; we are filled with compassion.

Determinist playwrights and film-makers stress the bitterness of life, the cruelty of the forces which overwhelm man, and man's enduring need for pity. They differ from Chekhov in that they are not as neutral in their attitude toward the destructive force. Chekhov refused to place blame anywhere. Nature is never regarded as hostile in herself, nor is society or the coming revolution. Chekhov once remarked that evil flows through people; it is the result of some inexplicable human chemistry that is just all wrong. But he never spells anything out; he offers the conditions of life with a stoic calm.

Deterministic tragedy stresses the process of destruction itself, and it usually proceeds from a more defined source — social environment, the economic system, or the biological urges within man. Even when the force is internal, however, there is always assumed to be an irreducible human essence that is being tragically invaded and devoured and that makes our pity worthwhile — as though man might possibly be born with will and the potential for doing something with his life, yet can only go so far before the virus attacks.

The work of three American dramatists — Eugene O'Neill (1888–1953), Tennessee Williams (born 1914), and Arthur Miller (born 1916) illustrates the nature of deterministic tragedy; and though it differs sharply from that of the classical and Elizabethan periods by robbing its heroes of the chance to engineer their own doom, it may well be the only possible tragic response available to modern dramatists.

Deterministic tragedy is humanitarian rather than humanistic. Its protagonists are not responsible for what happens to them; they are victims of the irresponsibility of existence. Oedipus and Hamlet asked no quarter. They set high standards for themselves and failed to measure up to them. O'Neill, Williams, and Miller offer compassionate portraits of unhappy souls who deserve our sympathy because, presumably, all of us are equally doomed. Theirs is the tragedy of an equalitarian age.

Because of this shared doom, a major problem is that of deciding who is worth writing a play about. Why this man, not that? The work which first brought O'Neill to fame suggests one of the strongest appeals of deterministic tragedy: its theatrical inventiveness and its exploitation of the technical resources of the modern stage. In *The Emperor Jones* (1920) O'Neill makes his impact on the audience through novelty of presentation.

The work established O'Neill's reputation as an innovator. The setting is the subconscious mind of a Negro, whose fast-talk artistry has helped him become lord and master of an uncharted island in the West Indies. Having overstepped his bounds and become a tyrant, Jones is being pursued all through the play by a number of forces: those who wish to depose him, as well as the more subtle and dangerous enemies — his own superstitions. The momentum of the play toward Jones's destruction is one of the most famous in modern drama, for it is accompanied by the ever-intensifying rhythms of tom-toms.

The play offers a nearly perfect example of yet another element of theater which determinism can provide by its very point of view —

namely, structure. The story of a Negro overlord, uneducated and presumptuous, would not in itself suggest the means of exciting a theater audience; but what really destroys Jones is his own primitive origins, the fears and superstitions which come alive as he plunges deeper into the jungle to escape his pursuers. The increasing boom-boom of the primitive self — the *id* in Freudian psychology — permits O'Neill to return to the ancient plot of the pretend sacrifice, the very plot from which formal tragedy was born.

Death of a Salesman and *A Streetcar Named Desire* also make liberal use of technical effects in an effort to elevate their subjects above the ordinary. Miller, in particular, whose theory of tragedy specifically insists that only the common citizen is a worthy protagonist for our times, surrounds his Willy Loman with a poetic production. From the haunting sound of the distant flute which begins the play, to the epilogue, in which Linda Loman places a simple wreath on the floor, stage front, the place where Willy's grave is supposed to be, the production never ceases to work upon the audience's emotions.

Lighting, music, and a striking setting also provide the basis for *Streetcar*. The convention of verisimilitude within which Chekhov mainly worked is no longer sufficient. If Williams is to establish Blanche Du Bois as extraordinary enough to write a tragedy about, the theatrical context must help to distinguish her. The locale of the play itself, the French Quarter in New Orleans, has a kind of ready-made theatricality about it, with its decadent architecture and its strange street cries like "Flowers for the dead" which Williams's heroine hears just before the catastrophe.

The sex drive itself gives Williams the chance to employ the pyramidal structure. From the moment Blanche arrives at her sister's flat and meets Stanley Kowalski, the fierce physical attraction of the man becomes the antagonist that slowly destroys her. Stanley is merely the embodiment of the animal in man, the sensuality with which Williams is rather constantly preoccupied, but at least the dramatist is able to objectify the source of his conflict. Scene after scene carries Blanche closer to the obligatory moment: sexual assault by Stanley and, finally, insanity. "We've had this date from the beginning," says Stanley; and suddenly one is struck by the realization that what is wrong with many modern tragedies is the inarticulation of the conflict. The great determinists of the American stage — O'Neill, Miller, and Williams — at their best are able to visualize the conflict in the strongest theatrical terms.

The Family Theme in Modern Drama

The family — its indissoluble ties and the clash of the generations — has provided the most consistently workable theme for naturalistic drama. If man is looked upon as being without bold outlines, without true freedom of will, family background helps to provide understanding of an important force in the formation of his destiny. As the world shrinks in size, as national and ethnic origins are said to mean less and less in our society and sensitive young artists of today regard themselves as footloose and drifting, the family comes more and more to be the only common experience which all members of a theater audience can share.

Modern literature has become increasingly autobiographical. Many a first novel by a new author has been a long, soul-searching backward glance over traveled roads. These personal accounts are unlikely to survive their age for the very reason that many naturalistic plays and films will not: the contemporary artist can be overwhelmed by the formlessness of his material. Thomas Wolfe is perhaps a notable exception to the rule which dooms most autobiographical writers to eventual obscurity.

Formlessness in the theater is not only a serious offense; it can be the unforgivable sin. Audiences must be held, and they are not likely to be when they lose all sense of where they are going.

The ego — the inner self of the playwright — is not often a feasible theatrical subject. It worked on the screen, in Federico Fellini's 8½, mainly because the movies are capable of infinitely more rapid movement than is the stage. Fellini's poetic camera kept turning up image after image, so that it was not the intellectual labyrinth of the ego which was being explored but rather the stream of consciousness of the artist. The images were in themselves objects of beauty, and if one wished to find symbolism, one was free to do so, but 8½ did not tie the audience down to an irresponsibly formless sequence of autobiographical scenes.

On the stage the nearly insurmountable obstacles of intense subjectivity on the part of the playwright are illustrated by Miller's *After the Fall* (1964). Like O'Neill in *The Emperor Jones*, Miller attempts to put a mind on the stage, a natural experiment in the age of Freud; but unlike O'Neill, he is exploring his own experiences. The theatrical razzle-dazzle of the play is impressive, as, once again, technical effects are called upon to save the day. Scene follows scene with machine-gun rapidity; characters appear as if by magic out of the shadows. The free form adopted by Miller allows maximum escape from the "trap" of the old box-set with its contrived entrances and exits, yet it also opens the floodgates for a sea of personal reminiscence to pour in upon the audience. *After the Fall* tries to turn the stage into the screen but succeeds only in re-emphasizing the fact that live theater requires a degree of order that the screen can exist without.

When the summing up is made in the case for twentieth-century drama, two American works, O'Neill's *Long Day's Journey into Night* and Williams' *The Glass Menagerie,* are likely to be among those dramas still being mentioned. Both are autobiographical but, unlike *After the Fall,* they do not overflow the family circle. In both plays the author as a young man is a major character but not the central figure, so that theatrical objectivity is maintained.

At the outset of *The Glass Menagerie*, Williams seems to have some doubts that his play will be precisely what an audience may want. His narrator, Tom, all but apologizes for the artless kind of experience about to unfold. He calls it a "memory play" and confesses that in memory things are not seen exactly as they were. This becomes Williams' saving grace, for his play is a series of relatively few scenes, most of which develop some aspect of family conflict. The work does not become a frenetic romp through a lifetime crammed with incident and people. Fortunately, the play came before Williams' extraordinary commercial success on Broadway and in Hollywood; he has only his family background to recall. Yet he is mature enough at this point to have gained a considerable amount of the dramatist's objectivity. A devout admirer of Chekhov, Williams in this play achieves a Chekhovian kind of compassionate insight into all of the characters and reminds us once more that the capacity for sharing the feelings of others is one of the few signs of greatness the modern dramatist can exhibit.

The family theme leads O'Neill to tragedy of a high order. Never denying that *Long Day's Journey* was a personal document, he dedicated to his wife "this play of old sorrow, written in tears and blood." Though the drama is long and carefully detailed in the manner of some of O'Neill's earlier, novelistic plays, he achieves a unity rare in modern drama. The self-centered Tyrone family itself — the father and the two sons — are bound together by their common fear that the mother's drug addiction will lead to disaster; as the three men clash among themselves, the conflicts-within-a-conflict further enhance the unity.

All of the action passes in the course of a single day, from early morning until late at night. This compression of time allows O'Neill to exploit the classical structure. The obligatory moment, Mary Tyrone's total surrender to her illness and total withdrawal from all contact with reality, is promised from the very first scene. Though O'Neill relives his own youth in the character of the consumptive Edmund Tyrone, who cannot seem to make his family realize that he is in dire need of medical help, this particular conflict never is allowed to become central. Upstairs in her bedroom the mother is heard walking back and forth; down below the men know all too well that, regardless of their conflicts, no one will escape the disaster which must destroy the entire family.

The play cannot quite reach the same star on which Oedipus stands because the mother's addiction is a force external to the three men, even though it dooms them all. O'Neill as a determinist has, more than any other playwright of this century, created a sense of fate to rival that of the Greeks. But his age lets him down. The force that destroys is still more important than the individual who is destroyed. The powerful final scene finds Mary, irrevocably lost, reliving her youth in a convent, while the three men sit there in deep anguish from which they will not emerge.

This scene suggests that the big tragic theme in naturalism is *too* big to be embodied in one man. *Long Day's Journey* may be seen as tragedy of general doom. Through the immediate drama of family conflict O'Neill reaches out toward larger truths. The apparently small scale assumes huge dimensions but also keeps the emphasis where it should be in the theater: on the characters as human beings, not on empty symbols or on the playwright's personality.

Expressionism

O'Neill's achievement in *Long Day's Journey* is rejected by some of the newer dramatists who scorn its strict use of verisimilitude and its classical unity. They point out that the big theme for our age cannot be reached by small-scale family drama. Some even deny that any of the theater forms which worked in the past can have any meaning today. They maintain that modern society is experiencing a complete break-down of unity, that modern man is lost, his life pointless, his universe uninterpretable; that the family is no longer the basic unit of society and so cannot serve as a symbol of it. If theater is to go on existing, they say, it must offer something entirely new. It must be prepared to sacrifice plot even in the Chekhovian sense, characterization in any established sense, dialogue which moves logically from one point to another, and episodes that have a beginning, a middle, and an end. Existence is absurd, and theirs must be "Theater of the Absurd."

Early in this century a theatrical movement known as *expressionism* had a strong vogue and took the first major step away from verisimilitude. The pioneer in this movement was August Strindberg (1849–1912), a Swedish naturalist who, like his American admirer O'Neill, was a tireless innovator. Sometimes his work is intensely realistic, but at other times what he had to say became more important than the creation of believable human beings on the stage. Expressionism in its purest form abandons all pretense at verisimilitude; the setting and the characters are heavily symbolic and usually admit of very specific interpretation. It is the work of an intellectual dramatist who is fully in command of his theme. He is not interested in arousing compassion for the human condition so much as he is in making his appeal to the audience through impact.

Expressionistic plays are bold and powerful. Since naturalism is the philosophy from which they generally proceed, the author's underlying pessimism is more forcefully conveyed than is the case when compassion for the characters is the desired goal. The naturalist, in other words, turns expressionist when his outrage toward the destructive force outweighs his concern for the suffering of those who are destroyed.

Expressionistic drama is characterized by a heavy-handed use of symbolism and Euripidean irony. O'Neill's *The Hairy Ape* (1922), showing strong Strindberg influence, begins on a luxury liner. The "first class" deck represents the human race at an advanced stage of evolution, while far below in the hold are the hero "Yank" and the other coal stokers, who symbolize the survival of the animal self. The ship also stands for the human psyche as a whole with the different levels of consciousness and responses to stimuli that are possible. O'Neill is clearly saying that man is only humanized in part. Wherever the ship goes, all the decks go with it. At any moment the uncivilized, irrational depths of the psyche may assert themselves.

The action of the plot begins to move when Mildred, a first class tourist, goes sightseeing at the bottom of the ship and is frightened by "Yank," whom she calls an ape. The label disturbs the stoker, and for the remainder of the play, he goes on a bizarre odyssey in New York in an effort to discover what he truly is and where he belongs. After being rejected by polite human society, he finally decides that his place may well be in the zoo with the other animals. Yet, in a Euripidean climax, "Yank" is strangled to death by a frenzied ape, who refuses to accept him either. Man is neither wholly human nor wholly animal. Man is an anomaly in the universe and can therefore never assert himself within it.

The expressionists sometimes are narrower in their scope and see man as a victim of society. Elmer Rice's *The Adding Machine* (1923) is an example of a deterministic tragedy handled in non-realistic, symbolic terms. The protagonist is Mr. Zero, and the constant centerpiece on the stage is the adding machine itself, exaggerated to monstrous size and representing American business as a mechanistic system which enslaves the worker. Rice's work is typical of expressionistic form but is more didactic than either Strindberg's or O'Neill's. It has something in common with the post World War I German expressionists, who reflected the bitter pessimism of the younger Germans inhabiting a conquered nation and envisioning a bleak future. Among the notable figures in the movement was Georg Kaiser (1878–1945), whose *From Morn to Midnight* (1916) was a pioneering work in expressionism. The story of an innocuous bank teller who steals a fortune in a desperate attempt to realize some happiness is presented with the terrifying symbols one might experience in a nightmare. Its unrelenting build to a tragic climax has much in common with that of *The Emperor Jones*, which can also be considered expressionistic.

Expressionism is dated now for several reasons. One is that its obvious symbolism was too easily imitated. Another is that its plays tended to say the same thing over and over. By the time Arthur Miller wrote *Death of a Salesman* in the 1940's, audiences found it no surprise that the little man was up against it in a capitalist society; they had experienced the novelty of expressionism's original impact. Though the towering skyscrapers behind Willy Loman's house represent an expressionistic element, the play creates a very real family and a very human hero.

"Epic Theater"

Closely allied to expressionist theater and undoubtedly influenced by it at the outset is the work of Bertolt Brecht (1898–1956), who, like Miller, also rejected it. Brecht, whose name is now associated with "epic theater" and the theory of alienation, developed a highly individual style of drama that often combines the elements of the medieval morality play and the modern musical comedy.

The morality play of the Middle Ages had no characters at all but rather symbolic representations of moral conditions: virtue, vice, fellowship, good deeds, gluttony, and so on. The conflict was one of values, not of persons. Brecht, a product of the Berlin unrest of the 1920's, found in Marxism a sensible blueprint for a happier future and used the theater, originally but not later, to hammer home his moralistic theses. His "epic" theater differs from expressionism, however, in that he believed the playwright had to detach himself completely from his work in order to see it steadily and see it whole and communicate effectively to his audience. He lost patience with the heavy-handed, idealistic fervor of the expressionists, preferring instead a drama that might be able to accomplish something. Yet, even though he thought of "epic" theater as one that was admittedly theatrical, not striving to weave an illusion or arouse the emotional attachment of the audience, his most popular works have elements of traditional success. *The Threepenny Opera* (1928) with its bitterly funny lyrics and the powerful music of Kurt Weill, and two fables from Brecht's later career, *The Good Woman of Setzuan* (1938) and *The Caucasian Chalk Circle* (1944), combine satire, gayety, and a moral to achieve a theatrical charm from which it is impossible to be alienated.

Brecht came to America in the 1940's to work in Hollywood and became in real life one of the theater's tragic figures. Ultimately shunned for the communism with which he had privately become disillusioned, and depressed by Hollywood's commercialism, which he found incompatible with the creation of art, Brecht went into a slow descent into obscurity.

In 1947, however, appeared his *Galileo*, which may ultimately be his master work. It is the most significant response by a dramatist to the atomic bomb. In telling the story of how Galileo, the scientific genius, became corrupted by his fear of the Church and "sold out" to its bureaucracy, Brecht is really talking about the scientists of today who placed the split atom, a supreme achievement of human genius, at the disposal of the state and so have enslaved the world. *Galileo* is non-communist, has no allegiance to any nation, reflects Brecht's exile. Far from alienation, it inspires great empathy for its powerful hero, a genius in ruin, who comes to represent modern man at his best and worst, destroyed by the very force of nature which he unleashed and by the state which he once created for his convenience. The reputation of this work is growing, but very slowly, because it has had few productions. It may well emerge as the naturalistic tragedy that all the others have been trying to write, with at last a protagonist who is a worthy opponent of the forces which crush him. Perhaps Brecht inadvertently found the key: the naturalist's sense of doom combined with the expatriate's lonely individualism.

Realism on the Screen

When film-making became big business just before 1920, it naturally manufactured products which had already proved successful with large theater audiences: melodrama and sentimentality. Regarded as a novelty on the public market rather than as an art form, the film sold those things which sold best. Just as Greek tragedy had taken time to evolve from the barest suggestion of actual drama in the work of Thespis to the perfection of *Oedipus the King,* so too was the screen medium at first a toy in the hands of an enthusiastic public before it was recognized as an artistic language in its own right.

Yet from the beginning, when the first image was projected onto a white sheet in 1895 — the same year in which Wilde's *The Importance of Being Earnest* and Ibsen's *Hedda Gabler* appeared and two years before *Cyrano* — the camera's potential was to be twofold: first, it would one day offer a photographic reproduction of reality better than the stage, which pretended sometimes to do so; and second, it would control the viewpoint of the audience, while the stage could not, by making the audience see whatever the director wished. The first potential was to make the screen the one and only medium of realism; the second helped to make it a medium of visual poetry, more subjective than the live theater could ever hope to be.

Even before sound came in 1927 and even before the jerky movements of the silents could be smoothed out, the cinema had established itself as an experimental form; and at first the public accepted all of the experiments and clamored for more. As early as 1903 the "cut" was introduced into film-making: it allowed the camera to show only as much of the action as the director considered significant. The science of film-editing was established, and, through it, a totally different image could appear, as if by magic, on the screen. In this way the audience could be kept more intensely interested and excited than had been possible when the camera had been used as a merely static instrument photographing what was actually a play. The film which so revolutionized both the art and the industry was *The Great Train Robbery,* directed by Edwin S. Porter, in 1903. It was clear from the work of such directors as Porter and the imaginative Frenchman Georges Méliès that the film director was the most important artist of the new medium. The script or screenplay on which a film is based provided the barest beginning for the total production. In the great movies which were to come, the story alone was far less memorable than the effects achieved by the skillful directors.

D. W. Griffith (1875–1948) is generally considered the first important craftsman of the movies, the first to use for strong dramatic effects those things which the camera had already learned how to do: move in close, move back, and cut from one action to another. *The Birth of a Nation* (1915) was a twelve-reel epic that proved how much action the screen could show. The cut was unique to film. No experimentation with free stage techniques could equal it. Brecht, who had tried to create "epic" theater by using large casts and many loosely-connected scenes, was, not surprisingly, lured to Hollywood by the possibilities he saw in the less restricted conventions of moving pictures.

The epic potential of the screen also helped to pave the way for the "bigger and better" slogans which would be the dominant creed of Hollywood from Griffith on. The escapism of screen life was irresistible during the war years. During the American twenties the familiar "little tramp" figure of Charlie Chaplin rose to the heights, but it was laughter he was selling, not necessarily the profundity which he developed underneath the comic façade. Along with Chaplin rose other big names, like Mary Pickford, Douglas Fairbanks, and Gloria Swanson. The American movie star became an international tradition.

The Birth of a Nation was not the extent of Griffith's work, and he should not be remembered for the one film alone. By presenting in 1912 *A Corner in Wheat,* a screen adaptation of Frank Norris' deterministic novel *The Pit,* Griffith showed that the movies were the place for the social criticism which Ibsen and Shaw brought to the theater. The entire population could be exposed to such a film with its clear-cut contrast between the pleasure-loving tycoon and the poor farmers whose lives he ruined. Mass communication was necessary to reach more people if social protest were to produce the reforms the meliorists wanted.

This film was among those which influenced the work of Sergei Eisenstein (1898–1948), the Soviet director who advanced the art of screen realism to a degree still admired today. There are two facets to this realism: one, the continuance of the "thesis" tradition to demonstrate an existing social evil; and two, the showing of only highly selected moments and actions in close and careful detail in order to offer a heightening of experience. Through the viewpoint of Eisenstein the audience saw more than they would if they had been actually present at events in real life. Not even the three-dimensional picture of the huge Cinerama screen has improved the insight into reality for which artists like Eisenstein became famous.

In 1925 Eisenstein's *Potemkin*, the story of a sailors' rebellion on a Russian battleship, showed how the camera eye could magnify small details, bring important moments into sharp focus, and hold onto them if necessary, stretching a sixty-second span of actual time into two or three minutes of screen time. The most memorable incident in the film occurs on a long flight of steps in Odessa, where the townspeople have gathered to cheer the sailors and are massacred by soldiers of the Czar. Instead of merely filming the massacre as it might have taken place in real life, Eisenstein keeps singling out details to heighten and prolong the effect of horror: a woman shot down while carrying her dead baby up the steps; a close-up of the bloodied face of a woman wearing glasses who has just been shot in the eye; a baby carriage rolling wildly down the steps in the midst of the unceasing rain of bullets. Above all, with this film Eisenstein showed that social protest needs more than ideas for its effect; it must have the visual persuasiveness which the screen can add.

The early realism of Eisenstein was seldom exploited in the American screen during the depression decade, 1930–1940, while, in contrast, live theater produced a number of important dramas and playwrights. Among the latter was Clifford Odets (1906–1963), whose *Waiting for Lefty* (1935) was performed at a taxi driver's union hall and is reported to have driven the audience into such a frenzy that they stood up finally and shouted "Strike!" On one occasion Hollywood almost matched the stage for significant social protest; this was *I am a Fugitive from a Chain Gang* (1933). The first major screen exposé of the Southern chain gang system, the film actually led to an investigation into the brutality which the camera was able to magnify. Audiences were spared none of the violent details of a story which followed, step by step, the degradation of a basically honest man, condemned through circumstantial evidence to years of abject slavery in what was shown to be a medieval and sadistic penal system.

Hollywood went, however, its customary escape route in most of the films of this period, and even Clifford Odets was lured by the promise of big money on the West Coast. Odets' gradual loss of the creative spark while writing screenplays must be counted as one of the major real-life tragedies in American theater; one of his last plays, *The Big Knife* (1949), was a bitter denunciation of Hollywood's insensitivity and demoralizing effect on talent.

The potential of the screen for heightening reality was ultimately realized as part of a major renaissance of the cinema, which had its beginnings in Europe after World War II. The Italian screen, in particular, pioneered in a movement known today as "neo-realism," but which was actually the application of the Eisenstein technique to stories which were basically naturalistic. In other words, the Italian neo-realists were not concerned with social protest as much as with insight into the lives of real human beings living in cities devastated by the war. About these films there is an air of futility, a realization that the time is long past for making improvements in society; what is left is compassion for men and women, trying to find a few fleeting moments of happiness in a harsh existence. In a sense neo-realism is the Chekhov microcosmic drama transferred to the screen.

No attempt is made to scale the heights of tragedy, as Miller, for example, tries to do in *Death of a Salesman*. One of the most impressive of these films, Vittorio de Sica's *The Bicycle Thief*, has the smallness of man as its very theme. Ricci is the hero, but the only reason *he* is singled out to have his story told is that his bicycle is stolen. Here is the furthest possible remove from the Greeks, with their proud image of a hero observed by the gods.

The milieu is most authentic, as if the director were simply walking with his camera along Italian streets and photographing what he sees. There is no sense of paid actors reciting prepared lines according to the director's master plan. And this milieu is one in which the possession of a bicycle gives a man importance and the chance to work and make enough money to put food on his table. It is the intense realism made possible by the medium itself which justifies both story and characters. So long as we can believe, it is not necessary to question.

Early in the film there occurs a sequence which demonstrates that de Sica's movie-making is a high order of art, needing no explicit moral implications or even greatness of writing to justify it. Ricci and his wife, in order to come up with enough money to get the bicycle, have to pawn all of their sheets. They go to an establishment which apparently specializes in buying and selling used bed linen. We do not know this at first, because the movie director allows us to see things in the order he deems desirable. We suppose it odd that anyone would have to resort to pawning his sheets. But the camera follows the pawnbroker as he carries the rolled-up sheets to add them to his inventory, and slowly the huge dimensions of the emporium are revealed — shelf upon shelf upon shelf, filled with nothing but sheets, all the way to the ceiling. It is no longer possible to disbelieve. The poverty of the city and its inhabitants is there, swiftly made real by the camera. From that moment Ricci becomes a worthy subject. Ricci lives.

The main part of the film shows Ricci and his small son searching through the streets of Rome for the bicycle stolen as Ricci was working the first day of his new job. They have the weekend. On Monday morning, if Ricci still has no bicycle, his job will be given to one of the many unemployed men seen at the beginning. The search carries them through Rome and a variety of encounters: with the police, busy but willing to help restore the bicycle if Ricci first locates it; the man in the union hall, reassuring, but involved in rehearsing some entertainers; a truck driver who comments on the rain; the people who are conducting a prayer meeting for the poor and who are annoyed by Ricci's attempt to find help at their mission; a well-dressed youngster in a restaurant, and so on; till they finally meet and accuse the thief, only to lose him when his neighbors in the tenement provide him with an alibi. Walking home, Ricci passes a soccer stadium with row upon row of bicycles parked outside. He seizes one, is pursued by onlookers, caught and released rather than arrested. The last words in the film are spoken by one of the men who caught him and who says to Ricci, "You're lucky."

De Sica's film is in the spirit of pure naturalism. It condemns no one; it blames no institution — society, big business, the church, or the law — for the things that happen. The film cannot be said to have a "point." It does not show that a man is made to commit a crime because of some deterministic force any more than it deals with right and wrong. The theft is a piece of irony that simply exists.

Neo-realism, though it gives the illusion of a direct photograph of the truth, is actually highly selective in its handling of details. It forces us to accept *its* vision of the real *because that is all we ever see;* in this respect it offers further corroboration of the fact that the movies constitute the only workable medium for verisimilitude.

The Avant-Garde on Stage

Every theatrical era has its avant-garde — new writers who come along and react strongly against existing conventions, established values, audience expectations, and the popularity of the accepted dramatists. In his time Aristophanes was avant-garde, though now his works represent the classic mode of comedy.

Even Shakespeare was a daring innovator compared to some of his lesser Elizabethan contemporaries. *King Lear,* for example, possesses a unity of structure, theme, and imagery which go far beyond what was needed to satisfy Elizabethan audiences. Its mood of pessimism is in striking contrast to the exuberance of the Renaissance which other artists demonstrate in their work.

The avant-garde generally crops up during times of upheaval, of great social, political, religious, or philosophical changes, especially when these are the results of the breakdown of some older order. During most of the nineteenth century, though there were important changes, they were accompanied by the idea of continual progress. The world seemed to be working *toward* a new and greater order, and the writers of the first three-quarters of the century tend to be full of hope and enthusiasm. In the theater there were decades upon decades of sentimental drama, reflecting the essential goodness of man and the fitness of the way the world is run. Thus playwrights like Oscar Wilde, resisting the enthusiasm of science, in the 1890's formed the core of the avant-garde of their time, despite the fact that the avant-garde plays of the '90's seem to have originated in happier and more innocent times than our own.

The mid-twentieth century is characterized by the most serious upheavals in human history: atoms are being split; civilization exists under the threat of nuclear devastation; our own country, which once seemed so indisputably to be carrying the hopes of the free world on its shoulders, is now being criticized for many of its policies both externally and internally; in society the family is no longer the solid rock foundation for the nation's stability; even the once-unquestioned relationship between the sexes is being re-evaluated in this age of women governors and male nurses.

In live theater the most exciting voices of the present are not those of social protest or of naturalism or determinism but rather those which deny that any previous modes of drama are adequate to express reality. They deny that "nature" is any kind of interpretable entity, benign or destructive or even neutral. They decry the meliorism of Ibsen on the grounds that mankind is unimprovable. They consider each human life as something that has occurred by itself and remains unrelated to other lives, the universe, or to its own times. On the whole, their views lead them to theatrical techniques which baffle and even outrage play viewers for whom live theater is still synonymous with the latest Broadway hit musical.

The avant-garde movement had one of its earliest pioneers in the Italian dramatist Luigi Pirandello (1867–1936), whose *Six Characters in Search of an Author* appeared in 1921 and broke ground for a tradition that has come to be called "anti-theater." The play dispenses with all customary elements usually involved in holding audiences: plot (even in the looser, Chekhovian sense), characters (in *any* sense generally understood by audiences), and theme (one that can be readily put into words). The play purports to be a rehearsal of another play, into which six strange people burst, insisting that they are characters created by a playwright who did not finish his play and demanding the use of the theater to play their story out. As the "real" actors attempt to impersonate the "unreal" characters, it becomes apparent that Pirandello is attacking both the common-sense and the purely scientific views of reality as being something "out there" which can be understood and to which we can relate meaningfully. When, finally, one of the characters shoots himself and is found to be actually dead, we are left with the intriguing suggestion that the reality of the theater may be something unique, with its own laws, and not any valid reflection of "out there" either through verisimilitude or the point-for-point symbolism of the expressionists.

The "anti-theater" contingent in our time has often been labeled Theater of the Absurd, and the phrase is useful so long as it is not made rigidly categorical and characterized in too great detail. The dramatists to whom the label has been applied share mainly a distinct unwillingness to be so categorized and made to seem the founders of new rules for the drama. Their whole purpose is to be free from rules, to be allowed to use the theater as a creative medium which cannot be "analyzed" or made to say coherent things about man and society and nature.

In some respects Theater of the Absurd is less bewildering and complex than it is unbelievably simple. In a world without meaning, purpose, or potential for bettering itself; in a reality that cannot be reflected in logical sentence structure, as so many modern poets contend, why should the drama be clearly meaningful?

Traditionalists — including the naturalists and determinists — point out that the "anti-theater movement," from Pirandello on, does not divorce itself from meaning (nothing can), that it is highly intellectual and *demands* interpretation, and that it seems to be an outgrowth of the philosophy of existentialism.

Existentialism contends that life is not to be explained in any of the traditional philosophical ways. Man simply exists; he is unique and alone, and consequently prey to doubts and fears. True wisdom comes when one experiences the anguish of realizing that all is absurd and that he must live his own version of a purposive life if he is to be saved from such anguish and retain a sense of identity for himself.

Since Theater of the Absurd originated in Europe and since Paris is today its capital, one might expect that it would strongly reflect existentialism in that by its very being it represents a deliberate, conscious assertion of the dramatist's self in the midst of chaos. Yet the obvious question might be: why should anyone other than the dramatist be interested?

A possible answer is that the Absurd section of avant-garde drama can be sub-divided: one group, represented by the work of Samuel Beckett, asks for compassion on the grounds that all of us are bound together by the same fundamental absurdity within which we exist; the other, represented by the work of Eugène Ionesco, uses absurdity as a technique and so is wildly funny even when it purports to be most anti-theatrical and ultimately *does* have something to say about society.

Ionesco's *Rhinoceros* (1960) shows men changing from human beings into tough, hard-skinned, snorting beasts — until only the protagonist has not joined the pack; and with no one to understand his language, he finds both words and reason obsolete. While Broadway audiences who saw Zero Mostel become a rhinoceros found a lesson against conformity in general, European audiences saw the re-enactment of the rise of Nazism. Avant-garde though it may be, *The Rhinoceros* has some kind of logic.

Even *The Lesson* (1951), with its ridiculous situation — a professor tutoring a young lady as she prepares to take an examination for a highly advanced degree and finally stabbing her to death because she cannot comprehend the principle of subtraction — can be seen to reflect the plight of the contemporary intellectual who cannot communicate even the simplest of his thoughts to a dull-witted middle class.

The most impressive work to come from the Absurd Theater to date is Beckett's *Waiting for Godot*, which had its American premiere in 1956 at the Coconut Grove Playhouse in Miami. The way the work of Irish-born Beckett was first introduced in this country is symptomatic of the gulf which often exists between the avant-garde artist and his audience, as well as a commentary on the general state of theater in America at the present time.

The very title of the play suggests the existential description of the human condition. It deals with two tramps in a park, who do not enjoy being in the park, but who cannot leave until they have seen a mysterious man named Godot. We do not know why they are to see this man; they do not know themselves. He is not — as some have hoped — a symbol of God. The play does not say that the world is waiting for God. The play says nothing. Godot is not anything. The tramps are waiting, just waiting. This is another way of expressing the notion of just existing. If the unseen Monsieur Godot is to be given a meaning, maybe we can say that he represents the way we talk about our meaningless existence — as if it *had* some purpose. Even saying "We are living for no reason" is to mention *some* kind of reason. It is too hard to bear to tell oneself that one is waiting for no one.

Waiting for Godot is an amazing work of art. There is probably no other play in the history of the theater that comes so close to being a perfect embodiment of the view of reality it assumes; for it is not *about* the anguish of waiting — it is the thing itself. And the viewer or the reader can enjoy every second of it as soon as he divorces himself from the habit of trying to abstract symbols and ultimate meanings from it.

The second aim of avant-garde drama — to bring us into contact with others who feel isolated — applies to this play above all others. In the two tramps we recognize echoes of the old vaudeville clowns from the Charlie Chaplin era; and like Chaplin himself, they affect us with warm feelings of humanity even as we are laughing at the idiotic things they do. When the viewer ceases to fear the play on the grounds that it is hopelessly intellectual for him, he comes to realize that it is as far from intellectualism as it is possible for a play to be. It is warmly human, because it *cares* about human anguish. And, in the final moments, Beckett has come up with a hauntingly beautiful visual metaphor of man's predicament.

The tramps have decided to hang themselves. Assuredly death would make as much sense for them as anything else, and it would free them from pain. But all they can use is the belt worn by one of them. When he removes the belt so that they can, by taking their own lives, go out with some dignity, his trousers fall down. A corny routine from the old burlesque show days becomes, in this new context, a great and poetic moment in modern theater. It is perhaps this warmth exuded by *Waiting for Godot* that lifts it above other avant-garde plays; for it *is* an emotional experience in the theater.

Proof of the impact of the play is that a performance by the San Francisco Actors' Workshop for the inmates of San Quentin prison was a smashing success. The audience, one might safely assume, was hardly a homogeneous one of dedicated theater-goers, much less devotees of the avant-garde; it was by and large a group of spectators who had nothing better to do, who wanted very badly to be entertained, who came to the play with no major philosophy of drama and probably few pre-conceptions. They either liked or did not like what they were watching at any given moment. This scene was amusing; that dialogue held the attention; this character was intriguing. Although audiences of sophis-ticated theater-goers would have been accustomed to certain kinds of theatricality, the San Quentin audience discovered that to enjoy theater it was not necessary to become involved with a specific protagonist moving in a specific direction towards an anticipated climax. Besides, as Martin Esslin has pointed out in his book *The Theater of the Absurd* (1961), the prisoners knew all too well the pain and anguish of the act of waiting. They were thus able to respond to the play as a humane document offer-ing no answers, asking only for an intuitive, not an intellectual, under-standing of the conditions of life that were being presented.

The Avant-Garde on the Screen

The screen is a natural dwelling place for both the absurd and other aspects of the avant-garde movement. If the emphasis is to be upon the drama as a deliberate assertion of the self (in the case of the movies, this would be the director), the screen medium, with its continually chang-ing perspective, focus, and images, has perhaps the greatest potential. The stage, despite Pirandello, Beckett, and Ionesco, still is handicapped by the physical presence of total figures for longer stretches of time than are necessary in the movies. Besides, the subjectivism which the existen-tial preoccupation with self incurs is more easily handled in a form whose realities are mainly determined by one man's peculiar vision, instead of by the combined efforts of playwright, director, and actors.

As early as 1930 Jean Cocteau (1891–1963) was experimenting with the French cinema. In *The Blood of a Poet* he used the camera to create a world of strange images, of things turning into other things, of objects which were composites of other objects torn apart and re-assembled by the imagination of the film director. It is Freudian, as all of Cocteau's films are, but not in a point-for-point sense. Like *Orpheus,* with its mirrors through which one can enter a land that does not exist anywhere in space, *The Blood of a Poet* was to be experienced, not interpreted. *Beauty and the Beast* was a retelling of the fairy tale with no intention other than to charm and fascinate through Cocteau's almost unending stream of imaginative touches, such as the long corridor of candelabra supported by human arms thrust through the wall in the palace of the Beast. Cocteau's existentialism might be called "artistic" as opposed to "philosophical"; he is a cinematic descendant of Oscar Wilde and his belief in art for art's sake.

The Swedish cinema became world famous and artistically respected largely through the work of Ingmar Bergman, around whom has grown a cult of devoted admirers and interpreters who hail his major works, including *The Seventh Seal* (1956), *Wild Strawberries* (1957), and *Virgin Spring* (1960), as masterpieces of symbolism. Bergman is in the avant-garde tradition because he is primarily a subjectivist using the camera to create the visual poetry of images.

There are, to be sure, religious overtones to his work, but he has repeatedly made clear his position that the viewer is free to make of his images what he wishes. He describes his approach to film-making:

> A film for me begins with something very vague — a chance remark of a bit of conversation, a hazy but agreeable event unrelated to any particular situation. It can be a few bars of music, a shaft of light across the street. These are split-second impressions that disappear as quickly as they come, yet leave behind a mood — like pleasant dreams.*

Bergman's work has taken two major forms: *The Seventh Seal* and *Virgin Spring* are medieval and have strongly allegorical elements along with an almost Rembrandtian use of black-and-white photography that elicits an emotional response in and for itself; and *Wild Strawberries,* which deals with one day in the life of an aging professor of medicine, goes backwards and forwards in time and in and out of the protagonist's mind in a manner that reminds one of what Arthur Miller attempted on the stage in *Death of a Salesman* and *After the Fall.* The difference is that film can create a far deeper illusion of truly subjective experience since it allows images to appear and disappear in a state much closer to that of actual stream of consciousness.

Fellini, now best known for his intense subjectivism, first made his presence felt with the neo-realism of *La Strada* (1954), a simple and touching tale of a traveling strong man and the slow-witted girl who assists him in his act. The film, tracing the development of the girl's adoration of her master in contrast with his egocentricity and incapacity for tender emotions, stresses insights into the two central characters and

---

* Ingmar Bergman in *Four Screenplays of Ingmar Bergman,* translated from Swedish by Lars Malmstrom and David Kushner, © 1960 by Simon and Schuster, p. xv.

evokes pity for both. It does not see them against the background of total society or nature or any of the destructive forces emphasized by the determinists. The very title of the movie (The Road) is indicative of Fellini's dedication to capturing the breath of life as it goes by and of using the film as a medium of complete authenticity.

In 8½, which has already been mentioned as a stream of consciousness movie, Fellini's hero is a director (presumably himself) who seems unable to commit himself any longer to the cause of neo-realism. He is the very personification of the avant-garde artist, and the conflict is between the artist's sense of responsibility to himself and the contention of the producers, who supply the money, that the artist belongs to them and to the public.

Even in 1960, when his *La Dolce Vita* appeared, it was evident that Fellini's way would not be toward greater and greater realism, especially that exploitation of sex which (according to the charges made in 8½) some of the Italian producers, with their eye on soaring international box-office receipts, were demanding. True, the film takes us on a three-hour odyssey through the world of present-day Roman decadence and of the lives of the "jet set," jaded pleasure seekers, and bored intellectuals who have no allegiance to any country. True, its hero — this time an existential novelist, but essentially the same self-figure Fellini was to use in 8½ — falls victim to the international set's continual thirst for new forms of erotic pleasures, which are graphically depicted in considerable detail. But the film continually departs from neo-realism and uses intriguing camera imagery that has a Bergmanesque ambiguity about it.

The famous opening image — a statue of Christ being transported through the air by helicopter — sets the pattern of the symbolism in the film. It was inevitably subjected to moralistic interpretation by many, as was the concluding image of the huge, dead, and unidentified fish which is washed ashore and stares from a terrifying, open eye at the various decadents assembled on the beach. Both images do seem on the verge of making definite statements, yet they retain the intense excitement of ambiguity, which is the soul of, not an impediment to, the enjoyment of the avant-garde. If one is tempted to interpret the Christ-helicopter contrast as a statement of the need for religion, one might just as easily see it as a reflection of the decadence of the Church itself. Was the eye of the fish a symbol of heavenly wrath at the moral iniquity of the international set? But what particular heaven that Fellini has ever committed himself to? The blankness of the stare seems as unyielding of a clear answer as existence itself.

Like his hero in both films, Fellini is unable to make a commitment in so sick a world as he finds all around him. This has become the theme of his work, and it typifies the position of the whole avant-garde movement of our time. To those who would question so unresolved a position, who would insist that 8½ is not even a complete film in the traditional sense, it could be said that a lack of commitment to a way of life or to a social context or to a definite philosophy is not a lack of commitment of oneself. The more displaced the artist feels in the world, the more intense is his introversion and the more arresting become his images and symbols. When one learns to recognize that the audience is all the richer for the artist's refusal to pin himself down or to be pinned down, one has learned to cope with and profit by the avant-garde.

Antonin Artaud, a French poet and essayist, has become one of the most articulate spokesmen for the new drama. He has coined the phrase "Theater of Cruelty" to refer to deliberate provoking of audience emotion by a continual series of shocks. A recent (1965) work which embodies Artaud's theory is Peter Weiss's *The Persecution and Assassination of Jean-Paul Marat as Performed by the Inmates of the Asylum of Charenton under the Direction of the Marquis de Sade.* In the following essay, "No More Masterpieces," Artaud presents some intriguing ideas.

❀ Antonin Artaud: *No More Masterpieces**

One of the reasons for the asphyxiating atmosphere in which we live without possible escape or remedy — and in which we all share, even the most revolutionary among us — is our respect for what has been written, formulated, or painted, what has been given form, as if all expression were not at last exhausted, were not at a point where things break apart if they are to start anew and begin fresh.

We must have done with this idea of masterpieces reserved for a self-styled elite and not understood by the general public; the mind has no such restricted districts as those so often used for clandestine sexual encounters.

Masterpieces of the past are good for the past: they are not good for us. We have the right to say what has been said and even what has not been said in a way that belongs to us, a way that is immediate and direct, corresponding to present modes of feeling, and understandable to everyone.

It is idiotic to reproach the masses for having no sense of the sublime, when the sublime is confused with one or another of its formal manifestations, which are moreover always defunct manifestations. And if for example a contemporary public does not understand *Oedipus Rex,* I shall make bold to say that it is the fault of *Oedipus Rex* and not of the public.

In *Oedipus Rex* there is the theme of incest and the idea that nature mocks at morality and that there are certain unspecified powers at large which we would do well to beware of, call them *destiny* or anything you choose.

There is in addition the presence of a plague epidemic which is a physical incarnation of these powers. But the whole in a manner and language that have lost all touch with the rude and epileptic rhythm of our time. Sophocles speaks grandly perhaps, but in a style that is no longer timely. His language is too refined for this age, it is as if he were speaking beside the point.

However, a public that shudders at train wrecks, that is familiar with earthquakes, plagues, revolutions, wars; that is sensitive to the disordered anguish of love, can be affected by all these grand notions and asks only to become aware of them, but on condition that it is addressed in its own language, and that its knowledge of these things does not come to it through adulterated trappings and speech that belong to extinct eras which will never live again.

Today as yesterday, the public is greedy for mystery: it asks only to become aware of the laws according to which destiny manifests itself, and to divine perhaps the secret of its apparitions.

Let us leave textual criticism to graduate students, formal criticism to esthetes, and recognize that what has been said is not still to be said; that an expression does not have the same value twice, does not live two lives; that all words, once spoken, are dead and function only at the moment when they are uttered, that a form, once it has served, cannot be used again and asks only to be replaced by another, and that the theater is the only place in the world where a gesture, once made, can never be made the same way twice.

If the public does not frequent our literary masterpieces, it is because those masterpieces are literary, that is to say, fixed; and fixed in forms that no longer respond to the needs of the time.

Far from blaming the public, we ought to blame the formal screen we interpose between ourselves and the public, and this new form of idolatry, the idolatry of fixed masterpieces which is one of the aspects of bourgeois conformism.

This conformism makes us confuse sublimity, ideas, and things with the forms they have taken in time and in our minds — in our snobbish, precious, aesthetic mentalities which the public does not understand.

How pointless in such matters to accuse the public of bad taste because it relishes insanities, so long as the public is not shown a valid spectacle; and I defy anyone to show me *here* a spectacle valid — valid in the supreme sense of the theater — since the last great romantic melodramas, i.e., since a hundred years ago.

The public, which takes the false for the true, has the sense of the true and always responds to it when it is manifested. However it is not upon the stage that the true is to be sought nowadays, but in the street; and if the crowd in the street is offered an occasion to show its human dignity, it will always do so.

If people are out of the habit of going to the theater, if we have all finally come to think of theater as an inferior art, a means of popular distraction, and to use it as an outlet for our worst instincts, it is because we have learned too well what the theater has been, namely, falsehood and illusion. It is because we have been accustomed for four hundred years, that is since the Renaissance, to a purely descriptive and narrative theater — storytelling psychology; it is because every possible ingenuity has been exerted in bringing to life on the stage plausible but detached beings, with the spectacle on one side, the public on the other — and because the public is no longer shown anything but the mirror of itself.

Shakespeare himself is responsible for this aberration and decline, this disinterested idea of the theater which wishes a theatrical performance to leave the public intact, without setting off one image that will shake the organism to its foundations and leave an ineffaceable scar.

If, in Shakespeare, a man is sometimes preoccupied with what transcends him, it is always in order to determine the ultimate consequences of this preoccupation within him, i.e., psychology.

Psychology, which works relentlessly to reduce the unknown to the known, to the quotidian and the ordinary, is the cause of the theater's abasement and its fearful loss of energy, which seems to me to have reached its lowest point. And I think both the theater and we ourselves have had enough of psychology.

I believe furthermore that we can all agree on this matter sufficiently so that there is no need to descend to the repugnant level of the modern and French theater to condemn the theater of psychology.

Stories about money, worry over money, social careerism, the pangs of love unspoiled by altruism, sexuality sugar-coated with an eroticism that has lost its mystery have nothing to do with the theater, even if they do belong to psychology. These torments, seductions, and lusts before which we are nothing but Peeping Toms gratifying our cravings, tend to go bad, and their rot turns to revolution: we must take this into account.

But this is not our most serious concern.

If Shakespeare and his imitators have gradually insinuated the idea of art for art's sake, with art on one side and life on the other, we can rest on this feeble and lazy idea only as long as the life outside endures. But there are too many signs that everything that used to sustain our lives no longer does so, that we are all mad, desperate, and sick. And I call for *us* to react.

This idea of a detached art, of poetry as a charm which exists only to distract our leisure, is a decadent idea and an unmistakable symptom of our power to castrate.

Our literary admiration for Rimbaud, Jarry, Lautréamont[1] and a few others, which has driven two men to suicide, but turned into café gossip for the rest, belongs to this idea of literary poetry, of detached art, of neutral spiritual activity which creates nothing and produces nothing; and I can bear witness that at the very moment when that kind of personal poetry which involves only the man who creates it and only at the moment he creates it broke out in its most abusive fashion, the theater was scorned more than ever before by poets who have never had the sense of direct and concerted action, nor of efficacity, nor of danger.

We must get rid of our superstitious valuation of texts and *written* poetry. Written poetry is worth reading once, and then should be destroyed. Let the dead poets make way for others. Then we might even come to see that it is our veneration for what has already been created, however beautiful and valid it may be, that petrifies us, deadens our responses, and prevents us from making contact with that underlying power, call it thought-energy, the life force, the determinism of change, lunar menses, or anything you like. Beneath the poetry of the texts, there is the actual poetry, without form and without text. And just as the efficacity of masks in the magic practices of certain tribes is exhausted — and these masks are no longer good for anything except museums — so the poetic efficacity of a text is exhausted; yet the poetry and the efficacity of the theater are exhausted least quickly of all, since they permit the *action* of what is gesticulated and pronounced, and which is never made the same way twice.

It is a question of knowing what we want. If we are prepared

---

[1] Arthur Rimbaud (1854–1891), Alfred Jarry (1873–1907), and Isidore Ducasse, Count of Lautréamont (1846–1870) were poets of the symbolist movement in France. All three lived unconventional, sensational lives.

for war, plague, famine, and slaughter we do not even need to say so, we have only to continue as we are; continue behaving like snobs; rushing en masse to hear such and such a singer, to see such and such an admirable performance which never transcends the realm of art (and even the Russian ballet at the height of its splendor never transcended the realm of art), to marvel at such and such an exhibition of painting in which exciting shapes explode here and there but at random and without any genuine consciousness of the forces they could rouse.

The empiricism, randomness, individualism, and anarchy must cease.

Enough of personal poems, benefiting those who create them much more than those who read them.

Once and for all, enough of this closed, egoistic, and personal art.

Our spiritual anarchy and intellectual disorder is a function of the anarchy of everything else — or rather, everything else is a function of this anarchy.

I am not one of those who believe that civilization has to change in order for the theater to change; but I do believe that the theater, utilized in the highest and most difficult sense possible, has the power to influence the aspect and formation of things: and the encounter upon the stage of two passionate manifestations, two living centers, two nervous magnetisms is something as entire, true, even decisive, as, in life, the encounter of one epidermis with another in a timeless debauchery.

That is why I propose a theater of cruelty. — With this mania we all have for depreciating everything, as soon as I have said, "cruelty," everybody will at once take it to mean "blood." But *"theater of cruelty"* means a theater difficult and cruel for myself first of all. And, on the level of performance, it is not the cruelty we can exercise upon each other by hacking at each other's bodies, carving up our personal anatomies, or, like Assyrian emperors, sending parcels of human ears, noses, or neatly detached nostrils through the mail, but the much more terrible and necessary cruelty which things can exercise against us. We are not free. And the sky can still fall on our heads. And the theater has been created to teach us that first of all.

Either we will be capable of returning by present-day means to this superior idea of poetry and poetry-through-theater which underlies the Myths told by the great ancient tragedians, capable once more of entertaining a religious idea of the theater (without meditation, useless contemplation, and vague dreams), capable of attaining awareness and a possession of certain dominant forces, of certain notions that control all others, and (since ideas, when they are effective, carry their energy with them) capable of recovering within ourselves those energies which ultimately create order and increase the value of life, or else we might as well abandon ourselves now, without protest, and recognize that we are no longer good for anything but disorder, famine, blood, war, and epidemics.

Either we restore all the arts to a central attitude and necessity, finding an analogy between a gesture made in painting or the theater, and a gesture made by lava in a volcanic explosion, or we must stop painting, babbling, writing, or doing whatever it is we do.

I propose to bring back into the theater this elementary magical idea, taken up by modern psychoanalysis, which consists in effecting a patient's cure by making him assume the apparent and exterior attitudes of the desired condition.

I propose to renounce our empiricism of imagery, in which the unconscious furnishes images at random, and which the poet arranges at random too, calling them poetic and hence hermetic images, as if the kind of trance that poetry provides did not have its reverberations throughout the whole sensibility, in every nerve, and as if poetry were some vague force whose movements were invariable.

I propose to return through the theater to an idea of the physical knowledge of images and the means of inducing trances, as in Chinese medicine which knows, over the entire extent of the human anatomy, at what points to puncture in order to regulate the subtlest functions.

Those who have forgotten the communicative power and magical mimesis of a gesture, the theater can reinstruct, because a gesture carries its energy with it, and there are still human beings in the theater to manifest the force of the gesture made.

To create art is to deprive a gesture of its reverberation in the organism, whereas this reverberation, if the gesture is made in the conditions and with the force required, incites the organism and, through it, the entire individuality, to take attitudes in harmony with the gesture.

The theater is the only place in the world, the last general means we still possess of directly affecting the organism and, in periods of neurosis and petty sensuality like the one in which we are immersed, of attacking this sensuality by physical means it cannot withstand.

If music affects snakes, it is not on account of the spiritual notions it offers them, but because snakes are long and coil their length upon the earth, because their bodies touch the earth at almost every point; and because the musical vibrations which are communicated to the earth affect them like a very subtle, very long massage; and I propose to treat the spectators like the snake-charmer's subjects and conduct them *by means of their organisms* to an apprehension of the subtlest notions.

At first by crude means, which will gradually be refined. These immediate crude means will hold their attention at the start.

That is why in the "theater of cruelty" the spectator is in the center and the spectacle surrounds him.

In this spectacle the sonorisation is constant: sounds, noises, cries are chosen first for their vibratory quality, then for what they represent.

Among these gradually refined means light is interposed in its turn. Light which is not created merely to add color or to brighten, and which brings its power, influence, suggestions with it. And the light of a green cavern does not sensually dispose the organism like the light of a windy day.

After sound and light there is action, and the dynamism of action: here the theater, far from copying life, puts itself whenever possible in communication with pure forces. And whether you accept or deny them, there is nevertheless a way of speaking which gives the name of "forces" to whatever brings to birth images of energy in the unconscious, and gratuitous crime on the surface.

A violent and concentrated action is a kind of lyricism: it summons up supernatural images, a bloodstream of images, a bleeding spurt of images in the poet's head and in the spectator's as well.

Whatever the conflicts that haunt the mind of a given period, I defy any spectator to whom such violent scenes will have transferred their blood, who will have felt in himself the transit of a superior action, who will have seen the extraordinary and essential movements of his thought illuminated in extraordinary deeds — the violence and blood having been placed at the service of the violence of the thought — I defy that spectator to give himself up, once outside the theater, to ideas of war, riot, and blatant murder.

So expressed, this idea seems dangerous and sophomoric. It will be claimed that example breeds example, that if the attitude of cure induces cure, the attitude of murder will induce murder. Everything depends upon the manner and the purity with which the thing is done. There is a risk. But let it not be forgotten that though a theatrical gesture is violent, it is disinterested; and that the theater teaches precisely the uselessness of the action which, once done, is not to be done, and the superior use of the state unused by the action and which, *restored,* produces a purification.

I propose then a theater in which violent physical images crush and hypnotize the sensibility of the spectator seized by the theater as by a whirlwind of higher forces.

A theater which, abandoning psychology, recounts the extraordinary, stages natural conflicts, natural and subtle forces, and presents itself first of all as an exceptional power of redirection. A theater that induces trance, as the dances of Dervishes induce trance, and that addresses itself to the organism by precise instruments, by the same means as those of certain tribal music cures which we admire on records but are incapable of originating among ourselves.

There is a risk involved, but in the present circumstances I believe it is a risk worth running. I do not believe we have managed to revitalize the world we live in, and I do not believe it is worth the trouble of clinging to; but I do propose something to get us out of our marasmus, instead of continuing to complain about it, and about the boredom, inertia, and stupidity of everything.

13 ❀ ❀ ❀

Styles of Acting

Each of the theaters of the past left a legacy of a particular style of production demanding a particular style of acting. If the plays survived, the method of presenting them also had to survive, though this method may have been modified from time to time. The varieties of drama and their acting techniques may be summarized in this way:

1) *Classical.* A tragedy of the Greek (or Roman) era.
2) *Elizabethan.* A tragedy by Shakespeare, Marlowe, and their contemporaries — originally presented in England from about 1575 to about 1640, when the Puritans closed the theaters.
3) *French classical.* A tragedy of Racine; by association (since Racine is the major neo-classical playwright) a tragedy composed during the neo-classical period that is not "heroic."
4) *Sentimental.* A work from the nineteenth-century middle-class theater; an element in a modern play which belongs in a nineteenth-century context.
5) *Professionalistic.* A play in the "well-made" form which Ibsen and Shaw perfected. Any modern play in which every element is carefully introduced as part of a well-oiled production machine. (*Note:* the use of the term "professionalistic" in this context is meant to identify a very specific kind of drama, which at the present time is sometimes called a "theater-piece." It is not to be confused with the word "professional" in reference to theaters in which all personnel are paid salaries.)
6) *Naturalistic.* A play which shows existence as operating solely in terms of natural forces. (Fidelity to the truth is the core of the production, but the conscious, precise planning of impact is also involved.)
7) *Kitchenistic.* A play in which theatrical impact is almost entirely forsaken in favor of giving the illusion of real life

through athentic but unnecessary details of everyday existence; any such element which tends to interrupt the dramatic, not necessarily probable, flow of
action.

8) *Tour de force.* A work such as a musical extravaganza or a one-
man show like *Cyrano de Bergerac* in which the
personality of the actor is more important than
fidelity to the truth.

9) *Stylized.* Any comedy which does not have a primarily naturalistic
basis or does not insist upon the convention of verisimilitude. Found primarily in satire of any period.

The special qualities of these forms of drama, together with their
philosophical and sociological bases, have already been discussed. In
order to become still more perceptive, the critical viewer must possess a
knowledge of the fundamental characteristics of the acting of each form.
Each of these modes of theater is not the equal of the other, and therefore
excellence in Elizabethan acting may be presumed to be superior to
good kitchenism. Whatever limitations may exist in the mode itself are
inevitably passed on to the actor.

Perspective is important. Knowing that declamation and exaggerated
enunciation are not consonant with the philosophy of naturalistic staging
will make the playgoer more conscious of having to listen carefully when
he attends a naturalistic production and less likely to criticize the actors
for slurring their words. Recognizing that classical productions demand
it, he will not be distracted by the actor's use of broad, unnatural gestures.
Accustomed to the acting styles current in movies and television, he must
not require every play or film he sees to be performed in a fashion he
can most easily accept.

He must also understand the four basic aspects of his profession: *voice,
face, gesture,* and *movement.* The viewer who is proficient in evaluating
a performance is one who knows how to tell when these four are being
used properly *with reference to the particular acting style demanded.*

Classical

Greek tragedy originated as ritual. Its earliest forms were undoubtedly
odes sung by a Chorus. Thus its language was basically sonorous — language at full throttle, intoned broadly and rhetorically by actors who had
to be heard by large numbers of people in the open air. The Greek
tragedians had to write speeches that communicated their meanings in
oratorical fashion — that is, without hair-splitting subtleties and fine
shadings.

The modern actor in a classical role still must do almost everything with
his voice. Even if he is playing Oedipus in a relatively small university

theater, even if he no longer has to shout in an amphitheater, he is none-theless appearing in a role which is sweepingly clear in its outlines, in which the exploration of psychological quirks in the character only hinders the actor. Whatever the character believes, he says in the broad-est possible terms.

With so much dependent upon the spoken word, its clarity rather than the sensuous beauty of its sound, classical acting is the most declamatory of styles. No matter what size the theater, it tends to retain its oratorical quality. The smallness of the auditorium does not shrink the themes of Greek tragedy. In fact the modern classical actor, aware of a proximity to the audience he does not need and cannot use, often seems excessively dignified and remote in order to preserve the heightened stature of the original play.

Plays written originally for masked actors naturally contain in the dialogue specific references to emotional states that are today normally conveyed through facial expression. The Messenger coming on to report an off-stage disaster usually prefaces his speech with an exclamation like "O horror!" Hence one of the perpetual dangers of classical performance today is the duplication of emotion. The Tyrone Guthrie production of

Greek chorus.

Oedipus, using a modern version of the ancient masks, was able to cir-cumvent the problem, but audiences for most contemporary productions should recognize that actors are bound to show on their faces the emo-tions they are talking about and be prepared to accept a heightening of feeling in the big moments as well as a heightening of natural speech patterns.

Since the face was concealed, the original Greek actors used broad gestures to assist further in communicating to thousands of spectators. The gesture of supplication, such as Haimon might have used in pleading with his father, would have been seen and understood by all. Creon's lack of gesturing would also have been significant; it would have had much to say about his arrogance, his unwillingness to compromise, the solidity of his position.

Classical gesturing remains highly economical — held to an absolute minimum and definitely subordinated to speech. The modern actor in a modern play, trained to be more natural in his bearing, tends to gesture as he pleases and so accustom the viewer to expect excessive gesturing in all productions. Such an expectation hampers the pleasure that can be found in a more controlled tradition.

The classical style thus emphasizes restraint and allows stage move-ments only when absolutely necessary. The four basic moves on the stage — crossing, turning, sitting, and rising — can never be left wholly up to the actor's discretion, but most modern dramas allow for these moves as logical consequences of the lines themselves.

In a classical production there is usually far less sitting down than in a modern play. Standing in a statuesque kind of repose is definitely a skill in this style of acting, while crossing from one location to another is normally full of heightened significance. The minimal amount of movement might dismay the contemporary viewer in his first encounter with classical acting. He might find it dull or static and equate stage motion with truly dramatic action.

One general rule can be taken into the theater which is offering a classical production: when the actor's creative energies are denied some of their usual outlets — such as walking about or gesturing — the held-in tensions can charge the air with their electricity. The raising of an arm can be more dramatic than the chariot races in *Ben-Hur.* The cry from *inside* the palace, as Medea recognizes what she has done to her children, can chill the spectator as much as a close-up of death in a lurid James Bond finale.

Elizabethan

Because it lacked elaborate technical aids to staging, the Elizabethan play depended on language; and Elizabethan acting developed a great vocal tradition to carry the all-important words of the play. There are now two schools in existence, traditional and modern. In the former, the actor rolls his r's and employs the "King's" English. He pronounces "fortune" as if it were "for tyune"; he says "fortnit" instead of "fortnight." English actors preserve the "grand" Shakespearean manner more than any others — as might be expected. The Royal Shakespearean Theater at Stratford, Shakespeare's birthplace, has become a monument for the preservation of the verbal authenticity in the performance of England's greatest dramatist. In this respect, this theater continues to set the standards by which Elizabethan speech can be evaluated in productions outside Britain.

There exists, however, a modern school, influenced by psychological acting methods, which stresses character revelation. An actor may be censured for glorying in the sound of his own voice when playing Shakespeare, with the result that many beginning actors, anxious to show that they are not being old-fashioned, deliver their lines in such a conversational tone that they sometimes fail to communicate. This failing is common in American productions of Shakespeare, for Americans lack the tradition of the King's English and are accustomed to emphasizing action more than language. The modified Elizabethan style makes the language of Shakespeare *move* rather than show itself off.

But for the connoisseur of Shakespeare there is no real lack of action in Elizabethan drama, either in the physical or in the verbal sense. The words pulsate with feeling, the feeling is complex and subject to rapid changes — in contrast to the speeches in classical drama, which are characterized by restraint. The complex fabric of Shakespearean poetry impels the actor to use *vocal dynamics* — sudden changes from loud tones to soft ones, sudden acceleration or deceleration, sometimes stopping abruptly.

All styles require such dynamics to a normal degree; without pausing, for example, the actor would be unable to breathe frequently enough to give him breath control. But all playwrights do not make the same demands as Shakespeare. The actor is forced into an incomparable vocal range, sometimes within a single speech.

Almost single-handedly Shakespeare invented the mandatory dramatic pause, one that is built into the speeches themselves. Though his medium is blank verse — unrhymed iambic pentameter — the alternation of light and heavy stress which constitutes this poetic meter does not impede the drama of strong moments in Shakespeare.

After Othello has smothered his wife, he hears a violent knocking on the door and says:

> Yes; 'tis Emilia: by and by. She's dead.
> 'Tis like she comes to speak of Cassio's death;
> The noise was high. Ha! no more moving?
> Still as the grave. Shall she come in? Were't good?

> I think she stirs again: no. What's best to do?
> If she come in she'll sure speak to my wife:
> My wife! my wife! what wife? I have no wife . . .

The first line scans perfectly. The pentameter is scrupulously maintained:

$$\breve{\text{Yes}}; \ '\text{tis} \ / \ \breve{\text{Emil}}/\breve{\text{ia}}: \ \text{by} \ / \ \breve{\text{and}} \ \text{by}. \ / \ \text{She's} \ \text{dead}.$$

But how could any actor speak the line as it scans? The "yes" is obviously a reply to the knocking. " 'Tis Emilia" must be spoken to himself — rapidly with great fear. Then "by and by" must be shouted to the closed door, to forestall further knocking. Finally, "she's dead" has to be a heartbroken realization, spoken from the depths of remorse — a pronouncement which can only follow a long, long pause, during which one can imagine Othello staring at the inert figure, perhaps even lightly touching it.

The next three lines suggest the same need for continual pausing. The sixth line not only scans perfectly but invites no vocal dynamics whatever:

$$\breve{\text{If}} \ \text{she} \ / \ \text{come} \ \text{in} \ / \ \text{she'll} \ \text{sure} \ / \ \text{speak} \ \text{to} \ / \ \text{my} \ \text{wife}:$$

If Shakespeare does not provide such lines, the whole principle of dynamics loses its effectiveness.

But then comes a line of unbearable poignancy:

$$\breve{\text{my}} \ \text{wife!} \ / \ \text{my} \ \text{wife!} \ / \ \text{what} \ \text{wife?} \ / \ \breve{\text{I}} \ \text{have} \ / \ \text{no} \ \text{wife}.$$

Any actor is defied to speak this line fluently. The minimum of three pauses is mandatory; more are possible. The word "wife" is used four times; one can readily suppose that the actor would experience increasing difficulty in getting the word out. Nor does it seem probable that "I have no wife" could be spoken as a unit. What a sentence for a man to have to speak who has just killed his wife — a man whose conscience has attacked him ferociously almost at once!

In addition to developing a finely tuned, exquisitely controlled vocal instrument to permit such stopping and starting, to permit the juxtaposition of loud and soft or fast and slow without loss of communication, the Shakespearean actor must be prepared to handle the most complex linguistic structure existing on the English-speaking stage. He must be able to articulate such tongue-twisters as Hamlet's "Speak the speech, I pray you, as I pronounced it to you, trippingly on the tongue . . ." or his fiercely impassioned outburst to Ophelia, "You jig, you amble, and you lisp and nick-name God's creatures and make your wantonness your ignorance." The audience must match the actor's vocal labors with a disciplined willingness to sit and listen.

Other Elizabethan Elements

Elizabethan theaters provided intimacy between actor and audience, in contrast to the distance existing between the Greek and Roman actors and their public. This proximity, together with the innate complexity of Shakespeare's language, made facial mobility very important. Because most modern stages are further away from the audience, Shakespearean actors often must resort to classical broadness. University theaters do more than the professional stage to keep alive the Shakespearean tradition, by offering annual Shakespeare festivals and using theater-in-the-round or facsimiles of the Elizabethan stage. In this way they try to bring the play to the audience as did Shakespeare's own company, the King's Men.

Elizabethan acting, at least for noble characters, demands a definite style of gesturing known as the "flourish." It is a matter of accentuating certain speeches by extending first one arm, then the other. There is also much bowing and curtsying as would be fitting in a predominantly aristocratic age. These outward trappings of nobility, however, are more than relics of the past; they are elegant touches of great beauty in themselves, like the colorful costumes which are a vital part of an Elizabethan play. The critical viewer does not expect the flourish to be like the natural gesturing required by modern acting standards.

He also appreciates the regality and grace of Elizabethan movement. Classical movement is stately and dignified and minimal; but, consistent with the dynamics of the language itself, movement, especially in Shakespeare, has an extraordinary range: from the aristocratic sweep of Queen Gertrude crossing the stage in a full gown of rich satin and velvet to the catlike springs of Hamlet as he bounds from one side of the stage to another in a momentary fit of enthusiasm for a newly conceived scheme.

The Elizabethan actor must therefore have as much bodily control as vocal control. He must be able to move suddenly, to suit an abrupt change in the mood of the language; he must be able to enter and exit quickly, but not clumsily, to maintain the sometimes rapid pace; he must be able to make a furtive stage cross terminate abruptly in a graceful bow, without the slightest loss of composure; he must be able to handle a sword with skill, walk (or sleep-walk) with royal dignity, swoon, "jig and amble" as he trades puns in a comic interlude, or fall dead from poison without evoking snickers from the back row. All these things must he do in the intimacy of a production which puts him under the close scrutiny of the audience. No style of acting makes greater demands on the actor.

Shakespearean acting, therefore, requires the devotion of a lifetime, with daily vocal and physical exercises as disciplined and rigorous as the

The stage of the Globe Theater as it probably appeared in Shake-speare's time.

training for opera and ballet. Since the United States has no permanent Shakespeare repertory theater, there is no group of American actors devoted to this one style of acting. It is seldom possible for an actor to achieve pre-eminence in Shakespearean interpretation without a constant dedication to self-improvement.

French Classical

The acting method appropriate for the tragic drama of the neo-classical period originated in the French theater of the seventeenth century, particularly in the dignified plays of Jean Racine, the greatest French tragedian. Neo-classicism was close in manner but not identical to the Greek and Roman style. It is close to ancient models in general play content and didactic purpose but different in theater design and audience. The differences affected the demands made upon the actor.

Since the theater was a lavish indoor, lighted auditorium with a stage at one end and the audience seated only in front of it, the actor was therefore less likely to address the audience than the Elizabethans had done. In addition, the audience was not the general public of either the classical or Elizabethan drama. Though they loved the more athletic theater of the heroic tragedies, with its near-parody version of Elizabethan exuberance in acting, they could also sit politely and listen to the tragedies of Racine which contain the least amount of stage action of any of the great works of the theater.

As Shakespeare epitomizes the English language, so does Racine the French. But the French admire him for his classic purity and restraint, not verbal dynamics. The vocal tradition of the French classical drama has become the basis of all French acting ever since. Even now in a French film, the English subtitles may sometimes speak of great violence, but the voices of the actors seldom register the emotions suggested by the words. The sound of the language has a lilting, musical effect and is to be enjoyed as language, not necessarily as a vehicle of emotion.

If a modern English-speaking actor in a naturalistic drama becomes excited or shrieks out in some kind of agony, we do not scorn his grating voice or say that he has destroyed the beauty of his language, but the French have always cherished and continue to cherish the beauty of theirs. The French acting tradition, it must be remembered, sprang from a culture that has an Academy, a group of linguistic authorities who act as a Supreme Court in all questions of usage and pronunciation.

A number of years ago a talented young student from the United States won a Fulbright grant to study French acting styles in both Paris and Aix-en-Provence. Because of her mastery of the language, she was given a fairly large part in a certain play; but under the stress of the performance, she reverted to the vocal methods instilled in her by her

American training. She shouted, screamed, wrenched her voice in despair, and was mentioned by the reviewers with hostility and scorn, but ultimately acquitted for being American and not knowing any better.

A sentence in French is meant to be spoken without any pausing or accents on particular words. It ripples and flows, charming the ear. Hence vocal technique in French classical acting is neither purely oratorical, as in classical drama, nor exceedingly "dramatic" in the Elizabethan sense. More than the others, it can be called musical technique.

French classical stage, with actress showing grace, elegance, and emotional control. Note the highly formalized setting and the use of perspective scenery.

The French tragic actor shows as little emotion in his face as he does in his voice. Neo-classical theaters, which were at least more intimate than Greek amphitheaters, nonetheless retained and even heightened classical impassivity of face. The aristocratic social norms of the period required well-bred people to keep their feelings to themselves. Even in the throes of passions which eventually destroy them, French classical actors maintain their regal bearing to the very end.

The social background of the neo-classical period continues to be reflected in the graceful, symmetrical movements of this acting school. It is not the grace of the Elizabethan; it is, rather, more closely allied to the classical ballet itself, in which movements are executed so as to exhibit the human form in a perfect light. Its aim is to evoke aesthetic pleasure by the dancer's triumph over human ungainliness and the dissipation of energy which characterizes the average person in his walking. In other words, its unlikeness to natural movement constitutes the major source of enjoyment. Similarly, French classical movement on the stage, like the suppressed emotionalism of the role itself, suggests a triumph over the naturally undisciplined bearing of people who are free from social restrictions. In its control it is meant to serve as a model which we can admire, even if we see no need to emulate.

If the word "civilized" had to be applied only once in the entire range of acting, it would be applied most effectively to the method of presenting French neo-classical tragedy, a display of upper-class behavior at its best. Today such a method is too rarefied for almost any but French audiences, and though Racine's plays are spoken of with reverence by those who read them there are few opportunities to see them performed on the English-speaking stage.

The Sentimental Tradition

The sentimental style of acting is supposed to be obsolete, but it should be catalogued so that theater-goers may recognize it and legitimately criticize it when it is revived except as parody. Melodramas of the popular theater in nineteenth-century Europe and America were written and performed with middle-class prejudices in mind. The actors' facial expressions, vocal tones, gestures, and movements were antique souvenirs of the Elizabethan theater which the audiences admired as "culture." Even though actors imitated the style appropriate to Shakespeare by flourishing, posing, and rolling their r's, the plays themselves had homely language and situations. The farmer's daughter, her would-be seducer, and the courageous fellow who paid off the mortgage were not necessarily elevated by their brush with the King's English. And since democratic traditions forbade the display of too much education, the actor with the grandest style was given the part of the villain.

Since sentimentality means the dishonest exploitation of the emotions, sentimental acting had a style carefully calculated to create emotional response within a largely unreflective audience. A conspicuous display of feeling was the mark of the well-bred person, so that, on the stage, the actor's emotions were conveyed through hand-wringing, face-clutching, mustache-twirling, a pointing finger, and a well-timed swoon.

Sentimental acting, in its contemporary versions, means cheating, getting the job done in the most obvious way. The amateur actor shows his inexperience when he communicates emotion by the hackneyed externals of nineteenth-century melodrama. Less obviously sentimental is the actor who approaches his role by thinking, "I play the scheming stepfather — you know, the one who just wants the wife's money and hates the kids." By pushing his character into a stereotype mold, he virtually eliminates any chance of creating a human being, and he resorts to very traditional external means to show an audience what he is.

Professionalistic

While all actors who have demonstrated skill at making audiences believe them and who are regularly paid for their services can be termed "professionals," there exists within the contemporary theater a division between the "professional" as a disciple of the "method" or the Stanislavsky System and as someone who regards himself as primarily a technician, a craftsman in the theater. The latter school can be called "professionalistic." While it does not always characterize its members in every role they play, it *is* capable of being broken down into certain identifiable techniques. Some actors tend to be more technical than others, even as some method actors tend to disparage excessively professionalistic elements in the work of their colleagues.

When a method actor says, for example, "Miranda Longmeadow is exclusively technical," he is in effect saying: "Miranda Longmeadow does not really believe what she is saying or doing on the stage. She performs with a calculated knowledge of the effect of every vocal inflection, movement and gesture, right down to the well-rehearsed lifting of an eyebrow." This is likely to be greatly exaggerated; it is doubtful whether any actor since Stanislavsky can perform without making some application of his own personality to the role.

Yet often the play itself determines the extent to which the method will work. Ibsen and Shaw, who have a great deal to say in their plays, eventually must prevail over the actor. He must remain quite conscious of the purpose of every line and speech in the total pattern of the drama. He aims at a certain kind of effect at every moment. Of course, all actors want to hold their audience, but it is characteristic of the method to insist that the audience meet it at least half way.

Thus the professionalistic *approach* is the one which places the greater stress upon the play as a whole and the impact it is calculated to have on an audience. Despite the number of method players who have achieved great fame in the theater, and despite the presence of method elements in almost any serious modern performance, the professionalistic approach is the one most characteristic of the Broadway stage today. Professionalistic or technical acting involves — to a greater extent than is true of method acting — precise concern with the externals: proper vocal pitch, gesturing, and significant movement. Those who excel in it have usually been thoroughly trained in classical and Elizabethan styles and have developed vocal and bodily control — in contrast to extreme method theater, which has been known to elevate to stardom someone who has had little or no formal training.

The professionalistic actor allows himself to feel a part only when it really counts, only in performance, while the method actor believes in living his role as soon as he can during the rehearsal period. The pressures of preparing a play for a Broadway opening, along with the business-like way rehearsals are conducted ("At one o'clock we shall do the death scene") force the performer to be sparing of his emotional energies during the time that the production details are being calculated. It is not at all uncommon for a technical actress to "die" from a stab wound inflicted by a jealous lover, go through bodily and vocal contortions, and then pop to her feet immediately and brightly ask the director, "Was that the kind of thing you meant, darling?"

There is a certain vocal quality well known to all theater-goers, a quality sometimes simply called "theatrical," denoting a resonant sound that is not classical or Elizabethan but not drawn from real-life either. It is heard in the voices of Judith Anderson, Alfred Lunt and Lynn Fontanne, Maurice Evans, Cornelia Otis Skinner, Tallulah Bankhead, and José Ferrer. Their diction is precise, and their voices rich. When a professionalistic actor appears as a guest on a television variety show, he is often paid the tribute of being called Mister, and he sounds more formal than the master of ceremonies who introduces him. Perry Como, Johnny Carson, and other "personalities" sound casual by comparison.

The professionalistic voice can do anything it wants; it can cry out so as to chill the spectator, or it can reach an abrupt termination in a hush that falls across the stage. It tends to hover just before a pause is reached; it does not come down on the final word of a sentence, but allows it to hang there in a ghostly reverberation. A speech from a play by Ibsen or from a modern "theater-piece" in the well-made play tradition is always hyper-intense at crucial moments. An example is the final scene in *A Doll's House*, when, after the selfish husband has told his sheltered wife that no man sacrifices his entire life for the one he loves, she hurls the line: "Millions of women have done so." Now a line like this simply is not left to the discretion of the actress — that is to say, she cannot underplay it or say it precisely as she might feel it in real life. She is required to put it neatly into the ears of the spectator in the last row of the second balcony and to pause dutifully while the impact is being registered.

Professionalistic drama today is seldom complex. It gets to the dramatic point, holds onto it for the appropriate length of time, then moves on. Facial expressions are less broad and stereotyped than those in sentimental drama, but they directly reflect the situation at hand. Intensity of focus is their major characteristic. Since the actor regards holding the audience enthralled as his sacred obligation in the theater, he has sometimes been known to sit before a mirror for hours practicing one glance; he can force the attention of five hundred spectators even on a shrugged shoulder. When he speaks a line of hypersignificance, he removes from his expression everything but the emotion appropriate to that line.

The theater of Ibsen reflected the manners and customs of the Victorian age, and the graceful, controlled movement of professionalistic acting today probably derives from Victorian middle-class gentility. Gesturing, in keeping with good Victorian custom, is sharply curtailed.

Modern technical actors gesture as they feel they must, so long as it does not detract from anything else. Whether the stage has gained or lost as a result of increased liberalism in the matter of the gesture must be decided by each theater-goer on the occasions when he is conscious of its specific use. Sometimes it will seem excessively melodramatic, but a gesture or the very evident lack of gesture can be the climax of a play.

There is a moment in Lillian Hellman's *The Little Foxes* (1939), when a scheming wife, knowing of her husband's heart condition, deliberately stirs him up and goads him into an attack. He clutches at his heart, staggers, falls, just a few feet from the table on which his medicine bottle stands. In this contrived situation we have to assume that the medicine in one particular bottle will suddenly, dramatically make the difference and save his life. Slowly, inexorably his hand moves upwards toward the bottle; all of the attention of all of the spectators must be on the man's hand as he finally makes the lightest kind of contact with the long-sought object — only to knock it over. Now attention shifts to the wife, because it is up to her to move *her* hand, pick up the bottle, give it to the dying man. Will she or will she not make these gestures? The reader who knows the characteristics of expert plotting may assume that the wife makes no gesture at all; the husband dies. Villainy triumphs until the final curtain, when the daughter makes her mother realize that she is not going to be able to live with herself. One can even imagine the mother, stricken for the first time with the pangs of self-recognition, putting out a tentative hand toward her child, only to have that gesture rejected.

Such a scene is a direct offspring of the concluding moment of Ibsen's *Ghosts*, in which the mother, Mrs. Alving, is faced with the choice of poisoning her son or having him live on as an imbecile. The entire play leads to this famous must-mustn't situation in which the mother either has to stretch out her hand to remove the poison tablets from the son's inner pocket or else refrain from making any gesture, thus committing herself to a lifetime of torture. Ibsen allows the final curtain to fall before the decision is made. It cannot be made; either alternative is unthinkable. But the choice of how she is to spend the rest of her life depends upon what she does with her hand.

Like speech and gestures, professionalistic movement is influenced by Victorian standards. The new drama of the nineteenth century rejected the overdone elegance of the past, but it never lost sight of the fact that the indoor theater with its artificially lit, over-bright stage, in contrast to the darkness surrounding the audience, made human movement subject to the most critical scrutiny. It became the professionalistic actor's duty to divest himself of all traces of former awkwardness, to become the embodiment of idealized movement proper in a well-behaved society.

Of all the nineteenth-century elements the concept of good stage movement has undergone the least change. Even if an actor is playing a drunk or a very slovenly person, he needs bodily control on the stage.

Method Acting

Whenever the theater is truly dramatic, it cannot be entirely life-like, and naturalistic or method acting is no more "real" than professional acting; yet it weaves an illusion so powerful that the elements of technical theatricalism have been known to disappear altogether. Its staunchest advocates freely admit their debt to Stanislavsky, founder of the Moscow Art Theater, who called his approach "the System."

"Psychological" would be another good label for this style of acting, well suited for the complex characters of Chekhov. In a play by Ibsen there was a consciousness on the part of the dramatist, the director, and the actor that every line and every event is taking place within the frame of the stage. But Chekhov was the least theatrical of all playwrights; in order to perform his work, Stanislavsky's actors had to forget much of what was traditional in the craft of acting. Here are some of the fundamentals of Stanislavsky's System, then and now:

1) The intensive training once required of voice, face, gesture and movement is replaced by the training of the "whole actor."

2) The actor proceeds on the assumption that his duty is to become a three-dimensional human being on the stage, rather than a unit of a theatrical pattern.

3) The play itself — or "script" — is a springboard, a point of departure for what will become a theatrical Whole greater than the sum of its parts.
4) The actor tends to relate the character to himself, not himself to the character. He asks, "What would I do if I were in that situation?" Such questions illustrate what Stanislavsky meant by calling his System the "As if" method.
5) Director and actor assume that *their* ideas about what lines mean or characters are thinking behind the lines proceed from the implications which the playwright has provided. Many method directors completely disregard the author's stage directions and direct commentary on his play on the grounds that what the author *consciously* wants in the production is not what he *really* wants.

With so many interpretations possible and with equal value given to all, there are frequent disputes between director and actor, author and director, and between author and actor. The strongest force out-argues the others, but the writer seldom prevails.

So far one of the major exponents of method acting in America has been the director Elia Kazan; and certainly the major school for the teaching of the method is the Actors' Studio in New York City, presided over by Lee Strasberg, who studied with Stanislavsky. They have trained or influenced some of the major talent in the American theater today, including Marlon Brando, Geraldine Page, Julie Harris, Paul Newman, Joanne Woodward, Kim Stanley, and Rip Torn. Though these personalities are highly paid professionals who possess a marketable technique of performing, none of them is especially known for the traditional elements of the actor's art. Brando and Newman, in particular, have been repeatedly censured for "mumbling" their lines.

Method acting has both the virtues and dangers of psychology itself: it can and does bring to light many subtleties that add to the pleasures of sensitive audiences, but it can also confuse, baffle, or disturb. Is it wise to encourage audience understanding of rarely encountered people and relationships? Does emphasis on interior feelings enhance the sensitivity of the insensitive, or alienate them further? And finally, is the emphasis on psychology overdone in an age perhaps needing a wider, more outward view of the world?

It becomes difficult properly to assess method performances, perhaps because they are so personal. The viewer may say, "I don't believe his performance because nobody in that predicament would behave in that manner." Yet the actor can retort, "Oh, but I would, and that's what I go on."

In watching method performers, the audience must listen very carefully, for nobody is allowed to over-articulate. Dialogue is muted, sometimes merely an undercurrent. At its best, the psychological approach lures the audience into a labyrinth of whispered half-meanings that does what theater after all is obliged to do — entertain, divert, enthrall. But its aim is to do so not in an obvious way. Method acting has done much to rid the stage of the unconvincing excesses which are often enduring trademarks of the professionalistic tradition.

"Kitchenistic" Non-Acting

A young actress once tried out for the part of Linda in *Death of a Salesman* by reading a famous, eminently actable speech from the epilogue which Arthur Miller calls "Requiem." Like most actresses she wanted the chance to be alone in front-stage center, saying farewell to her husband, who lies in his grave:

> Forgive me, dear. I can't cry. I don't know what it is, but I can't cry. It seems to me that you're just on another trip. I keep expecting you, Willy dear, I can't cry. Why did you do it? I search and search and I search, and I can't understand it, Willy. I made the last payment on the house today. Today, dear. And there'll be nobody home. (*A sob rises in her throat.*) We're free and clear. (*Sobbing more fully, released.*) We're free ... We're free ... We're free ...

At the casting session she was able to sob at will and had enough vocal control to remain audible; she held back the tears until just the right moment. In fact, during the reading of this speech, there was dead silence in the theater (a rare occurrence at tryouts); when she finished, no one spoke. The director and his staff were clearly moved. It seemed inevitable that she would get the part; yet, another actress was named to play Linda.

The reason? The girl simply could not manage the kitchenistic moments in the play. She did not question the verdict, for she had even admitted that lines like "Be careful on the stairs, dear!" or "The cheese is on the middle shelf!" were beyond her ability. The actress who got the part of Linda was not as touching on opening night as the first girl had been at the readings, but she was at home in the kitchen of Willy Loman's house.

Kitchenistic acting requires a special kind of skill that training in the other styles does not help. The actors who dislike it argue that they cannot concentrate solely on the build towards a big moment amid the authentic-sounding hen cluckings somewhere outside. At first, the kitchenistic element in acting (though it too was called "natural") was hailed as a great advance; nobody suspected or feared that it could become a menace to the theater.

In one of the television commercials a rather unattractive woman, someone's idea of a typical next-door neighbor, correctly chooses the pile of laundry that was not cleaned with Brand X, utters a little cry of surprise, then begins to laugh from the nervous excitement of it all. The paid actors in the commercials like the ones who perform the soap operas, all have mastered the skill of kitchenism; all know how to give the illusion that they have just walked in off the street. Shakespeare's actors never tried to give this illusion, nor did those who performed Ibsen, nor even did Stanislavsky's psychological actors. In kitchenism we have not acting but mimicry, not theatrical magic but photographic fidelity, not truth but authenticity.

Kitchenism seems to take less out of an actor than any other style of performing. Relaxation is its major characteristic. Other notable characteristics are frequent and insignificant pausing; a strange use of low, sometimes nearly inaudible vocal tones; frequent sighing and other noises which are substituted for words; and, above all, the actor's taking in a deep breath before speaking almost every line. Kitchenism is rigorously anti-intellectual; it strives to avoid all traces of acting styles that might be associated with any sophisticated form of drama.

It is not, however, to be condemned altogether. In Paddy Chayevsky's *Marty* the actors were required to reproduce faithfully certain *types* which they either had observed or were familiar with. The boredom of their lives is a significant one, and thus the actors' crystallization of the characters performs a valuable service. Not only is *Marty* kitchenistic in style, it is *about* kitchenism. The authenticity of the acting makes us regret the narrowness of the lives being depicted.

But kitchenism becomes unacceptable when the material warrants more dramatic treatment or when it uses its mask of authenticity to present highly unauthentic subject matter, such as the sugary portrait of the typical American home offered in the "family" television series. *Marty* stands almost alone, as though it had done all that kitchenism could ever do. Kitchenistic acting and writing do not lend themselves to endless variations; their very soul is a lack of variety.

Tour de Force

The great stars of the musical comedy stage, such as Mary Martin, Robert Preston, Carol Channing, and Jackie Gleason, possess an inner "something" that is hard to define. It has been called "charm" and "star quality," but the best definition may have been given in one of Ethel Merman's songs: "You either have it, or you've had it." The show-biz people base their art not on the laws of human nature but on the laws of the theater. They are the ones who say "break a leg" or "knock 'em dead tonight," — the traditional theater slogans for "Good Luck." With professional performers, the obligation to the audience is an obsession.

Since the great stars of the British and American popular stage normally appear in long-run hits, they become extraordinarily attuned to the subtle shadings of audience reactions. Ordinary actors recognize their responsibility as being primarily the total play with its motivations and important moments all duly considered. They rarely look directly at the audience; rather they play to each other. Even the Elizabethan actor, coming to the front of the stage and delivering a soliloquy to the audience, will be serious or smile according to the nature of the lines he is speaking; the integrity of the character must not be violated.

Show-biz actors, however, do not really play characters. A part of themselves is a radiant individualism that arouses an instant "glow" within their audience. Their two chief characteristics are an almost constant smile and an infectious, dynamic enthusiasm that ultimately exhaust the viewer. Theirs is a great and honorable tradition, but their art is always left in the theater. The implications of what they have said and done do not creep out into all areas of our lives. They have given us a few hours of pleasure.

Occasionally, however, a performance may have a peculiar brilliance about it, that has too much characterization to be show-biz but is too brittle, too glossy to be deeply related to the laws of human nature. José Ferrer's Cyrano de Bergerac is one example. The famous death of Cyrano in the convent garden, with blossoms falling tenderly all about, is not the result of a tragic catastrophe. It is a thing of beauty as pure theatrical hokum. The actor's performance is therefore a *tour-de-force*. The phrase sometimes suggests a certain emptiness behind the spectacular quality, but this need not be the case in the theater. The depth, however, is a theatrical one. A tour-de-force performance maintains almost constant rapport with the viewer, a phenomenon which is impossible to achieve in any other kind of theater except show biz.

Stylized

Thus far nothing has been said about acting in comedy. Two major traditions now exist in the theater which govern performances that are mainly intended to inspire laughter: one belongs to the professionalistic school, which strives to calculate in advance where the humor of a play lies and how it may best be served so as to entertain the audience. This approach nonetheless believes the actor must remain honest — within the framework of the play — and not "mug" or play to the audience whenever he feels he needs another laugh. He must not carry to extremes such comic devices as the double take, the slow burn, the choking cough, or the pratfall. The professionalistic approach to comedy does not wholly divorce it from the general theatrical law of plausibility, maintaining that the best comic performers are those who are equally adept in more serious forms of drama, that even the pie-in-the-face sequence must be carefully motivated or else the proceedings will degenerate into preposterousness.

The reason that the professionalistic style of comic acting tends to dominate modern stage practice is that most popular modern comedies have been in themselves deeply influenced by the well-made play tradition of the nineteenth century. They use authentic settings and even many kitchenistic elements in the dialogue. The situation may be basically incongruous, but not necessarily improbable. Thus if the plot is about a man and a woman sharing an apartment to pool their expenses but trying to maintain a Platonic relationship, it is *Lysistrata,* twentieth-century style, but not, for all that, relieved of its obligation to show some fidelity to real life.

The other major tradition is that of stylized acting — appropriate for the continued performances of Aristophanes, Molière, or Wilde, as well as the comedies of Shakespeare and the neo-classical comedies of manners. All of them demand high style in the playing, as opposed to more natural handlings of the four basic aspects of acting: voice, face, gesture, and movement. They differ from classical and Elizabethan schools of acting in demanding even more broadness and, under certain circumstances, "prettier" movements, speech, and action.

Since comedy is still performed on a stage, under the close scrutiny of an audience, the theory behind stylized playing is that whatever incongruities may exist in lines and situations to provoke laughter cannot be extended to the physical externals. Thus an actor pretending to be an awkward buffoon with two left feet has to possess more bodily control than an actor in a straight part. A drunken fall on the stage affords no pleasure to the viewer when it is not executed with finesse. Nobody wants to pay to see a highly convincing imitation of the real thing with all its ineptitude and waste of energy. Beside, the actor who lacks the experience of speaking and moving with style calls attention to the basic absurdity of what he is doing and so breaks the contract with the audience that everything on the stage — even nonsense — must inspire complete belief. The theory of stylized acting rests its case on the conviction that, since the great comedy of the theater has been a most civilizing art, its performance logically demands a hyper-civilized (that is, essentially classical) use of the voice and body.

Since words are a major source of humor in comedy, the actor's skill in delivering his speech is important and can be as much a reason for admiration of his performance as the humor itself. Stylized speech, when it is found in comedy, is of two main varieties: witty delivery and patter.

The effectiveness of theatrical wit depends upon the actor's seriousness and seeming indifference to the comic potential of what he is saying. Dame Edith Evans as Lady Bracknell in *The Importance of Being Earnest* and as Miss Western in *Tom Jones* (both are films of high style) provides examples of what witty acting is all about. The actress' magnificently immobile face, which never breaks into the slightest suggestion of a smile, allows her to say the most outrageous things without ever sacrificing her lofty dignity. When she accuses Jack Worthing of carelessness after he has announced dolefully that he has lost his parents, she reaches the summit of theatrical incongruity without admitting for a moment that she is not serious. Her voice could be that of a queen and imparts to the homeliest phrase an aristocratic elegance which is funny without losing dignity — as when Miss Western denounces her drunken brother as a "country stewpot." The marvelous sound of "sti-oo" comes to us straight from the Royal Shakespearean Theater and makes us laugh all the harder for that very fact.

Patter is an improbable barrage of polysyllable words that the average person could not efficiently handle without long practice. The trained comic actor makes the verbal feat sound easy; we laugh because we know that such complicated and rapid speech is not normally easy and because the actor — in a fashion similar to Lady Bracknell's high-toned, deadpan delivery of her lines — does not appear to notice that his word pattern and his virtuoso delivery of it are at all out of the ordinary. W. S. Gilbert is the most famous of all creators of patter in the theater, and the actor who attempts to master it has the twofold difficulty of having to sing as well as to enunciate.

> I am the very model of a modern Major-General,
> I've information vegetable, animal and mineral,
> I know the kings of England, and I quote the fights historical,
> From Marathon to Waterloo, in order categorical;
> I'm very well acquainted too with matters mathematical,
> I understand equations, both the simple and quadratical,
> About binomial theorem I'm teeming with a lot o' news —
> With many cheerful facts about the square of the hypotenuse.

So sings the Major-General in *The Pirates of Penzance* (1879), who has the added benefit of absurd rhymes like "lot o' news" and "hypotenuse" to help make us laugh. But actors who can "put their voices" anywhere they please in a theater, who can stop on a dime, who can accelerate to such a point that most people cannot understand them do not need the rich patter material provided by Gilbert; they can speed up the normal tempo of a speech so that it has the effect of patter and can thus insure a greater response from the audience.

Here is a brief list of the more commonly discernible characteristics of the vocal tones in stylized comic acting:

1) *The aristocratic sound.* Many works — like the comedy of manners, for example, feature characters who are able to dazzle the audience by their superior erudition.

2) *Vocal control.*

3) *Vocal incongruity* — as when the tone of voice is inappropriate to the statement. In John Huston's memorable film *Beat the Devil,* a steward on a British ship walks among the passengers, striking a

triangle and announcing in the deadest possible voice, "The ship is sinking."

4) *The high-low pattern.* This is sometimes known as "undercutting." One character will build a speech to a high emotional pitch; another will reply with no emotion at all. Or the same character may abruptly reverse himself in the middle of his own speech. Example: someone in frenzied desperation cries out, "You wouldn't!"; and then drops immediately to a flat "You would."

The face of the actor in stylized playing is less mobile than it is in all forms of acting except the classical. It broadly states the case, whether it be that of jealous husband, man-hungry widow, or earnest suitor. The intricacies of character psychology have no place in this kind of drama. There is never any doubt concerning what the actor is thinking or what the audience is to understand. But this does not make the facial aspect of stylized art any the less important. Indeed the great comic players on the world's stages are as famous for their facial control as for their voices, e.g., W. C. Fields, Bert Lahr, Fernandel and Charlie Chaplin, and the great French mime Marcel Marceau, who does all of his communicating with face and body alone. When the broadness of an expression is relied upon, every detail of that expression naturally comes under scrutiny. Any part of it — the eye, the mouth, the lips — that fails to communicate something is seen at once for its shortcomings.

Many of the great comic actors are as well-known for their faces as others are for their voices. Since the aim of stylized playing is to evoke laughter or at least to encourage high spirits, gesturing cannot be indiscriminate. An actor who is said to have "style," has gestures that are significant, pointed, appropriate to the occasion. Most of the world's great comedies take place in highly artificial surroundings — like the Forest of Arden in *As You Like It* — and everything said or done must shine with precision. Gesturing is generally of two varieties: graceful, as for Shakespeare, whose comedies have more romance and charm than they do physical humor; and flamboyant, as for Aristophanes, Molière, and the comedies of manners, where everything has to be "overdone" well — in exquisite exaggeration.

The exquisiteness, the precision, the finesse — while not necessarily sources of humor in themselves — also play their part in evoking pleasurable responses from the audience. If comedy in its fundamental and traditional sense is satire, if it has an underlying serious purpose, then it follows that it cannot be slambang, "knock 'em dead" theater. Its classical grace must alternate with the humor so that the seriousness does not altogether disappear amid the roaring of an audience. Being entertained at a comedy is not directly dependent upon the volume and number of laughs as one gag follows another. Only in the business world of commercial television does a laugh meter determine the worth of a show. The discriminating spectator likes to laugh, but he does not want to obscure his understanding of what he came to the theater to see in the first place: a great comedian in a great play.

Here is an example of how one popular actor uses the Stanislavsky Method in preparing a role.

 Sidney Poitier: *Actors Talk about Acting**

POITIER: . . . . I used the Stanislavsky Method in preparing my work, something which I am privileged to use over a *long* period of time before I go on the stage, or before I go on in front of a camera. Which means that instead of employing the Stanislavsky Method for two hours a night in a theatre, I employ it for two or three months in the preparation of that work, so that when I go on the stage, or in front of a camera, my function becomes organic and instant and natural, spontaneous and full, because I have a frame of reference for every want, every need, every desire that is registered on my emotion boards.

INTERVIEWER: Could you be specific here, and just take us through a single part you prepared for?

POITIER: Well, let's take the last thing I did on the stage; let's take *A Raisin in the Sun*. I received the script almost a year before we went into production, right? And I read it, naturally, many, many times and I knew, generally, after ten or twenty readings, what the circumstances of the play were. I knew what the individual characters were like, generally. I understood my character kind of generally. Now I needed time to make my understanding of my character specific. In so doing I must understand all of the contributing elements that go to making up this character. First I must understand what are the driving forces in the man. In order to understand that, you must find out what are his political, social, economic, religious milieus, and how they contribute to the personality idiosyncrasies or whatever. And in so examining, I find that this, first, is a Negro man thirty-six years old, living in Chicago on the South Side — which of itself is quite significant in the building of a character, because only a particular kind of Negro lives on the South Side in this particular kind of circumstances, see? So that narrows the field already. And then we take: Why is this man living here? Is he here by choice? What is his relation

---

* From *Actors Talk About Acting*, edited by Lewis Funke and John E. Booth. © Copyright 1961 by Lewis Funke and John E. Booth. Reprinted by permission of Random House, Inc.

to his community? What is his relation to his religion, if he has one? What is his relation to his economic disposition? Is it one in which he finds enough elasticity to function and maintain his manhood or is it a constant badge or remembrance of his inadequacies — you follow? — and all these things can be found in the script, or at least if they're not there they can be made compatible with what is in the script at one point or another. So that — after months of actually making specific this man in his milieu — then I come to the final conclusion of what are his wants. And when I find what are his general wants, I find what is his most specific want or wants. And they aren't many — so with his most specific want, I now have the man in total. I know what his reaction would be to everything done and said in the play — see? I know what and how he feels about his neighborhood, so that any question or reference to it strikes a certain chord in a man. Now with this kind of information, I then proceed to familiarize myself with the pros and cons of his life and his wants. I try to experience them, so by the time I'm ready to perform, I don't go in a corner — at least I don't have to go in a corner and concentrate and conjure up some mysterious magic. I walk on the stage and it happens. And I don't work Method because it's too late now to work Method. If you're not ready, forget it. You walk on the stage and you perform, because what begins to happen out there is that you find that you have taken on the milieu of the character, and you then begin to seek out and fulfill the very wants that are burning inside *you* now, which are his wants. Once you're on the stage you have no time, because the stage is to experience — you follow? — the stage is to experience . . . Once the curtain goes up and there is an audience out there, you, the artist, your responsibility is to experience, and only through your experiencing are you able really to transmit — you follow? There are many kinds of actors. There are actors who can get on a stage, but they can never quite enthrall, nor can they ever quite involve or hypnotize, but they can give a workmanlike job. Well, *if they're not gifted,* they don't enthrall and they don't involve, because they themselves are not able to involve on the level required by the artist.

INTERVIEWER: What is the difference between these two?

POITIER: There is a basic difference to my mind between the two. And ofttimes it's not because of the difference in talent. It's sometimes — it always is the difference in the humanity of the individual, you see. There is a phrase used by jazz musicians, and they call it "soul." It is a reference to a certain kind of humanity — of the sensitivity of humanity — that is overstocked in one person. They use the word soul because there are certain gifted, brilliant musicians who have a kind of human compassion that — they are so inarticulate in every other phase of life, they can only express through their music, and hence they are terribly important musicians and gifted. With actors, I think — there are some actors who have a great degree of "soul power." There are actors who have not as much and there are actors who are void of it. Now, the fine actors who are void of it are called technicians. They are quite capable of making you *realize* you are in a theatre watching a terribly gifted technician at work, and you say, "Ahh, he's marvelous." If he had the added gift of soul, you would forget you're in a theatre, that's the difference.

Here is an example of the Professionalistic theory of acting styles as enunciated by Josef von Sternberg, director of *The Blue Angel* (1930) and other screen masterpieces.

❀ Josef von Sternberg *On the Art of Control**

Acting is not the memorizing of a text while wearing a disguise, nor the facility to simulate anything at a moment's notice, but the reconstruction of motives that are the cause of action and words. This is not easy, easy though it may be for the actor to forget his own suffering by shouldering that of another. At his best he is not only an interpreter, not only a carrier of ideas originating in others, but can invest his impersonation with a depth of understanding beyond the playwright's knowledge. He can be a superb mechanic and take the written word plus the director's instructions to combine the two with the components of his own person, and thus give fluency and cohesion to thoughts that would not float over the footlights without his skill. He can impress us with the meaning of the simplest word though we may have heard it a thousand times before without recognizing its significance. It is not when he spouts Shakespeare without slurring a syllable that he wins his spurs, not when he has absorbed Kabuki and Stanislavsky in order to read a television commercial, but when he has learned to muffle his flamboyance, and so to control what he does that he can combine both actor and commentator. He then can make us feel compassion, not for himself but for the one whose history we witness.

* Reprinted from *Fun in a Chinese Laundry* by Josef von Sternberg by permission of The Macmillan Company, Publishers. Copyright © Josef von Sternberg, 1965.

14 ❀ ❀ ❀

The Craft of Theater

There is nothing disillusioning about looking backstage; rather, the critical viewer discovers a heightened sense of appreciation of theater there. He recognizes that the most solid-looking stage set is made of muslin, a beautiful queen's gown may contain a dozen snaps for a quick change, a glass of bourbon is really only cold tea, and a violent stabbing scene has been carefully rehearsed so that the victim knows exactly where to fall, how to fall safely, and how to make his body give the illusion that it has been pierced by a knife. The critical viewer avoids the sign of the popcorn syndrome — too complete an absorption in what he is seeing. Enjoying the craft of theater at work helps to prevent a loss of critical identity and offers in itself one of the additional pleasures of theater-going.

The Method-Professional Director

A young German director, an associate of Max Reinhardt, who came to prominence in the Berlin theater of the 1920's, was given as his first assignment the task of directing a play in which Elisabeth Bergner was to play the lead. After the second or third rehearsal the star handed in her resignation on the grounds that the young director was impossible to work with. When asked whether he had been "giving her trouble," the star replied that, on the contrary, her director had not seemed to notice that she was alive. The great Reinhardt then confronted his protegé with the accusation and was told that the star was simply so magnificent that specific direction had seemed extraneous and insulting. Advised that he would either direct Miss Bergner or be removed from the assignment, the young man the next day kept interrupting the star to change certain of her movements. She was delighted and withdrew her resignation.

Even the greatest performer feels insecure on stage during the rehearsal period of a play unless there is a competent director sitting at the back of the theater carefully scrutinizing every movement and listening to the interpretation of every line. When the curtain rises on opening night, the audience sees only the finished product and, at curtain calls, applauds only the players. But few performers merit enthusiastic applause without a director's constant help.

This dependence on the director is quite new. It is unlikely that the

Greek actors were directed at all in the contemporary sense of the word, and the Elizabethan and seventeenth-century acting companies had managers who normally played the leading roles. They saw to it that everyone kept out of their way and did not prevent them from attracting most of the audience attention, which was their due. During the time of Molière, in keeping with the rigid class system of society itself, the manager-lead would play stage front all night long, while lesser members of the cast would occupy stations further upstage according to the importance of their roles.

One of the earliest directors in the modern sense and certainly the first major director was André Antoine (1857–1943), founder of the Theâtre Libre in Paris. More than any other single theater personality, Antoine helped to make Ibsen an international success.

Pioneering in the "fourth wall" or "illusionistic" theater that strove for verisimilitude on the stage and consciously attempting to rid the drama of sentimentality and melodrama, Antoine raised the director to a position of pre-eminence. It became the director's task to subdue the actor's natural tendency to exhibit himself on stage, for the entire tradition of the nineteenth-century theater up to Antoine's time had stressed the actor's dulcet tones and rhetorical flights. Seeing a performance during the early 1800's would have been something like attending the opera today. One waited for the big speeches and roundly applauded them as audiences do their favorite arias. There was never any doubt as to the pure theatricality of the theater. With productions of Ibsen, however, Antoine recognized the need for greater acting restraint and for the director's interpretation of the entire production so as to communicate its serious thesis. The director's rising importance parallels the change from the theater of sentimentality to the theater of the later nineteenth century which saw itself as serious art.

Stanislavsky went further than Antoine. In addition to visualizing, analyzing, and interpreting the play, he made the director's function that of providing the proper "atmosphere" during rehearsals, of taking the art of theater so seriously that it became almost a religion to the members of his company. More than any other force in the history of theater, Stanislavsky is responsible for that complete dedication which distinguishes the "total" actor from the performer for whom theater is a pleasant way to earn a generous living. What Aristotle was to the aesthetics of tragedy, Stanislavsky was to the aesthetics of directing. He was not only a competent craftsman but a philosopher of the drama. He saw the play as an organic whole, having evolved from the depths of the playwright. It was not to be chopped up into "meaning," "symbol," or even this speech or that scene as high points to be especially punched out in performance. Just as the play emerged living from its creator's hands, it had to be approached in the same spirit by the director and his actors.

Ever since Stanislavsky, the craft of play directing has been over-whelmingly influenced by his philosophy of drama and by his devotion to the truthfulness and integrity of stage life. Whether a director is staging *Hamlet* in an authentic Elizabethan style or *The Cherry Orchard* itself, he tends to follow the principles which Stanislavsky set down. A good term for the general approach to directing which dominates the modern theater is *method-professional.* Essentially this means that, unlike the purely method actor who might lose himself altogether in his role, the director must never lose sight of the obligation of the theater to its audience.

An actor may perform for purely personal reasons, just as Edgar Rice Burroughs, unable to walk and confined to his bed, created Tarzan, the super hero, as a vicarious means of escape from his condition. The director, however, must be fully conscious at every moment that his aim is to create a unified whole which will have certain effects upon the audience at certain definite places. Indeed method acting cannot work at all without professional directing, without the sure, steady hand of a deliberate craftsman who leaves nothing to chance.

The amateur theater, to be sure, is filled with many directors who call themselves "method" but who, paradoxically enough, have none at all. Their concept of Stanislavsky is to give the actor almost unlimited freedom on the stage, to allow him to experiment and build his part in hit or miss fashion. If the play "goes" with the audience on opening night, nobody is more surprised than the director. While everyone in the theater knows that audiences are hard to predict, a method-professional director can normally tell whether a production is going to work or not.

New York is now filled with many teachers of acting who claim to be apostles of Stanislavsky himself, and there are stories — probably exaggerated — of what they demand. Fledgling actors are said to spend months to years learning about "life" before they ever perform actual roles. One such school recommended to its students that they deliberately court real-life experiences that would help them feel the anguish of great sexual longing, which the head of the school had decided was the major theme in modern drama. A young actress at another such school is reported to have spent her first year of study attempting to lose her own self-consciousness by pretending to be various non-human entities. She was a bottle of milk, a polar bear in the zoo, and an ancient oak tree. "Think milk!" she was told. "Think milk and you become milk!" If these stories are true, it is doubtful that Stanislavsky would have comprehended some of the curricula developed in his name.

There is, of course, a vast difference between directing highly paid actors and directing university or community groups. Tyrone Guthrie, one of the major directors in theater today, has said that he regards his function at rehearsals as being somewhat akin to that of the chairman of the board. He is dealing with people who know their business, who take it upon themselves to analyze their characters before they appear for the first rehearsal. His job is to assemble the whole production, to stand back and make certain that the actors develop their roles so that a true ensemble effect is gained — that is, the illusion that the people on the stage are truly relating to each other, not simply saying lines and moving. It is seldom the director's responsibility to super-impose his own vision of each character upon the actor who has been selected for the part, presumably because of his skill and experience.

The university or community director, however, has a teaching function as well. In general, he is dealing with players who are not adept at calling up past experiences and past insights and making immediate, concentrated applications to present roles. He is also dealing with people who have not yet acquired the vocal and physical control needed to free the actor for the important business of impersonating someone else on the stage. The fledgling actor will sometimes move awkwardly across the stage, sound too loud or too soft, have difficulty enunciating a tongue-twisting bit of dialogue, fail to find the "hot" or intensely lighted areas, or else find these too obviously. In addition, this director is often working with backstage people who do not quite know how to light a stage so as to bring out the values of the production or to select a costume so that it helps, not hinders, the performer. He must therefore be everywhere and consider all phases of the production. If performances on the non-professional level are sometimes found wanting, the reason may not be purely the "talent" (an unmeasurable quantity) of the actors but rather the diffusion of the director's responsibilities.

How the Director Reads the Play

When an established director, who is in a position to choose either commercial or uncommercial plays, decides to direct a given drama, he is motivated by any one of a number of guiding principles. If the play is an established classic of the theater — Ibsen's *A Doll's House*, for example — he reads the play to decide whether it is still worth doing. He looks for those elements in the play to which modern audiences might yet be able to relate. Above all, he attempts to determine whether the play's reputation is based upon its age and significance in theater history or whether it does in fact possess a real theater sense that endures.

University directors are sometimes pressured into staging a play because it is academically reputable and because the students need the opportunity to see a play that they study. The director may want to find a wholly fresh new approach to the play, one which will revitalize it altogether. At times this approach results in a grotesque distortion of the original, but at other times, what had been a candidate for library dust now becomes super-charged with theatrical electricity.

A Doll's House, for example, is a play whose original thesis is now outmoded. The double standard is no longer a major issue, and few wives nowadays need to pretend to be as foolish and helpless as Nora. But with the rise to power of woman, there has been a decline in the prestige of man — particularly man as husband. *A Doll's House* could easily be re-interpreted in the light of these sociological changes, so that the husband becomes the central figure, a tragic victim of his own mistaken idea of self-importance, a victim of the failure of his masculinity. For audiences familiar with *Who's Afraid of Virginia Woolf?* the relationship between Ibsen's husband and wife could be refurbished and rendered as good as new.

In the commercial theater the task of the director includes being able to read a new script in order to determine how stageworthy it is. Directors differ in their response to the often-asked question, "What makes you decide to do a certain play?" Sometimes they are attracted by one particular scene, which they can clearly visualize on the stage and which they know will have a tremendous impact on the audience. Sometimes the script seems to challenge anyone to make it come to life. Sometimes the theme itself is so original, the issue so provocative and the position taken so bold and controversial that the director cannot resist trying it.

In general, however, most directors insist that before everything else a play must have "heart," a useful term which theater people understand, though it is not easy to define in so many words. It is something, they argue, that is "there" or else not; when it is, there is no mistaking it. It is a quality in a play that makes one instantly care about the people in it — or at least the hero. It is not to be confused with anything sentimental. "Heart" means the thing is alive — it exists — it dares the viewer not to be concerned. Some directors have used the phrase "a sense of urgency." In the works of George Bernard Shaw, for example, "heart" is the undeniable brooding presence of a lofty wisdom, an incisive genius that forces the attention and commands the respect.

Bad scripts have a forced quality about them. They are lumbering robots, not living organisms. The basic situation, the idea of the protagonist — *something* was not there to begin with, and the dialogue simply prattles on about events toward which the critical viewer remains indifferent. A sense of urgency generally communicates itself almost from the outset, and a perceptive director seldom has to read beyond the first act. George Abbott, one of the most famous directors of slick comedy, put the matter aptly when he stated that most plays are bad anyway and that all first plays are bound to be bad. That the detection of "heart" is difficult is shown in the sobering statistic that ninety per cent of all plays that open every year on Broadway close after only short runs.

When Liza Doolittle, the ragged flower girl of *My Fair Lady*, first steps into the spotlight and sings "Wouldn't It Be Loverly?" there is "heart." Everyone in the world wants to protect her from the rain and the cold —

and all the more because she is a tough little spitfire who asks for no pity. From that point on, the audience is hers. It is impossible not to care what happens to her. And there is immediate interest when Greta Garbo in *Ninotchka* (1939), playing a lady Russian commissar sent to Paris on a mission, steps into the lavish hotel suite reserved for her and asks in a flat voice, "What part of the room do I occupy?"

The director is likely to be sold on the validity of the play almost at once in such cases, though not likely to admit it. He needs further justification. For example, something ought to *happen* in the play and not just here and there; there should be a solid, unmistakable line of direction running through the play from exposition to obligatory moment; if there is not, he looks for some compensating factor. He knows that the closer a plot comes to a pyramidal structure, the easier it will be to make an impact on the audience. But a play such as Thornton Wilder's *Our Town* undoubtedly won over its director because of its total lack of dramatic structure and unique method of telling its story: a bare stage, with the Stage Manager acting as narrator, leaning casually against the proscenium arch, smoking a pipe, and weaving his spell.

After urgency and structure, the next principle the director searches for is *imbalance*. Does the play move along precisely as one would expect? Or does it have a "difference" that is not just put there for its own sake? "Balance" often means that the audience has seen all the characters and heard all the dialogue in other plays before. In tragedy imbalance can be the principle of Euripidean irony, for example, King Lear entering with the corpse of his youngest daughter, who had so much to live for. Or it can be an additional horror not required by the steady build toward an inevitable climax, such as Oedipus' re-entrance from the palace with his eyes gouged out. Stanislavsky pointed to the principle of imbalance as one of the major aspects of good characterization, advising actors to look for the strength of weak characters and the weakness of strong characters so as to bring the whole play closer to the truth of human beings.

The director also asks whether the work contains a must factor and a mustn't factor (see Chapter Three). Does it suggest movement in a certain direction that will fascinate the audience but create at the same time a contrary desire? A play about the trial and execution of the hero might have little else, but it would have a must-mustn't.

A director who reads O'Neill's *Long Day's Journey into Night* finds an immediate sense of urgency (a young man trying to persuade his mother that he has consumption, only to be ignored); a pyramidal structure (a long day's journey toward the mother's inevitable total surrender to drugs); the principle of imbalance (a scene in the fourth act in which the older brother strikes the younger brother violently and knocks him to the floor — out of love, not hate — and the final scene in which the mother's surrender is found to be as bad as we had feared); and the must-mustn't factor (an inevitable consequence of the plot's revolving around the mother's intensifying need for drugs).

Testing Dialogue

The first reading also attempts an evaluation of the workability of the dialogue on the stage. While the act of reading is for most people a purely literary experience the aim of which is to find the thought behind the words, the director cares about how the words will sound when they are spoken. Conversations in real life are so wordy, repetitious, and rambling, they cannot be the models for good dramatists — not even for those who try most to capture the authentic rhythms of actual speech. The director looks for dialogue that is more than adequate. He knows that audiences admire certain lines in plays for two reasons, and the director is aware of both: 1) something fresh and unexpected has been put into words which surprise and delight; or 2) an old sentiment has been given striking new phrasing. "God is love" would not be a good line from a play because the phrasing is trite; "God is dead" has become equally stale and would have no more effect upon a sophisticated audience.

What constitutes workable stage language is not reducible to a set of rules. If it were, there might be fewer failures in the professional theater. Even the most experienced director can make a mistake by over-estimating the impact that an author's writing will have upon the audience. Excessive cleverness can sink a play as well as lift it to the heights. A sophisticated comedy in which nearly every line is a quip or an epigram will soon bore; a serious play, with a serious social theme, can become tiresome if all the speeches are ladened with profundities. Thus:

JOE: (grimly) I'll have to go away and leave you. We've just got to face it, Cindy.

CINDY: (crying out) It's all so wrong! Why must there be fighting and killing? Why do men hate? Why can't there be love? Why can't two decent people like us have a chance? Why? Why?

At this point the director is likely to close the script — if indeed he has not done so before. He objects to the dialogue not because he favors war and hate but because he doubts the plausibility of those sentiments being spoken by Joe and Cindy. He wants a play that will show, not tell.

Young playwrights are often afflicted by *signifiphelia,* the disease of taking themselves too seriously and believing they will be able to lead the world out of darkness by forcing it to hear a sermon. Samuel Beckett, whose *Waiting for Godot* may endure as one of the great stage works of the twentieth century, was well into maturity when he composed the play. He did not make the mistake of trying to say too much about the human predicament. It is hard for young writers to realize the weakness of the overly explicit statement. One character's insistence to another "If only we could communicate —" is likely to sound as embarrassing on stage as it would in real life.

One play which has entertained audiences for three-quarters of a century is Wilde's *The Importance of Being Earnest,* and one of its most famous sequences is the "muffin scene," with the two young heroes, Jack and Algernon, sitting at a table and eating muffins as fast as they can. Here are two lines from the scene as it was originally written:

> JACK: There is certainly no chance of your marrying Miss Cardew.
> ALGERNON: I don't think there is much likelihood, Jack, of you and Miss Fairfax being united.

Here is an example of how a lesser playwright — one without heart — might have continued the scene:

> JACK: What makes you say that?
> ALGERNON: Because you don't really love her. You don't know how to love anyone. In fact, what you are is in love with love.
> JACK: How dare you say I don't know how to love when you've never been serious with any girl?
> ALGERNON: I'm in love with Cecily.
> JACK: And do you intend to marry her?
> ALGERNON: Is that any of your business?
> JACK: Why shouldn't it be? I'm her guardian.
> ALGERNON: Isn't she a free agent? Can't she love whom she pleases?
> JACK: Anyone else but you. I know you too well.
> ALGERNON: We'll see about that, Jack!
> JACK: Yes, we certainly shall!

There is nothing really wrong with the dialogue, except that there is nothing right with it either. And the director wants the play to work every second. Everything has to be right. He sometimes applies the "cab driver test" — that is, he scans the play at first very rapidly, scene after scene, to see whether any exchange of dialogue notably seizes him or notably repels him with its leadenness. In the bad version above, the dialogue is nothing more than a pair of fat oxen pulling the story along. But Jack and Algernon are vain, shallow young men who live for pleasure, and the truth of *this* play depends on their being shown continually *having* pleasure.

Here is the way Wilde continued the scene:

	Director's thoughts
JACK: Well, that is no business of yours.	(*The sassy retort is imbalance.*)
ALGERNON: If it was my business, I wouldn't talk about it. (*Begins to eat muffins.*) It is	(*Algernon's comeback is further imbalance.*)

very vulgar to talk about one's business. Only people like stockbrokers do that, and then merely at dinner parties.

(Most people can accept a moralization as entertaining as this one.)

JACK: How you can sit there, calmly eating muffins when we are in this horrible trouble, I can't make out. You seem to me to be perfectly heartless.

(Turns the muffin-eating into a major calamity.)

ALGERNON: Well, I can't eat muffins in an agitated manner. The butter would probably get on my cuffs. One should always eat muffins quite calmly. It is the only way to eat them.

(Responds to "calmly" rather than to supposed gravity of the situation.) *(Another absurd moralization.)*

JACK: I say it's perfectly heartless your eating muffins at all under the circumstances.

(They still go on about muffins instead of the original subject.)

ALGERNON: When I am in trouble, eating is the only thing that consoles me. Indeed, when I am in really great trouble, as any one who knows me intimately will tell you, I refuse everything except food and drink. At the present moment I am eating muffins because I am unhappy. Besides, I am particularly fond of muffins.

(This is the closest to soul-searching Algernon ever gets in the entire play.)

(The gastronomical truth and the comic shock after "refuse everything" negate the soul-searching anyway.)

JACK: Well, that is no reason why you should eat them all in that greedy way. *(Takes muffin from Algernon.)*

ALGERNON: *(offering teacake)* I wish you would have teacake instead. I don't like teacake.

(Algernon becomes even more outrageous and hence likeable, since he lacks all the cliché characteristics of a likeable person.)

JACK: Good heavens! I suppose a man may eat his own muffins in his own garden.

(Reasonable. We're with you, Jack.)

ALGERNON: But you have just said it was perfectly heartless to eat muffins.

(Algernon strangles him with his own logic.)

JACK: I said it was perfectly heartless of you, under the circumstances. That is a very different thing.

(Jack rises again.)

ALGERNON: That may be. But the muffins are the same. (*He seizes the muffin dish from Jack.*)

(*Algernon has the last word, as expected, since he is sponging on Jack and has no right to the last word.*)

Unlike the bad version of this scene, Wilde's continually does the *expectedly unexpected.* It departs from the subject of the amorous involvements of the two young men and never returns, preferring instead to deal with muffin-eating and its ethical ramifications. Bad playwrights do not visualize the scene on an actual stage; they experience it in some imaginary real setting. They come to think of their characters as having independent existence, and their dialogue comes to be what they *would* say, instead of what they *should* say in theatrical time and space. Because theater is a matter of what is possible, not necessarily what is probable, the director is interested in what he can believe in. He will not forgive a lifeless scene merely because statistically it *could* happen. Besides, Jack and Algernon are the very kind of people who *would* become involved in the question of the right and wrong of muffin-eating. Wilde does not violate the law of plausibility.

Closely associated, in the director's preliminary consideration of the play, is the moral honesty or dishonesty of the situation and its ultimate resolution. If the script seems to promise that a sexually repressed girl must eventually surrender to a passion for a promiscuous lover, he will not "buy" a sudden change in the man's character and an obligatory moment that evades the issue altogether by taking the couple to the altar. The director runs in terror from the *deus ex machina.*

He condemns melodrama — the division of the characters into good and bad — even as he deplores sentimentality — the cheap exploitation of audience emotion by resorting to time-honored tricks. Nor does he limit his definition of sentimentality to its nineteenth century emphasis on tears. He knows that contemporary spy thrillers depicting tireless love-making and unimpassioned brutality are also exploiting emotions cheaply. He knows that the script which calls for gushing blood or intense close-ups of panting faces and full, moist lips coming together in graphic demonstrations of kissing can also merit the label "sentimental."

Probably the major quality which the chosen script must possess is a sense of truth. The ideal playwright — even one who wears a comic mask — has a mature vision of life; he sees the strength in its weakness and the weakness in its strength. He continually catches the director off-guard by the deftness of his insight and his refusal to be taken in by a cliché view of existence. The ideal director is not just a businessman in the theater. He is an informed citizen of the world, a man of erudition and many interests, a man who can analyze American foreign policy as well as a scene in a play. Such a man knows what the important minds of today are thinking. He knows this is not a period of easy optimism and that the major voices in the theater are those of the naturalists, the determinists, and the avant-garde. To the reading and evaluation of a new script he brings the judgment which helps him to understand before he opens to page one what are the boundaries of belief available to the writer who is aware of his world.

For a serious director the pale distillation of a play into a disciplined, orderly, analyzable outline will never yield stage life. The illusion of truth on the stage is born from the enthusiasm of the director's responding to a play he believes in. Good theater can result from the careful, conscious craftsmanship of a man hired to do a certain job, but great theater never can.

The Director's Vision

Once the method-professional director, who dominates serious theater today, has chosen his script, his task becomes far more business-like. He has gone beyond "I *must* do this show!" and has reached "*How* am I going to do it?" While each director has developed his own peculiar style and certain working habits during rehearsal, there are a few steps in the evolution of the finished product which almost all directors take in common.

First, the director closets himself with the script, reading it over and over and over; no longer concerned only with its general sense of truth, no longer content in the knowledge that it has a big scene or two, he must probe every line, every pause between lines *to make certain that the sense of truth is maintained.* He also tries to find a definite destination for the play, one which he can articulate to himself. A predominantly literary analysis of *The Cherry Orchard,* for example, might disclose a play of beautiful subtlety, of infinite ambiguity, one with a distinctly lyrical atmosphere; yet these observations will not put the play on the stage. The director knows he will not be able to say to his cast at the first rehearsal, "We must be beautiful, subtle, and lyrical."

From Stanislavsky he has learned that a play must have a "super-objective" — his term for obligatory moment. Even avant-garde plays, which in literary analysis are exempt from the classical pyramidal structure, must offer the director a destination. Perhaps he is to stage *Waiting for Godot,* which "culminates" (a word that cannot really be applied to this play outside the practical theater) in the scene of the tramps attempting suicide and failing. He will not tell his cast, "This play is about two lonely men who become disillusioned with life and thus attempt suicide." He may say, instead, something like this: "In this play you are forced to stay here on this bleak and cheerless stage. You would like to leave. You cannot bear it another moment. Yet you absolutely must stay. Is that clear? At precisely the right moment — that is, just when you have all but forgotten there is a way out, you remember that you can hang your-selves. From then on, the play will take care of itself."

Anticipating that the actors may ask *why* they must suppose they cannot leave the stage (note that it is not the *park*, the actual setting of the play, which the director talks about), the director will find a reason to give them. If he says, "You are waiting for Godot," all will be lost. The proceedings will become enveloped by clouds of abstraction, and the actors will end up simply mouthing words. Thus he may say, "You cannot leave the stage because you have nothing better to do. You must concentrate in the beginning on that one idea. Forget whatever plans you may have for after the rehearsal. If you look forward to a late supper or a meeting with friends, erase them from your mind. Anticipate nothing. Become as bored as you possibly can be. Think back to a time when you really *had* nothing better to do and you thought you never would have."

Once he has decided where the play must go, the director relates each character separately to the common destination, helping each actor to see how he is to be affected or not affected by it. If *A Doll's House* is to be staged, for example, with the new interpretation, the common destina-tion or super-objective of the play might be phrased: "A husband finally awakens to the realization that he has been deluded by a false image of his masculine superiority, and he does not know what to do." The whole purpose of the wife in the play must now be articulated in terms of the husband's discovery. The director would realize that in the final scene he must have the actress become very assertive, aggressive, dynamic; the latent strength of the woman must emerge, absolutely disarming and bewildering the husband. And then, scene by scene, he investigates what the two central characters, as well as the minor characters, are doing which will move the proceedings one step closer to the common destina-tion.

At this initial stage of his practical analysis of the script, the director makes some astonishing discoveries; especially does he recognize that some scenes may simply not work. That is, they do not carry the play towards its super-objective. They go off on a tangent and cloud the whole issue. When it is a question of a brand new play, the director normally insists that these scenes be rewritten so as to serve the plan of the produc-tion to which the director has committed himself.

He is not, of course, always right. Tennessee Williams' *Cat on a Hot Tin Roof* (1955) was originally published with two different versions of the third act: the one that was approved by the author but discarded for production and the alternate demanded by the director, Elia Kazan. In his introduction, Williams, by strongly suggesting that he was in basic disagreement with his director about the act, brought into the open the struggle between author and interpreter and the sometimes enormous gulf between page and stage.

In theaters of the past — before the rise to eminence of the director — the playwright was king. Great dramas of the past have survived as literature without having been radically altered in rehearsal by the director's craft. Published scripts of the future may well continue to offer written and acted versions side by side. The written script-as-literature and the director's working script as a blueprint for an actual production may become separate entities. There may even come a time when the predominant and authoritative text of a play will be the director's.

Even when the work as published is substantially the same as the work in live performance, the identity of the words does not guarantee identity of interpretation. Many times an author does not indicate, specifically, how he wants a line read, or he does, but the indicated interpretation does not fit into the director's general scheme. The greatest playwrights of past and present have an extraordinary ear for the spoken word and an instinctive feeling for the rhythms of speech; but they cannot predict all of the stage circumstances. The sheer physical distance between actors may be greater or less at any point than the dramatist originally imagined; the length of time it takes the speaker of a line to move across the stage can alter the entire tempo of the speech and perhaps necessitate a change in its meaning.

A very obvious example of the problem of interpretation is the most famous speech in the theater: Hamlet's "To-be-or-not-to-be" soliloquy. It is standard fare for English classes; almost every aspiring actor recites it in acting school. No speech has ever been subjected to so much analysis and psychoanalysis. Yet Shakespeare offers not the slightest hint of what purpose the speech is intended to serve relative to the plot in general and the hero in particular. The problem is further complicated by an early printed version of *Hamlet* which indicates that the prince enters, reading the speech from a book. Some commentators have suggested that it is therefore not a soliloquy at all but was intended to show the audience that Hamlet realizes he is being spied on at this moment and reads the thoughts of others rather than say his own. The modern director, approaching the monumental task of transferring *Hamlet* from page to stage, has to make a definite decision about "To be or not to be" as well as many other passages which in print contain sublime poetry and complex thoughts but which become ambiguous in terms of live performance.

If the play is a modern one, like *Cat on a Hot Tin Roof*, and the director has the playwright there in the theater, there develop inevitable disagreements which usually revolve around

1) the playwright's tendency to over-verbalize — when a significant look or gesture, the director knows, will work better
2) the playwright's frequent desire to insist upon certain implications or stated meanings which he wants to say to an audience but which the director knows will impede the action and perhaps not harmonize with his own understanding of the play's destination

3) the playwright's own analysis of his characters which may differ sharply from the knowledge of human nature that the director and his actors together bring to their tasks

It is not a matter of who is "right" — the director or the dramatist — but rather of what works on the stage and what does not work. The director's primary concern is to achieve such workability.

From Blueprint to Production

The second step in the evolution of the stage life of a play is casting. In the professional theater the director usually knows in advance who will play the major roles, and this knowledge has already affected his preliminary analysis of the script in terms of its ultimate destination and the workability of its parts. Frequently the availability of a talented performer can even determine the choice of scripts for production.

In the non-professional theater the casting of a play can become the major step in the whole production process, and much depends on chance. The director knows where he wants to go and how he intends to get there. But the decisions have been made on the basis of an ideal vision of the performance. When he arrives at the theater for try-outs, he scans the faces of those who have come to read for parts and finds none that resemble his personal images of the characters.

In university theaters the casting problem is intensified because the actors available to the director are usually in the same youthful age group; yet from them he must select a Hamlet or a King Lear or a Willy Loman. No matter how much natural talent a young performer may possess, the director cannot expect a vast amount of life experience from him or the long years of training which develop flexibility in the use of voice and body. Thus the university director is also an educator, teaching the actor his profession as well as readying a specific play for performance.

The first rehearsals in both professional and non-professional theaters are devoted to a reading of the script aloud by the cast, with the director stopping frequently to indicate the script changes that he has made, advise on line interpretations, but, particularly, to establish his vision of the production. It is here that the actors have their major opportunity to raise questions and make their own contributions. This prerogative of the players is more scrupulously observed in the professional theater, where the leading actors have made an intense study of the script themselves and have many important and workable suggestions to offer. Compromises and concessions are made at this point, so that by the time the actors are ready to get to their feet and begin walking through the action, the plan of the production is quite clear to all of the artists (including the set designer, the lighting designer, and the costumer, each of whom is beginning to work on his phase of the production).

The rehearsals which follow the reading and analysis of the script are devoted to the foundation for the rest of the production. During the course of these rehearsals director and cast decide upon:

1) when, why, and where each character will move
2) what he will do when he arrives at his new location
3) what his change of location will mean to the other players on the stage
4) the "business" that each character engages in at appropriate places (such as the pouring of a drink or the lighting of a cigarette)
5) the fundamental pacing of the play — that is, when dialogue and action are to be quickened, when slowed down, and when the actors are to pause

Some directors plan movement, "business," and pacing in advance and in considerable detail. Others sketch these out roughly but wait until the cast is ready to walk before making final decisions. Others prefer to improvise as they go through the script.

At this time, the director is guided by two major concerns: motivation and visual impact. The crossing from one place to another and the actor's standing or sitting have to be what the character would do in real life under the same circumstances. The actor is not given permission to move, sit, or rise merely because he would like to. If his instincts on the stage cause him to differ with the director, he must be able to justify his position. As a rule professional actors do not have to be steered around the stage, because they are experienced in perceiving the logical motivations which govern actions.

In the professional theater a typical rehearsal conversation might sound like this:

ACTRESS. How would it be if I sat down at this point?
DIRECTOR. Why would you?
ACTRESS. Well, I think that here I have decided I am not going to win the argument with my husband.
DIRECTOR. True, but would you want to indicate to him your resignation with so definite a movement?
ACTRESS. I believe so. Frankly, I don't care what he thinks; I never have.
DIRECTOR. Yes, I see what you mean. All right. Try it; let's see if it works.

If the movement does in fact work, it will seem inevitable, so organic to character and situation that the audience will not even be conscious of it.

The pacing or timing of the play has so many variables that it is the one aspect of the whole production about which the director is least certain. No one can predict at the outset whether the leading lady will have a splitting headache on opening night that will distract her and cause her to reply a half-second too early here or pause too long there. Or perhaps an actor will miss his entrance by a fraction of a second. On the stage even the slightest passage of time in a vacuum can be detrimental to the whole effect. A flippant remark that is not tossed off at precisely the right moment can be enough to arouse uneasy feelings within the critical viewer, who says to himself: "Something is wrong."

Directors lose more sleep over the pace of a play than over any other single element. Having decided that the play is worth staging, having mentally filled every moment of it with stage life before the first rehearsal was called, the director must see to it that it works every second.

Ever since Stanislavsky, directors have customarily broken the script down into "units" or "beats." The reader of a printed script finds the work divided into "scenes," but the director and the cast cannot operate in terms of such large segments. The "unit" is the irreducible atom of the play; it has a beginning, a middle, and an end. Thus: a mother enters to find her son smoking.

MOTHER. You're smoking.
SON. That's obvious.
MOTHER. You know my rules against smoking.
SON. I do.
MOTHER. And yet you disobey them.
SON. Yes.
MOTHER. If you are to live under my roof, you will do as I say.
SON. No! I'm tired of your rules. I'm tired of living in a morgue. I hate this house and every room in it. I hate you, Mother!

Now, regardless of what reply follows from the Mother, the director recognizes that the son's outbursts must be the end of a beat. A break in the continuous flow of action is mandatory. The mother will stare at him; she will not be able to reply for a second or two. Then the characters move to the next beat, which will have a climax of its own, and so on.

The movement of the play from minor climax to minor climax is a rhythmic one. In a serious play the action on stage is punctuated by the pauses which usually occur at the conclusion of each unit; in a farce comedy each beat ends in a line, expression, gesture, or movement which evokes laughter; thus *its* rhythm is the alternation of listening and laughing. The skillful director knows that, if a serious play goes too long without a pause, the rhythm will be less dramatic, less keenly felt, and similarly that, if a comedy goes too long without a laugh or at least a smile, it has some dead spots.

Once all the preliminary decisions have been made, once the pacing scheme has been built into the plan of production, a point is reached at which further change can be made for only pressing reasons. Lines have been memorized; even the most autocratic director begins to loosen his tight hold on the cast. It is now necessary for the play to "build." Actors must begin to concentrate on the truth of what they are saying and doing. Stage life begins to breathe.

These rehearsals constitute the intermediate phase in the preparation of the play. The director interrupts the scenes less and less; when he does, it is to signify that a line or a movement has not convinced him. "Sincerity," "plausibility," "dishonesty" — these are the terms used most often. In purely amateur theater, where it is all the director can do to have the cast know its lines and a set painted in time for the rising of the curtain, certain statements and terminology run throughout the entire rehearsal period: "I was supposed to be over here" or "He forgot to kiss me."

The final phase of the rehearsal period is extremely trying, because two forces come together which can never be instantly harmonious. On the one hand, the actors, who have lived with their characters long enough to be ready to begin living on the stage in earnest, must now be concerned about last-minute costume adjustments, hair-style changes, make-up that does not quite fit the conception of the part. They have grown accustomed to working on a bare stage, but now they must re-adjust to the unfamiliar surroundings of the set. In professional and university theaters, directors introduce costumes little by little and work against the set as it is being built. In low-budget amateur theaters, costumes, make-up, and scenery usually arrive all together for the dress rehearsal, and everything has a good chance of going wrong at the same time.

But theater on all levels works towards a dizzying, intensified pre-opening pace. Nerves become taut, tempers sometimes become short; everyone experiences that inner straining, that impatience to open which is frequently combined with a terror of opening. That the excitement floods over into even the most polished of professional companies suggests that the final life of the play on stage is charged with the electricity from all this nervous energy. The major difference between professional, non-professional, and amateur theater on opening night is the degree to which this energy can be controlled and used to heighten the entire production.

The Scenic Elements: Sets, Lights, and Costumes

Though the impact of a play comes largely from the combined efforts of the actors and the director, the scenic elements in themselves deserve to be noticed. Sometimes they can make an evening spent on a dull play seem to have been almost worthwhile. In general, the three scenic elements of setting, lighting, and costuming ought to be, like stage movement, unnoticed in themselves — except as the critical viewer, who can be both absorbed and detached, enjoys taking note of their merits.

In its color and construction, in its way of occupying space, a set must be pleasing to look at in a way that does not distract from the total production. It must conform to the style of production the director wants, allow the actors freedom to move about with a minimum of awkwardness,

Scene from Death of a Salesman *after the original, multi-leveled setting by Jo Mielziner, making possible the dramatist's freedom from the restrictions of verisimilitude.*

and, above all, add an effect that cannot be gained from the language of the play itself.

A distinction has to be made between the all-purpose set and the symbolic set. The all-purpose set has little to do with the mood of the play. The same fashionable living room would do for a drawing room comedy, a love story or a murder mystery and the appreciative applause would be more for its interior decoration than for its suitability. But the famous set designed by Jo Mielziner for the original New York production of *Death of a Salesman* showed the skeletal house of the Loman family with the skyscrapers of New York City looming over it as though they might at any moment tumble down and crush the little salesman. In this production, setting became a constant, brooding fatalism that was implied in the writing but obviously required visual reinforcement.

The "mass" of a set is the manner in which it occupies space. The contemporary theater has a number of types. Some plays require backgrounds that are obviously two-dimensional, that can, for example, be painted on a curtain or backdrop; others are best performed against sets that reproduce the actual appearance of real life and must be three-dimensional. The Loman house in the Mielziner set was an example of "constructivism" — that is, it was composed of wooden frames, not filled in and not made to appear realistic. But since the play moves back and forth in time, since it continually breaks with the convention of verisimilitude, an unrealistic set was required.

Many directors and scene designers try interesting experiments, particularly in the matter of breathing new life into classics. The all-time record for experimentation is held by a production of *Hamlet* which featured a modern swimming pool as its major set piece and had the actors performing in bathing suits. The criterion in such experiments is the extent to which the novel set adds a workable freshness to the production; if it serves only to distract the audience, it must be judged a failure.

Lighting has become integral to modern theater production, as well as television and cinema production. It was first found in the seventeenth-century theaters of England and France, which were able to put a roof over the head of drama by the use of the chandelier. In the beginning the lighting of the stage would have come from the same source as the lighting of the auditorium itself — overhead candles. The purpose of lighting was purely utilitarian — to make the action on stage visible.

The nineteenth-century theaters used footlights — first, candles with shields so that the flickering flames would not constitute a menace and would not distract by being too readily seen; then, electric bulbs, also hidden from view by shields. Footlights served essentially the same purpose as the chandelier; but they also, in the era of electricity, tended to heighten the degree of luminosity on the stage to an unnatural degree.

The modern theater continues to use the contrast between a lighted stage and a darkened auditorium as a means of channeling the attention. But now stages are lighted, not only from the floor or from overhead, but from every conceivable direction, including the rear of the auditorium, the sides out front, the wings, and overhead at various angles.

Stage lighting, like all the other aspects of the theater, has become both art and science. It retains its functional quality of making the performers visible, but the intensity of their visibility varies from play to play and often from moment to moment within the same play.

In a sparkling comedy the technician merely throws the switch and brings up the lights to near-maximum intensity. The brightness of the stage enhances the liveliness of the stage action. It helps to raise the spirits of the audience almost immediately. In the typical "general lighting" of a show that is not of notable profundity or one that uses the convention of verisimilitude (so that lighting intensity can change only through naturalistic motivation such as the coming of twilight or dawn) the shadows that are caused in real life by the undirected falling of light are eradicated. The stage is divided into certain geometric areas, and each one is "covered" by beams of light coming from at least two directions, which wash the shadows away.

In a play of some complexity, however, and one that does not employ verisimilitude, the director can use lighting to enhance mood, to narrow the attention of the audience and focus it on one specific place or one specific actor so that not one bit of impact has to be lost. In a modern production of *Hamlet* the changes of lighting intensity, the alternation of light and shadow on the stage can symbolize visually the devious intrigues on which the plot is based as well as the complexity of the hero's inner self.

Like the set and the blocking, the lighting should function so organically within the spirit of the whole that most viewers will not be aware that lights are going down in some areas and coming up in others. This general rule does not necessarily hold for purely theatrical spectacles such as musical comedy. These sometimes depend upon extremely sensuous lighting effects such as the turning of the whole stage red or blue for a particular number in the show.

Costuming, by its style and color schemes, helps the director to enhance his general vision of the production. Taking advantage of the universal connotations of certain colors, one director of *Mourning Becomes Electra* (1931) showed the heroine in black at first, while her adulterous mother wore red; later in the play the heroine's wearing red signified her triumph over her mother and the assumption of her mother's personality. But a Juliet wearing a bright red dress for her first entrance would certainly confuse both the audience and Romeo. These examples of color significance are not meant to suggest that costuming exists for the emotional guidance of the audience in a point-for-point relationship: mean character, dark clothes; virginal heroine, white clothes; rugged he-man hero, rough-looking gray tweed.

An Iago dressed in light blue with pink accessories would not suggest the Machiavellian figure that he is. But putting him in black each time he appears would be too expected and would lose impact. Since he is referred to as "honest Iago" throughout the play, the whole essence of his character is the disparity between what he seems and what he is; therefore the style and color of his clothes must suggest the capacity for friendship and being trusted. Intermediate shades would serve better than extreme light or dark, particularly since he can plan Othello's destruction better by not calling attention to himself.

Even in the lightest comedy, certain subtleties are insisted upon, so that the effect of clothes styles and colors is cumulative rather than instantaneous. The heroine of a romantic comedy might secretly long for amorous adventure but be inhibited by her Puritanic upbringing. The dress in which we first see her might have a tasteful simplicity about it — in keeping with the character's background — yet it might also contain a streak of bright color, to suggest an eventual capacity for romantic warmth. On the other hand, in a scene in which the heroine must actually demonstrate such warmth, the costumer, in conference with the director, might decide that the girl's native fear of love will drive her unconsciously to wear a plainjane outfit that offers not a trace of hope to potential boyfriends. In other words, the costumer, like the director and the actors, is guided by the inner life of the characters. Like color, the style of the costume is decided upon from an analysis of the play itself. Othello is normally dressed in sumptuous robes for his first appearance, when he appears before the Senate. His clothes have to be those of a noble figure who is proud of what he is, sure of himself, and undesirous of hiding anything. But as the tragedy progresses, and he loses confidence and control, his costumes must become simpler and drabber to indicate that he has become slave more than master. In the final scene he reaches the complete opposite of the rich color and elaborate style in which he was costumed at the outset: he appears in a pure white robe with simple, Grecian lines. Here is visual symbolism to underscore the irony of the murder: Othello believes he is committing a sacrifice. He approaches the death of his wife solemnly not passionately, religiously not diabolically. And finally, as both he and Desdemona lie there in death, the whiteness of the garments is a reminder of the purity of Othello's love and his ideals, both of which have been so tragically wasted.

Splitting the Screen Illusion

The screen has a scientific exactitude which the stage cannot match. Because scenes can be re-shot, a film does not depend on the simultaneous excellence of all participants. Therefore the viewer should have the right to expect precision in every department and to judge the whole movie as a total, unchangeable fact. If a play is dull, the critical viewer knows, the fault may lie in the script itself, the director's misconception of it, the wrong choice of actor for the leading man, or any one of a number of factors. He can derive some pleasure from locating the source of the problem. But if a movie or television show is dull, the fault is mainly in outside factors such as the economics of the popular theater. A bad movie may be the result of faithfully transferring to the screen a deliberately unoriginal script.

When a movie or television play is good, the director is almost solely responsible for it. The very method of shooting a film makes it impossible for much of the credit to be placed elsewhere. If something works because of the magic of its stars, the director has been responsible for using that magic in just the right way.

In a very real sense, a work of screen cannot be misdirected. A film is only what a director lets a camera photograph, so that the product can only be acceptable or not acceptable. A miscasting of an actor cannot ruin a film, because it is inconceivable to imagine the film without him. It does not even exist without him. With another actor, it is a different product altogether. A stage play, on the other hand, is not made up of shots and angles, and established plays exist as literature almost apart from performance; they have a constant identity that permits critical dissection.

All the critical movie-goer can do is realize that what he is seeing is not the way something is, but the way someone sees it. The camera's eye is the director's eye. There is no question of the viewer's wanting to see something "another way" because then it becomes another something.

For the purpose of enjoying a casual evening in the local movie house or before the television set, the critical viewer finds it best to forget as much as possible about looking behind the scenes. Sometimes he cannot help himself. If he is not enjoying a movie he may try to salvage some pleasure by noting how special lighting or sound have added to the dishonesty of the whole story: how, for example, when it is necessary for the audience to dislike a wife she is made to appear unpleasant (in mannish clothes) and photographed with all her imperfections. The sound track can even make the click of her heels too loud. Later, when it suits the director to make her sympathetic, she looks soft and feminine, and happy music even accompanies her walk. The technique would probably not be noticed if the movie were honest. When the movie is generally implausible, the tricks reveal themselves.

Usually the critical viewer would rather not be aware of the machine that parted the Red Sea in *The Ten Commandments* (1957) or of the menacing music that accompanies the cowboy hero searching a deserted shack. If to his happy surprise he is able to become involved in the pounding excitement of Ben-Hur's struggle to win the chariot race, he knows enough to take his moments of legitimate pleasure and run — and learning that an extra in the scene was really killed during the filming of the sequence does not enhance his enjoyment.

The pleasure of critical awareness is greatest in the re-seeing of a favorite film, when the knowledge that a particular shot is coming up next can alert the viewer to watch more closely and speculate on how the impact may have been achieved. The picture may be about a young man who has a casual encounter with an older woman but who gradually comes to love her. The second time around the critical viewer may note that imperceptibly the woman seems to look younger as the story progresses. He realizes that on first viewing he had simply felt a deepening of the relationship and a sympathy for the characters. Now he recognizes how camera technique changed the woman's appearance from scene to scene. But whether the effect was achieved through make-up or by placing gauze in front of the camera lens or through lighting alone is unimportant. It is enough to detect the sure hand of the director at work.

❀ Josef von Sternberg *On the Reward of Acting**

It is unavoidable at this point to repeat that an actor is rewarded with attention out of all proportion to his responsibility. I do not wish to imply that he is paid too much for his services, as this phase of his reward does not concern me; to delude the masses is always profitable. It is, however, important to point out the absurdity of receiving the profits of speculation in emotions, when neither the emotions nor the speculation are the actor's. Lest this observation be so misleading that it gives rise to the suspicion that I envy the applause an actor receives, this is not so. The painter does not resent the praise received by the colors on his canvas. "This spot of red is wonderful," cannot displease the artist who placed the red in his design. However, there is a slight difference: the spot of red, having been praised, does not vilify the artist.

* Reprinted from *Fun in a Chinese Laundry* by Josef von Sternberg by permission of The Macmillan Company, Publishers. Copyright © Josef von Sternberg, 1965.

The power of the screen director is overwhelming. If most films are bad (and statistics overwhelmingly support this gloomy truth), what is astonishing is that so many can be good at all. The odds are against one man's being able to shoulder the burden of having to entertain an audience that is potentially the entire world. The stage director is dealing with a far narrower segment of humanity and assumes a degree of sophistication in his audience that the movie or television director cannot. By having to appeal to the lowest common denominator, the commercial screen today presents for the most part, not an artist's personal vision — as the films of Bergman and Fellini definitely do — but rather a continual use of cinematic elements that always seem to work.

In short, it is risky enough to have one man responsible for the final screen product, even when that man is a dedicated artist. He can so easily go off kilter, leaving us baffled instead of with the kind of realization we can have in the theater, when we know why something about a scene or an interpretation of a speech has not worked. Small wonder then that the screen industry in its normal, commercial sense is highly conservative, fearing that incommunicability will be the inevitable result of allowing the director to do more than has been known to be understandable and reasonably entertaining in the past.

When a film or television play does seem to offer a personal vision of importance, one that is able to touch us, the praises should be loud and long. The critical viewer must extricate himself from the spell of a fine screen achievement long enough to pay tribute to an artist who was able to take blazing lights, rolling cameras, overhanging microphones, miles of wires — all plainly visible to the actor who cannot be expected to forget for one minute that film-making is a business to him — and turn these into a language whereby he has expressed himself.

❀   **Constantin Stanislavsky:** "The Beginnings of My System" from *My Life in Art.**

The actor must first of all believe in everything that takes place on the stage, and most of all he must believe in what he himself is doing. And one can believe only in the truth. Therefore it is necessary to feel this truth at all times, to know how to find it, and for this it is unescapable to develop one's artistic sensitivity to truth. It will be said, "But what kind of truth can this be, when all on the stage is a lie, an imitation, scenery, cardboard, paint, make-up, properties, wooden goblets, swords and spears. Is all this truth?" But it is not of this truth I speak. I speak of the truth of emotions, of the truth of inner creative urges which strain forward to find expression, of the truth of the memories of bodily and physical perceptions. I am not interested in a truth that is without myself; I am interested in the truth that is within myself, the truth of my relation to this or that event on the stage, to the properties, the scenery, the other actors who play parts in the drama with me, to their thoughts and emotions.

The actor says to himself:

"All these properties, make-ups, costumes, the scenery, the publicness of the performance, are lies. I know they are lies, I know I do not need any of them. But *if* they were true, then I would do this and this, and I would behave in this manner and this way towards this and this event."

I came to understand that creativeness begins from that moment when in the soul and imagination of the actor there appears the magical, creative *if*. While only actual reality exists, only practical truth which a man naturally cannot but believe, creativeness has not yet begun. Then the creative *if* appears, that is, the imagined truth which the actor can believe as sincerely and with greater enthusiasms than he believes practical truth, just as the child believes in the existence of its doll and of all life in it and around it. From the moment of the appearance of *if* the actor passes from the plane of actual reality into the plane of another life, created and imagined by himself. Believing in this life, the actor can begin to create.

Scenic truth is not like truth in life; it is peculiar to itself. I understood that on the stage truth is that in which the actor sincerely believes. I understood that even a palpable lie must become a truth in the theatre so that it may become art. For this it is necessary for the actor to develop to the highest degree his imagination, a childlike naïveté and trustfulness, an artistic sensitivity to truth and to the truthful in his soul and body. All these qualities help him to transform a coarse scenic lie into the most delicate truth of his relation to the life imagined. All these qualities, taken together, I shall call the *feeling of truth*. In it there is the play of imagination and the creation of creative faith; in it there is a barrier against scenic lies; in it is the feeling of true measure; in it is the tree of childlike naïveté and the sincerity of artistic emotion. The feeling of truth, as one of the important elements of the creative mood, can be both developed and practised. But this is neither the time nor the place to speak of the methods and means of such work. I will only say now that this ability to feel the truth must be developed to such an extent that absolutely nothing would take place on the stage, that nothing would be said and nothing listened to, without a preparatory cleansing through the filter of the artistic feeling of truth.

If this was true, then all my scenic exercises in loosening the muscles as well as in concentration had been performed incorrectly. I had not cleansed them through the filter of spiritual and physical truth. I took a certain pose on the stage. I did not believe in it physically. Here and there I weakened the strain. It was better. Now I changed the pose somewhat. Ah! I understood. When one stretches himself in order to reach something, this pose is the result of such stretching. And my whole body and after it my soul, began to believe that I was stretching towards an object which I needed very much.

It was only with the help of the feeling of truth, and the inner justification of the pose, that I was able more or less to reach the loosening of the muscles in actual life and on the stage during performances.

From that time on all my scenic exercises in the loosening of muscles and in concentration passed under the strict control of my feeling of truth.

❀ Curtain Calls

Here is a selected list of terms and phrases which have been used in this book, together with a brief reminder of what should be remembered about each.

alienation: the state of being detached from or emotionally uninvolved in the action of a drama.

ambiguity: a line, character, scene, or symbol in a play or film that can be interpreted in a number of ways, none of which is necessarily "the right" way.

anachronism: any element in a play or film which does not belong to the historical period of the action.

antagonism: the force which tries to impede the hero's progress toward a goal; it can be embodied in a character, but in great tragedies it is usually a quality within the hero's own personality.

avant-garde: dramatic trends which are ahead of their time; in our era the movement can be found in the Theater of the Absurd, as well as in the films of Ingmar Bergman and Federico Fellini, among others, which stress imagery and the subjective expression of the director himself and tend to show little formal plotting.

biography: the life of the playwright can offer some insight into the nature of his work but should not be insisted upon; theater is of necessity an objective medium, so that a dramatist is not always putting himself into his plays.

blank verse: unrhymed iambic pentameter; the poetic form employed by

Shakespeare: e.g., "My wife / My wife / what wife? / I have / no wife."

It is important to remember that Shakespeare is so much master of the form that the actor's emotional delivery of his lines is not inhibited by the regularity of the rhythm.

box set: the standard stage scenery of nineteenth-century drama — and still common in the popular melodramas and romantic comedies on Broadway; created by linking a number of "flats" together and painting them so as to give the illusion of a real interior.

catharsis: the condition of being purged of emotions; a feeling of tranquility which Aristotle maintained was the aim of tragedy and which can be considered the aim of drama in general.

chorus: a group of masked actors who represented in Greek drama the voice of the common man or the voice of reason; sometimes referred to as the "ideal spectator" and in use today occasionally through individual characters who communicate the author's views.

331

classical: used to identify Greek or Roman drama or dramatic elements or any elements which are conscious imitations of these; also the style of acting appropriate to productions of Greek or Roman plays.

closet drama: a literary work employing many of the conventions of drama but of such proportions that it cannot be staged; also refers to dramatic works that are considered too philosophical and lacking in action for live performance.

comedy of manners: a rarefied kind of comedy, popular during the seventeenth century, which holds up for admiration the behavior of upper class people and for ridicule those who do not measure up to aristocratic standards; specializes in witty dialogue and the playboy or rogue hero.

communication: a frequently misunderstood term with reference to the theater; audience involvement in what is taking place — not necessarily limited to intellectual understanding of what the play "means."

conflict: the opposition of forces which creates the drama; in general, it involves an object of sympathetic concern against something or someone that attempts to hinder his progress toward a goal; only in weak plays and films is this opposition a matter of all good against all bad.

context: the historical period in which a work was written or filmed and whose prevailing values it inevitably reflects.

convention: any artificial element of a play or film that we agree to accept as real, e.g., images on a screen, passage of time, a Greek chorus, an Elizabethan soliloquy.

criticism: the analysis, interpretation, and evaluation of drama; it is *not* limited to derogation.

determinism: a pessimistic brand of naturalism in which the process of human destruction by some natural force becomes the subject of a drama; illustrated by the work of Eugene O'Neill and Tennessee Williams.

deus ex machina: an obvious contrivance introduced by an author for an expedient and desirable, but not probable, resolution to a plot. Example: a convenient bolt of lightning to kill the evil-doer.

didacticism: a moralizing element in a play or film; with rare exceptions, such as the work of Ibsen or Shaw, not a major function of the theater. Found in classical and neo-classical plays, as means of instructing audiences.

Dionysus: Greek god of vegetation; rites performed in his honor became the festivals from which the tragic theater of Athens evolved.

dishonesty: any clear evasion of his obligation to the audience on the part of a dramatist or film director, especially in regard to the sudden and implausible imposition of traditional moral values, such as "Crime does not pay."

Elizabethan: the era and style of theater of Shakespeare; Queen Elizabeth reigned from 1558 to 1603.

empathy: the phenomenon whereby the audience projects itself into the action on stage or screen; through the years this has been considered the most desirable way of enjoying drama but has been challenged in our time by the alienation theory.

epic theater: associated with the work of Bertolt Brecht, the major exponent of the alienation theory; emphasizes the thought content of a drama and makes use of large casts, multiple sets, music — in short, any obviously theatrical element since a strong illusion of reality does not serve the aims of alienation.

episodic plot: a casual, not logical, arrangement of incidents; the opposite of the pyramidal or classical plot structure.

Euripidean irony: a cruel twist of fate not promised earlier in the drama.

exposition: the presentation of the background material necessary for an understanding of the action; usually found in the beginning of the play, exposition should be a compelling way of attracting attention to the characters and situation.

expressionism: a form of drama, popular earlier in this century as a reaction against the theater of verisimilitude, in which characters, incidents, and sets are strongly symbolic and clearly interpretable; a vehicle of the determinists.

family theme: one of the strongest bases for modern drama; it helps the naturalists and determinists to localize sharply the source of dramatic conflict, which, when it is society or even nature as a whole, can become exceedingly vague and not conducive to theatrical excitement.

French classical: the stately, restrained tragic drama of Racine, modeled rigidly after the Greek unities of time, place, and action; containing a minimum of on-stage action; stressing the verbal analysis of an emotional problem, but not a display of emotion; also refers to the style of acting which stresses control and excessive under-playing.

genre: French term meaning category of play or film, such as tragedy, comedy of manners, musical comedy.

Globe: the theater for which most of Shakespeare's greatest works were written; built in 1599.

groundlings: the commoners who stood in the pit to witness an Elizabethan production.

hero: the central figure, the one with whom we are in sympathy; term should be understood not only in its narrow connotations of nobility of soul and willingness to sacrifice for others; classical and Elizabethan heroes are not always models for the audience to admire.

heroic tragedy: a spectacular form of entertainment popular during the neoclassical period (last half of seventeenth century); made uninhibited use of technical effects.

hubris: a Greek term for "pride"; the major flaw of the hero in a classical tragedy.

Ibsensian irony: the gradual realization on our part that we have been mistaken in our understanding of the point that Ibsen is making; a technique developed further by Shaw.

imagery: has two important usages in drama: 1) the word pictures created in the mind of the listener or reader of Shakespeare in particular; 2) the main element of cinema art, that which clearly distinguishes it from the stage; the actual language of films is the camera image, and at its best it is not reducible to a verbal equivalent.

incongruity: a situation, character, or line of dialogue that violates our sense of what is reasonable or fitting; the basis of theatrical comedy at its best.

intensification: the main part of a drama using the pyramidal plot structure; it follows the prologue and terminates in the obligatory moment.

joke: a form of verbal incongruity that is less clever than wit.

kitchenism: homely details of 'ordinary' life — especially middle-class existence — introduced into plays and movies to give a sense of authenticity but which may bog the plot down in a morass of small talk.

"meaning": a term so abused and confused in the theater that it is best not employed at all.

meliorism: the philosophy, popular at the end of the last century, that nature and society were improvable; forms the basis of the thesis plays of Ibsen and Shaw.

melodrama: a non-comic play or film which revolves around the opposition of clearly good and clearly bad characters.

message: the lowest form of thesis that a play can have; usually a trite sentiment like "Delinquency begins in the home"; to be sharply distinguished from the theses of Ibsen or Shaw, who expected action to be taken; generally the property of very obvious and very empty works that steer clear of controversy.

"method": modern name for the Stanislavsky system of acting, especially in America; emphasis is put on the actor's relating himself honestly to his role.

moral: a message that involves some traditional standard of ethical conduct and is usually a tag stuck on at the end of a melodrama which has been exploiting the delights of evil.

musical play: a popular form of theatrical entertainment, frequently the source of morale-boosting and a re-affirmation of some traditional ideal, such as "Somehow things will work out for the best."

must-mustn't: a strange phenomenon whereby we want something to happen and do not want something to happen at the same time; the tension between the two is a distinct form of pleasure.

naturalism: a belief underlying most of the drama of the twentieth century that only natural forces prevail; these can be outer (in the form of natural phenomena or society or war) or inner (in the form of drives and passions that man cannot control); the naturalists do not believe that man can make significant changes in his environment; some naturalists, notably Chekhov, find the world neutral, neither friendly not actively hostile to man, while the determinists tend to stress such hostility; the term should *not* be construed to refer to a realistic method of theatrical presentation.

neo-classicism: the literary movement of the late seventeenth century which went back to the Greeks and Romans for models; it includes the French classical tragedy of Racine as well as the heroic tragedies and the comedies of manners.

obligatory moment: the third part of the pyramidal plot structure; the biggest single action in an entire drama, that which has been promised from the outset.

orchestra: a Greek term meaning "dancing place"; the circular area in front of the stage building where the Chorus sang and danced.

pit: the ground floor, surrounding the Elizabethan stage on three sides, where the commoners stood.

philosophy: systematic statements about the nature of existence and man. It is not the primary function of the drama to philosophize.

pleasantness: the atmosphere of most nineteenth- and twentieth-century comedy; features good-natured rather than bitingly satirical humor on the grounds that it is cruel to make fun of people; an outgrowth of nineteenth century primitivism and its belief that man is naturally benevolent.

plot: the arrangement of incidents in a certain way; it differs from the story of a drama as an architect's blueprint differs from the house itself; it is always important to decide whether one has liked or disliked the plot or the story.

popcorn syndrome: the affliction of being too easily pleased.

professional: term denoting that a person is being paid for theatrical services.

professionalism: the quality of expertly crafted drama or carefully calculated performances; in acting, "professionalistic" is often contrasted with "method."

prologue: the first part of the pyramidal structure, in which the exposition is offered.

proscenium: the opening of the stage in almost all modern theaters; that which takes the place of the fourth wall of the setting, through which the audience sees the action.

protagonism: the focal point of audience sympathy in a drama, almost always embodied in the person of the hero.

recognition: that which takes place at the end of most tragedies; the hero understands the reasons for his downfall; this is the reason we are able to pity him.

repertory theater: one that maintains a resident company which plays a number of works in succession, as opposed to a long run.

resolution: the fourth and final part of the pyramidal plot structure; usually contains the recognition; a stumbling block for modern dramatists, who often have a hard time reaching a point of distinct finality.

roadblock: a prejudice (such as political or ethnic) which interferes with the proper evaluation of a play or film.

sacrifice: the ancient rite from which, according to one theory, the theater really sprang.

satire: serious criticism through ridicule; the classical function of comic theater, but difficult to find today.

satyr play: the fourth play submitted by the ancient Greek dramatists in competition for the annual prize awarded at the festival of Dionysus; sometimes called the "comic afterpiece," this is the ancestor of comedy in the theater; a ribald and irreverent play.

sentimentality: the dishonest exploitation of audience emotion, whether it be through the death of a child or the close-up in a movie of a brutal killing.

skene: name of the stage building on which the episodes in Greek tragedy were performed.

soliloquy: a speech delivered by an actor directly to the audience in which he objectifies his thoughts; a convention of the Elizabethan theater, given its greatest treatment by Shakespeare.

Sophoclean irony: the major device of the pyramidal plot structure, whereby the audience knows from the beginning what the obligatory moment will be but the hero does not; the most famous example is provided by *Oedipus the King.*

stereotype: sometimes known as a "stock character"; an overdone kind of characterization, whereby the function of a character in a drama is made immediately evident by certain superficial and time-honored attributes; thus there are the meddling mother-in-law, the cruel stepfather, the man-chasing girl friend of the heroine, the wisecracking secretary, or the absent-minded professor.

stylized: the acting technique for most of the great comedies; it stresses beauty and fluidity of movement and gesture, and even awkwardness has a certain grace to it.

symbol: an object or character in a drama which intrigues the imagination by offering the possibility of multiple meanings; at its worst it has a point-for-point reference to a definite idea; a famous example of symbolism at its best is the breaking string heard at the very end of *The Cherry Orchard.*

Theater of the Absurd: one of the major areas of the avant-garde in drama today; it zealously refuses to employ verisimilitude or definite symbolism; generally predicated on the existential view of existence as being without meaning, it embodies the state of meaninglessness in dialogues and situations that seem to be nonsensical and are frequently funny; it is not to be interpreted or philosophically dissected but to be enjoyed in and for itself, even as the existentialist believes man must make an existence for himself out of nothing.

theme: the abstraction of the subject matter of a play; the more general a statement we can make for it, the more significant the work is likely to be; a statement like "The play is about a mother who tries to run her son's life" does not indicate that the play has a theme, but a statement like "The play concerns the conflict between the generations" *does.*

thesis: a specific point of view which the author wants us to take home and act upon; the important attribute of the socially-minded plays of Ibsen and Shaw, which were written out of the conviction that improvements in society were necessary and possible.

Thespis: the first known dramatist and actor; a sixth-century B.C. figure, none of whose works survives today.

understanding: another abused term; should properly denote the act of maintaining one's involvement or interest in the drama because the direction of the plot and the motivations behind the actions are clear and plausible; it should not be used narrowly to mean comprehension of a drama's meaning.

unities: time, place, action; conventions associated with the classical and neoclassical drama — except for the heroic tragedies.

verisimilitude: the major convention developed during the nineteenth century and still the major convention of the drama; the imitation of the surface appearance of reality through authenticity in setting and costume and presumably language.

villain: a specific kind of antagonistic force which grew out of medieval Christian literature and which became very popular on the stage during Shakespeare's time; another term for this figure in Elizabethan drama is "Machiavellian"; classical drama has no such convention, but the drama has seldom been entirely free from it since it was introduced; Shakespeare humanized the figure in such characters as Iago and Richard III, giving them plausible motivations; in general villainy tends to be a force in melodramas only.

well-made play: an overly precise and calculated plot structure, outgrowth of nineteenth-century melodrama, but employed by Ibsen as the vehicle of thesis drama.

wit: the highest form of verbal humor in comedy; it is linguistic incongruity that nevertheless emerges from a rational context and appears at first to be logical; e.g., Lady Bracknell's accusing Jack Worthing of "carelessness" after he tells her that he has lost his parents.

✿ Selected Bibliography

CRAFT

Fischer, Edward, *The Screen Arts: A Guide to Film and Television Appreciation,* Sheed and Ward: New York, 1960.

Funke, Lewis and Booth, John E., *Actors Talk About Acting,* Random House: New York, 1961.

Guthrie, Sir Tyrone, *A Life in the Theatre,* McGraw-Hill Book Co. New York, 1959. (A distinguished stage director describes his own career, the function of the director, and actual stars and productions.)

Jones, Margo, *Theatre-in-the-Round,* McGraw-Hill Paperbacks: New York, 1965. (A history of in-the-round staging by a famous American director.)

Jones, Robert Edmond, *The Dramatic Imagination, Reflections and Speculations on the Art of the Theatre,* Theatre Arts Books: New York, 1941.

Kingson, Walter K. and Cowgill, Rome, *Television Acting and Directing,* Holt, Rinehart and Winston, Inc.: New York, 1965.

Montagu, Ivor, *Film World,* Penguin Books: Baltimore, 1964. (Film as Science, Art, Commodity, and Vehicle.)

Stanislavsky, Constantin, *My Life in Art,* Little, Brown: New York, 1924. Current edition 1948, Theatre Arts Books.

HISTORY

Esslin, Martin, *The Theatre of the Absurd,* Anchor Books, Doubleday: New York, 1961.

Gassner, John and Allen, Ralph G., *Theatre and Drama in the Making,* Houghton Mifflin Co.: Boston, 1964. (Historical background to important theatrical periods told through authors' notes, prefaces to plays, criticism, and other primary material.) (2 vols.)

Kitto, H. D. F., *Greek Tragedy,* Anchor Books, Doubleday: New York, 1954. (A modern study of the works of Aeschylus, Sophocles, and Euripides, combining history and criticism.)

Harbage, Alfred, *As They Liked It, A Study of Shakespeare's Moral Artistry,* Harper Torch Book edition, 1961.

Spencer, Theodore, *Shakespeare and the Nature of Man,* The Macmillan Co.: New York, 1961.

Weber, Eugene, *Paths to the Present: Aspects of European Thought from Romanticism to Existentialism,* Dodd, Mead & Co.: New York, 1960.

CRITICISM

Alpert, Hollis, *The Dreams and the Dreamers: Adventures of a Professional Movie-Goer,* The Macmillan Co.: New York, 1962.

Brustein, Robert, *Seasons of Discontent: Dramatic Opinions 1959–1965,* Simon & Schuster, Inc.: New York, 1965.

Fergusson, Francis, *The Idea of a Theater, A Study of Ten Plays* (includes structural analysis of *Oedipus, Hamlet, Ghosts,* and *The Cherry Orchard*), reprinted in Doubleday Anchor Books: Princeton, N.J., 1949.

Kerr, Walter, *How Not to Write a Play,* Simon and Schuster: New York, 1955. (Finds weakness in current plays caused by imitators of Ibsen's social themes and Chekhov's psychological inaction.)

Krutch, Joseph Wood, *The Modern Temper,* Harcourt, Brace & World, Inc.: New York, 1956. (Includes the famous essay "The Tragic Fallacy," comparing old and modern heroes.)

Meserve, Walter, ed., *Discussions of Modern American Drama,* D. C. Heath and Company: Boston, 1965.

Michel, Laurence and Sewall, Richard B., ed., *Tragedy: Modern Essays in Criticism,* Prentice-Hall, Inc.: Englewood Cliffs, N. J., 1963.

Schumach, Murray, *The Face on the Cutting Room Floor, The Story of Movie and Television Censorship,* William Morrow and Company: New York, 1964.

❄ Primary Sources, Selected Chronological List

COLLECTIONS

Fitts, Dudley, ed. *Greek Plays in Modern Translation*, The Dial Press: New York, 1947.

Neilson, William Allan and Hill, Charles Jarvis, *The Complete Plays and Poems of William Shakespeare*, Houghton Mifflin Company: Boston, 1942.

Landis, Paul, ed., *Six Plays by Corneille and Racine*, The Modern Library: New York, 1931.

Felheim, Marvin, ed., *Comedy*, Harcourt, Brace & World, Inc.: New York, 1962. (Includes comedies by Aristophanes, Shakespeare, Molière, Sheridan, Chekhov, Shaw, Wilde, and Christopher Fry.)

Gassner, John, ed., *A Treasury of the Theatre (From Henrick Ibsen to Arthur Miller)*, Simon and Schuster: New York, 1950.

Reinert, Otto, ed., *Drama, An Introductory Anthology*, Little Brown & Co.: Boston, 1964.

Weales, Gerald, ed., *Eleven Plays*, W. W. Norton & Company: New York, 1964. (An anthology which is neither historical nor exemplary of genre but made up of plays "modern in tone" and according to increasing difficulty.)

Corrigan, Robert W., ed., *The New Theatre of Europe*, Delta Books: New York, 1962 and 1964, (2 vols.).

❊ Theater Chronology

CLASSICAL	THEATERS, CONVENTIONS, AUDIENCES
Age of Pericles (5th Century B.C.)	amphitheater: *audience on stone benches, remote from actors*
Aeschylus (525–456 B.C.)	tragedy: *chorus; masks; little on-stage action; elevation of language*
Sophocles (496–406 B.C.)	
Euripides (485–406 B.C.)	
Aristophanes (448–380 B.C.)	comedy: *satiric criticism of contemporary events*

Roman Drama

The Romans made important contributions to theater architecture and to comedy. Their theaters were in the shape of a bowl and had steep seating; the seats were attached to the stage at either side, so that the Roman audience was much closer to the actors than was the Greek. The stage was more like a theater stage of today. Plautus (254–184 B.C.) was Rome's greatest comic playwright, and Seneca (4 B.C.–65 A.D) was her greatest tragedian.

Medieval Church Drama

For hundreds of years the drama lay buried with other lost treasure of classical civilization. When it emerged in the ninth and tenth centuries, it was as church drama which celebrated events in the Bible and in the life of Christ (mystery plays), and in the lives of the saints (miracle plays).

ELIZABETHAN	
Reign of Elizabeth (1558–1603)	*round or octagonal playhouse; stage thrust into middle of pit where groundlings stood; upper classes in balconies or on stage itself; no scenery and few props; audience very close to actors*
Marlowe (1564–1593)	
Shakespeare (1564–1616)	
	soliloquy; aside; boys in women's roles; on-stage violence; complex poetic language

NEO-CLASSICAL	
Louis XIV (1643–1715)	*indoor theater; use of chandeliers for lighting; proscenium stage; audience exclusively upper class*
Molière (1622–1673)	
Dryden (1631–1700)	

NEO-CLASSICAL	THEATERS, CONVENTIONS, AUDIENCES
Racine (1639–1699)	*perspective scenery; women on stage; return to classical unities; elegance of language; little on-stage action*

EIGHTEENTH CENTURY	
George Lillo (1693–1739)	*predominantly middle-class audience; sentimentality; melodrama*
Gotthold Ephraim Lessing (1729–1781)	

NINETEENTH CENTURY	
Victoria (1837–1901)	*Thesis play; explosive social issues; employed well-made play structure; meliorism*
Henrik Ibsen (1828–1906)	
George Bernard Shaw (1856–1950)	
Anton Chekhov (1860–1904)	*naturalism; symbolism; psychological or "method" acting*

TWENTIETH CENTURY STAGE	
Eugene O'Neill's *The Hairy Ape* (1922)	*expressionism; rejection of verisimilitude; determinism*
Clifford Odet's *Waiting for Lefty* (1935)	*American social realism of the 1930's*
Thornton Wilder's *Our Town* (1940)	*bare stage; return to Elizabethan free stage techniques; further rejection of verisimilitude*
Tennessee Williams' *The Glass Menagerie* (1945)	*episodic structure so characteristic of contemporary drama; the "family theme"*
Bertolt Brecht's *Galileo* (1947)	*the scientist as tragic hero*
Arthur Miller's *Death of a Salesman* (1949)	*the common man as tragic hero*
Samuel Beckett's *Waiting for Godot* (1952)	*Theater of the Absurd; no conventional plot at all; dialogue seemingly nonsensical*

TWENTIETH CENTURY FILMS	
Edwin S. Porter's *The Great Train Robbery* (1903)	*first film to tell a story; first film to use the "cut"*

TWENTIETH CENTURY FILMS	THEATERS, CONVENTIONS, AUDIENCES
Sergei Eisenstein's *Potemkin* (1925)	*film editing developed; camera imagery; prolongation of the cinema moment; heightened authenticity beyond resources of stage*
It Happened One Night (1934)	*Hollywood romantic comedy; wish-fulfillment; the star system*
Jean Cocteau's *Orpheus* (1950)	*complex Freudian imagery; fusion of fantasy and verisimilitude in a world of cinematic reality that fully exploits the camera's creative potential*
Ingmar Bergman's *The Seventh Seal* (1956)	*use of medieval settings; imagery and symbolism*
Ben Hur (1959)	*wide screen Hollywood epic; the ultimate in verisimilitude*
Federico Fellini's *La Dolce Vita* (1960)	*neo-realism, as well as imagery and symbolism*

Index